Chas. Edward Potter.

GENEALOGIES

OF

SOME OLD FAMILIES

OF

CONCORD, MASSACHUSETTS

AND

THEIR DESCENDANTS

IN PART TO THE PRESENT GENERATION

VOLUME I
Barrett, Blood, Brooks, Brown, Bulkeley, Buttrick, Conant, Davis, Farrar, Flint,
Hartwell, Hayward, Hosmer, Hubbard, Jones, Minott, Potter,
Prescott, Wheeler, Willard, and Wood

Edited by
Charles Edward Potter

HERITAGE BOOKS
2007

HERITAGE BOOKS
AN IMPRINT OF HERITAGE BOOKS, INC.

Books, CDs, and more—Worldwide

For our listing of thousands of titles see our website
at
www.HeritageBooks.com

A Facsimile Reprint
Published 2007 by
HERITAGE BOOKS, INC.
Publishing Division
65 East Main Street
Westminster, Maryland 21157-5026

Originally published

Boston:
Alfred Mudge & Son, Printers
24 Franklin Street
1887

International Standard Book Number: 978-0-7884-0161-9

PREFACE.

THE desire to know of the principal incidents in the lives of our progenitors, as well as the places of their births, and their origin, has induced a goodly number to make such researches for personal accounts of those persons and families who migrated to this country and became the first permanent settlers, as the records preserved have afforded; though in many cases these investigations have discovered but a meagre account, yet they have nevertheless encouraged the compilation of many of the family genealogies that have been published.

It is the purpose of this work, "Old Families of Concord, Massachusetts, and their Descendants in Part to the Present Generation," to give genealogies of some of the families who first settled there, and of their descendants; but it is in no wise intended to give an account of Concord, its settlement, history, or growth, excepting as may appear in the personal relations of some herein noted.

The genealogical tables begin with items respecting the families of Barrett, Blood, Brooks, Brown, Bulkeley, Buttrick, Conant, Davis, Farrar, Flint, Hartwell, Hayward, Hosmer, Hubbard, Jones, Minott, Potter, Prescott, Wheeler, Willard, and Wood, all of whom were known early in the settlement.

"The plantation of Musketaquid (Concord) was settled by Rev. Peter Bulkeley, from Odell, England, associated with Simon Willard, a merchant from Horsmonden, England, who brought with them about twelve families, other families joining the plantation within a few years succeeding. Excepting Bulkeley and Flint, they were plain people, of humble station in their own country, and of small means, who hoped in the New World to better their condition, and to enjoy unmolested the simpler form of religious worship that their tastes and consciences approved."

The original homes of the pioneers had been widely separated: Rev. Peter Bulkeley came from Bedfordshire; Simon Willard, James Hosmer, and probably Luke Potter were from Kent; William Buttrick, from Kingston on Thames; and Thomas Flint and William Wood, probably from Derbyshire.

To make a record of the descendants of any one of these families to the present time, extending as it does over a period of more than two hundred and fifty years, and to make such a record tolerably complete, is a matter attended with much difficulty. As much as could be obtained from imperfect records, and that which has come from various other sources, are recorded. That the early settlers in many cases are not directly connected with English ancestry is readily explained by the experience of Samuel Gardner Drake, as given in his "Founders of New England" : —

"Whoever goes to England expecting to find the genealogy of any particular family settled in America at an early date, is pretty sure, in at least nine cases out of ten, to meet with disappointment. The reason of this uncertainty is easily explained. In the first place, persons who emigrate are not often possessors of real estate, and hence deeds and wills seldom furnish indications referable to them; they leave no deeds or wills in the fatherland by which they can be traced. In the next place, very few emigrants from England were landholders, for the reason that for ages little or no land has been for sale in quantities within the reach of persons of moderate estates. As the great body of emigrants to New England took no pains to transmit to their descendants any account of their ancestors, or even the places whence they came, it is pretty evident they had nothing to expect from the one, or any special regard

"Thus genealogy becomes a *science*, and the learned pursued it as a useful and necessary branch of knowledge; and as such it is generally pursued. There are those who pursue it with a notion that they are heirs to a great estate in England, left by some unknown ancestor. They may thus add something to the science of genealogy, and enlarge their own knowledge, while they will find no necessity to enlarge their pockets."

Many works of this class have proved a disappointment to those for whom they were primarily designed, owing to the complicated manner of indicating the succession of families. The compiler believes that his simple method of tabulating the records (patent applied for) will make it an easy matter to trace out the direct lines of descent, and the collateral branches as well. A particular advantage, aside from the readiness with which family connections are traced, is that all the essential genealogical facts of each family are discovered at the first glance, while the blank spaces indicate if any data is wanting. In these blank spaces the names or dates missing may be written, if ever ascertained; or in the cases of the persons now living, the records of the facts of marriage and death may be inserted as they occur; and there is added also to the volume several pages in blank, particularly intended to be used for the record of future generations of any families that the possessors of the volume may wish, together with any biographical notes desired for preservation.

The compiler desires particularly to acknowledge his indebtedness for the very considerable assistance rendered to him by Mr. Charles Francis Potter, of Boston, to whose indefatigable efforts (and at his own expense) many of the complete records of families in the work are due; and to Mr. George Tolman, the accomplished genealogist of Concord, for his valuable aid, not forgetting also Shattuck's "History of Concord," and Walcott's "Concord in the Colonial Period," — works to which every one must refer for information respecting Concord and its history.

LIST OF ILLUSTRATIONS.

OLD FAMILIES, CONCORD, MASSACHUSETTS.

BARRETT.

PAGE.¹	NAMES.²	NOS.³	BIRTHS.⁴	DEATHS.⁵	MARRIAGES.⁶	TO WHOM MARRIED.⁷
5	Humphrey Barrett,	1	England, 1592	Nov. 7, 1762		Mary ——; –1663.⁸

HUMPHREY AND MARY ( ) BARRETT. 1.⁹

PAGE.	NAMES.	NOS.	BIRTHS.	DEATHS.	MARRIAGES.	TO WHOM MARRIED.
	John,	2	England,	1652		Elizabeth ——; –1690.
5	Thomas,	3	"			July 17, 1661	1. Elizabeth Paine; –1694.
5	Humphrey, Jr.,	4	"	1630	Jan. 3, 1715–16	Mar. 23, 1674–5	2. Mary Potter. No. 545.¹⁰
5		5	"				

THOMAS AND ELIZABETH ( ) BARRETT. 3.

PAGE.	NAMES.	NOS.	BIRTHS.	DEATHS.	MARRIAGES.	TO WHOM MARRIED.
	Oliver,	6	Concord, about 1648	Sept. 13, 1671	Unmarried.	
	Mary,	7	" " 1650	July 18, 1711	Dec. 4, 1671	James Smeadley; 1650–1724; son John and Ann.

HUMPHREY AND ELIZABETH (PAINE) BARRETT. 4.

PAGE.	NAMES.	NOS.	BIRTHS.	DEATHS.	MARRIAGES.	TO WHOM MARRIED.
	Mary,	8	Concord, Nov. 9, 1662	1688	Mar. 4, 1688	Josiah Blood. No. 51.

HUMPHREY AND MARY (POTTER) BARRETT. 5-545.

PAGE.	NAMES.	NOS.	BIRTHS.	DEATHS.	MARRIAGES.	TO WHOM MARRIED.
5	Joseph, Capt.,	9	Concord, Jan. 31, 1679	Apr. 4, 1763	Dec. 24, 1701	Rebecca Minott. No. 506.
5	Benjamin,	10	" May 7, 1681	Oct. 25, 1728	Jan. 3, 1704–5	Lydia Minott. No. 507.

CAPT. JOSEPH AND REBECCA (MINOTT) BARRETT. 9-506

PAGE.	NAMES.	NOS.	BIRTHS.	DEATHS.	MARRIAGES.	TO WHOM MARRIED.
10	Mary,	11	Concord, Apr. 6, 1706	Sept. 25, 1778		Dea. George Farrar. No. 301.
	Joseph,	12	" Jan. 30, 1707–8		Married.	Had issue, two daughters.
	Rebecca (no issue),	13	" July 12, 1710	Feb. 8, 1733	Jan. 31, 1731–2	Elnathan Jones. No. 4745.
16	Oliver, Lieut.,	14	" Jan. 17, 1712	Apr. 4, 1788	Dec. 8, 1737	Hannah Hunt; 1716–74; dau. John and Mary (Brown).
18	Humphrey,	15	" Aug. 28, 1715	Mar. 24, 1783	Dec. 9, 1742	Elizabeth Adams; 1722–91; dau. Daniel and Elizabeth (Minott).
14	Elizabeth,	16	" Jan. 9, 1717	Apr. 23, 1799	1736	Col. Charles Prescott. No. 5? . [(Wheeler).
21	John,	17	" Feb. 14, 1719–20	Apr. 19, 1790	Nov. 15, 1744	Lois Brooks; 1723–1805; dau. Joshua and Lydia
	Samuel,	18	" July 6, 1725	Jan. 18, 1727–8		

BENJAMIN AND LYDIA (MINOTT) BARRETT. 10-507.

PAGE.	NAMES.	NOS.	BIRTHS.	DEATHS.	MARRIAGES.	TO WHOM MARRIED.
23	Benjamin,	19	Concord, Nov. 15, 1705	Oct. 23, 1738	About 1730	Rebecca Jones. No. 4278.
30	Thomas, Dea.,	20	" Oct. 2, 1707	June 20, 1779	" 1730	Mary Jones. No. 4281.
35	James, Col.,	21	" July 31, 1710	Apr. 11, 1779	Dec. 21, 1732	Rebecca Hubbard. No. 462.
10	Lydia,	22	" Aug. 2, 1712	June, 1802	Jan. 13, 1732	Dea. Samuel Farrar. No. 303.
	Rebecca,	23	" Mar. 29, 1714	Prob. young.		
48	Timothy,	24	" Jan. 2, 1716	Jan. 4, 1800		1. Mrs. Dina Witt; –1754.
	(no issue),	25			Sept. 27, 1758	2. Anna Vaughn; –1779.
	(no issue),	26				3. Rebecca Brown.
	Mary,	27	" Dec. 27, 1717	1737		Aaron Parker; 1713–62.
48	Stephen,	28	" Apr. 18, 1720		May 15, 1750	Elizabeth (Hubbard) How. No. 464.

NOTES.—The Genealogical Tables are continued in this uniform manner throughout.

¹ The figures to the left of the lines indicate the pages on which the descendants are recorded.

² The names of the children of each family.

³ Numbers for reference to each name.

⁴ Places and dates of births. The places are in the State of Massachusetts, unless otherwise noted.

⁵ Dates of deaths.

⁶ Dates of marriages.

⁷ To whom married.

⁸ Year of birth – year of death.

⁹ The numbers at the end of the lines, indicating heads of families, refer to their direct ancestry family.

¹⁰ Numbers following names in this manner indicate where the name may be found recorded in full.

BLOOD.

6	James Blood,	29	England,	Nov. 17, 1683		Ellen ——; –1764.

JAMES AND ELLEN ( ) BLOOD. 29.

	Name	No.	Birth	Death	Marriage	Spouse
6	James,	30 / 31		Nov. 26, 1692	Oct. 26, 1657 / Nov. 19, 1679	1. Hannah Purchiss; –1677; dau. Oliver, of Lynn. / 2. Isabel (Farmer) Wyman; dau. John Farmer.
6	Richard,	32		Dec. 7, 1683		Isabel ——.
	John,	33		Oct. 30, 1692	Unmarried.	
6	Robert,	34 / 35		Oct. 27, 1701	Apr. 8, 1653 / Jan. 8, 1690	1. Elizabeth Willard. No. 716. / 2. Hannah Parker; –1716.
9	Mary,	36	Concord, July 12, 1640		Dec. 12, 1660	Lieut. Simon Davis. No. 258.

JAMES AND HANNAH (PURCHISS) BLOOD. 30.

Name	No.	Birth	Death	Marriage	Spouse
Sarah,	37	Concord, Mar. 5, 1659–60			Capt. Will Wilson, of Concord.
James,	38	"	Aug. 26, 1663		
Elenor,	39	"	Aug. 1, 1674		
Hannah,	40	"	Nov. 25, 1676		

RICHARD AND ISABEL ( ) BLOOD, 32.

Name	No.	Birth	Death	Marriage	Spouse
Mary,	41		Apr. 19, 1662		
James,	42 / 43		Sept. 13, 1692	Sept. 7, 1669 / Dec. 20, 1686	1. Elizabeth Longley; dau. William, of Lynn. / 2. Abigail Kemp.
Nathaniel,	44			June 13, 1670	Hannah Parker; 1647–1728; dau. Capt. James.
Elizabeth,	45			Dec. 1, 1686	Thomas Tarbell; 1667–1719.

ROBERT AND ELIZABETH (WILLARD) BLOOD. 34–716.

	Name	No.	Birth	Death	Marriage	Spouse
8	Mary,	46	Concord, Mar. 4, 1655			John Buttrick. No. 198.
	Elizabeth,	47	" June 14, 1656	Mar. 7, 1734	Feb. 1, 1679	Samuel Buttrick. No. 199.
	Sarah,	48	" Aug. 1, 1658			Daniel Colburn.
6	Robert,	49	" Dec. 20, 1660		May 12, 1690	Dorcas Wheeler.
	Simon,	50	" July 5, 1662	Apr. 4, 1692	Unmarried.	
6	Josiah,	51 / 52	" Apr. 6, 1664	July 2, 1731	Mar. 4, 1688 / Feb. 3, 1690	1. Mary Barrett. No. 8. / 2. Mary Torrey; 1657–; dau. James and Ann.
	John,	53	" Oct. 29, 1667	Oct. 24, 1689	Unmarried.	
	Elenor,	54	" Apr. 14, 1669	June 19, 1690	"	
6	Samuel,	55	" Oct. 16, 1672		Apr. 1, 1701	Hannah Davis. No. 270.
6	James,	56	" Nov. 3, 1673	May 17, 1738	Dec. 26, 1701	Abigail Wheeler; –1748.
	Ebenezer,	57	" July 4, 1676	Died young.		
	Jonathan,	58 / 59 / 60	" July 1, 1679	Jan. 5, 1778	Apr. 20, 1733	1. Sarah ——; –1715. / 2. Abigail ——; –1729. / 3. Rebecca Wood.

ROBERT AND DORCAS (WHEELER) BLOOD. 49.

Name	No.	Birth	Death	Marriage	Spouse
Dorcas,	61	Concord, Apr. 10, 1691			
Thomas,	62	" Oct. 11, 1692	Dec. 28, 1692		
Ebenezer,	63	" Dec. 8, 1693			

JOSIAH AND MARY (TORREY) BLOOD. 52.

Name	No.	Birth	Death	Marriage	Spouse
Elizabeth,	64	Concord, May 2, 1692	Oct. 10, 1708		
Mary,	65	" May 2, 1692		Jan. 19, 1714	James Colburn.
Josiah,	66	" May 30, 1694	Oct. 21, 1711		
John,	67	" Apr. 6, 1696			Sarah ——.
Abigail,	68	" June 15, 1698			
Robert,	69	" Apr. 26, 1700			Sarah ——.
Ephraim,	70	" June 12, 1702			
Stephen,	71	" Feb. 22, 1703–4			Mary ——.
Zachariah,	72	" June 10, 1707		Feb. 9, 1737–8	Elizabeth Wheeler.
Elizabeth,	73	" July 7, 1709			
Anna,	74	" Mar. 30, 1712			

SAMUEL AND HANNAH (DAVIS) BLOOD. 55–270.

Name	No.	Birth	Death	Marriage	Spouse
Hannah,	75	Concord, Sept. 6, 1700			
Elenor,	76	" Feb. 10, 1701–2			
Samuel,	77	" Jan. 19, 1703–4			
Sarah,	78	" Dec. 19, 1705	May 17, 1769	Jan. 23, 1740–1	Francis Wheeler. No. 661.
Mary,	79	" Jan. 13, 1707–8			
Elizabeth,	80	" Apr. 20, 1710			
Simon,	81	" Dec. 28, 1712		Feb. 15, 1739	Abigail Flint. [(Buttrick).
Phineas,	82	" June 5, 1717		Oct. 16, 1735	Elizabeth Allen; 1717–; dau. Ebenezer and Eliz.
Oliver,	83	" Sept. 20, 1719			
Lucy,	84	" July 26, 1723			

JAMES AND ABIGAIL (WHEELER) BLOOD. 56.

Name	No.	Birth	Death	Marriage	Spouse
Abigail,	85	Concord, July 30, 1703			
James,	86	" Oct. 5, 1705	May 4, 1710		
Simon,	87	" Sept. 6, 1707	Sept. 1711		
James,	88	" Mar. 23, 1710–11	Jan. 10, 1748	Unmarried.	
Martha,	89	" Feb. 9, 1712–13			
Esther,	90	" Sept. 4, 1718			

BROOKS.

6	Capt. Thos. Brooks	91		May 21, 1667		Grace ——; –1664.

CAPT. THOMAS AND GRACE ( ) BROOKS. 91. (Continued page 7.)

	Name	No.	Birth	Death	Spouse
	Hannah,	92		Dec. 13, 1647	Thomas Fox; –1664.
7	Joshua,	93		Oct. 17, 1653	Hannah Mason; dau. Capt. Hugh.
7	Caleb,	94 / 95	1632	Apr. 10, 1660	1. Susanna Atkinson; 1641–1668; dau. Thomas. / 2. Hannah Atkinson; 1643–; dau. Thomas.
7	Gershom,	96		Mar. 12, 1666–7	Hannah Eckels; –1710–11; dau. Richard and Mary.
7	Mary,	97		Oct. 4, 1693	Capt. Timothy Wheeler. No. 629.
	Thomas,	98			

| | Hugh, | 99 | | | | |
| | John, | 100 | | | | |

JOSHUA AND HANNAH (MASON) BROOKS. 93.

	Name	No.	Born	Died	Married	Spouse
	John,	101	1657	May 18, 1697		
	Noah,	102	Concord, 1666	Feb. 1, 1739	1685	Dorothy Potter. No. 543.
13	Grace,	103	" Mar. 10, 1660–1	1753	1686	Judah Potter. No. 546. [(Cooper).
	Daniel,	104	" Nov. 15, 1663	Oct. 18, 1733	Aug. 9, 1692	Ann Meriam; 1669–1757; dau. John and Mary
	Thomas,	105	" May 5, 1666	Sept. 9, 1671		[Mary (Upham).
	Esther,	106	" July 4, 1668	1742	Aug. 17, 1692	Benjamin Whittemore; 1669–1734; son John and
	Elizabeth,	107	" Dec. 16, 1672			[(Simonds).
	Job,	108	" July 26, 1675	May 18, 1697		
	Hugh,	109	" Jan. 1, 1677	Jan. 18, 1746	Apr. 9, 1701	Abigail Barker; 1683–; dau. John and Judith
	Joseph,	110	" 1681	Sept. 17, 1759	June 26, 1704	Rebecca Blodget.
	Hannah,	111	"			Benjamin Pierce.

CALEB AND SUSANNA (ATKINSON) BROOKS. 94.

	Name	No.	Born	Died	Married	Spouse
	Susanna,	112	Concord, Dec. 27, 1761	Oct. 23, 1686	Unmarried.	
	Mary,	113	" Nov. 18, 1663	Died young.		
	Mary,	114	" Apr. 3, 1666	Aug. 22, 1726		Nathaniel Ball; 1663–1725; son Nathaniel and Mary.
	Rebecca,	115	" Nov. 9, 1667	Died young.		
	Sarah,	116	" Dec. 16, 1668			

CALEB AND HANNAH (ATKINSON) BROOKS. 95.

	Name	No.	Born	Died	Married	Spouse
	Ebenezer,	117	Concord, Feb. 21, 1669–70			
	Samuel,	118	" Sept. 1, 1672			

GERSHON AND HANNAH (ECKELS) BROOKS. 96.

	Name	No.	Born	Died	Married	Spouse
	Mary,	119	Concord, May 6, 1667			Edward Bridge.
	Hannah,	120	" Mar. 24, 1668–9	Dec. 12, 1696		[Abigail (Meriam).
	Joseph,	121	" Sept. 16, 1671		Jan. 31, 1703	Abigail Bateman; 1677–1705; dau. Thomas and
	Tabatha,	122	" Mar. 31, 1674			
	Daniel,	123	" Mar. 14, 1678–9			
	Elizabeth,	124	" Feb. 18, 1680–1	Apr. 15, 1762	Dec. 6, 1705	Ebenezer Meriam; son John and Mary (Cooper).

BROWN.

	Name	No.	Born	Died	Married	Spouse
7	Thomas Brown,	125		Nov. 3, 1688		Bridget ——; –1700–1.

THOMAS AND BRIDGET ( ) BROWN. 125.

	Name	No.	Born	Died	Married	Spouse
7	Boaz,	126	Concord, Feb. 14, 1641–2	Apr. 7, 1724	Nov. 8, 1664	Mary Winship; dau. Edward and Jane.
		127			Oct. 10, 1716	Abigail (Ballard) Wheat.
7	Jabez,	128	"	1692		Deborah ——.
	Mary,	129	" Mar. 26, 1646		June 21, 1669	William Woodward.
7	Eleazer,	130	" July 6, 1649		Feb. 9, 1674–5	Dinah Spalding.
7	Thomas,	131	" 1651	Apr. 4, 1718	Nov. 12, 1677	Ruth (Vinton) Jones. See No. 475.

BOAZ AND MARY (WINSHIP) BROWN. 126.

	Name	No.	Born	Died	Married	Spouse
	Boaz,	132	Concord, July 31, 1665			Abigail ——.
7	Thomas,	133	" May 12, 1667	May 13, 1739		Rachel Poulter.
	Mary,	134	" Oct. 31, 1670			
	Edward,	135	" Mar. 20, 1672–3	Mar. 15, 1710–11		Elizabeth Hapgood
	Mercy,	136				—— Everett.
	Mary,	137	" May 24, 1678			
	Jane,	138	Stow, Sept. 4, 1684			

JABEZ AND DEBORAH ( ) BROWN. 128.

	Name	No.	Born	Died	Married	Spouse
	Thomas,	139			Apr. 3, 1706	Mary Hayward.
	Jabez,	140				Sarah ——.
	Josiah,	141	Stow, June 23, 1685			Abigail.
	Mary,	142				
	Sarah,	143				

ELEAZER AND DINAH (SPALDING) BROWN. 130.

	Name	No.	Born	Died	Married	Spouse
	Eleazer,	144	Chelmsford, Apr. 2, 1676	Apr. 3, 1755		Abigail Chandler; –1768; dau. Roger.
	Dinah,	145	" Feb. 4, 1677–8			
	Thomas,	146	" May 9, 1680			
	Benjamin,	147	" Feb. 27, 1682–3			
	Bridget,	148	" July 7, 1685			
	Deliverance,	149	" Dec. 4, 1689			

THOMAS AND RUTH (JONES) BROWN. 131.

	Name	No.	Born	Died	Married	Spouse
75	Ruth,	150	Concord, Feb. 8, 1678–9	Mar. 22, 1764	Nov. 10, 1698	Samuel Jones. No. 483.
	Mary,	151	" Nov. 18, 1681	July 14, 1750		John Hunt; –1765; son Nehemiah and Mary (Tool).
	Rebecca,	152	" Mar. 5, 1683–4		Sept. 26, 1704	Jonathan Hubbard. No. 450.
64	Thomas,	153	" Aug. 28, 1686	Mar. 13, 1717–18	Nov. 22, 1709	Hannah Potter. No. 551.
64	Ephraim,	154	" Apr. 21, 1689	Feb. 6, 1749–50	Aug. 28, 1719	Hannah Wilson; –1768; dau. William.
	Elizabeth,	155	" Mar. 8, 1691–2	Dec. 28, 1717	Sept. 22, 1713	Jonathan Hartwell. No. 367.

THOMAS AND RACHEL (POULTER) BROWN. 133.

	Name	No.	Born	Died	Married	Spouse
10	Rachel,	156	Concord, Feb. 16, 1691–2	Mar. 4, 1691–2		
	Mary,	157	" Mar. 20, 1692–3		June 15, 1717–18	Thomas Flint. No. 330.
54	John,	158	" Sept. 18, 1694	Mar. 6, 1750	Feb. 23, 1714–15	Elizabeth Potter. No. 555.
	Rachel,	159	" Mar. 10, 1695–6			Jonathan Harris.
	Jonathan,	160	" July 30, 1698	1745	Sept. 5, 1718	Sibell Dudley.
	Thomas,	161	" June 14, 1700	Nov. 28, 1700		
	Hannah,	162	" June 5, 1702			—— Russell.
	Abigail,	163	" Mar. 12, 1703–4			Jonathan Davis.
	Dinah,	164	" Feb. 12, 1705–6		Nov. 13, 1735	Henry Jefts.
	Thomas,	165	" Dec. 24, 1707	1762	Feb. 18, 1729	Mary Holyoke.
	Mercy,	166	" Apr. 22, 1710	June 10, 1737		David Whitaker.

BULKELEY.

8 8	Rev. Peter Bulkeley	{ 167 { 168	England, Jan. 31, 1582-3	Mar. 9, 1658-9	About 1613 " 1634	1. Jane Allen; dau. Sir Thomas, of Goldington, Eng. 2. Grace Chetwoode; dau. Sir Rich'rd, Chetwoode, "

REV. PETER AND JANE (ALLEN) BULKELEY. 167.

8	Edward, Rev. Thomas, John, Rev. Joseph, William, Richard,	169 170 171 172 173 174	England,	Jan. 2, 1696 1689		Sarah Jones; dau. Rev. John Jones.

REV. PETER AND GRACE (CHETWOODE) BULKELEY. 168.

8 8	Gershon, M. D. Eleazer, Peter, Maj. Dorothy,	175 176 177 178	Concord, 1636 " " Aug. 12, 1643 " Aug. 2, 1640	Dec. 2, 1713 May 24, 1688	Oct. 26, 1659 Apr. 16, 1667	Sarah Channey; 1631-; dau. Dr. Chas. and Catharine [(Eyre). Rebecca Wheeler. No. 687.

REV. EDWARD AND   (   ) BULKELEY. 169.

	John, Peter, Jane (no issue), Elizabeth,	179 180 181 182 183	Concord, " " Jan. 3, 1640-1 "	Apr. 28, 1706	Mar. 20, 1683-4 Dec. 7, 1665	Capt. Ephraim Flint. No. 323. 1. Rev. Joseph Emerson; -1680. 2. John Brown, of Reading, Mass.

DR. GERSHON AND SARAH (CHANNEY) BULKELEY. 175.

	Peter, Edward, Charles, John,	184 185 186 187	Concord, Nov. 7, 1660 " " "		July 14, 1702	Dorothy Prescott. No. 586.

MAJ. PETER AND REBECCA (WHEELER) BULKELEY. 177.

   14	Edward, Joseph, Capt. John, Rebecca,	188 189 190 191 192	Concord, Mar. 18, 1667-8 " Sept. 7, 1670 " July 10, 1673 " Aug. 24, 1681	Died young.	May 12, 1691 July 9, 1701	1. Rebecca (Jones) Minott. No. 481. 2. Silence Jeffrey. Abigail ——. Jonathan Prescott, Jr. No. 584.

BUTTRICK.

8	Wm. Buttrick,	{ 193 { 194 { 195	England, About 1617	June 30, 1698	 1646 Feb. 21, 1667	1. Mary ——. 2. Sarah Bateman; -1664. 3. Jane Goodnow.

WILLIAM AND SARAH (BATEMAN) BUTTRICK. 193.

   8	Mary, William, John, Samuel, Edward, Joseph, Sarah, Mary,	196 197 198 199 200 201 202 203	Concord, Sept. 19, 1648 " " Sept. 21, 1653 " Jan. 12, 1654-5 " Jan. 6, 1656-7 " Oct. 29, 1657 " July 27, 1662 " June 17, 1664	Nov. 1, 1648 Aug. 8, 1726 Jan. 15, 1656-7 Apr. 21, 1726 Apr. 21, 1665	 1677	Mary Blood. No. 46. Elizabeth Blood. No. 47. —— Barrett (probably John Barrett, of Chelmsford).

SAMUEL AND ELIZABETH (BLOOD) BUTTRICK. 199-47.

    10 8	Elizabeth, Samuel, William, Sarah, Abigail, Jonathan, Dea.	204 205 206 207 208 209	Concord, Aug. 25, 1679 " Jan. 31, 1681-2 " Apr. 15, 1683 " Nov. 7, 1684 " Nov. 21, 1687 " Apr. 4, 1690	 Sept. 16, 1711 Oct. 7, 1746 Mar. 23, 1767	 May 7, 1713 Dec. 19, 1718	[munds). Mercy Hett; 1680-; dau. Thomas and Dorothy (Ed- John Flint. No. 328. Elizabeth Wooley; -1772.

DEA. JONATHAN AND ELIZABETH (WOOLEY) BUTTRICK. 209.

	Samuel, Mary, Jonathan, Capt. Joseph, Nathan, Elizabeth, Abigail, John, Maj. Rachel, Ephraim, Daniel, Lois, Sarah, Willard,	210 211 212 213 214 215 216 217 218 219 220 221 222 223	Concord, Nov. 16, 1718 " Apr. 18, 1720 " Jan. 30, 1721-2 " Jan. 9, 1723-4 " Sept. 27, 1725 " Aug. 21, 1727 " Aug. 20, 1729 " July 20, 1731 " Nov. 12, 1733 " Feb. 15, 1735-6 " Apr. 3, 1738 " June 2, 1740 " Aug. 10, 1742 " Nov. 12, 1746	Jan. 14, 1814 May 18, 1775 Dec. 29, 1803 Dec. 25, 1812 May 16, 1791 Apr. 15, 1785 Feb. 24, 1743 Apr. 27, 1783 July 12, 1827	Sept. 18, 1744 July 14, 1756 July 23, 1751 Dec. 12, 1757 Dec. 21, 1753 June 24, 1760 Unmarried. Unmarried. Nov. 22, 1769	Lucy Wheeler; 1723-1803. Mary Brown. No. 3624. Sarah Brown. No. 3625. [ter). No. 556. Grace Wheeler; 1730-; dau. Joseph and Sarah (Pot- Charles Flint. No. 346. Abigail Jones. Esther Blood; 1748-1775; dau. John and Esther.

CONANT.

    8	CONANT.	224 225 226 227 228	First generation, Roger Conant, from England. Second generation, Lot and Elizabeth (Walton) Conant. Third generation, John and Bethiah (Mansfield) Conant, of Beverly, Mass. Fourth generation, Lot and Martha (Cleaves) Conant, of Beverly, Mass. Fifth generation, Andrew and Elizabeth ( ) Conant, of Concord, Mass.

ANDREW AND ELIZABETH (   ) CONANT. 228   (Continued page 9.)

 9 9 9	Elizabeth, Andrew, Nathan, Keziah, Nathan, Lydia, Silas,	229 230 231 232 233 234 235 236	Concord, Feb. 10, 1723-4 " Aug. 22, 1725 " Feb. 2, 1730-1 " Feb. 1, 1732-3 " Mar. 18, 1734-5 " Oct. 27, 1737 " Aug. 15, 1740	 Sept. 17, 1805 July 30, 1733 Died young. Apr. 3, 1803	 Nov. 30, 1748 Dec. 30, 1762	[nah (Dakin). 1. Ruth Brooks; 1729-1770; dau. Thomas and Han- 2. Mary ——; -1818; æ. 84. Lois Potter. No. 567.

8

	Name	No.	Birth	Death	Marriage	Spouse / Notes
	Eli,	237	Concord, Mar. 16, 1741-2	May 26, 1801	Dec. 23, 1767	Elizabeth Gardner.
	Ruth,	238	" Mar. 25, 1745	Mar. 14, 1760		
	Abel,	238	" Apr. 5, 1747		May 7, 1771	Catharine Johnson; –1780.
	Nathan,	239	" June 23, 1751			

ANDREW AND RUTH (BROOKS) CONANT. 230.

	Name	No.	Birth	Death	Marriage	Spouse / Notes
	Zebulon,	240	Concord, Oct. 29, 1749			

ANDREW AND MARY ( ) CONANT. 231.

	Name	No.	Birth	Death	Marriage	Spouse / Notes
	Nathan,	241	Concord, Sept. 30, 1777			
	Andrew,	242	" May 7, 1773	Jan. 31, 1813	June 16, 1803	Lydia Miles; 1780-1825; dau. Oliver and Martha.
	Thaddeus,	243	" Nov. 1, 1771	Jan., 1803		

SILAS AND LOIS (POTTER) CONANT. 236-567.

	Name	No.	Birth	Death	Marriage	Spouse / Notes
	Elizabeth,	244	Acton, Oct. 7, 1764			
67	Samuel Potter,	245	" Mar. 27, 1767	Nov. 6, 1815	Oct. 23, 1789	Rebecca Tuttle; 1766-1835; dau. Simon and Rebecca.
	Keziah,	246	" Sept. 29, 1769		Dec. 29, 1791	Elisha Jones.
	Charlotte,	247	" Apr. 4, 1772		Apr. 22, 1791	Joseph Dole. [Lucy (Conant).
68	Lois,	248	" July 5, 1774	Oct. 31, 1841	Aug. 27, 1795	Capt. Reuben Hayward; 1767-1838; son Josiah and
68	Silas,	249	" Oct. 25, 1776	May 13, 1840	Aug. 11, 1796	1. Abigail Lawrence; 1778-1805. [(Conant).
69		250			May 5, 1807	2. Mary Hayward; 1775-1855; dau. Josiah and Lucy
	Andrew,	251	" Mar. 9, 1782	Feb. 8, 1803		
69	James,	252	" May 26, 1788		Nov. 4, 1810	Seba Davis.

DAVIS.

	Name	No.	Birth	Death	Marriage	Spouse / Notes
9	Dolor Davis,	253	England, about 1600	June, 1673	1624	1. Margery Willard. No. 697. [Hull.
	(no issue),	254				2. Joanna (Hull) Bursley; 1620–; dau. Rev. James

DOLOR AND MARGERY (WILLARD) DAVIS. 253-697.

	Name	No.	Birth	Death	Marriage	Spouse / Notes
	John,	255	England, about 1626	1703	Mar. 15, 1648-9	Hannah Lynnell; dau. Robert.
	Mary,	256	" " 1631		June 15, 1653	Thomas Lewis; son George.
	Elizabeth,	257	" " 1633	Died young.		
9	Simon, Lieut.,	258	America, " 1636	June 14, 1713	Dec. 12, 1660	Mary Blood. No. 36.
9	Samuel,	259	"		Jan. 11, 1665-6	1. Mary Medows; –1710.
		260			Oct. 18, 1711	2. Ruth Taylor; –1720.
	Ruth,	261	"			Stephen Hall.

LIEUT. SIMON AND MARY (BLOOD) DAVIS. 258-36.

	Name	No.	Birth	Death	Marriage	Spouse / Notes
9	Simon, M. D.,	262	Concord, Oct. 12, 1661		Feb. 14, 1689	1. Elizabeth Woodhis; –1711; dau. Henry.
		263			Oct. 19, 1714	2. Mary Wood.
	Mary,	264	" Oct. 3, 1663		May 28, 1691	Deliverance Wheeler, of Stow.
	Sarah,	265	" Mar. 11, 1665-6		Nov. 13, 1695	Thomas Wheeler, of Concord.
	James,	266	" Jan. 19, 1668	Sept., 1727	1701	Ann Smedley; –1760.
	Elenor,	267	" Oct. 22, 1672		May 14, 1699	Samuel Hunt.
	Ebenezer,	268	" June 1, 1676			1. Dinah ——.
		269				2. Mrs. Sarah French; –1751.
6	Hannah,	270	" Apr. 1, 1679		Apr. 1, 1701	Samuel Blood. No. 55.

DR. SIMON AND ELIZABETH (WOODHIS) DAVIS. 262.

	Name	No.	Birth	Death	Marriage	Spouse / Notes
	John, M. D.,	271	Concord, Nov. 19, 1689	Nov. 16, 1762	Dec. 17, 1713	Abigail Dudley.
69	Simon,	272	" Sept. 7, 1692		June 1, 1719	Hannah (Potter) Brown. No. 552.
	Henry,	273	" Feb. 23, 1694-5			
	Elizabeth,	274	" Mar. 28, 1698	Nov. 15, 1706		
	Mary,	275	" Nov. 8, 1701			
	Samuel,	276	" Mar. 6, 1703			
	Eleanor,	277	" Mar. 4, 1705-6			
	Peter,	278	" Sept. 25, 1707			

SAMUEL AND MARY (MEDOWS) DAVIS. 259.

	Name	No.	Birth	Death	Marriage	Spouse / Notes
	Mercy,	279	Concord, Sept. 27, 1666	Dec. 18, 1667		
	Samuel,	280	" Jan. 21, 1669		Mar. 2, 1697-8	1. Abigail Read; –1709.
		281			1710	2. Mary Law.
	Daniel,	282	" Mar. 26, 1673	Feb. 11, 1741	Apr. 27, 1699	Mary Hubbard. No. 449.
	Mary,	283	" Aug. 12, 1677		Apr. 26, 1699	John Stearns.
70	Eleazer,	284	" May 26, 1680	Aug. 10, 1721	May 7, 1705	Eunice Potter. No. 549.
	Simon, Lieut.,	285	" July 9, 1683	Feb. 16, 1763	1713	Dorothy ——; –1776.
	Stephen.	286	" Mar. 30, 1686		Mar. 26, 1713	Elizabeth Fletcher.

FARRAR.

	Name	No.	Birth	Death	Marriage	Spouse / Notes
9	John Farrar,	287	Propr's, Lancaster, 1653	Nov. 3, 1669	About 1640	Ann ——.
9	Jacob Farrar,	288		Aug. 14, 1677		

JACOB AND ANN ( ) FARRAR. 288.

	Name	No.	Birth	Death	Marriage	Spouse / Notes
9	Jacob,	289	England, about 1642	Aug. 14, 1677	About 1668	Hannah Hayward. No. 389.
	John,	290			June 30, 1667	Mary ——.
	Henry,	291		Feb. 10, 1675-6		
	Mary,	292			Feb. 22, 1671-2	John Houghton, Jr.
	Joseph,	293	Lancaster,	Aug. 22, 1675		

JACOB AND HANNAH (HAYWARD) FARRAR. 289-389.

	Name	No.	Birth	Death	Marriage	Spouse / Notes
	Jacob,	294	Lancaster, Apr. 29, 1669	Apr. 29, 1722	1692	Susanna Redit; –1737-8.
9	George,	295	" Aug. 16, 1670	May 15, 1760	Sept. 9, 1692	Mary Howe; –1761.
	John,	296	" 1672	Aug. 19, 1707	Dec. 6, 1699	Elizabeth Meriam.
	Henry,	297	" 1674			
	Joseph,	298	"			

GEORGE AND MARY (HOWE) FARRAR. 295. (Continued page 10.)

	Name	No.	Birth	Death	Marriage	Spouse / Notes
	Joseph,	299	Concord, Feb. 28, 1693-4	About 1731	1715	Mary ——.
	Daniel,	300	" Nov. 30, 1696	1755		Hannah Fletcher.
10	George, Dea.,	301	Lincoln, Feb. 16, 1705	May 28, 1777		Mary Barrett. No. 11.

	Name	No.	Place	Birth	Death	Marriage	Spouse / Notes
	Mary,	302	Lincoln	Oct. 12, 1706	Sept. 29, 1759		Nathan Brown; 1704-; son Eleazer and Abigail
10	Samuel, Dea.,	303	"	Sept. 28, 1708	Apr. 17, 1783	Jan. 13, 1732	Lydia Barrett. No. 22. [(Chandler). No. 144.

DEA. GEORGE AND MARY (BARRETT) FARRAR. 301-11.

	Name	No.	Place	Birth	Death	Marriage	Spouse / Notes
	Rebecca,	304	Concord	Jan. 18, 1729		Feb. 7, 1749	Timothy Brown. No. 3629.
	Geo., Rev. (no issue),	305	"	Nov. 23, 1730	Sept. 17, 1756		
	Mary,	306	"	July 6, 1732	Sept. 19, 1759	Apr. 8, 1756	Nathan Parks; -1771.
	Sarah,	307	"	Aug. 11, 1733	July 28, 1736		
	Sarah,	308	"	Oct. 4, 1736			
	Elizabeth,	309	"	Feb. 2, 1738-9		May 3, 1763	Stephen Hosmer, Jr. No. 441.
	Humphrey,	310	"	Feb. 28, 1740-1		Apr. 26, 1770	Lucy Farrar. No. 318.
	Joseph, Rev.,	311	"	Jan. 20, 1744	Apr. 5, 1816	July 28, 1779	Mary Brooks; 1755-1854.
	Love,	312	"	June 13, 1749	Sept. 9, 1756		

DEA. SAMUEL AND LYDIA (BARRETT) FARRAR. 303-22.

	Name	No.	Place	Birth	Death	Marriage	Spouse / Notes
	Lydia,	313	Lincoln	Sept. 2, 1735		Mar. 6, 1755	William Bond.
73	Samuel. Dea.,	314	"	Feb. 14, 1737	Sept. 19, 1829	Oct. 13, 1772	Mercy Hoar; -1829.
	Stephen, Rev.,	315	"	Sept. 8, 1738	June 23, 1809	1764	Eunice Brown; -1818.
	James,	316	"	July 24, 1741	July 11, 1767	Unmarried.	[and Hannah.
	Rebecca,	317	"	Aug. 13, 1743	Apr. 1, 1829	Nov. 29, 1764	John Preston, M. D.; 1738-1803; son Capt. Samuel
73	Lucy,	318	"	Apr. 27, 1745	Jan. 1832	Apr. 26, 1770	Humphrey Farrar. No. 310.
73	Timothy,	319	"	June 28, 1747	Feb. 21, 1849	Oct. 14, 1779	Anna Bancroft; -1817.
	Mary,	320	"	July 5, 1754	Sept. 2, 1756		

FLINT.

	Name	No.	Place	Birth	Death	Marriage	Spouse / Notes
10	Thomas Flint,	321		1603	Oct. 8, 1653		Abigail ——; -1689.

THOMAS AND ABIGAIL ( ) FLINT. 321.

	Name	No.	Place	Birth	Death	Marriage	Spouse / Notes
10	John, Col.,	322	Concord,		Dec. 5, 1686	Nov. 12, 1667	Mary Oakes; -1690; dau. Edward and Jane.
	Eph'm,Cap. (no issue),	323	"	Jan. 14, 1642	Aug. 3, 1723	Mar. 20, 1683-4	Jane Bulkeley. No. 181.

COL. JOHN AND MARY (OAKES) FLINT. 322.

	Name	No.	Place	Birth	Death	Marriage	Spouse / Notes
	Mary,	324	Concord	Oct. 26, 1668	May 31, 1675		
	Thomas,	325	"	Dec. 12, 1670	May 29, 1675		
	John,	326	"	Mar. 31, 1673	June 6, 1675		
	Abigail,	327	"	Jan. 11, 1674-5		Nov. 21, 1701	Capt. Daniel Esterbrook; 1677-1737; son Rev. Jos. [and Mary (Mason).
10	John,	328	"	July 18, 1677	Oct. 25, 1746	May 7, 1713	Abigail Buttrick. No. 208.
	Mary.	329	"	Aug. 11, 1680	May 24, 1748		Timothy Green.
10	Thomas,	330	"	Jan. 16, 1682-3	Apr. 1, 1755	Jan. 15, 1717-18	Mary Brown. No. 157.
	Edward,	331	"	July 6, 1685	Nov. 15, 1754		Love (Minott) Adams. No. 515.

JOHN AND ABIGAIL (BUTTRICK) FLINT. 328-208.

	Name	No.	Place	Birth	Death	Marriage	Spouse / Notes
	Ephraim,	332	Concord,	Mar. 4, 1713-14	Dec. 26, 1762	Mar. 31, 1743	Ruth Wheeler.
	Abigail,	333	"	Feb. 24, 1715-16			
	Mary,	334	"	Dec. 17, 1717	May 20, 1719		
	Sarah,	335	"	May 3, 1720			[Abigail (Chandler). No. 144.
	John,	336 / 337	"	May 12, 1722	Jan. 20, 1792	Jan. 12, 1744-5	1. Hepzibah Brown; 1725-1785; dau. Eleazer and 2. Submit (Bateman) Hunt; dau. John and Anna [(Wheeler) Bateman.
	Hannah,	338	"	Sept. 23, 1724			
	Jane,	339	"	Apr. 23, 1727			

THOMAS AND MARY (BROWN) FLINT. 330-157.

	Name	No.	Place	Birth	Death	Marriage	Spouse / Notes
	Dorothy,	340	Concord	Oct. 1, 1718			
	Mary,	341	"	Dec. 20, 1719			
	Thomas,	342	"	Apr. 19, 1722			
	Lucy,	343	"	Oct. 3, 1725	Aug. 30, 1727		
	Henry,	344	"	Apr. 6, 1724		Feb. 19, 1750	Sarah Wheeler.
	Josiah,	345	"	Mar. 13, 1726-7	Dec. 9, 1783	Dec. 8, 1763	Hannah Meriam; -1789.
	Charles,	346	"	July 27, 1729	Sept. 11, 1758	Dec. 21, 1753	Elizabeth Buttrick. No. 215. [(Wheeler).
	John,	347	"	May 23, 1731		Apr. 24, 1759	Mary Bateman; 1739-40-; dau. John and Anna
	Edward, M. D.,	348	"	Mar. 28, 1735	Nov. 13, 1818	Jan. 8, 1758	Mary How; -1817; dau. Daniel.
	Ruth,	349	"			1766	Capt. Bardwell Smith.

HARTWELL.

	Name	No.	Place	Birth	Death	Marriage	Spouse / Notes
10	William Hartwell,	350			Mar. 12, 1690		Jasan ——; -1695.

WILLIAM AND JASAN ( ) HARTWELL. 350.

	Name	No.	Place	Birth	Death	Marriage	Spouse / Notes
10 10	John,	351 352	Concord,	Feb. 23, 1640-1	Jan. 12, 1702-3	June 1, 1662	1. Priscilla Wright; -1681. 2. Elizabeth ——; -1704.
10	Samuel,	353	"	Mar. 26, 1645		Oct. 26, 1665	Ruth Wheeler. No. 633.
	Jonathan,	354	"				
	Nathaniel,	355	"				
	Martha,	356	"	Apr. 25, 1649			
	Mary,	357	"				Jonathan Hill.
	Sarah,	358	"				

JOHN AND PRISCILLA (WRIGHT) HARTWELL. 351.

	Name	No.	Place	Birth	Death	Marriage	Spouse / Notes
	Ebenezer,	359	Concord,	Feb. 23, 1666-7		Mar. 17, 1690-1	Sarah Smedley.
	John, Jr.,	360	"	Apr. 15, 1669		June 7, 1697	Sarah Shepard; 1674-; dau. Abraham.
	Samuel,	361	"	Oct. 9, 1673	Dec. 31, 1694		
	Sarah,	362	"	Apr. 12, 1677		Apr. 19, 1698	Ebenezer Lamson.
	Joseph,	363	"	Jan. 24, 1680	Nov. 3, 1743		Ruhamah Cutter.
	William,	364	"	Feb. 20, 1678-9			

JOHN AND ELIZABETH ( ) HARTWELL. 352.

	Name	No.	Place	Birth	Death	Marriage	Spouse / Notes
	Elizabeth,	365	Concord,	Dec. 23, 1684			
	Edward,	366	"	May 23, 1689			
	Jonathan,	367 368	"	Feb. 15, 1691-2		Sept. 22, 1713	1. Elizabeth Brown. No. 155. 2. Sarah Wheeler.

SAMUEL AND RUTH (WHEELER) HARTWELL. 353. (Continued page 11.)

	Name	No.	Place	Birth	Death	Marriage	Spouse / Notes
	Samuel,	369	Concord,	Oct. 6, 1666	Nov. 27, 1744	Nov. 23, 1692	Abigail Stearns; -1709.

	Name	No.	Birth	Death	Marriage	Spouse
	Mary,	370	Concord, Feb. 16, 1667–8			
	Ruth,	371	" Oct. 17, 1669			
	William,	372	" Aug. 19, 1671	Dec. 11, 1742		Ruth ——.
11	John,	373	" June 18, 1673			
11	Hannah,	374	" Oct. 8, 1675	Jan. 5, 1755	Feb.13,1695–6	Thomas Hosmer. No. 425.
	Elizabeth,	375	" Oct. 23, 1677			
	Sarah,	376	" July 10, 1679			
	Abigail,	377	" May 1, 1681			
	Rebecca,	378 / 379	" Feb. 14, 1682–3	Mar. 29, 1776	Oct. 23, 1705	1. Simeon Hayward. No. 408. 2. —— Temple.
	Jane,	380	" Nov. 30, 1684			
	Joseph,	381	" Apr. 23, 1691	Mar.16,1693–4		
	Jonathan,	382	"			

HAYWARD.

	Name	No.	Birth	Death	Marriage	Spouse
11	Geo. Hayward,	383		Mar. 29, 1671		Mary ——; –1692–3.

GEORGE AND MARY ( ) HAYWARD. 383.

	Name	No.	Birth	Death	Marriage	Spouse
	Mary,	384				
11	John,	385	Concord, Dec. 20, 1640		June 2, 1671	Anna White.
11	Joseph,	386 / 387	" Mar. 26, 1643	Oct. 13, 1714	Oct. 26, 1665 / Mar. 23, 1676	1. Hannah Hosmer. No. 418. 2. Elizabeth Treadwell.
11						
	Sarah,	388	" Mar. 19, 1645			
9	Hannah,	389	" Feb. 20, 1646–7			Jacob Farrar. No. 289.
	Simeon,	390	" Jan. 22, 1648–9			Elizabeth ——.
	George,	391	" July 2, 1654	Dec. 16, 1675	Unmarried.	

JOHN AND ANNA (WHITE) HAYWARD. 385.

	Name	No.	Birth	Death	Marriage	Spouse
	Mary,	392	Concord, Dec. 5, 1671			
	George,	393	" July 20, 1673		Jan. 17, 1695–6	Hannah Chadwick; dau. John and Sarah.
	Mary,	394	" May 13, 1677		Oct. 31, 1698	John Willard. No. 708.
	Judith,	395	" Apr. 25, 1675		Aug. 30, 1699	Philip Goss.
	James,	396	" Jan. 27, 1678–9			
	John,	397	" June 7, 1680		Feb. 17, 1708–9	Susanna Dakin; 1689–; dau. John and Sarah.
	Hannah,	398	" Aug. 30, 1682			
	Sarah,	399	" June 16, 1689			

JOSEPH AND HANNAH (HOSMER) HAYWARD. 386–418.

	Name	No.	Birth	Death	Marriage	Spouse
	Joseph,	400	Concord, Aug. 17, 1666			
	Mary,	401	" Sept. 27, 1667			
	John,	402	" Feb. 2, 1669			
	Hannah,	403	" June 14, 1670			
	George,	404	" Mar. 3, 1672			
	Dorothy,	405	" Jan. 23, 1673–4			

JOSEPH AND ELIZABETH (TREADWELL) HAYWARD. 387.

	Name	No.	Birth	Death	Marriage	Spouse
	Ebenezer,	406	Concord, June 22, 1679			
	James,	407	" May 1, 1681			
	Simeon,	408	" June, 1683	May 18, 1719	Oct. 23, 1705	Rebecca Hartwell. No. 378.
	Abial,	409	" Sept. 12, 1691			

HOSMER.

	Name	No.	Birth	Death	Marriage	Spouse
11	James Hosmer,	410 / 411 / 412	England, 1607	Feb. 7, 1685		1. Ann ——; –1608. 2. Mary ——; –1641. 3. Ellen or Alice ——; –1646.
11						
11						

JAMES AND MARY ( ) HOSMER. 411.

	Name	No.	Birth	Death	Marriage	Spouse
	Mary,	413	About 1633	Died young.		
	Ann,	414	" 1635			
11	James,	415	" 1637	April, 1676	Oct. 13, 1658	Sarah White; dau. John.
	Mary,	416	Concord, Jan. 10, 1639–40	Aug. 18, 1642		

JAMES AND ELLEN ( ) HOSMER. 412.

	Name	No.	Birth	Death	Marriage	Spouse
11	Stephen,	417	Concord, Nov. 27, 1642	Dec. 15, 1714	May 24, 1667	Abigail Wood. No. 730.
11	Hannah,	418	" 1644	Dec. 15, 1675	Oct. 26, 1665	Joseph Hayward. No. 386.
	Mary,	419	" Apr. 14, 1646	Oct. 1, 1719		Thomas Smith; 1640–; son Thos. and Mary (Knapp).

JAMES AND SARAH (WHITE) HOSMER. 415.

	Name	No.	Birth	Death	Marriage	Spouse
	James,	420	Concord, Oct. 23, 1660			
	Mary,	421	" Apr. 26, 1664	Dec. 24, 1725		Samuel Wright.
	Dorothy,	422	" June 10, 1667	Jan. 22, 1667–8		
	Hannah,	423	" Oct. 2, 1669	Dec. 9, 1672		
	Sarah,	424	" 1771	Apr. 7, 1724	June 8, 1681	Capt. Thomas How; 1656–1733; son John and Mary.
11	Thomas,	425	" July 6, 1672	Nov. 2, 1754	Feb.13,1695–6	Hannah Hartwell. No. 374.

STEPHEN AND ABIGAIL (WOOD) HOSMER. 417–730.

	Name	No.	Birth	Death	Marriage	Spouse
	Mary,	426 / 427	Concord, May 2, 1668		Jan. 27, 1690 / Dec. 5, 1721	1. Samuel Wheeler. No. 648. 2. John Bellows.
15	Abigail,	428	" Nov. 6, 1669	Dec. 27, 1717	Aug. 14, 1695	George Wheeler. No. 646. [(Bannister).
	John,	429	" Aug. 31, 1671	1751	May 12, 1699	Mary Billings; 1680–1–; dau. Nathaniel and Jane
	Ruth,	430	" Aug. 28, 1675			
	Dorothy,	431	" Dec. 10, 1677		Mar. 8, 1711	John Wheeler. [(Bannister).
12	Stephen,	432	" June 27, 1680		Feb. 26, 1707	Prudence Billings; –1770; dau. Nathaniel and Jane
	James,	433	" June 27, 1685	Sept. 28, 1685		
	Hannah,	434	" Dec. 9, 1682			

THOMAS AND HANNAH (HARTWELL) HOSMER. 425–374.

	Name	No.	Birth	Death	Marriage	Spouse
	Hannah,	435				
	Sarah,	436				
73	Thomas,	437	1710		1731	Prudence Hosmer. No. 440.
	Mary,	438				
	James,	439	1708			Elizabeth Davis.

STEPHEN AND PRUDENCE (BILLINGS) HOSMER. 432.

	Name	No.	Born	Died	Married	Spouse / Notes
73	Prudence,	440				Thomas Hosmer. No. 437.
	Stephen, Capt., {	441				1. Meliscent Wood.
67		442	1709			2. Elizabeth Farrar. No. 309.
	Jonathan,	443				
	Josiah,	444				
	Jane,	445				
	Ephraim,	446				

HUBBARD.

		No.				
12	First generation,		George and Mary Hubbard, of Glastonbury, Conn.			
	Second "	447	John and Mary (Meriam) Hubbard, of Hartford, Conn.			

JOHN AND MARY (MERIAM) HUBBARD. 447.

	Name	No.	Born	Died	Married	Spouse / Notes
12	Jonathan,	448	Jan. 3, 1659	July 1, 1728	Mar. 15, 1681-2	Hannah Rice; dau. Samuel and Eliz. (King).

JONATHAN AND HANNAH (RICE) HUBBARD. 448.

	Name	No.	Born	Died	Married	Spouse / Notes
	Mary,	449	Concord, June 3, 1682		Apr. 27, 1699	Daniel Davis. No. 282.
	Jonathan,	450	" Aug. 18, 1683			Rebecca Brown. No. 152. [orah.
	Hannah,	451	" Apr. 20, 1685	May 23, 1725		John Temple; 1680-1-1734; son Abraham and Deb-
	Samuel, {	452	" Apr. 27, 1687	Dec. 12, 1753	Dec. 8, 1709	1. Sarah Clark; 1681-1720; dau. Samuel and Rachel.
12		453				2. —— [becca (Minott).
	Joseph, Capt.,	454	" Feb. 8, 1688-9	Apr. 10, 1768	Nov. 10, 1713	Rebecca Bulkeley; 1696-1772; dau. Joseph and Re-
	Elizabeth,	455	" June 16, 1691	Dec. 25, 1757	Jan. 12, 1709-10	Samuel Heywood; 1687-1750; son John and Sarah.
	John,	456	" Mar. 12, 1692-3		Nov. 14, 1716	Hannah Blood. [(Wooster).
	Daniel,	457	" Nov. 20, 1694		Dec. 5, 1717	Dorothy Dakin; 1698; dau. Joseph and Dorothy
12	Thomas,	458	" Aug. 27, 1696			Mary ——.
	Abigail,	459	" Jan. 23, 1698		Jan. 18, 1721-2	Samuel Fletcher. [(Barron).
	Ebenezer,	460	" Dec. 28, 1700	May 21, 1755		Mary Billings; 1704-1763; dau. Samuel and Mary

CAPT. JOSEPH AND REBECCA (BULKELEY) HUBBARD. 454.

	Name	No.	Born	Died	Married	Spouse / Notes
35	Joseph,	461	Concord, Jan. 11, 1714-15		Aug. 18, 1743	Abigail Brown.
	Rebecca,	462	" July 11, 1717	Oct. 18, 1806	Dec. 21, 1732	Col. James Barrett. No. 21.
	Elizabeth, {	463	" Sept. 25, 1720	May 12, 1802	Mar. 24, 1740	1. Israel How.
48		464			May 15, 1750	2. Stephen Barrett. No. 28.
	Lucy,	465	" Dec. 14, 1722			
	Abigail,	466	" Feb. 20, 1724-5		Mar. 15, 1742	David Howe.
	Peter,	467	" Nov. 14, 1727	Apr. 6, 1753	Dec. 20, 1750	Mary Adams; 1730-; dau. Daniel and Eliz. (Minott).
	Thomas, Capt.,	468	" June 8, 1730		Nov. 1, 1753	Abigail Brown; 1733-; d. Eph'm & Abigail (Wheeler).
	Lucy,	469	" June 8, 1730	Oct. 12, 1810	Dec. 12, 1749	John Adams; 1723-; son John and Love (Minott).
	Hannah,	470	" Jan. 18, 1735-6		May 19, 1757	Benjamin Estabrook.

THOMAS AND MARY ( ) HUBBARD. 457.

	Name	No.	Born	Died	Married	Spouse / Notes
	Nathan,	471	Concord, Feb. 23, 1723-4		Apr. 2, 1745	Mary Patterson.
	Mary,	472	" June 21, 1725			

JONES.

	Name	No.	Born	Died	Married	Spouse / Notes
12	John Jones,	473		June 22, 1673		Dorcas ——; -1709. (She married 2d Wm. Buss.)

JOHN AND DORCAS ( ) JONES. 473.

	Name	No.	Born	Died	Married	Spouse / Notes
12	Samuel,	474	Cambridge, 1648	1717	Jan. 16, 1672	Elizabeth Potter. No. 544. [No. 131.)
12	Ephraim,	475	Concord, June 6, 1650	1676	May 7, 1673	Ruth Vinton. (She married 2d Thomas Brown.
	Elizabeth,	476	" Feb. 12, 1652		Dec. 21, 1671	Joseph Buss; 1649-1680; son William and Ann.
	Joseph,	477	" June 8, 1654			[(Wheeler).
12	John,	478	" July 6, 1656	Feb. 14, 1725-6	May 5, 1681	Sarah Farwell; 1662-; daughter John and Sarah
	Dorcas,	479	" May 19, 1659		June 12, 1697	Samuel Stone.
	Rebecca, {	480	" Mar. 8, 1662-3	July 17, 1712	Feb. 9, 1688	1. James Minott.
		481				2. Capt. Joseph Bulkeley. No. 189.

SAMUEL AND ELIZABETH (POTTER) JONES. 474-544.

	Name	No.	Born	Died	Married	Spouse / Notes
	Susanna,	482	Concord, 1673	Died young.		
75	Samuel,	483	" Sept. 5, 1674	Nov. 5, 1755	Nov. 10, 1698	Ruth Brown. No. 150.
82	Nathaniel,	484	" 1676	Mar. 22, 1745	Sept. 1, 1696	Mary Rait; 1675-1749; dau. John and Susanna.
83	Ephraim,	485	" Apr. 30, 1679	Oct. 7, 1710	Apr. 18, 1701	Hepzabah Chandler.
	Joseph,	486	" July 25, 1682		1705	Hannah ——.
	John,	487	" 1684		Unmarried.	

EPHRAIM AND RUTH (VINTON) JONES. 475.

	Name	No.	Born	Died	Married	Spouse / Notes
	John,	488	Concord, Mar. 23, 1674			[(Sparhawk).
	Mary,	489	" Mar. 29, 1677		Sept. 26, 1696	Joseph Adams; 1673-1718; son Samuel and Hester

JOHN AND SARAH (FARWELL) JONES. 478.

	Name	No.	Born	Died	Married	Spouse / Notes
	Sarah,	490	Concord, June 4, 1686		Dec. 20, 1705	Daniel Hoar; -1773; son Daniel and Mary (Stratton).
	John,	491	" Jan. 6, 1690		July 25, 1716	Anna Brooks; 1695-1753; dau. Daniel and Ann
	Timothy,	492	" Apr. 6, 1694	Mar. 12, 1762 Mar. 10, 1697-8		[(Meriam).
	Bartholemew,	493	" Feb. 15, 1696-7	Sept. 16, 1738	July 4, 1720	Ruth Stow; 1701-2-; dau. Nath'l and Ruth (Meriam).

MINOTT.

	Name	No.	Born	Died	Married	Spouse / Notes
12	George Minott,	494	England, Aug. 4, 1594	Dec. 24, 1671		Martha ——; -1657.

GEORGE AND MARTHA ( ) MINOTT. 494.

	Name	No.	Born	Died	Married	Spouse / Notes
12	John, Capt., {	495	Apr. 2, 1626	Aug. 12, 1669	May 19, 1647	1. Lydia Butler; -1667; dau. Nicholas and Joice.
		496				2. Mary (Dassett) Biggs; -1676; dau. John Dassett.
	James, {	497	Dec. 31, 1628	Mar. 30, 1676	Dec. 9, 1653	1. Hannah Stoughton; 1637-1670; dau. Col. Israel.
		498			May 21, 1673	2. Hepzabah Corlet; d. Elijah and Barbara (Cutter).
	Stephen,	499	May 2, 1631	Feb. 16, 1671	Nov. 10, 1654	Truecourse Davenport; 1635-1692; dau. Richard and
	Samuel,	500	Dec. 18, 1635	Dec. 18, 1690	June 23, 1670	Hannah Howard; dau. Robert and Mary. [Eliz.

CAPT. JOHN AND LYDIA (BUTLER) MINOTT. 495.

	Name	No.	Born	Died	Married	Spouse / Notes
13	James,	501	Sept. 14, 1653	Sept. 20, 1735		Rebecca Wheeler; dau. Capt. Timothy.
	John,	502	Jan. 22, 1647	Jan. 26, 1690	Mar. 11, 1670	Elizabeth Brick; -1690; dau. Edward.
	Martha,	503	Sept. 22, 1657	Nov. 23, 1678	Unmarried.	
	Stephen,	504	Aug. 10, 1662		Dec. 1, 1686	Mary Clark; dau. Christopher.

	Samuel,	505		July 3, 1665			Hannah Jones.

JAMES AND REBECCA (WHEELER) MINOTT. 501.

	Name	No.	Place	Birth	Death	Marriage	Spouse / Notes
5	Rebecca,	506	Concord,	Feb. 9, 1685	June 23, 1738	Dec. 24, 1701	Capt. Joseph Barrett. No. 9.
5	Lydia,	507	"	Mar. 12, 1687		Jan. 3, 1705	1. Benjamin Barrett. No. 10.
		508					2. Samuel Stow.
	Mary,	509	"	Nov. 16, 1689	Sept. 3, 1760	Dec. 26, 1706	Ebenezer Wheeler. No. 656. [(Potter). No. 543.
	Timothy,	510	"	June 18, 1692	Nov. 30, 1778		1. Mary Brooks; 1699–1760; dau. Noah and Dorothy
		510					2. Mrs. Beulah Brown; –1786.
13	James, Col.,	511	"	Oct. 17, 1694	Feb. 6, 1759	Nov. 14, 1716	1. Martha Lane; 1694–1735; dau. John and Susanna.
13		512				1736	2. Eliz. Merrick; –1746; dau. Tilley and Eliz. (Wilder).
	Elizabeth,	513	"	Jan. 29, 1697	Nov. 12, 1764	Apr. 23, 1715	Capt. Dan. Adams; –1780; s. Jos. and Marg't (Eames).
	Martha,	514	"	Apr. 3, 1699	Jan. 18, 1739	Apr. 30, 1719	James Lane; 1696–; son John and Susanna.
	Love,	515	"	Apr. 15, 1702		Dec. 13, 1722	John Adams; –1725; son Joseph and Marg't (Eames).
	Mercy,	516	"	Apr. 15, 1702		Dec. 13, 1722	Samuel Dakin; 1700–; son Joseph and Dorothy (Wooster). [ful (Wheeler).
13	Samuel,	517	"	Mar. 25, 1706	Mar. 17, 1766	Mar. 7, 1731–2	1. Sarah Prescott; 1712–1737; dau. Jonas and Thank-
13		518	"			1738	2. Dorcas Prescott; 1714–1803; dau. Jonas and Thankful (Wheeler).

COL. JAMES AND MARTHA (LANE) MINOTT. 511.

	Name	No.	Place	Birth	Death	Marriage	Spouse / Notes
	John,	519	Concord,	Aug. 31, 1717	July 31, 1802	Jan. 26, 1744	Sarah Stow; 1717–1796; dau. Samuel and Sarah.
	Rebecca,	520	"	May 15, 1720	Oct. 8, 1761	Aug. 12, 1741	Benjamin Prescott; 1717–1788; son Rev. Benjamin and Elizabeth (Higginson).
	James,	521	"	Jan. 20, 1726	Aug. 2, 1773		1. Rebecca Stow.
		522					2. —— Blanchard.

COL. JAMES AND ELIZABETH (MERRICK) MINOTT. 512.

	Name	No.	Place	Birth	Death	Marriage	Spouse / Notes
	Martha,	523	Concord,	Feb. 1, 1737–8		Jan. 24, 1757	Rev. Josiah Sherman; 1729–1789; son William and
	Ephraim,	524	"	June 17, 1742		Sept. 25, 1764	Abigail Prescott. No. 615. [Mehitable.
	Elizabeth,	525	"				

SAMUEL AND SARAH (PRESCOTT) MINOTT. 517.

	Name	No.	Place	Birth	Death	Marriage	Spouse / Notes
	Samuel,	526	Concord,	Dec. 23, 1732			Elizabeth Davis. [(Cotton).
	Jonas,	527	"	Apr. 25, 1735	Mar. 20, 1813		Mary Hall; 1738–1792; dau. Rev. Willard and Abigail
	Thankful Sarah,	528	"	Mar. 4, 1737		June 12, 1755	Dea. Amos Dakin; 1731–2–; son Sam'l 2d and Mary.

SAMUEL AND DORCAS (PRESCOTT) MINOTT. 518.

	Name	No.	Place	Birth	Death	Marriage	Spouse / Notes
30	Dorcas P.,	529	Concord,	Mar. 24, 1739	Apr. 17, 1767	Jan. 15, 1761	Thomas Barrett. No. 1556.
84	George,	530	"	Apr. 23, 1741	Apr. 13, 1808	Jan. 17, 1765	Rebecca Barrett. No. 1896.
	(no issue),	531				Dec. 12, 1776	Elizabeth Barrett. No. 849.
	(no issue),	532				Apr. 11, 1782	Lydia (Barrett) Mann. No. 1018.
'32	Rebecca,	533	"	Jan. 14, 1744	1838	Oct. 15, 1799	Charles Barrett. No. 1559.
	Daniel,	534	"	Aug. 29, 1748	Dec. 20, 1753		[nah (Pierce).
	Mary,	535	"	Oct. 5, 1755			Elnathan Jones; 1737–1793; son Elnathan and Han-

POTTER.

	Name	No.	Place	Birth	Death	Marriage	Spouse / Notes
13	Luke Potter,	536	England,	1608	Oct. 13, 1697		1. Mary ——; –1644.
13		537				Oct. 13, 1644	2. Mary Edmunds; –1710; dau. Walter.

LUKE AND MARY ( ) POTTER. 536.

	Name	No.	Place	Birth	Death	Marriage	Spouse / Notes
	Eunice,	538	Concord,	Mar. 2, 1640	Died young.		
	Eunice (no issue),	539	"	Apr. 2, 1641	Nov. 24, 1708	Oct. 14, 1660	John Fry; –1696; son Andrew.
	Rebecca,	540	"	Oct. 2, 1643	Oct. 11, 1643		

LUKE AND MARY (EDMUNDS) POTTER. 537.

	Name	No.	Place	Birth	Death	Marriage	Spouse / Notes
	Luke,	541	Concord,	May 30, 1646	Aug. 13, 1661		
	Samuel,	542	"	Apr. 1, 1648	Mar. 31, 1676	Jan. 8, 1673	Sarah Wright; dau. John and Priscilla.
	Dorothy,	543	"	Apr. 9, 1650		1685	Noah Brooks. No. 102.
12	Elizabeth,	544	"	1652	Dec. 14, 1694–5	Jan. 16, 1672	Samuel Jones. No. 474.
5	Mary,	545	"	1656	Nov. 17, 1713	Mar. 23, 1674–5	Humphrey Barrett, Jr. No. 5.
13	Judah,	546	"	1657	June 20, 1731	Dec. 6, 1686	Grace Brooks. No. 103.
	Francis,	547	"		Nov. 17, 1761		
	Bethiah,	548	"	Nov. 4, 1659			

JUDAH AND GRACE (BROOKS) POTTER. 546–103.

	Name	No.	Place	Birth	Death	Marriage	Spouse / Notes
70	Eunice,	549	Concord,	Dec. 10, 1688	July 27, 1770	May 7, 1705	1. Eleazer Davis. No. 284.
		550					2. Richard Wheeler. No. 668.
64	Hannah,	551	"	Dec. 20, 1690	Dec. 1, 1782	Nov. 22, 1709	1. Thomas Brown. No. 153.
69		552				June 1, 1719	2. Simon Davis. No. 272.
	Luke,	553	"	Mar. 18, 1692–3	Sept. 25, 1784	Unmarried.	
	Mary,	554	"	Oct. 24, 1695	Sept. 1, 1696		
64	Elizabeth,	555	"	July 23, 1699		Feb. 23, 1714–5	John Brown. No. 158.
	Sarah,	556	"	Feb. 16, 1701–2	June 24, 1748	1723	Joseph Wheeler; 1695–1732.
13	Samuel,	557	"	Jan. 2, 1704–5	Feb. 15, 1800	About 1726	Elizabeth ——; 1708–1790.

SAMUEL AND ELIZABETH ( ) POTTER. 557.

	Name	No.	Place	Birth	Death	Marriage	Spouse / Notes
	Elizabeth,	558	Concord,	Oct. 16, 1727	Jan. 1, 1729–30		
	Samuel,	559	"	Dec. 1, 1729	Dec. 18, 1729		
85	Ephraim,	560	"	Dec. 27, 1731	Mar. 8, 1815	Sept. 19, 1752	1. Sarah Taylor; 1727–1792.
	(no issue),	561					2. Jane Curtis; –1837. [(Farrar).
87	Lydia,	562	"	June 7, 1733	Nov. 7, 1826	Dec. 5, 1764	James Russell; 1723–1801; son James and Susanna.
	Elizabeth,	563	"	June 15, 1735		Jan. 24, 1760	Noah Brooks; 1733–1809; son Thomas and Hannah
	Samuel,	564	"	Apr. 26, 1738	Apr. 21, 1762		[(Dakin).
90	Jonas,	565	"	Feb. 6, 1740	Mar. 7, 1821	Dec. 30, 1766	Persis Barrett. No. 1898. [(Wesson).
90		566				Oct. 24, 1782	Sarah Jones; 1754–1834; dau. John and Abigail
9	Lois,	567	"	May 2, 1744	Nov. 12, 1815	Dec. 30, 1762	Silas Conant. No. 236.
94	Grace,	568	"	Aug. 10, 1746	Mar. 10, 1827	Jan. 22, 1765	John Prescott. No. 613.
	Mary,	569	"	July 22, 1749			

PRESCOTT.

	Name	No.	Place	Birth	Death	Marriage	Spouse / Notes
13	John Prescott,	570			1683		Mary Platts.

JOHN AND MARY (PLATTS) PRESCOTT. 570.

(Continued page 14.)

	Name	No.	Place	Birth	Death	Marriage	Spouse / Notes
	Mary,	571	Bap.	Feb. 24, 1630		1648	Thomas Sawyer.

	Sarah,	572 573	Bap. 1637		Aug. 2, 1658	1. Richard Wheeler, of Lancaster. 2. —— Rice.
	Lydia,	574 575	Watertown, Aug. 15, 1641		May 28, 1658	1. Jonas Fairbanks. 2. Elias Barron.
	Martha,	576	Bap. Mar. 12, 1632	Jan. 24, 1656		John Rugg.
	John, Jr.,	577	" Apr. 1, 1635		Mar. 11, 1668	Sarah ——.
14	Jonathan,	578 579 580 581	1643	Dec. 5, 1721	Aug. 3, 1670 Dec. 23, 1675 Dec. 18, 1689 Aug. 18, 1718	1. Dorothy ——. 2. Elizabeth Hoar; –1687; dau. John. 3. Rebecca (Wheeler) Bulkeley. No. 688. 4. Ruth Brown; –1740.
	Hannah,	582			May 4, 1660	John Rugg.
	Jonas,	583	1648	Dec. 31, 1723	Dec. 14, 1672	Mary Loker; –1735; dau. John and Mary (Draper).

JONATHAN AND ELIZABETH (HOAR) PRESCOTT 579.

14	Jona'n, Jr., M.D.,	584	Concord, Apr. 5, 1677	Oct. 28, 1729	July 9, 1701	Rebecca Bulkeley. No. 192.
	Elizabeth,	585	" Sept. 27, 1678		July 1, 1696	John Foule.
	Dorothy,	586	" Mar. 31, 1681	1748	July 14, 1702	Edward Bulkeley. No. 185.
	John,	587	" May 13, 1683	Jan. 28, 1706		
	Benj., Rev.,	588 589 590	" Sept. 16, 1687	May 28, 1777	Oct. 20, 1715	1. Elizabeth Higginson; 1696–1723. 2. Mercy Gibbs; –1744; dau. Rev. Henry. 3. Mary (Pepperell) Coleman; dau. Sir Wm. Pepperell.
	Mary,	591	" Aug. 14, 1685		Apr. 16, 1702	John Miles; son John.

DR. JONATHAN AND REBECCA (BULKELEY) PRESCOTT. 584-192.

	Jonathan,	592	Concord, June 3, 1702			Mary ——.
	Rebecca,	593	" Aug. 14, 1704			
	John, M.D.,	594	" May 8, 1708	Dec. 30, 1743		Ann Lynde; –1795; dau. Nathaniel.
	Peter,	595	" Apr. 17, 1709	1784	1735	Elizabeth Call.
14	Charles, Col.,	596	" Aug. 15, 1711	Feb. 2, 1779	1736	Elizabeth Barrett. No. 16.
	Elizabeth,	597	" Dec. 2, 1713		June 24, 1731	Rev. David Hall.
	Dorothy,	598	" May 13, 1716	July 5, 1784		
14	Abel, M.D.,	599 600	" Apr. 7, 1718	Oct. 24, 1805		1. Abigail Brigham. 2. Mrs. Mary Burton.
	Mary,	601	" July 3, 1720			
	Lucia,	602	" Aug. 25, 1723	Apr. 20, 1725		
	Benjamin,	603	" April, 1724	May, 1745		

COL. CHARLES AND ELIZABETH (BARRETT) PRESCOTT. 596-16.

	Elizabeth,	604 605	Concord, Aug. 31, 1737			1. Jesse Hosmer. 2. Capt. Aaron Jones, of Weston.
	Lucy,	606	" Dec. 21, 1738	Dec. 22, 1819	Unmarried.	
	Mary,	607	" Aug. 9, 1742	May 4, 1797		
	Charles,	608	" Sept. 24, 1744	May 10, 1810		
	Rebecca,	609	" Sept. 19, 1746			Joseph Hayward.
	John,	610	" Oct. 18, 1748	Sept. 12, 1753		
	Ann,	611	" June 7, 1750			Amos Baker.
	Amy,	612	"			Jesse Hosmer.

DR. ABEL AND ABIGAIL (BRIGHAM) PRESCOTT. 599.

94	John,	613	Concord, Apr. 23, 1743	Mar. 12, 1821	Jan. 22, 1765	Grace Potter. No. 568.
	Benjamin,	614	" Apr. 4, 1745	Aug. 23, 1830	Nov., 1768	Dorothy Wheeler.
	Abigail,	615	" June 12, 1747	Feb. 27, 1825	Sept. 25, 1764	Ephraim Minott. No. 524.
	Dorothy,	616	" July 27, 1753		Unmarried.	
	Lucy,	617	" Apr. 24, 1757		Dec. 6, 1776	Hon. Jonathan Fay.
	Jonathan,	618	" June 11, 1755	Aug. 22, 1810	Unmarried.	
	Abel,	619	" Apr. 12, 1749	Sept. 3, 1775		
	Samuel, M.D.,	620	" Aug. 19, 1751	Died Halifax.		

WHEELER.[1]

14	George Wheeler,	621	England,		1687	Katharine ——; –1684-5.
15	Lt. Jos. Wheeler,	622 623	" 1610			1. Elizabeth ——; –1643. 2. Sarah ( ) Meriam; –1670-1; widow Joseph.
15	Obadiah Wheeler,	624	" 1608	Oct. 27, 1671		Susanna ——; –1679.
15	Ephr'm Wheeler,	625	(Removed to Fairfield 1644)	1670		(Left 4 sons, 6 daughters.)
	Thomas Wheeler,	626	(" " " 1644)	1654		(Left sons Thomas, John, and two daughters.)
Capt. Thomas Wheeler,		627	England,	Dec. 10, 1676		Ruth Wood. No. 724.
Capt. Timothy Wheeler,		628 629	" 1604	July 10, 1687		1. Jane ——; –1642-3. 2. Mary Brooks. No. 97.
	James Wheeler,	630	(Removed to Stow.)	Jan. 31, 1721		Sarah ——.

[1] The relationship of these eight families is not known.

GEORGE AND KATHARINE ( ) WHEELER. 621.

14	William,	631	Prob. England,	Dec. 31, 1683	Oct. 30, 1659	Hannah or Anna Buss; 1641-2-; d. Wm. and Anna.
	Thomas,	632	" "	1687	Oct. 10, 1657	Hannah Harrod (or Harwood).
	Ruth,	633	" "	Dec. 9, 1713	Oct. 26, 1665	Samuel Hartwell. No. 353.
	Elizabeth,	634	" "	June 14, 1704	Oct. 1, 1656	Francis Fletcher; son Robert.
	Hannah,	635	" "			—— Fletcher.
	Sarah,	636	Concord, Mar. 30, 1640	Dec. 12, 1713	Oct. 26, 1665	Francis Dudley.
15	John,	637	" Mar. 19, 1643	Sept. 27, 1713	Mar. 25, 1663	Sarah Larkin; 1647-1727; d. Dea. Edw'd and Joanna.
	Mary,	638	" Sept. 6, 1645	Dec. 24, 1678	Oct. 26, 1665	Eliphalet Fox; –1711; son Thomas and Rebecca.

WILLIAM AND HANNAH (BUSS) WHEELER. 631.

	Hannah,	639	Concord, Oct. 23, 1660	Died young.		
	Rebecca,	640	" Feb. 25, 1661-2			Nicholas Shevally.
	Elizabeth,	641	" Jan. 2, 1663		June 15, 1682	Samuel Fletcher.
15	William,	642	" Feb. 8, 1665	May 29, 1752		Sarah ——; –1744.
	Hannah,	643	" Apr. 15, 1669	Apr. 8, 1673		
	Richard,	644	" Sept. 19, 1672	Mar. 31, 1689		
	John,	645	"			
15	George,	646 647	"	July, 1737	Aug. 14, 1695 Dec. 3, 1719	1. Abigail Hosmer. No. 428. 2. Abigail Smith; –1728; dau. Thomas.

JOHN AND SARAH (LARKIN) WHEELER. 637.

	Name	No.	Place	Birth	Death	Marriage	Spouse / Notes
16	Samuel,	648	Concord,	July 6, 1664	Dec. 20, 1717	Jan. 27, 1690	Mary Hosmer. No. 426.
	Sarah,	649	"			July 22, 1691	John Meriam; 1666–; son John and Mary (Cooper).
	Edward,	650	"	July 17, 1669	Feb. 17, 1733–4	Nov. 23, 1697	Sarah Meriam; 1675–1738; dau. Samuel and Eliz.
	Joanna,	651	"	Dec. 21, 1671	Died young.		[(Townsend).
	Mary,	652	"	Sept. 16, 1673		Apr. 15, 1697	Jacob Wood. No. 728.
	Lydia,	653	"	Oct. 27, 1675		May 19, 1692	1. Timothy Wheeler; 1667–1718; s. Thos. and Sarah.
		654				Apr. 21, 1720	2. Nathaniel Stow; s. Nathaniel and Ruth (Meriam).
	Esther,	655	"	Dec. 1, 1678		May 5, 1698	Samuel Prescott.
	Ebenezer,	656	"	June 3, 1682		Dec. 26, 1706	Mary Minott. No. 509. [No. 583.
	Thankful,	657	"	June 3, 1682	Nov., 1716	Oct. 5, 1699	Jonas Prescott; 1678–1750; son Jonas and Mary.

WILLIAM AND SARAH ( ) WHEELER. 642.

	Name	No.	Place	Birth	Death	Marriage	Spouse / Notes
15	William,	658	Concord,	Jan. 9, 1693–4	Sept., 1769		Mercy ——; –1760.
15	Joseph,	659	"	Feb. 2, 1695–6			[(Brooks).
	Francis,	660	"	Feb. 8, 1697–8	Nov., 1774		1. Mary Meriam; 1707–1737; dau. Jos. and Dorothy
		661				Jan. 23, 1740	2. Sarah Blood. No. 78.
	Hezekiah,	662	"	June 13, 1700	May 5, 1759	Apr. 12, 1732	Sarah Buss.
	Nathaniel,	663	"	Sept. 18, 1702			Abigail Conant.
	Elizabeth,	664	"	Oct. 2, 1704			
	Sarah,	665	"	Mar. 8, 1706–7	Nov. 26, 1707		
	Jeremiah,	666	"	Nov. 22, 1709	Aug. 3, 1783		Esther ——.

GEORGE AND ABIGAIL (HOSMER) WHEELER. 646–428.

	Name	No.	Place	Birth	Death	Marriage	Spouse / Notes
	Richard,	667	Concord,			Feb. 21, 1720	1. Jemmima French.
		668					2. Eunice (Potter) Davis. No. 550.
		669					3. Mrs. Anne Bateman.
	James,	670					
	Peter,	671					

FRANCIS AND MARY (MERIAM) WHEELER. 660.

	Name	No.	Place	Birth	Death	Marriage	Spouse / Notes
	Francis,	672		Feb. 22, 1724–5	Dec. 14, 1727		
	Mary,	673		Aug. 27, 1726	June 21, 1736		
	Francis,	674		July 3, 1728	June 25, 1778		Mary ——; –1831.
	Rhoda,	675		Aug. 24, 1730		Jan. 22, 1750	Abraham Smith.
	Nathaniel,	676		Apr. 29, 1732	July 11, 1736		
	Meriam,	677		Jan. 3, 1733–4			
	Solomon,	678		Nov. 5, 1735	Nov. 30, 1736		

FRANCIS AND SARAH (BLOOD) WHEELER. 661.

	Name	No.	Place	Birth	Death	Marriage	Spouse / Notes
	Sarah,	679		June 22, 1742		June 24, 1773	Keziah Wellington; –1830.
	Samuel,	680		Oct. 5, 1743	Jan. 23, 1832		Lydia Merriam; 1747–; dau. Josiah and Lydia.
	Phineas,	681		Apr. 30, 1745	June 18, 1814		Redit Jones; 1741–2–1826; s. Ebenezer and Priscilla.
	Hannah,	682		Jan. 23, 1746–7	Apr., 1788	July 30, 1776	Sarah Meriam; 1753–1825; dau. Josiah and Lydia.
	Noah,	683		Jan. 25, 1749–50	Feb. 23, 1834		

LIEUT. JOSEPH AND ELIZABETH ( ) WHEELER. 622.

	Name	No.	Place	Birth	Death	Marriage	Spouse / Notes
	Ephraim,	684	Concord,	Apr. 14, 1640	July 10, 1642		
	Joseph,	685	"	Dec. 1, 1641	July 18, 1642		
	Mary,	686	"	Sept. 20, 1643	Sept. 20, 1643		

LIEUT. JOSEPH AND SARAH (MERRIAM) WHEELER. 623.

	Name	No.	Place	Birth	Death	Marriage	Spouse / Notes
8	Rebecca,	687	Concord,	Sept. 6, 1645		Apr. 16, 1667	1. Peter Bulkeley. No. 177.
		688					2. Jonathan Prescott. No. 580.

OBADIAH AND SUSANNA ( ) WHEELER. 624.

	Name	No.	Place	Birth	Death	Marriage	Spouse / Notes
	Joshua,	689					Elizabeth ——.
	John,	690	Concord,	Jan. 27, 1640–1			
	Ruth,	691	"	Apr. 23, 1642			
	A son,	692	"	Nov. 25, 1643	Nov. 29, 1643		
	Samuel,	693	"	Feb. 22, 1644–5		Nov. 10, 1673	Mary Perry.
	Susanna,	694	"	Mar. 17, 1648–9			—— Shipley.
	Obadiah,	695	"		Apr. 21, 1676	July 17, 1672	Elizabeth White.
	Josiah,	696	"		Apr. 21, 1676	Unmarried.	

WILLARD.

	Name	No.	Place	Birth	Death	Marriage	Spouse / Notes
9	Margery Willard,	697	England,				Dolor Davis. No. 253.
15	Maj. Simon "	698	"	1605	Apr. 24, 1676		1. Mary Sharpe; dau. Henry and Jane.
		699					2. Elizabeth Dunster.
		700					3. Mary Dunster.

MAJ. SIMON AND ( ) WILLARD. 698. (Continued page 16.)

	Name	No.	Place	Birth	Death	Marriage	Spouse / Notes
	Josiah,	701		1674		Mar. 20, 1656–7	Hannah Hosmer; dau. Thomas
	Simon,	702	Concord,	Nov. 23, 1649	June 23, 1731	About 1679	1. Martha Jacob.
		703				July 25, 1722	2. Priscilla Buttolph.
	Samuel,	704	"	Jan. 31, 1640	Sept. 12, 1707	Aug. 4, 1664	1. Abigail Sherman; d. John and Mary (Lawrence).
		705				1679	2. Eunice Tyng; –1720; dau. Edward.
	Henry,	706	"	June 4, 1655	Aug. 27, 1726	July 18, 1674	1. Mary Dakin.
		707				1689	2. Dorcas Cutler.
	John,	708	"	Feb. 12, 1656–7		Oct. 31, 1698	Mary Hayward. No. 394.
	Daniel,	709	"	Dec. 12, 1658	Aug. 23, 1708	Dec. 6, 1683	1. Hannah Cutler; –1690–1.
		710				Jan. 4, 1692	2. Mary Mills; dau Josiah.
	Joseph,	711	Lancaster,	Jan. 4, 1660	June, 1721	Jan. 8, 1690	Mary Brown.
	Benjamin,	712	"	1665		1690	Sarah Larkin; dau. John.
	Mary,	713	England,			1649	Joshua Edwards.
	Jonathan,	714	Lancaster,	Dec. 14, 1669	1706		
	Dorothy,	715				Unmarried.	
6	Elizabeth,	716			Aug. 29, 1690	Apr. 8, 1653	Robert Blood. No. 34.
	Sarah,	717	Concord,	June 27, 1642	Jan. 22, 1677–8		Nathaniel Howard.
	Abovehope,	718	"	Oct. 30, 1646	Dec. 23, 1663	Unmarried.	

	Mary,	719	Concord, Sept. 7, 1653		May 23, 1693	Capt. Thomas Brintnall; son Thomas and Esther.
	Hannah,	720	Lancaster, Oct. 6, 1666		Unmarried.	
	Elizabeth,	721	"		"	

WOOD.

16	William Wood,	722		May 14, 1671		

WILLIAM AND ( ) WOOD. 722.

16	Michael,	723		May 13, 1764		
	Ruth,	724				Capt. Thomas Wheeler. No. 627.

MICHAEL AND MARY ( ) WOOD. 723.

	Abraham,	725				
	Isaac,	726				Elizabeth.
	Thompson,	727				Martha.
16	Jacob,	728	Mar. 3, 1691-2	Oct. 6, 1723	Apr. 15, 1697	Mary Wheeler. No. 652.
	John,	729			Nov. 13, 1677	Elizabeth Vinton.
11	Abigail,	730	Apr. 10, 1642	Jan. 5, 1717	May 24, 1667	Stephen Hosmer. No. 417.

JACOB AND MARY (WHEELER) WOOD. 728-652.

	Jacob,	731	Nov. 3, 1698			
	Mary,	732	July 14, 1700			
	Ephraim,	733	Feb. 4, 1701-2	Mar. 20, 1789		
	Dorcas,	734	Feb. 10, 1703-4			Mary Buss; 1706-7-; daughter Peter and Rachel.
	Hannah,	735	Aug. 29, 1705			

LIEUT. OLIVER AND HANNAH (HUNT) BARRETT. 14.

	Rebecca,	736	Bolton, Jan. 7, 1738-9	Mar. 26, 1823	Jan. 3, 1762	Dea. David Nourse; 1739-1825.
	Hannah,	737	" Feb. 19, 1741	Feb. 2, 1830	Jan. 18, 1764	William Sawyer; -1822.
	Bathsheba,	738	" Apr. 2, 1744		June 5, 1769	Ahobiab Sawyer; 1742-.
16	Oliver,	739	" July 22, 1746	May 11, 1817	Mar. 6, 1775	Sarah Whitcomb, 1754-1834.
	Ruth,	740	" Dec. 24, 1749	Dec. 16, 1841	Oct. 20, 1772	Jonathan Nourse; 1754-1827.
	Abigail,	741	" Aug. 8, 1752	Nov. 24, 1839	Jan. 7, 1772	Calvin Sawyer; 1750-.

OLIVER AND SARAH (WHITCOMB) BARRETT. 739.

16	Hannah,	742	Bolton, Dec. 16, 1775	Aug. 22, 1856	May 28, 1793	Maj. Barnard Nourse; 1771-1851.
	John,	743	" July 23, 1777	Sept. 4, 1799	Unmarried.	
17	Oliver, Major,	744	" Nov. 27, 1780	Jan. 17, 1859	Jan. 28, 1806	Lucy Fairbanks, 1786-1874.
17	Becke,	745	" May 3, 1783	Oct. 25, 1853	May, 1804	1. Eleazer Houghton; 1776-1814.
		746			May, 1816	2. Phineas Fairbanks; 1774-1843.
18	Asa,	747	" Nov. 8, 1787	Jan. 17, 1878	May 8, 1814	Sally Bennett; 1794-1863.

MAJ. BARNARD AND HANNAH (BARRETT) NOURSE. 742.

	Rufus,	748	Bolton, Sept. 24, 1793		Unmarried.	
16	Hannah,	749	" Aug. 5, 1797	Nov. 21, 1824	Nov. 8, 1818	Levi Sawyer, M. D.; 1781-1841.
16	Caleb,	750	" June 18, 1804	Mar. 6, 1884	Sept. 13, 1826	Orissa Holman; 1805-1859.

DR. LEVI AND HANNAH (NOURSE) SAWYER. 749.

	Zipporah,	751	Aug. 13, 1819			
16	Sterling Konisky,	752	Nov. 20, 1821		Nov. 6, 1846	Sarah B. Whitcomb.
	Rufus,	753	Dec. 31, 1823			

STERLING K. AND SARAH B. (WHITCOMB) SAWYER. 752.

	Alice Jane,	754	Bolton, Feb. 20, 1848	Aug. 20, 1854		
	Mary Lincoln,	755	" Sept. 24, 1861	July 11, 1863		
	Geo. Whitcomb,	756	" Oct. 30, 1852			
16	Charles Howe,	757	" July 11, 1856		Aug. 31, 1880	Mary E. L. Bowers.

CHARLES H. AND MARY E. L. (BOWERS) SAWYER. 757.

	Zipporah Hattie,	758	Bolton, Aug. 24, 1881			
	George Konisky,	759	" Aug. 25, 1885			

CALEB AND ORISSA (HOLMAN) NOURSE. 750.

16	Hannah,	760	Bolton, Mar. 25, 1828		June 18, 1848	Rev. George S. Ball; 1823-.
16	Rufus C.,	761	" May 25, 1830	Nov. 26, 1862	Apr. 6, 1853	Abby A. Hall; 1831-1885.
	Caleb E.,	762	" July 1, 1831	Sept., 1867	Sept., 1861	Hattie J. Munroe; -1867.
17	Orissa H.,	763	" Dec. 4, 1832		Apr. 6, 1853	Andrew J. Barton.
	Ellen A. (no issue),	764	" Oct. 27, 1834		May 7, 1861	John Whitney.

REV. GEORGE S. AND HANNAH (NOURSE) BALL. 760.

	Clinton D.,	765	Bolton, Oct. 2, 1849			
16	Susan A.,	766	Upton, July 26, 1852		Feb. 3, 1876	George A. Wood; 1854-.
	Lydia W.,	767	" Nov. 6, 1854			
	George W.,	768	Plymouth, May 25, 1857			
	Lizzie H.,	769	Upton, Oct. 28, 1863			
	Walter S.,	770	" Mar. 17, 1867			

GEORGE A. AND SUSAN A. (BALL) WOOD. 766.

	Florence Lincoln,	771	Upton, Dec. 12, 1876			
	Eliza Maria,	772	" Sept. 20, 1878			
	Merton Arba,	773	" Apr. 29, 1880			
	Anna Barnard,	774	" Apr. 24, 1882			
	Lois Ilione,	775	" Mar. 16, 1884			

RUFUS C. AND ABBY A. (HALL) NOURSE. 761.

16	Rufus E.,	776	Bolton, Jan. 30, 1854	Jan. 18, 1874		
	Charles W.,	777	" Mar. 19, 1856		May 6, 1879	Lucy F. Sanford; 1860-.
	Fred T.,	778	" July 16, 1860			
	Rufus C.,	779	" Oct. 27, 1862			

CHARLES W. AND LUCY F. (SANFORD) NOURSE. 777.

	Florence S.,	780	Milton, Apr. 22, 1880			

ANDREW J. AND ORISSA (NOURSE) BARTON. 763.

	Name	No.	Place	Birth	Death	Marriage	Spouse
	Alexander,	781	Upton,	July 26, 1854			
	Fred.,	782	"	Sept. 10, 1856			
	Abbie S.,	783	"	Feb. 6, 1858	Dec. 19, 1879		
	Alice R.,	784	"	Jan. 26, 1861			
	Anna O.,	785	"	Dec. 28, 1862	Nov. 1, 1882		

MAJ. OLIVER AND LUCY (FAIRBANKS) BARRETT. 744.

	Name	No.	Place	Birth	Death	Marriage	Spouse
	Sarah (no issue),	786	Bolton,	Dec. 5, 1806		Feb. 18, 1830	Joel Sawyer; 1805–.
17	Rebecca,	787	"	Mar. 26, 1810		Oct. 17, 1839	Horatio F. Newton; 1807–.
17	Humphrey (no issue),	788	"	Mar. 26, 1810	Dec. 3, 1885	Nov. 27, 1854	Marion E. Munroe; 1832–.
	Oliver,	789	"	Feb. 24, 1813		Oct. 15, 1840	Abby B. Sawyer; 1819–1881.
	Lucy,	790	"	Feb. 24, 1813	Aug. 14, 1816		
	John,	791	"	Nov. 23, 1816	Sept. 7, 1818		
17	Jabez,	792	"	Nov. 23, 1816	Nov. 27, 1873	Nov. 4, 1841	Helen Jewett; 1820–.
17	Roswell,	793	"	Dec. 16, 1819		May 2, 1854	Sarah Josephine Barrett. No. 841.
	Asa,	794	"	Nov. 15, 1822	Nov. 26, 1829		
17	Achsah,	795	"	May 24, 1827		Oct. 27, 1853	John F. Sawyer; 1825–1882.

HORATIO F. AND REBECCA (BARRETT) NEWTON. 787.

	Name	No.	Place	Birth	Death	Marriage	Spouse
	George B.,	796	Bolton,	Dec. 8, 1842		July 6, 1880	1. Helen Burnes; 1847–1881.
		797				July 23, 1882	2. Emma Rice; 1856–.
	Fidelia,	798	"	Jan. 23, 1845			
17	Maria Augusta,	799	"	Oct. 19, 1847		Sept. 11, 1876	Andrew L. Nourse.
	Henry B.,	800	"	Aug. 3, 1849			

ANDREW L. AND MARIA A. (NEWTON) NOURSE. 799.

	Name	No.	Place	Birth	Death	Marriage	Spouse
	Arthur Henry,	801	Bolton,	July 6, 1877			
	Richard Edgar,	802	"	Nov. 28, 1878			
	Fidelia Elizabeth,	803	"	Oct. 22, 1880			
	Grace Maria,	804	"	Nov. 5, 1882			

OLIVER AND ABBY B. (SAWYER) BARRETT. 789.

	Name	No.	Place	Birth	Death	Marriage	Spouse
17	Edward G.,	805	Bolton,	July 27, 1841		Oct. 24, 1867	Mary Bulfinch; 1846–.
	Louisa C.,	806	"	Apr. 25, 1845			
17	Fred O.,	807	"	Oct. 16, 1848		Mar. 9, 1876	Mary B. Wyatt; 1852–.

EDWARD G. AND MARY (BULFINCH) BARRETT. 805.

	Name	No.	Place	Birth	Death	Marriage	Spouse
	Charles F.,	808		Sept. 29, 1868	Nov. 7, 1869		
	Louis G.,	809		Sept. 2, 1870			
	Annie L.,	810		June 2, 1873			
	Edith M.,	811		Aug. 27, 1876			
	Grace F.,	812		Aug. 25, 1878			

FRED. O. AND MARY B. (WYATT) BARRETT. 807.

	Name	No.	Place	Birth	Death	Marriage	Spouse
	Alice G.,	813		June 2, 1877			
	Charles F.,	814		May 17, 1880			

JABEZ AND HELEN (JEWETT) BARRETT. 792.

	Name	No.	Place	Birth	Death	Marriage	Spouse
	Helen,	815	Bolton,	Oct. 9, 1842	May 5, 1859		
17	Frank,	816	"	Sept. 19, 1847	Oct. 13, 1880	Dec. 2, 1871	Ellen F. Rogers; 1848–.
17	John H.,	817	"	Sept. 6, 1851		Dec. 6, 1876	Ella F. Munson; 1855–.
	Lucy S.,	818	"	July 3, 1861			

FRANK AND ELLEN F. (ROGERS) BARRETT. 816.

	Name	No.	Place	Birth	Death	Marriage	Spouse
	Herbert S.,	819		July 27, 1873	Aug. 13, 1873		
	Mabel S.,	820		May 9, 1875			

JOHN H. AND ELLA F. (MUNSON) BARRETT. 817.

	Name	No.	Place	Birth	Death	Marriage	Spouse
	Bertha M.,	821	Hudson,	July 2, 1881			
	Frank Herbert,	822	"	Apr. 5, 1884			

ROSWELL AND SARAH J. (BARRETT) BARRETT. 793–841.

	Name	No.	Place	Birth	Death	Marriage	Spouse
	Ella V.,	823		Dec. 20, 1858			

JOHN F. AND ACHSAH (BARRETT) SAWYER. 795.

	Name	No.	Place	Birth	Death	Marriage	Spouse
	Abby G.,	824		Dec. 15, 1861	July 3, 1862		
	Charles J.,	825		Oct. 7, 1866			
	Lucy H.,	826		July 11, 1869			

ELEAZER AND BECKE (BARRETT) HOUGHTON. 745.

	Name	No.	Place	Birth	Death	Marriage	Spouse
17	Partmon, Hon.,	827		May 3, 1806		June 25, 1833	Orlinda A. Prince.
17	Cyrene,	828		May 7, 1808			Simon D. Cunningham; 1810–1884.

HON. PARTMON AND ORLINDA A. (PRINCE) HOUGHTON. 827.

	Name	No.	Place	Birth	Death	Marriage	Spouse
17	Sarah P.,	829		Mar. 14, 1836	June 3, 1872	Oct. 3, 1869	Andrew W. Bibber.
	Henry P.,	830		June 8, 1842	July 17, 1842		

ANDREW W. AND SARAH P. (HOUGHTON) BIBBER. 829.

	Name	No.	Place	Birth	Death	Marriage	Spouse
	Edith P.,	831		July 23, 1870			
	Sarah P. H.,	832		Dec. 24, 1871	Oct. 14, 1876		

SIMON D. AND CYRENE (HOUGHTON) CUNNINGHAM. 828.

	Name	No.	Place	Birth	Death	Marriage	Spouse
	Ellen A.,	833					E. A. Emes.
	George H.,	834	Bolton, Aug. 14, 1832			Nov. 29, 1854	Mary F. Tirrell.
17	Harriet Augusta,	835	So. Boston, Sept. 22, 1837	May 3, 1874		Sept. 22, 1864	John R. Summer.

JOHN R. AND HARRIET A. (CUNNINGHAM) SUMMER. 835.

(Continued page 18.)

	Edith Houghton,	836	Bristol, N. H., Oct. 9, 1866			
	Clara Davis,	837	Concord, Aug. 13, 1868			
	Walter Dickerson,	838	E. Weymouth, Aug. 1, 1870	Dec. 11, 1874		
	Herbert Ross,	839	" Dec. 9, 1872			

ASA AND SALLY (BENNETT) BARRETT. 747.

17	Charles,	840		Mar. 6, 1815	Mar. 9, 1815		
18	Sarah Josephine,	841		Sept. 20, 1818		May 2, 1854	Roswell Barrett. No. 793.
18	Francis Oliver, {	842	Balt., Md., Apr. 8, 1831			Nov. 12, 1863	1. Sarah Louise Post; 1836–1878. [Mary.
18	{	843				Oct. 31, 1882	2. Mary Caroline Gwyn; 1845–; dau. Charles R. and

FRANCIS O. AND SARAH L. (POST) BARRETT. 842.

	Alberta Louise,	844	Balt., Md., Aug. 18, 1864	June 9, 1865	
	James Post,	845	" Jan. 17, 1866		
	Francis Reese,	846	" Oct. 6, 1868	Nov. 11, 1870	
	Henry Wellington	847	" Oct. 6, 1873	Aug. 19, 1874	

FRANCIS O. AND MARY C. (GWYN) BARRETT. 843.

	Francis Oliver, Jr.	848	Balt., Md., July 7, 1885

HUMPHREY AND ELIZABETH (ADAMS) BARRETT. 15.

18	Elizabeth (no issue),	849	Concord, Apr. 10, 1745	Apr. 10, 1789	Dec. 12, 1776	Dea. George Minott. No. 531. [(Raymond).
	Rebecca,	850	" Feb. 13, 1746	June 28, 1796	Jan. 18, 1770	Reuben Hunt; 1744–1816; son Simon and Mary
	Mary,	851	" Nov. 18, 1748	Dec. 16, 1777		Jonas Lee; 1745–1816; son Dr. Jos. and Ruth (Jones).
	Sarah,	852	" Sept. 18, 1750	Aug. 14, 1751		[(Prescott).
	Humphrey (no issue),	853	" May 23, 1752	Mar. 13, 1827	July 6, 1780	Rebecca Heywood; 1752–1829; dau. Jonas and Ann
46	Sarah,	854	" Feb. 16, 1754		June 22, 1775	Stephen Barrett. No. 1899. [Hannah (Simmons).
	Martha,	855	" May 21, 1756	Nov. 28, 1792	Feb. 27, 1780	Dea. Joshua Brooks; 1755–1790; son Joshua and
20	Ruth,	856	" Dec. 25, 1760	July 26, 1795	Feb. 23, 1786	Jonas Heywood, Jr.; 1721–1808.
21	Abel,	857	" Oct. 28, 1764	Jan. 2, 1803	Dec. 1, 1796	Lucy Minott. No. 4852.

REUBEN AND REBECCA (BARRETT) HUNT. 850.

18	Humphrey, Capt., {	858	Concord, Nov. 30, 1770		Jan. 14, 1802	1. Betsey Heywood. No. 1009.
18	{	859			Jan. 3, 1812	2. Sally Prescott; 1786–; dau. Willoughby and Eliz.
	Ruth,	860	" Sept. 18, 1772	June 14, 1811	Feb. 19, 1797	Daniel Parker.
	Reuben,	861	" Nov. 16, 1774	Feb. 18, 1777		
	Rebecca,	862	" Mar. 15, 1776		May 12, 1808	James Wright. [and Eliz.
19	Mary,	863	" Apr. 20, 1778	Dec. 9, 1818	Oct. 29, 1809	John Lynde Prescott; 1775–1826; son Willoughby
20	Martha,	864	" Dec. 23, 1779	May 17, 1865	Apr. 3, 1806	William Abrams; 1782–1819.
	Miriam,	865	" Sept. 9, 1781	Sept. 20, 1781		
20	Reuben, {	866	" Jan. 11, 1783	May 11, 1866	Oct. 27, 1814	1. Eliza Tufts; –1817.
20	{	867			Mar. 10, 1819	2. Sarah Snow.
20	Simon,	868	" Oct. 11, 1784	June 1, 1865	July 22, 1818	Hannah B. Rogers; 1785–1882.
	Abel,	869	" Mar. 8, 1787		Unmarried.	
	Betsey,	870	" Jan. 23, 1789	June 25, 1817	Feb. 12, 1816	Thomas Dix.

CAPT. HUMPHREY AND BETSEY (HEYWOOD) HUNT. 858–1009.

18	Mary Heywood,	871	Concord, Nov. 8, 1802	June 5, 1838	Jan. 9, 1827	Stedman Buttrick; 1796–1874; son James and Lucy.
18	Rebecca,	872	" Aug. 29, 1804		Dec. 7, 1826	David Buttrick; 1800–. [and Lydia.
19	Elizabeth Taylor,	873	" June 2, 1807	Jan. 15, 1864	May 31, 1831	David Wheeler Buttrick; 1804–1851; son Col. John
	Martha Ann,	874	" July 30, 1810	Sept. 24, 1810		

CAPT. HUMPHREY AND SALLY (PRESCOTT) HUNT. 859.

19	Ann Maria,	875	Concord, Dec. 6, 1812		Sept. 7, 1841	Reuben Moore; –1856.
19	Emeline Prescott,	876	" May 29, 1814	June 28, 1875	July 17, 1845	Barzillai Nickerson Hudson; 1813–1885.
19	Sarah Augusta,	877	" 1816	Nov. 18, 1849	Feb. 20, 1840	Capt. John B. Moore; son Abel and Ruth.
	Marinda,	878	" Dec. 27, 1818	Feb. 5, 1880	Nov. 25, 1845	Charles Henry Hurd; 1819; son Isaac, Jr., and Mary.
	Harriet Parker,	879	" Aug. 24, 1822			
	Louisa Jane,	880	" Jan., 1824	July 11, 1826		
19	Almira Caroline,	881	" May 7, 1826	May 11, 1877	Feb. 11, 1851	Capt. John B. Moore; son Abel and Ruth.
	Chas. Humphrey,	882	" Nov. 10, 1830			

STEDMAN AND MARY H. (HUNT) BUTTRICK. 871.

18	Lucy Jane,	883	Concord, July 12, 1827		Feb. 8, 1853	John Hosmer; son Edmund and Sally (Pierce).
	Adeline Eliza,	884	" Oct. 16, 1828			
	Harriet,	885	" Oct. 27, 1829			
	Susan Barrett,	886	" Oct. 30, 1830	Sept. 3, 1847		
	Alden,	887	" Dec. 25, 1831	June 3, 1863		
	Annie M. (no issue),	888	" Dec. 30, 1832	Oct. 22, 1854	July 5, 1853	Nathaniel G. Groton.
	William,	889	" Apr. 22, 1834		Jan. 17, 1861	Emma Florence King.
	Caroline M.,	890	" Dec. 15, 1835	Dec. 18, 1836		
	George,	891	" Mar. 6, 1837			
	Charles H.,	892	" May 30, 1838	May 15, 1839		

JOHN AND LUCY J. (BUTTRICK) HOSMER. 883.

	George Stedman,	893	May 13, 1855
	John Frederick,	894	Dec. 10, 1859

DAVID AND REBECCA (HUNT) BUTTRICK. 872.

18	Humphrey H.,	895	Concord, May 3, 1827		Sept. 25, 1856	Lucy A. Tolman.
19	Charles,	896	" Aug. 23, 1828		Apr. 9, 1856	Elizabeth Cowdin.
19	Martha A.,	897	" Jan. 11, 1830		Dec. 16, 1852	William M. Holden.
	David H.,	898	" Feb. 9, 1833	Died young.		
19	David H.,	899	" Jan. 11, 1834		Sept. 14, 1862	Julia A. Thayer.
19	Maria E.,	900	" May 24, 1835	June 30, 1870	Oct. 3, 1860	Chandler B. Lane.
	Francis,	901	" Jan. 11, 1837	Aug. 6, 1863		
19	Gorham,	902	" Jan. 11, 1840		Sept. 29, 1863	Charlotte Hall.
19	Caroline R.,	903	" May 27, 1845		Jan. 24, 1866	George F. Hall.

HUMPHREY H. AND LUCY A. (TOLMAN) BUTTRICK. 895.

(Continued page 19.)

19	Thomas S.,	904	Concord,	Aug. 4, 1857		June 27, 1883	Anna E. Smith.
19	Henrietta M.,	905	"	Mar. 29, 1859		Oct. 15, 1884	Herbert W. Hosmer.
	Kate P.,	906	"	Dec. 14, 1860	July 13, 1883		

THOMAS S. AND ANNA E. (SMITH) BUTTRICK. 904.

Kate S.,	907		July 17, 1884	
Humphrey S.,	908		Feb. 17, 1886	

HERBERT W. AND HENRIETTA M. (BUTTRICK) HOSMER. 905.

Herbert B.,	909	July 23, 1885	

CHARLES AND ELIZABETH (COWDIN) BUTTRICK. 896.

Charles F.,	910		Sept. 24, 1858	
Arthur W.,	911		Sept. 7, 1868	Nov. 8, 1877

WILLIAM M. AND MARTHA A. (BUTTRICK) HOLDEN. 897.

Sarah Frances,	912	Concord,	Oct. 10, 1853	
David B.,	913	"	May 19, 1857	Sept. 5, 1865
William M.,	914	"	May 2, 1859	Sept. 18, 1865
George W.,	915	"	Apr. 15, 1868	

DAVID H. AND JULIA A. (THAYER) BUTTRICK. 899.

19	Martha A.,	916	Apr. 19, 1863		Jan. 13, 1881	George W. Trowbridge.
	David H.,	917	Aug. 17, 1865	Apr. 30, 1869		
	George O.,	918	Dec. 29, 1867	May 5, 1869		
	Julia M.,	919	July 10, 1871			
	Annie M.,	920	Dec. 29, 1872	Aug. 15, 1882		
	Carrie A.,	921	Feb. 25, 1875			
	John A.,	922	Mar. 16, 1880			

GEORGE W. AND MARTHA A. (BUTTRICK) TROWBRIDGE. 916.

Alice M.,	923	May 16, 1881	

CHANDLER B. AND MARIA E. (BUTTRICK) LANE. 900.

Chandler W.,	924	May 25, 1861		
Lydia R.,	925	Jan. 13, 1863	Nov. 26, 1884	Wilfred B. Jones.
Arthur B.,	926	Sept. 7, 1867		

GORHAM AND CHARLOTTE (HALL) BUTTRICK. 902.

Francis L.,	927	Nov. 2, 1864	
David,	928	Feb. 12, 1868	
Clifford,	929	Aug. 1, 1871	

GEORGE F. AND CAROLINE R. (BUTTRICK) HALL. 903.

Carrie B.,	930	Apr. 7, 1867	
Gilbert C.,	931	Mar. 26, 1877	

DAVID W. AND ELIZABETH T. (HUNT) BUTTRICK. 873.

19	Edwin Augustus,	932	Lowell,	Nov. 4, 1832		Feb. 6, 1855	Harriet Ann Cooley; 1837–; dau. Lucius and Mary.
19	Albert Henry,	933	"	Dec. 19, 1840	Feb. 1, 1870	Sept. 25, 1864	Esmeralda Gordon; dau. Thomas and Lucina.

EDWIN A. AND HARRIET A. (COOLEY) BUTTRICK. 932.

Mary Elizabeth,	934	Chicopee,	Dec. 25, 1859	
Harriet Cooley,	935	"	Jan. 11, 1864	
John Lucius,	936	"	July 10, 1866	July 16, 1866
Caroline Hunt,	937	"	Nov. 10, 1867	May 6, 1883

ALBERT H. AND ESMERALDA (GORDON) BUTTRICK. 933.

Flora E.,	938	Medford,	Dec. 20, 1864	
Ada Eliza,	939	"	Jan. 5, 1869	Nov. 10, 1870

REUBEN AND ANN MARIA (HUNT) MOORE. 875.

Ella Maria,	940	Concord,	Oct. 2, 1844		
George Henry,	941	N.Hartl'nd,Vt.,	Jan. 20, 1848	Dec. 14, 1870	Emma Smith.
Charles Reuben,	942	Champlain,N.Y.,	Feb.10,'51	Feb. 8, 1882	Hattie MacDonald.

BARZILLAI N. AND EMELINE P. (HUNT) HUDSON. 876.

Hannah Rebecca,	943	Concord,	Jan. 13, 1847

CAPT. JOHN B. AND SARAH AUGUSTA (HUNT) MOORE. 877.

	Caroline Augusta,	944	Concord,	Dec. 4, 1840	Aug. 24, 1872	Charles E. Lovett.
19	Emma Frances,	945	"	Sept. 12, 1843	Sept. 22, 1870	Col. Charles W. Davis.
19	Mary H.,	946	"	Apr. 16, 1847	Nov. 23, 1869	William Horace Morse.

COL. CHARLES W. AND EMMA F. (MOORE) DAVIS. 945.

Bradley Moore,	947	Chicago,	Nov. 19, 1871

WILLIAM H. AND MARY H. (MOORE) MORSE. 946.

Wm. Horace, Jr.,	948	Aug. 10, 1872	
Arthur Moore,	949	Nov. 26, 1873	
Robert Stearns,	950	Mar. 16, 1878	Mar. 20, 1878
Howard Moore,	951	Jan. 16, 1881	
Charles Levi,	952	July 3, 1883	
John Moore,	953	Dec. 5, 1885	

CAPT. JOHN B. AND ALMIRA C. (HUNT) MOORE. 881.

John Henry,	954	Concord,	Mar. 22, 1854

JOHN LYNDE AND MARY (HUNT) PRESCOTT. 863.

(Continued page 20.)

Sumner,	955	Norridg'wock,Me.,Dec.3,1808	June, 1814

	Name	No.	Born	Died	Married	Married to / Notes
20	Rebecca,	956	Norridgewock, Me., Oct. 10, 1816	Feb. 25, 1884	Oct. 3, 1833	Capt. George Warren; –1881; son Charles E.
	Mary Ann,	957	" Feb. 29, 1812	Oct. 20, 1840		Unmarried.
20	Eliza,	958	" June 13, 1813		Mar. 17, 1836	Augustus Brick; –1846.
20	Franklin,	959	" Mar. 23, 1816		Mar. 12, 1846	Jane Ware.
	Abel, Hon.,	960	" June 30, 1818		Jan. 19, 1847	Mary Ann Rollins.

CAPT. GEORGE AND REBECCA (PRESCOTT) WARREN. 956.

	Name	No.	Born	Died	Married	Married to / Notes
	Charles Edwin, {	961	Norridgewock, Me., Oct. 17, 1834		Sept. 10, 1865	1. Ellen A. Farmer.
		962			Jan. 22, 1885	2. Mary S. Hale.
	Emelyn Goodwin,	963	" Aug. 22, 1836		Apr. 21, 1863	William W. Bixby.
20	Mary Caroline,	964	" Apr. 17, 1842	Apr. 16, 1879	Oct. 31, 1866	Henry L. Bixby.

HENRY L. AND MARY CAROLINE (WARREN) BIXBY. 964.

	Name	No.	Born
	Elizabeth Rebecca,	965	Aug. 13, 1867
	Abel Prescott,	966	Aug. 18, 1870

AUGUSTUS AND ELIZA (PRESCOTT) BRICK. 958.

	Name	No.	Born	Died	Married	Married to / Notes
20	Frank Augustus,	967	Oct. 23, 1837		May 25, 1862	Augusta W. Williams.
	Mary E.,	968	May 18, 1839			
	Ann Maria,	969	Jan., 1841	1842		
20	Charles Henry,	970	Jan. 11, 1844		Jan. 8, 1867	Mary Emily Starrett.
	Albert,	971	Dec. 21, 1845	Nov. 17, 1846		

FRANK A. AND AUGUSTA W. (WILLIAMS) BRICK. 967.

	Name	No.	Born	Died
	Charles Albert,	972	May 27, 1863	
	Jennie Anthony,	973	June 19, 1865	
	Mabel Prescott,	974	June 11, 1868	Dec. 28, 1868
	Martha Hunt,	975	Dec. 30, 1870	
	Walter Williams,	976	Feb. 26, 1873	

CHARLES H. AND MARY E. (STARRETT) BRICK. 970.

	Name	No.	Born
	Alice Prescott,	977	Mar. 2, 1885

FRANKLIN AND JANE (WARE) PRESCOTT. 959.

	Name	No.	Born
	Elizabeth Foster,	978	May 29, 1848

WILLIAM AND MARTHA (HUNT) ABRAMS. 864.

	Name	No.	Born	Died	Married	Married to / Notes
100	Martha,	979	Dec. 4, 1806	Jan. 23, 1819		
100	Eliza, {	980	Nov. 29, 1809	Mar. 5, 1867	Nov. 4, 1827	1. Henry Jordan; –1837.
		981			1844	2. Clifton Ashton Garrett; –1849.
20	William Hunt, {	982	May 16, 1811	May 27, 1846	Jan. 22, 1839	1. Louisa Dunseth; –1842.
20		983			Nov. 7, 1844	2. Sarah A. Brown.

WILLIAM H. AND LOUISA (DUNSETH) ABRAMS. 982.

	Name	No.	Born	Died
	J. Stroader,	984	Cinn., Ohio, Oct. 20, 1840	Dec. 4, 1841
	Louisa Dunseth,	985	" May 24, 1842	Aug. 14, 1843

WILLIAM H. AND SARAH A. (BROWN) ABRAMS. 983.

	Name	No.	Born	Married	Married to / Notes
20	Mary E.,	986	Cinn., Ohio, Oct. 2, 1845	June 4, 1868	Samuel Baird Huey; 1842-.

SAMUEL B. AND MARY E. (ABRAMS) HUEY. 986.

	Name	No.	Born
	Arthur Baird,	987	Phila., June 14, 1870
	Williams Abrams,	988	" Aug. 18, 1872
	Emma Harvey,	989	" Sept. 29, 1874
	Sam'l Culbertson,	990	" Dec. 11, 1877
	Malcolm Sidney,	991	Spring Lake, N.J., Aug. 3,'85

REUBEN AND ELIZA (TUFTS) HUNT. 866.

	Name	No.	Born	Died	Married	Married to / Notes
	Eliza A.,	992	Charlestown, Sept. 20, 1815	1845	1842	Warren Tapley.
	Reuben,	993	" Dec. 9, 1816	Mar. 17, 1867		

REUBEN AND SARAH (SNOW) HUNT. 867.

	Name	No.	Born	Died
	Sarah,	994	Charlestown, Feb. 8, 1820	Dec. 10, 1858
	Martha Rebecca,	995	" Nov. 7, 1822	

SIMON AND HANNAH B. (ROGERS) HUNT. 868.

	Name	No.	Born	Married	Married to / Notes
20	Thomas H.,	996	Camden, Me., Apr. 13, 1820		
20	Simon, Jr.,	997	" Feb. 2, 1826	Aug. 6, 1854	Jane C. Arey; 1829–1883.
20	Hannah R.,	998	" June 11, 1833		Rev. John L. Locke; –1875.
20	Abel,	999	" Apr. 19, 1835	Dec. 17, 1866	Evelina Knight; dau. Elbridge G. and Myra H.

SIMON AND JANE C. (AREY) HUNT. 997.

	Name	No.	Born	Died
	Ada I.,	1000	Hudson, Wis., Aug. 4, 1855	Died in infancy.
	Clara R.,	1001	" Feb. 24, 1857	Nov. 18, 1863
	Mary P.,	1002	" June 20, 1859	
	Leonard B.,	1003	" Nov. 22, 1870	

REV. JOHN L. AND HANNAH R. (HUNT) LOCKE. 998.

	Name	No.	Born
	Herbert Hunt,	1004	Aug. 2, 1872

ABEL AND EVELINA (KNIGHT) HUNT. 999.

	Name	No.	Born
	Walter Reid,	1005	Camden, Me., Nov. 15, 1867
	Ralph Hudson,	1006	" Dec. 9, 1868
	Edward Jarvis,	1007	" Sept. 25, 1872
	Eva Sawtelle,	1008	" May 19, 1874

JONAS AND RUTH (BARRETT) HEYWOOD. 856.

	Name	No.	Born	Died	Married	Married to / Notes
18	Betsey,	1009	Dec. 22, 1786			Capt. Humphrey Hunt. No. 858.
	Rebecca,	1010	Dec. 24, 1788		Nov. 17, 1808	John Howe.

ABEL AND LUCY (MINOTT) BARRETT. 857-4852.

	Name	No.	Born	Died	Married	Spouse
	Humphrey,	1011	Concord, Sept. 18, 1797	June 2, 1818		

JOHN AND LOIS (BROOKS) BARRETT. 17.

	Name	No.	Born	Died	Married	Spouse
21 21 22	Joseph, Capt., {	1012 1013	Concord, Jan. 5, 1745	Dec. 20, 1831	Nov. 4, 1798	1. Sarah Brooks; 1752–1794; dau. John and Lucy. 2. Sarah (Witherell) Scott; 1759–1845. [(Flagg).
	John,	1014	" Aug. 2, 1748	Sept. 22, 1815	Nov. 29, 1780	Experience Ball; –1848; dau. Caleb and Experience
	Hepzabah,	1015	" Oct. 3, 1750		May 23, 1775	Samuel White; son Mark. [young.)
	Lois,	1016	" Dec. 14, 1752	Nov. 17, 1778	Unmarried.	
	Lydia, {	1017 1018 1019	" May 25, 1755	Jan. 20, 1832	Apr. 11, 1782 Dec. 6, 1792 Dec. 12, 1809	1. Silas Mann; 1745–1788. (Had 2 children who d. 2. Dea. George Minott. No. 532. 3. Capt. Chandler Page.
	(no issue), (no issue),					
	Hannah,	1020	" July 5, 1757		June 28, 1786	Ephraim Chamberlain; 1756–.
	Persis,	1021	" Oct. 20, 1759		Dec. 28, 1790	Nathaniel Boynton. No. 1164.
	Anna,	1022	" Nov. 16, 1761	1841		
	Rebecca Elizab'h,	1023	" Dec. 5, 1764	Nov. 17, 1793	Unmarried.	

CAPT. JOSEPH AND SARAH (BROOKS) BARRETT. 1012.

	Name	No.	Born	Died	Married	Spouse
21	Joseph,	1024	Mason, N. H., Jan. 25, 1774	Oct. 31, 1852	Oct. 3, 1809	Mary Appleton; 1775–1853; d. Isaac and Mary (Adams).
21	John, Capt.,	1025	" Aug. 21, 1775	Aug. 22, 1856	Dec. 12, 1822	Lucy Joslyn; 1786–1866; dau. Daniel.
21	Elisha,	1026	" Dec. 7, 1776	July 21, 1857	Nov. 27, 1803	Abigail Russell; 1788–1852.
	Sarah,	1027	" Oct. 12, 1778	May 21, 1820	Feb. 24, 1779	Nehemiah Russell.
22	Mercy,	1028	" Aug. 5, 1780	Dec. 21, 1867	Jan. 30, 1807	Mark Safford; 1782–1844; son John and Mehitable.
	Abel,	1029	" June 3, 1782			
22	Hannah,	1030	" Sept. 13, 1783	Nov. 17, 1861	Sept. 29, 1798	Amos Davis; –1834.
	Jonas,	1031	" Dec. 31, 1784	Jan. 22, 1787		
22	Mary,	1032	" Jan. 8, 1787	Nov. 1, 1869	May 12, 1814	Nathan Stow; 1793–1841; son Nathan and Abigail.
	Rebecca (no issue),	1033	" May 26, 1789		Mar. 6, 1817	William Ward.

CAPT. JOSEPH AND SARAH (WITHERELL-SCOTT) BARRETT. 1013.

	Name	No.	Born	Died	Married	Spouse
22	Asa Scott,	1034	Mason, N. H., Apr. 5, 1800	Nov. 24, 1878	Oct. 17, 1832	Arvilla C. Wheeler.
	Louisa,	1035	" Sept. 26, 1803	Sept. 4, 1870	May 26, 1832	Stephen Walker; 1803–1874.

JOSEPH AND MARY (APPLETON) BARRETT. 1024.

	Name	No.	Born	Died	Married	Spouse
	Joseph Appleton,	1036	Bakersf'd, Vt., July 22, 1812	Apr. 20, 1833		
	Emily Maria,	1037	" Oct. 23, 1814	June 11, 1833	Unmarried.	[Hannah.
21	Mary Narcissa,	1038	" Aug. 24, 1816		Aug. 3, 1836	Samuel Watson Bent; 1812–1861; son Samuel B. and
21	Dora Everett,	1039	" Jan. 10, 1820		June 23, 1842	Dr. Edw. Spalding; 1813–; s. Dr. Matthias and Rebecca.

SAMUEL W. AND MARY N. (BARRETT) BENT. 1038.

	Name	No.	Born	Died	Married	Spouse
	Sam'l Arthur, A.M.,	1040	July 1, 1841			
	Joseph Appleton,	1041	Feb. 22, 1843	Aug. 12, 1869		

DR. EDWARD AND DORA E. (BARRETT) SPALDING. 1039.

	Name	No.	Born	Died	Married	Spouse
	Mary Appleton,	1042	Nashua, N. H., Mar. 20, 1848			
	Edward Atherton,	1043	" Oct. 13, 1852	Nov. 10, 1863		
	Dora Narcissa,	1044	" July 25, 1857			

CAPT. JOHN AND LUCY (JOSLYN) BARRETT. 1025.

	Name	No.	Born	Died	Married	Spouse
21	Lucy,	1045	Grafton, Vt., Oct. 1, 1823		Sept. 8, 1847	Francis Daniels; 1809–1877; s. Leon'd & Eliz. (Cutler).
21	John Humphrey,	1046	" Sept. 5, 1825		Sept. 12, 1867	Augusta L. Perry; 1840–; d. Dr. Chas. and Lousia [(Chamberlain).
21	Susan Hall,	1047	" Nov. 7, 1826	June 17, 1855	June 4, 1850	J. S. D. Taylor; 1818–1873; s. Dr. Jonathan & Aseneth.
21	Charles, Hon.,	1048	" Jan. 28, 1830		Dec. 5, 1859	Caroline Sanford; 1834–; d. Wm. R. & Emily (Bascom).

FRANCIS AND LUCY (BARRETT) DANIELS. 1045.

	Name	No.	Born	Died	Married	Spouse
21	Francis Barrett,	1049	Grafton, Vt., Oct. 31, 1848		June 19, 1878	Harriet Louise Seymour; 1856–; dau. Rev. Chas. H.
21	Leonard,	1050	" Feb. 4, 1852		Mar. 26, 1883	Annie S. Greg; 1860–. [and Caroline.
	John,	1051	" June 19, 1854		1884	Minnie Staples.
	Charles,	1052	" Aug. 11, 1856			
	Lucy J.,	1053	" Nov. 5, 1858			
	Susan Elizabeth,	1054	" May 18, 1861			

FRANCIS BARRETT AND HARRIET LOUISE (SEYMOUR) DANIELS. 1049.

	Name	No.	Born	Died	Married	Spouse
	Caroline Seymour,	1055	Dubuque, Ia., Apr. 6, 1879			
	Lucy Barrett,	1056	" June 26, 1880			

LEONARD AND ANNIE S. (GREG) DANIELS. 1050.

	Name	No.	Born	Died	Married	Spouse
	Maud Errol,	1057	Kan. City, Mo., Jan. 7, 1884			

JOHN HUMPHREY AND AUGUSTA L. (PERRY) BARRETT. 1046.

	Name	No.	Born	Died	Married	Spouse
	John Francis,	1058	Lincoln, Neb., Nov. 10, 1872			

J. S. D. AND SUSAN HALL (BARRETT) TAYLOR. 1047.

	Name	No.	Born	Died	Married	Spouse
	Dorsey,	1059	Dec. 24, 1852			

HON. CHARLES AND CAROLINE (SANFORD) BARRETT. 1048.

	Name	No.	Born	Died	Married	Spouse
	Charles Sanford,	1060	Grafton, Vt., Oct. 25, 1860			
	John,	1061	" Nov. 28, 1866			
	Lucy Emily,	1062	" June 7, 1874	Mar. 15, 1875		

ELISHA AND ABIGAIL (RUSSELL) BARRETT. 1026.

	Name	No.	Born	Died	Married	Spouse
22	George Minott,	1063 1064	Mason, N. H., May 9, 1805	Apr. 3, 1883	June 18, 1835 1879	1. Elvira Bancroft; dau. Dea. Daniel and Sukey. 2. Nellie Townsend; dau. Lafayette and Lucinda.
	Sophronia,	1065	" Sept. 10, 1808	Jan., 1848	Aug. 18, 1833	Amos Scripture.
	Lucy R.,	1066	" June 22, 1813	Oct. 31, 1843	Nov., 1835	Winslow Ames.
	Abigail,	1067	" June 9, 1816	Jan. 11, 1878	Sept. 12, 1837	Amos H. Hosmer. [(Jones).
22	Elisha Brooks, {	1068 1069	" Nov. 18, 1818		May 19, 1842 Dec. 4, 1859	1. Lucy S. Cutler; 1819–1856; dau. Daniel and Sally 2. Caroline (Cragin) McClure; 1831–.

GEORGE MINOTT AND ELVIRA (BANCROFT) BARRETT. 1063.

	Name	No.	Birth	Death	Married	Spouse
	Everett E.,	1070	Grafton, Vt., 1839	Nov. 23, 1857	Unmarried.	

ELISHA BROOKS AND LUCY S. (CUTLER) BARRETT. 1068.

	Name	No.	Birth	Death	Married	Spouse
	Frank Herbert,	1071	Mar. 30, 1851	May 29, 1879	Sept., 1875	Hattie Farrar.

MARK AND MERCY (BARRETT) SAFFORD. 1028.

	Name	No.	Birth	Death	Married	Spouse
	Lucy (no issue),	1072	Washington, N. H., Feb. 19, 1808	July 20, 1842	June 6, 1833	John Cummings.
	Ward D. (no issue),	1073	" Apr. 24, 1810	May 25, 1884	June 27, 1850	Sarah W. Boot.
	John B.,	1074	" Nov. 9, 1811	Oct. 21, 1833		
22	Mary,	1075	" Feb. 3, 1814	Sept. 20, 1885	Aug. 17, 1837	Samuel Daniels; 1808-.
22	Joseph,	1076	" June 17, 1816		July 24, 1841	Mary Fifield.
22	Mark,	1077	" July 1, 1818		Aug. 10, 1844	Eliza Lamphrey.
	Harriet,	1078	" June 2, 1822			
	George W.,	1079	" Nov. 29, 1823	Oct. 21, 1853		

SAMUEL AND MARY (SAFFORD) DANIELS. 1075.

	Name	No.	Birth	Death	Married	Spouse
	George Barrett,	1080	May 11, 1839	Mar. 5, 1884	Mar. 10, 1870	Carrie M. Abbott.
	Mary Lucy,	1081	Aug. 15, 1845		Jan. 1, 1865	James Chandler Fairbank.

JOSEPH AND MARY (FIFIELD) SAFFORD. 1076.

	Name	No.	Birth	Death	Married	Spouse
	John L.,	1082	Sept. 22, 1844		Sept. 26, 1871	Sarah Eglatine.
	Joseph B.,	1083	Mar. 11, 1846		Dec. 29, 1880	Jennie L. Hatch.

MARK AND ELIZA (LAMPHREY) SAFFORD. 1077.

	Name	No.	Birth	Death	Married	Spouse
	George A.,	1084	July 9, 1848		July 9, 1876	Mary M. Blake.

AMOS AND HANNAH (BARRETT) DAVIS. 1030.

	Name	No.	Birth	Death	Married	Spouse
	Nathan,	1085	Groton,			

NATHAN AND MARY (BARRETT) STOW. 1032.

	Name	No.	Birth	Death	Married	Spouse
103	Mary,	1086	Concord, Feb. 16, 1816	May 4, 1868	June 2, 1843	Lorenzo Eaton; 1815-; son Silas and Nancy (Stone).
	Lydia Barrett,	1087	" Dec. 27, 1817	June 2, 1836		
	Harriet,	1088	" Feb. 17, 1821			[well].
104	Nathan Brooks,	1089	" Nov. 28, 1822		Nov. 18, 1856	Elizabeth Brown; 1827-; dau. John and Sally (Cogs-
	Sarah Abigail,	1090	" Oct. 19, 1824			
	Caroline,	1091	" Nov. 7, 1827			

ASA SCOTT AND ARVILLA C. (WHEELER) BARRETT. 1034.

	Name	No.	Birth	Death	Married	Spouse
22	Melinda E.,	1092	Grafton, Vt., Aug. 4, 1833		May 25, 1856	George W. Crawford.
	Merinda,	1093	" Apr. 28, 1835	Sept. 2, 1836		
22	Charles Henry,	1094	" Aug. 17, 1837	Apr. 27, 1878	May 1, 1860	Elisa J. Holden.
22	Arvilla L.,	1095	" Aug. 15, 1839		Jan. 1, 1861	Edmund Dinsmore; 1832-.
	Victoria E.,	1096	" Sept. 23, 1841			W. H. Fuller.
	Marcellus M.,	1097	" Sept. 18, 1843	Oct. 25, 1884		
	John De Zue,	1098	" Jan. 3, 1846			[Mary.
22	Lucy E.,	1099	" Apr. 28, 1848		Dec. 17, 1877	Alexander H. Eustace; 1850-; son Christopher and
	Franklin W.,	1100	" Dec. 29, 1851		May 20, 1872	Lucy J. Reed.
	J. Arthur,	1101	" Jan. 7, 1854	Sept. 14, 1879		

GEORGE W. AND MELINDA E. (BARRETT) CRAWFORD. 1092.

	Name	No.	Birth	Death	Married	Spouse
	George Willie,	1102	Alstead, N. H., Apr. 4, 1857		Sept. 18, 1883	Charlotte E. Ballance.
	Ernest E.,	1103	Bellows Falls, Vt., Aug. 31, 1858		Feb. 11, 1885	Cora E. Gilson.
	Katie T.,	1104	" Oct. 19, 1860		Oct. 24, 1878	Hiram F. Noyes.
	Minnie M.,	1105	Rutland, Vt., Feb. 8, 1863			

CHARLES HENRY AND ELIZA J. (HOLDEN) BARRETT. 1094.

	Name	No.	Birth	Death	Married	Spouse
	Frank M.,	1106	Mar. 19, 1861			
	Fernand H.,	1107	Sept. 27, 1867			
	Willie N.,	1108	May 9, 1869	Oct. 3, 1873		
	Carlos,	1109	Dec. 28, 1872	Feb. 1, 1874		
	Leola,	1110	May 12, 1876			

EDMUND AND ARVILLA L. (BARRETT) DINSMORE. 1095.

	Name	No.	Birth	Death	Married	Spouse
	Elmira E.,	1111	Nov. 19, 1861	Mar. 19, 1864		
	Myra E.,	1112	1863		Nov. 26, 1883	Ernest Mack.
	George Calvin,	1113	1866			
	Gertrude May,	1114	May 23, 1872	Dec. 14, 1874		

ALEXANDER H. AND LUCY E. (BARRETT) EUSTACE. 1099.

	Name	No.	Birth	Death	Married	Spouse
	Mabel A.,	1115	Hansville, N. H., Feb. 24, 1878			

JOHN AND EXPERIENCE (BALL) BARRETT. 1014.

	Name	No.	Birth	Death	Married	Spouse
	John, Rev. (no issue),	1116	Concord, Sept. 30, 1781	Dec. 3, 1849		Charlotte Kendall. [Sarah.
23	Joshua, Rev.,	1117	" Feb. 28, 1783	1868	Nov., 1826	Sarah Newhall; 1790-1854; dau. Daniel A. B. and
22	Daniel,	1118	" Sept. 28, 1784	Dec. 2, 1857	Mar. 31, 1818	Elizabeth Flint; 1786-1873; d. Edward and Hepzabah.
	Lois,	1119	" May 22, 1786		June 12, 1805	Rev. Wm. Frothingham; 1819-1852; s. Wm. & Mary.
23	Silas,	1120	" June 16, 1788	Nov. 17, 1851	Feb. 22, 1819	1. Elizabeth Aiken; 1798-1848; dau. Peter and Eliz.
		1121				2. Hannah G. Hoyt; -1878.
23	Joel,	1122	" Oct. 9, 1789	Feb. 2, 1863	Jan. 10, 1822	Sarah R. Wyman; 1796-1859.
	Miriam,	1123	" June 15, 1793	Feb. 27, 1817		
	Lydia,	1124	" Sept. 6, 1795	June 19, 1820		
	Lucy,	1125	" Sept. 20, 1797	Sept. 28, 1815		

DANIEL AND ELIZABETH (FLINT) BARRETT. 1118.

	Name	No.	Birth	Death	Married	Spouse
	Elizabeth Almira,	1126	Concord, Mar. 3, 1820			
	Daniel,	1127	" Apr., 1826	Sept., 1827		
23	Ann E.,	1128	" Aug. 5, 1829		May 13, 1852	Jeremiah Farmer; 1816-.

JEREMIAH AND ANN E. (BARRETT) FARMER. 1128.

	Hattie A.,	1129	June 10, 1853			
	Lizzie M.,	1130	May 29, 1860			

REV. JOSHUA AND SARAH (NEWHALL) BARRETT. 1117.

	Joshua Payson,	1131	Nov., 1828	1874		
	Daniel Newhall,	1132	Jan., 1831			
	Sarah Mansfield,	1133	June, 1833			

SILAS AND ELIZABETH (AIKEN) BARRETT. 1120.

23	John Lyman,	1134	Mt. Taber,Vt., July 29, 1824		May 8, 1855	Mary Stillman Whitney; 1825-.
	Eliz'th Goodhue,	1135	" Aug. 17, 1826	Nov. 29, 1848		
	Albert Aiken,	1136	Windham,Vt.,Nov. 27, 1820	July 17, 1847		
	Lucy Ann,	1137	Mt. Taber,Vt., July 26, 1830			
	Henry Martyn,	1138	Putney, Vt., May 14, 1834	May 28, 1860		
	George Barney,	1139	June, 1837	May 31, 1839		

JOHN LYMAN AND MARY STILLMAN (WHITNEY) BARRETT. 1134.

23	Harriet Elizabeth,	1140	Farmerville,La.,July 9,1863		Sept. 3, 1883	Andrew C. Campbell; son Andrew and Margaret.

ANDREW C. AND HARRIET E. (BARRETT) CAMPBELL. 1140.

	Lyman Barrett,	1141	June 16, 1884			

JOEL AND SARAH R. (WYMAN) BARRETT. 1122.

	Sarah Doubt Wyman,	1142	Concord, Nov. 11, 1822		Nov. 29, 1849	Adams F. Warren.
23	Elizabeth Brooks,	1143	" Dec. 14, 1823		Oct. 16, 1844	Joseph H. Blake; 1816–1885; s.|Jedediah and Sarah.
23	Ann Everett,	1144	" June 6, 1825		Nov. 30, 1848	William H. Devens.
	John,	1145	" July 6, 1826		May 17, 1860	Julia Ann Robbins; 1819–; dau. Eli and Hannah.
	Caroline Augusta,	1146	" Nov. 29, 1827	Jan. 1, 1862	Unmarried.	

JOSEPH H. AND ELIZABETH B. (BARRETT) BLAKE. 1143.

	Sarah Wyman,	1147	Concord, Mar. 8, 1846	Aug. 13, 1846		
	Rosville,	1148	" May 12, 1847		Dec. 18, 1870	Mary E. Smith.
	Frank Warren,	1149	" Aug. 29, 1853			

WILLIAM H. AND ANN E. (BARRETT) DEVENS. 1144.

	Florence Aldrich,	1150	Littleton, Apr. 6, 1850			
	Clifford,	1151	" Oct. 22, 1852			
	William,	1152	" June 26, 1855			
	Wyman,	1153	Concord, N. H., Nov. 2, 1857			
	Annie Barrett,	1154	" Feb. 22, 1860			
	Ellsworth,	1155	" Mar. 8, 1862	Aug. 8, 1879		
	Adams,	1156	Concord, Feb. 10, 1866			

BENJAMIN AND REBECCA (JONES) BARRETT. 19-4278.

23	Rebecca, { (no issue),	1157	Concord, Feb. 14, 1730–1	Mar. 30, 1805	1750	1. Nathaniel Boynton; 1724–1798.
		1158			July 10, 1800	2. Timothy Prescott; 1728–1808; son Jonas.
	Lydia,	1159	" Mar. 16, 1732–3	Mar. 24, 1733		
23	Benjamin, {	1160	" Jan. 9, 1734–5	Sept. 14, 1811	Nov. 24, 1761	1. Sarah Meriam; 1735–1781. [(Locke).
		1161				2. Hannah Jones; 1742–1831; dau. Wm. and Sarah
26	Jonas, Lieut., {	1162	" Sept. 24, 1737	Jan. 31, 1803	Nov. 19, 1776	1. Mary Fletcher; 1739–1877; dau. Timothy.
26		1163				2. Urania Locke; 1758–1838; d. James and Hannah.

NATHANIEL AND REBECCA (BARRETT) BOYNTON. 1157.

	Nathaniel,	1164	1763			Anna Barrett. No. 1022.

BENJAMIN AND SARAH (MERIAM) BARRETT. 1160.

23	Benjamin, {	1165	Ashby, June 21, 1762	Nov. 6, 1842		1. Bridget Lawrence; –1793.
23		1166				2. Rhoda (Stearns) Wheeler; 1756-.
	Jonas Prescott,	1167	" Sept. 2, 1764	Oct. 31, 1781		
	Mary,	1168	" Mar. 25, 1767	Aug. 22, 1841	Feb. 18, 1790	Josiah Whitney; –1842.
	Cynthia,	1169	" Nov. 7, 1769	Feb. 20, 1784		
	John Beaton,	1170	" Dec. 5, 1774	Apr. 5, 1800		
	Joseph Meriam,	1171	" Sept. 30, 1778	Jan. 21, 1806	May, 1803	Sally Green.

BENJAMIN AND BRIDGET (LAWRENCE) BARRETT. 1165.

23	Jonas Prescott,	1172	Ashby, Mar. 10, 1783	June, 1822	Dec. 30, 1803	Sally Foule; 1782–1817.
24	Benjamin,	1173	" June 18, 1786	Aug. 3, 1837	Feb. 7, 1809	Nancy Stone; 1786–; dau. Oliver and Nancy.
24	Charles, Col., {	1174	" Feb. 21, 1788	June 8, 1855	Sept. 19, 1811	1. Sarah Hastings; 1792–1815.
24		1175			Aug. 5, 1817	2. Betsey Johnson; 1799–1862.
25	Oliver, {	1176	" Jan. 31, 1790	1880	Jan. 14, 1812	1. Betsey Stone; 1792–1842.
		1177				2. Mrs. Sophia Wheeler.
		1178				3. Mrs. —— Jefts.
25	Ezra,	1179	" May 11, 1791	Jan. 1, 1843	Nov. 17, 1817	Rhoda Johnson; 1789; dau. Col. Reuben and Rhoda.
25	Polly, {	1180	" Aug. 29, 1792	Feb. 8, 1857	Dec. 3, 1820	1. Sam'l Wiggins; 1790–1832; s. Phineas & Mehitable.
		1181			June 24, 1834	2. Wm. Richardson; 1791–1872; s. Abel and Tabitha.
	Thomas,	1182	" 1793	Sept. 26, 1793		

BENJAMIN AND RHODA (STEARNS) BARRETT. 1166.

	Sally,	1183	Ashby, 1795			
26	Cynthia,	1184	" May 26, 1797	Mar. 15, 1881	Dec. 5, 1816	Isaac Foster; 1795–1838.

JONAS PRESCOTT AND SALLY (FOULE) BARRETT. 1172.

24	Harriet,	1185	Woburn, Sept., 1804		Nov. 5, 1826	Samuel Fox.
24	James Foule,	1186	" Apr. 16, 1806	Dec. 9, 1851	Apr. 15, 1829	Mary G. Raymond; 1813-.
	Edwin,	1187	" 1808	Oct. 17, 1808		
21	Jonas Prescott,	1188	" Dec., 1809		Sept. 7, 1831	Ann Augusta Reed.
	Mary Foule,	1189	" Apr. 16, 1812			William Hart.
	Marshall,	1190	" 1814	Apr. 5, 1884	Unmarried.	

SAMUEL AND HARRIET (BARRETT) FOX. 1185.

	Harriet Jones,	1191				Charles C. Woodman.

JAMES FOULE AND MARY G. (RAYMOND) BARRETT. 1186.

24	Jonas Prescott,	1192	Woburn, July 26, 1831		June 1, 1855	Sarah F. Skinner; 1833–; dau. Stephen and Sarah.
	Adelia,	1193	" July 24, 1833	Sept. 14, 1834		
	Sarah Adelia,	1194	" June 30, 1840	Aug. 26, 1840		
24	Albert Polk,	1195	" July 14, 1844		Dec. 25, 1868	Mary F. Norcross; 1847–; dau. Geo. L. and Lucy H.
	Cynthia Eliza,	1196	" Mar. 15, 1847	Aug. 9, 1847		
	James Foule,	1197	" Mar. 8, 1851		Aug. 18, 1833	Elizabeth J. Garrett; 1859–; dau. Hugh and Maria.

JONAS P. AND SARAH F. (SKINNER) BARRETT. 1192.

24	Jonas Francis,	1198	Woburn, June 26, 1858		Nov. 21, 1876	Ella A. Sweetzer.
	Ralph Lewis,	1199	" Oct. 20, 1870			

JONAS FRANCIS AND ELLA A. (SWEETZER) BARRETT. 1198.

	Willis Stephen,	1200	Jan. 24, 1877	Apr. 21, 1880
	Frank Everett,	1201	May 1, 1878	July 21, 1878
	Elsie Prescott,	1202	July 22, 1879	
	Cora Sweetzer,	1203	Mar. 7, 1882	
	Nellie Frances,	1204	June 30, 1884	

ALBERT POLK AND MARY F. (NORCROSS) BARRETT. 1195.

	J. Lewis,	1205	Nov. 4, 1869
	Lucy J.,	1206	Aug. 21, 1871
	George A.,	1207	Sept. 8, 1874
	Henry H.,	1208	May 9, 1878

JONAS PRESCOTT AND ANN AUGUSTA (REED) BARRETT. 1188.

	John Foule,	1209	Oct. 14, 1832		
	Mary Jane,	1210	Dec. 30, 1834	May 26, 1861	Unmarried.
	Charles Robert,	1211	Feb. 10, 1840	Dec. 8, 1857	
	Josephine,	1212	Oct. 9, 1842	Sept. 12, 1861	
	Ann Augusta,	1213	Jan. 6, 1846	Dec. 17, 1846	

BENJAMIN AND NANCY (STONE) BARRETT. 1173.

	Oliver Stone,	1214	Ashburnham, Dec. 9, 1809	Nov. 10, 1810		
	Nancy Stone,	1215	" Dec. 14, 1811	Sept. 17, 1828		
24	Joseph,	1216	" Jan. 13, 1813		Feb. 10, 1840	Louisa Newton; 1812–.
	Mary,	1217	" Aug. 24, 1815	Nov. 8, 1816		
	Mary (no issue),	1218	" July 26, 1817	Dec. 31, 1839	1839	S. Dexter Smith.
24	Lucy,	1219	" June 28, 1819		June 14, 1842	Martin Johnson.
	Ephraim,	1220	" Aug. 24, 1821	Nov. 20, 1821		
	Benjamin,	1221	" Oct. 4, 1822	Apr. 24, 1823		
	Edward S.,	1222	" Feb. 17, 1824		June 23, 1860	Nancy Brigham.
24	Julia M.,	1223	" Mar. 18, 1826		Apr. 11, 1849	Samuel C. White.
24	Caroline,	1224	" Feb. 15, 1828		June 25, 1851	Francis A. White.

JOSEPH AND LOUISA (NEWTON) BARRETT. 1216.

	Mary Caroline,	1225	June 9, 1841	June 10, 1843
	Mary Caroline,	1226	Nov. 9, 1845	
	Charles Benjamin,	1227	Nov. 14, 1847	
	Frank Edward,	1228	July 12, 1850	
	Jennie Eliz.,	1229	Dec. 27, 1852	
	Helen Louise,	1230	Mar. 28, 1855	

MARTIN AND LUCY (BARRETT) JOHNSON. 1219.

	Ellen Augusta,	1231	Ashburn'm, Aug. 29, 1843		Aug. 9, 1876	George V. Barrett. No. 2554.
	Sarah Louisa,	1232	Fitchburg, Sept. 22, 1845		Sept. 21, 1872	John W. Dowden.
	Lydia Frances,	1233	" Nov. 21, 1847	Mar. 30, 1848		
	Abbie Caroline,	1234	" Aug. 23, 1851			
	Fannie Eveline,	1235	" Sept. 10, 1854			
	Mary Barrett,	1236	Lunenburg, June 8, 1861			

SAMUEL C. AND JULIA (BARRETT) WHITE. 1223.

24	Julia Maria,	1237	Mar. 19, 1852		Oct. 6, 1880	George H. Gale.
	Louisa,	1238	Dec. 8, 1857			
	Edward,	1239	Apr. 6, 1862			
	Harriet Stone,	1240	Oct. 21, 1868			

GEORGE H. AND JULIA M. (WHITE) GALE. 1237.

	Charles White,	1241	Bergen Point, N. J., Mar. 31, '83
	Helen Avery,	1242	Sept. 12, 1885

FRANCIS A. AND CAROLINE (BARRETT) WHITE. 1224.

	Charles Frederick,	1243	Roxbury, May 27, 1856
	William Howard,	1244	Brookline, Sept. 21, 1858
	Francis Winthrop,	1245	" Dec. 17, 1860
	Sophia Buckland,	1246	" Dec. 16, 1862

COL. CHARLES AND SARAH (HASTINGS) BARRETT. 1174.

	Charles Hastings,	1247	Ashburn'm, Jan. 2, 1812		Mar. 17, 1836	Emma Flint; 1814–.
	Sarah Jewett,	1248	" Jan. 28, 1814	Oct. 19, 1843	1834	Myrick Stevenson.

COL. CHARLES AND BETSEY (JOHNSON) BARRETT. 1175.

25	Francis J., Col.,	1249	Ashburn'm, Aug. 7, 1818	Oct. 10, 1851	May 7, 1839	Nancy Bemis; 1817–1864.
	Elizabeth F.,	1250	" Sept. 21, 1820	Aug. 27, 1837		
	Almira Child,	1251	" Feb. 12, 1823	Aug. 25, 1837		
25	George Henry,	1252	" Nov. 28, 1833		Nov. 30, 1854	Mary S. Greenwood; 1833–.

COL. FRANCIS JOHNSON AND NANCY (BEMIS) BARRETT. 1249.

Emma Almira,	1253	Ashburnh'm, Sept. 13, 1840			Oct. 10, 1865	J. H. Wilkins.
Charles Francis,	1254	" Apr. 13, 1842	July 4, 1843			
Eliz. Tollansbee,	1255	" Apr. 7, 1844				

COL. GEORGE HENRY AND MARY S. (GREENWOOD) BARRETT. 1252.

Grace Greenwood,	1256	Ashburnham, July 16, 1861	May 7, 1881		

OLIVER AND BETSEY (STONE) BARRETT. 1176.

25	Oliver Stone,	1257	Ashburnham, July 13, 1812			Sept. 2, 1834	Lucy Wyman; 1814–1877. [Betsey.
	John Otis,	1258	" Apr. 18, 1815			Apr. 30, 1839	Harriet S. Richardson; 1816–1882; dau. Josiah and
	Cyn. Eliza (no issue),	1259	" Mar. 24, 1817	June 1, 1862		Sept. 24, 1843	Joseph Jackson Waters; 1806–1880.
	Geo. Benj. (no issue),	1260	" May 10, 1819	1870		Nov. 24, 1857	1. Nancy Haradan; 1820–1861.
	(no issue),	1261					2. Anna Potter.
	Clar'sa Davis, (no iss.),	1262	" May 22, 1821			Apr. 17, 1850	Rodolphus Priest; 1828–.
25	Thomas Parker,	1263	" July 5, 1823	Jan. 27, 1872		Mar. 26, 1848	Sophia Sawtelle; 1829–.
25	Eph. Cobleigh,	1264	" July 26, 1825				1. Martha Tenney; 1825–1827.
	(no issue),	1265					2. Mrs. Howard Nutting.
	Emily Augusta,	1266	" Aug. 8, 1827	July 30, 1829			
	Henry A.,	1267	" Sept. 7, 1830	June 2, 1831			
25	Emily Ann,	1268	" Nov. 14, 1831				William H. Potter; –1879.
	N'cy Stone (no issue),	1269	" May 2, 1835			Apr. 17, 1857	1. Oliver W. Norris; 1830–1861.
	(no issue),	1270				Feb. 10, 1870	2. Amasa Whitney; –1884.
	Owen Tracey,	1271	" Oct. 5, 1838	Nov. 5, 1879			Louisa Stone.

OLIVER STONE AND LUCY (WYMAN) BARRETT. 1257.

	Elizabeth Jane,	1272	Ashburnh'm, June 10, 1835	May 2, 1844		
25	Henry Oliver,	1273	" June 28, 1843		July 9, 1863	Mary Forsyth.
	Charles Gregg,	1274	" Dec. 15, 1847	Mar. 13, 1848		
25	Clara Adelaide,	1275	" June 16, 1850		Nov. 18, 1875	John E. Staples.
	Ella Sophia,	1276	" Aug. 1, 1854		June 3, 1880	Earl S. Sloan.

HENRY O. AND MARY (FORSYTH) BARRETT. 1273.

Lizzie May,	1277		Sept. 24, 1865	Dec. 25, 1884	Charles W. Seavey.
Henry Wyman,	1278		Oct. 25, 1867		
Nellie Louise,	1279		June 30, 1869		

JOHN E. AND CLARA A. (BARRETT) STAPLES. 1275.

Alice Wyman,	1280		Apr. 15, 1878
Harry Oliver,	1281		Apr. 14, 1880

THOMAS PARKER AND SOPHIA (SAWTELLE) BARRETT. 1263.

Elmer Clinton,	1282		May 26, 1852
Ida Clara,	1283		July 27, 1856

EPHRAIM C. AND MARTHA (TENNEY) BARRETT. 1264.

Frank H.,	1284		Aug. 9, 1851		Lizzie Brodden.
Edgar Clarence,	1285		Jan. 16, 1853		
Eva Marion,	1286		Oct. 22, 1856	Nov. 11, 1862	
Nellie Bacon,	1287		Apr. 14, 1858	Nov. 17, 1862	

WILLIAM H. AND EMILY ANN (BARRETT) POTTER. 1268.

Wm. Herbert,	1288		Aug. 2, 1863

EZRA AND RHODA (JOHNSON) BARRETT. 1179.

25	Edward Harris,	1289	Warner, N.H., Sept. 17, '18			Oct. 27, 1845	Charlotte Eastman Ladd; 1824–.
25	Maria Boardman,	1290	" June 7, 1820	Feb. 22, 1853		Dec. 16, 1841	Samuel Aiken.
	Caroline Jewett,	1291	" May 27, 1823	Feb. 13, 1844			
	John Woods,	1292	" July 25, 1825	Aug. 18, 1862		Unmarried.	

EDWARD HARRIS AND CHARLOTTE EASTMAN (LADD) BARRETT. 1289.

25	Frank Edward,	1293	Franklin, N.H., July 24, '47			Feb. 7, 1871	Libbie M. Mason; 1849–.
25	Walter Scott,	1294	Plym'th, N.H., Aug. 24, '49			Aug. 3, 1881	Eva M. Champlin; 1856–.
25	Herbert Ezra,	1295	Springfield, Ill., Jan. 31, '52			Feb. 2, 1876	Melrose Abby Shafner; 1857–.
	Carrie Maria,	1296	Utica, Minn., Jan. 17, 1855				
	William Johnson,	1297	" Sept. 14, 1859				
	George Hamilton,	1298	" Aug. 18, 1861	Mar. 5, 1862			
	Rollo Fayette,	1299	" Mar. 3, 1864				
	George Ames,	1300	" Feb. 23, 1869				

FRANK EDWARD AND LIBBIE M. (MASON) BARRETT. 1293.

Roy Frank,	1301	Minneap., Minn., Sept. 18, '76	
Raymond Mason,	1302	" Nov. 24, 1884	

WALTER SCOTT AND EVA M. (CHAMPLIN) BARRETT. 1294.

Floy Madge,	1303	Nov. 6, 1882	Jan. 3, 1884

HERBERT E. AND MELROSE A. (SHAFNER) BARRETT. 1295.

Grant Millard,	1304	Feb. 25, 1884

SAMUEL AND MARIA BOARDMAN (BARRETT) AIKEN. 1290.

Mary Augusta,	1305	Oct. 5, 1842	Mar. 21, 1844
Chas. Augustus,	1306	Sept. 6, 1846	

SAMUEL AND POLLY (BARRETT) WIGGINS. 1180.

Maria,	1307	Bath, Me., Oct. 11, 1822	
Emily Jewett,	1308	" Nov. 19, 1824	June 5, 1825
Cynthia,	1309	" Dec. 30, 1825	Oct. 23, 1833

ISAAC AND CYNTHIA (BARRETT) FOSTER. 1184.

	Name	No.	Birthplace/date				Spouse
	Isaac Barrett,	1310	Forestville, N. Y., Nov.10, 1817		May 6, 1843	Unmarried.	
	Cynthia Maria,	1311	" Oct. 31, 1819			Jan. 6, 1841	Philemon R. Fairchild; 1817–1861.
	Celia Augusta,	1312	" Nov. 13, 1821			Mar., 1839.	Lewis B. Moore; –1885.
	Pamelia,	1313	" June 11, 1824	Sept. 5, 1827			
	Mary Helen,	1314	" July 8, 1826	Sept. 25, 1827			

LIEUT. JONAS AND MARY (FLETCHER) BARRETT. 1162.

	Name	No.	Birthplace/date				Spouse
	Mary,	1315	Ashby,	July 14, 1767		Dec. 18, 1788	Thomas Chamberlain.
	Lydia,	1316	"	Oct. 20, 1768	Nov. 20, 1768		
26	Lucy,	1317	"	Sept. 15, 1769	Oct. 20, 1861	May 25, 1790	William Johnson; 1761–1841.
	Rebecca (no issue),	1318	"	Feb. 15, 1771	Feb. 22, 1793	Jan. 17, 1792	John Rice; 1768–.
	Elizabeth	1319	"	Aug. 18, 1772	May 25, 1777		
26	Jonas, Dea. (no issue), {	1320	"	Mar. 7, 1774	Dec. 30, 1863	Sept. 28, 1798	1. Sally Chamberlain; –1798.
		1321				Apr. 30, 1801	2. Susan Taylor; 1779–1842.
		1322				1844	3. Nancy Boynton; 1792–1854.
	Nathan,	1323	"	Aug. 22, 1775	Apr. 10, 1777		

WILLIAM AND LUCY (BARRETT) JOHNSON. 1317.

	Name	No.	Birthplace/date				Spouse
26	Lucy,	1324	Ashby,	Apr. 17, 1791	Nov. 7, 1831		Capt. Goodhue.
	Rebecca,	1325	"	May 16, 1793	May 18, 1869	May 15, 1816	Eleazer Rice; 1790–1850.
	Sally,	1326	"	Feb. 29, 1796	Nov. 21, 1796		
26	William,	1327	"	Mar. 2, 1798	Feb. 27, 1881	Dec. 4, 1823	Betsey Wright; 1800–.
26	Sarah, {	1328	"	Jan. 2, 1802	Aug. 6, 1885	Nov. 4, 1824	1. Ephraim Hayward.
		1329				Mar. 22, 1856	2. Paul Hayward.
	Mary,	1330	"	July 22, 1804	June, 1807		
	Eliza,	1331	"	Feb. 4, 1807			
	Urania,	1332	"	July 12, 1810	Jan. 27, 1883		Levi Burr.
26	Harriet Atwood,	1333	"	Apr. 23, 1814	Dec. 24, 1878	Aug. 30, 1837	Stevens Hayward.

ELEAZER AND REBECCA (JOHNSON) RICE. 1325.

	Name	No.	Birthplace/date				Spouse
	Emily A.,	1334	Ashby,	Feb. 20, 1819		Apr. 21, 1841	Ashel Boyden; –1877

ASHEL AND EMILY A. (RICE) BOYDEN. 1334.

	Name	No.		Birth date			Spouse
	Louise,	1335		July 3, 1845			
	Edward C.,	1336		May 2, 1850			
	Herbert E.,	1337		Aug. 23, 1856		Nov. 28, 1878	Lucy Wilmot.

WILLIAM AND BETSEY (WRIGHT) JOHNSON. 1327.

	Name	No.	Birthplace/date				Spouse
	Edward Kendall,	1338	Ashby,	Oct. 5, 1827		July 19, 1866	Lucy M. Thayer; 1835–1870.
26	Augustus William,	1339	"	July 30, 1832	Sept. 7, 1855	Feb. 2, 1854	Georgiana Swain; –1882.

AUGUSTUS W. AND GEORGIANA (SWAIN) JOHNSON. 1339.

	Name	No.		Birth date			
	William Augustus,	1340	Ashby,	Dec. 24, 1854			

EPHRAIM AND SARAH (JOHNSON) HAYWARD. 1328.

	Name	No.		Birth date			Spouse
	Elizabeth Gates,	1341		Feb. 20, 1840		Jan. 1, 1862	Martin Webber. No. 1420.
26	Charles Herbert,	1342		Dec. 31, 1831		Jan. 1, 1855	Myra Jane Webber. No. 1415.

CHARLES H. AND MYRA J. (WEBBER) HAYWARD. 1342-1415.

	Name	No.		Birth date			
	Jennie Estella,	1343	Ashby,	May 18, 1863			

STEVENS AND HARRIET A. (JOHNSON) HAYWARD. 1333.

	Name	No.	Birthplace/date				
	Helen Adelia,	1344	Boxboro,	Dec. 13, 1846			
	Lucy Adell,	1345	"	Aug. 31, 1852			

DEA. JONAS AND SUSAN (TAYLOR) BARRETT. 1321.

	Name	No.	Birthplace/date				Spouse
	Sally H.,	1346	Ashby,	June 10, 1802	Died young.		[(Taylor).
26	Jonas H., {	1347	"	Mar. 11, 1805	Dec. 28, 1853	July 19, 1833	1. Sarah Jones; 1807–1838; dau. Elisha and Persis
26		1348					2. Laura E. Gates.
	Susan,	1349	"	Sept. 25, 1808	Mar. 24, 1842	Nov. 9, 1832	Isaac Whitney; s. David.
	Caleb,	1350	"	Feb. 2, 1815	Feb. 5, 1815		
	Rowenna,	1351	"	Mar. 11, 1816			
	John, {	1352	"	Nov. 29, 1817		1842	1. Emma Ward; 1820–1862; dau. Caleb.
		1353					2. Marietta Wetherbee; dau. Joseph W. and Nancy.
	Seth,	1354	"	July 29, 1822	July 31, 1832		
	Myra T.,	1355	"	Apr. 17, 1828	May 6, 1833		

JONAS H. AND LAURA E. (GATES) BARRETT. 1348.

	Name	No.	Birthplace/date				
	Charles H.,	1356	Ashby,	June 8, 1841	Aug. 31, 1849		
	Sarah E.,	1357	"	Sept. 7, 1843	Sept. 19, 1849		
	Mary S.,	1358	"	Aug. 30, 1850	Dec. 30, 1868		

ISAAC AND SUSAN (BARRETT) WHITNEY. 1349.

	Name	No.		Birth date			Spouse
26	Lucius,	1359		Feb. 24, 1836		Jan. 28, 1865	Harriet J. Longhead; 1840–; dau. James and Harriet.
	John Howard,	1360		July 5, 1840	May 14, 1864		

LUCIUS AND HARRIET J. (LONGHEAD) WHITNEY. 1359.

	Name	No.		Birth date			
	Susan Hamlin,	1361		July 1, 1866			
	Gertrude Lawrence,	1362		Dec., 1867			
	Clara Louise,	1363		Oct., 1873			

LIEUT. JONAS AND URANIA (LOCKE) BARRETT. 1163.

(Continued page 27.)

	Name	No.	Birthplace/date				Spouse
27	Betsey, {	1364	Ashby,	Nov. 24, 1781	Jan. 30, 1847	Mar. 5, 1803	1. John Morse; 1769–1806.
27		1365				Nov. 27, 1808	2. John Crosby; 1767–1863; s. Joseph and Hannah.
27	John,	1366	"	Jan. 23, 1783	Oct. 24, 1810		
27	Amos,	1367	"	Mar. 12, 1785	Nov. 7, 1865	1813	Lucy Wheeler; 1793–1845.
28	Olive, {	1368	"	Oct. 8, 1786	Jan. 1, 1869	July 3, 1808	1. Benjamin Damon; –1822; s. Jacob and Anna.
		1369					2. Dea. Nathan Wheeler; 1781–1881.

29	Nathan,	1370	Ashby,	Nov. 19, 1788	Apr. 6, 1877	May 26, 1816	1. Lydia L. Sawyer; 1792–1819.
29		1371				Nov. 19, 1838	2. Harriet Ware; 1799–.
29	Lydia,	1372	"	Nov. 16, 1790	Dec. 13, 1875	Jan. 12, 1815	Charles Richardson; 1789–1859.
	Rebecca,	1373	"	Apr. 27, 1793	June 2, 1794		
30	Urania,	1374	"	Jan. 12, 1796	Feb. 19, 1880	Apr. 21, 1824	Lyman Griswold; 1793–.
	Samuel, M. D.,	1375	"	Mar. 27, 1798	June 1, 1833		

JOHN AND BETSEY (BARRETT) MORSE. 1364.

	Betsey,	1376	Ashby,	May 25, 1804	Sept. 9, 1817		
27	Olive,	1377	"	Mar. 30, 1806	July, 1876	Oct. 23, 1828	Jeremiah Morton; 1778–1854.

JEREMIAH AND OLIVE (MORSE) MORTON. 1377.

27	John Dwight,	1378	Athol,	Oct. 3, 1830		Oct. 7, 1862	Maria C. Wesson.
	Austin Jeremiah,	1379	"	Sept. 8, 1832	Mar. 8, 1833		

JOHN D. AND MARIA E. (WESSON) MORTON. 1378.

	Arabel,	1380	Boston,	Dec. 10, 1863			
	George Carpenter,	1381	"	Sept. 23, 1868			
	Clara,	1382	"	Dec. 21, 1870			

JOHN AND BETSEY (BARRETT-MORSE) CROSBY. 1365.

27	John Morse,	1383	Athol,	Aug. 30, 1809	Oct. 30, 1881	Jan. 7, 1834	Amelia Cobb; dau. David and Sally.
	Lucinda Kendall,	1384	"	Oct. 4, 1812	Oct. 22, 1839	Jan. 27, 1835	Daniel R. Cobb; son David and Sally.
27	Urania Barrett,	1385	Putney, Vt.,	Oct. 19, 1815		May 9, 1837	John Henry Humphrey; 1813–1870; s. John & Hannah.
27	Theo. Franklin,	1386	"	Apr. 9, 1821		May 25, 1842	Stella A. White; dau. Alfred and Tabitha.
	Francis Locke,	1387	"	Aug. 21, 1822	Feb. 11, 1825		

JOHN MORSE AND AMELIA (COBB) CROSBY. 1383.

	David Oscar,	1388	Putney, Vt.,	June 27, 1835	Dec. 6, 1839		[Almira.
27	Sarah Elizabeth,	1389	"	Dec. 13, 1840		Dec. 11, 1876	Lewis H. Grover; 1848–1878; son. John N. and
27	John Marshall,	1390	"	Apr. 26, 1842		Jan. 20, 1869	A. Gertrude Reed; 1851–.
27	Emogene Amelia,	1391	"	Jan. 11, 1845		Dec. 21, 1871	William Geer; 1826–; son Noah B. and Sally.

LEWIS H. AND SARAH E. (CROSBY) GROVER. 1389.

	Frank C.,	1392	Sept. 17, 1877	July 6, 1878	
	Grace Amelia,	1393	Nov. 14, 1878		

JOHN MARSHALL AND A. GERTRUDE (REED) CROSBY. 1390.

	Harry Morse,	1394	Dec. 10, 1872		
	Eva Marion,	1395	July 9, 1882		
	John Marshall,	1396	Jan. 1, 1884	Apr. 1, 1884	

WILLIAM AND EMOGENE A. (CROSBY) GEER. 1391.

	Edward Knapp,	1397	Nov. 24, 1878		

JOHN H. AND URANIA B. (CROSBY) HUMPHREY. 1385.

	John,	1398	Athol,	Aug. 29, 1838	Mar. 8, 1862		
	Hannah Elizabeth,	1399	"	Dec. 23, 1847	Sept. 27, 1849		
27	Flora Urania,	1400	"	Feb. 2, 1851		Mar. 2, 1869	James J. Corson.
	Crawford Nightingale,	1401	"	July 16, 1856	Aug. 27, 1857		

JAMES J. AND FLORA URANIA (HUMPHREY) CORSON. 1400.

	Anna Urania,	1402	Apr. 15, 1870		
	Ida Smith,	1403	Dec. 3, 1875		

THEODORE F. AND STELLA A. (WHITE) CROSBY. 1386.

	Chas. Theodore,	1404	Putney, Vt.,	Aug. 5, 1844	May 14, 1869	
	Willett Eugene,	1405	"	Mar. 5, 1846		
	Stella Annette,	1406	"	Nov. 16, 1852		

AMOS AND LUCY (WHEELER) BARRETT. 1367.

	Nancy,	1407	Ashby,	Aug. 13, 1813	Aug. 6, 1814		
27	Diantha Jane,	1408	"	July 19, 1815		Oct. 3, 1832	George Webber; 1819–1861.
28	Elizabeth Morse,	1409	"	July 13, 1817		June 2, 1847	Col. John Metcalf Everett; 1803–1884.
28	Philander G.,	1410	"	May 30, 1819		Nov. 25, 1849	Sarah Wilson; dau. Benjamin and Maria.
28	Jonas Adison,	1411	"	Apr. 18, 1821		June 1, 1847	Zoa Sherwin; 1822–; dau. Levi and Hannah. [tha.
28	Amos Augustus,	1412	"	May 7, 1823		Sept. 12, 1853	Martha Ann Thurston; 1826; dau. Nahum and Mar-
	Angeline Lucy,	1413	"	Aug. 17, 1826			
28	Emily Maria,	1414	"	Aug. 3, 1830		Mar. 26, 1857	Joseph Fox; 1828–; son Dr. Abel and Mary.

GEORGE AND DIANTHA JANE (BARRETT) WEBBER. 1408.

26	Myra Jane,	1415	Ashby,	Jan. 31, 1835		Jan. 1, 1855	Charles Herbert Hayward. No. 1342.
	Amos Augustus,	1416	Townsend,	Aug. 26, 1836			1. Adelia Prescott.
		1417					2. Alice Millard.
27	Frank G.,	1418	"	Apr. 13, 1838		Aug., 1861	1. Clara M. Dougherty.
		1419				Mar., 1873	2. Mrs. Elizabeth S. Burgen.
	Martin,	1420	"	Dec. 26, 1839		Jan. 1, 1862	Elizabeth Gates Hayward. No. 1341.
27	Sarah Elizabeth,	1421	"	May 31, 1841		July 6, 1859	Joel Foster Hayward.
	Lucy Diantha,	1422	"	Jan. 6, 1843		May 3, 1869	Joseph C. Morin.
	Fanny Ann,	1423	"	Oct. 8, 1844			
	Nancy Malvina,	1424	"	Mar. 12, 1846	June 26, 1855		
	John Stratton,	1425	"	Dec. 11, 1848			
28	Martha Dolly,	1426	"	Oct. 26, 1850		Sept. 29, 1869	Silas Wood Davis.
28	Mary Ellen,	1427	"	Aug. 16, 1854		June 15, 1875	Warren Blanchard.

FRANK G. AND CLARA M. (DOUGHERTY) WEBBER. 1418.

	Herbert Eugene,	1428	Oct. 16, 1863		
	Edward D.,	1429	June, 1868		

JOEL F. AND SARAH E. (WEBBER) HAYWARD. 1421.

(Continued page 28.)

	Name	No.	Born	Died	Married	Spouse / Notes
	Cornelia,	1430	Aug. 8, 1860			
	Cordelia,	1431	July 26, 1861	Jan. 31, 1876		
	James P.,	1432	July 15, 1863			
	Stevens,	1433	May 13, 1867			
	J. Foster,	1434	July 23, 1870			
	Minnie H.,	1435	Mar. 15, 1874			
	Martha J.,	1436	July 29, 1877			
	Poland E.,	1437	Dec. 31, 1883			

SILAS WOOD AND MARTHA DOLLY (WEBBER) DAVIS. 1426.

	Name	No.	Born	Died	Married	Spouse / Notes
	Henry Wood,	1438	Ashby, Feb. 13, 1871			
	Grace Myra,	1439	New London, Wis., Mar. 31, 1875			
	Irving Herbert,	1440	" Nov. 25, 1876			

WARREN AND MARY ELLEN (WEBBER) BLANCHARD. 1427.

	Name	No.	Born	Died	Married	Spouse / Notes
	Joseph Warren,	1441	Fitchburg, July 5, 1879	June 15, 1880		
	John Locke,	1442	" June 8, 1881			
	Loring Webber,	1443	" July 23, 1884			

COL. JOHN M. AND ELIZABETH M. (BARRETT) EVERETT. 1409.

	Name	No.	Born	Died	Married	Spouse / Notes
	Melatiah,	1444	Foxboro', June 20, 1848	Aug. 23, 1849		
	Metcalf,	1445	" June 20, 1848	Oct. 29, 1878	Apr. 20, 1871	Elizabeth Schmidt; –1883.
	John,	1446	" May 26, 1852			
	Elizabeth,	1447	" Jan. 29, 1859		Oct. 23, 1885	Albert W. Coleman.

PHILANDER G. AND SARAH (WILSON) BARRETT. 1410.

	Name	No.	Born	Died	Married	Spouse / Notes
28	George Milton,	1448	Sept. 15, 1850		Nov. 30, 1871	Mary Jennie Newcomb; 1853–; d. Geo. D. and Mary.
28	S. Lizzie,	1449	Dec. 5, 1852		Oct. 17, 1877	Elmer D. Goddard; 1852–; s. Martin L. and Louisa D.
28	Frederick L.,	1450	Aug. 20, 1854		Apr. 19, 1882	Lutheria L. Goddard; 1859–; d. Martin L. & Louisa D.
	Eliza E.,	1451	June 24, 1856		May 7, 1885	Wallace Johnson Hutchins.
	Arthur L.,	1452	Sept. 6, 1857			
28	Ida M.,	1453	May 16, 1860		Aug. 1, 1883	Willard L. Harris; 1852–; son Leonard.

GEORGE MILTON AND MARY JENNIE (NEWCOMB) BARRETT. 1448.

	Name	No.	Born	Died	Married	Spouse / Notes
	Philip Henry,	1454	May 26, 1872	Aug. 4, 1872		
	Herbert Franklin,	1455	June 4, 1873			

ELMER D. AND S. LIZZIE (BARRETT) GODDARD. 1449.

	Name	No.	Born	Died	Married	Spouse / Notes
	Mary Eliza,	1456	Aug. 20, 1883			

FREDERICK L. AND LUTHERIA L. (GODDARD) BARRETT. 1450.

	Name	No.	Born	Died	Married	Spouse / Notes
	Edward Luther,	1457	Sept. 11, 1883			

WILLARD L. AND IDA M. (BARRETT) HARRIS. 1453.

	Name	No.	Born	Died	Married	Spouse / Notes
	Ida Stella,	1458	Nov. 22, 1884			

JONAS ADISON AND ZOA (SHERWIN) BARRETT. 1411.

	Name	No.	Born	Died	Married	Spouse / Notes
28	Sherwin Hustis,	1459	Ashby, Mar. 5, 1850		June 15, 1882	Anna L. Heywood; 1852–; d. James and Isabella M.
	Alice Raymond,	1460	Great Fall, Me., Sept. 29, 1852		Dec. 10, 1881	William H. Howe; 1842–; son Oliver and Martha.
	Clifford Marsden,	1461	Lawrence, July 26, 1854		June 15, 1881	Cora A. Hatch; 1855–.
	Emily Rosetta,	1462	Dec. 19, 1858	June 5, 1859		

SHERWIN HUSTIS AND ANNA L. (HEYWOOD) BARRETT. 1459.

	Name	No.	Born	Died	Married	Spouse / Notes
	Myrtle Florence,	1463	May 20, 1884			

AMOS AUGUSTUS AND MARTHA ANN (THURSTON) BARRETT. 1412.

	Name	No.	Born	Died	Married	Spouse / Notes
	Augusta Angenette,	1464	Lawrence, Oct. 16, 1855	Apr. 14, 1865		
	Albion Roscoe,	1465	" Dec. 14, 1858	Aug. 15, 1860		
	Florence Marion,	1466	" May 18, 1861	Apr. 5, 1865		
	Isabella Thurston,	1467	" Nov. 13, 1864			

JOSEPH AND EMILY MARIA (BARRETT) FOX. 1414.

	Name	No.	Born	Died	Married	Spouse / Notes
	Frederick Joseph,	1468	Ipswich, N. H., Jan. 8, 1859	Aug. 7, 1859		
	Josephine Angeline,	1469	Cambridge, Aug. 28, 1860	Dec. 18, 1860		
	Mary Estelle,	1470	" Dec. 10, 1861			
	Lizzie Etta,	1471	" Oct. 11, 1868	Mar. 11, 1873		
	Mabel Barrett,	1472	" Dec. 20, 1870	Feb. 3, 1872		

BENJAMIN AND OLIVE (BARRETT) DAMON. 1368.

	Name	No.	Born	Died	Married	Spouse / Notes
28	Jonas Barrett,	1473	Ashby, May 16, 1809		Apr. 15, 1838	Joanna Randall.
28	John Edwin, {	1474			1837	1. Laura A. Kendall; –1842.
28	{	1475				2. Philomel Wiley; 1827–.
29	Thirza Maria,	1476	" Jan. 31, 1813	Oct. 7, 1883	Dec. 15, 1834	Charles Eaton; 1809–1858.
29	Urania Locke, {	1477	" Nov. 12, 1815		June 1, 1836	1. Sylvester Wood; 1810–1841; son Isaac and Nabby.
29	{	1478			Nov. 22, 1843	2. William S. Humphrey; 1812–1871.
	Sarah Kendall,	1479	" July 9, 1817			
	Lydia Livermore,	1480	" Apr. 23, 1819	Died young.		

JONAS B. AND JOANNA (RANDALL) DAMON. 1473.

	Name	No.	Born	Died	Married	Spouse / Notes
	Lydia Clementine,	1481	Ashby, July 3, 1841		Oct. 20, 1879	Paul Gates.
	Ida Frances,	1482	" June 20, 1849			
	Sarah Ann,	1483	" Apr. 30, 1852		May 8, 1878	Francis M. Butterfield.

JOHN EDWIN AND LAURA A. (KENDALL) DAMON. 1474.

	Name	No.	Born	Died	Married	Spouse / Notes
	Susan M.,	1484	Ashby, June 1, 1838		Nov. 9, 1858	Leroy H. Atwood.
	Edwin Waldo,	1485	" Apr. 19, 1842			

JOHN EDWIN AND PHILOMEL (WILEY) DAMON. 1475.

	Name	No.	Born	Died	Married	Spouse / Notes
	John Franklin,	1486	Oct. 24, 1853		Oct., 1885	Jenny Robinson.
	James Myron,	1487	Feb. 8, 1858			

CHARLES AND THIRZA M. (DAMON) EATON. 1476.

	Name	No.	Birth	Death	Marriage	Spouse
29	Olive Adelia, {	1488	Rindge, N.H., Nov. 20, 1835		Nov. 9, 1859	1. Charles S. Graves; –1867.
		1489			Dec. 2, 1869	2. Ezra D. Cilley.
29	Charles Irving, {	1490	" Sept. 19, 1837		Dec. 22, 1871	1. Emma A. Barton; –1874.
29		1491			Nov. 25, 1875	2. Ellen S. Bean.
	Myron Wilbur, {	1492	Ashby,		Nov. 25, 1865	1. Elizabeth Gilchrist; –1869.
		1493			May 16, 1870	2. Jennie Gerrish.
29	Francis Herbert,	1494	Rindge, N.H., Feb. 10, 1843		Mar. 31, 1870	Juliette C. Hall.
29	Willis Damon,	1495	Peterboro', N. H.,		Dec. 21, 1863	Myranda Lynch.

CHARLES S. AND OLIVE A. (EATON) GRAVES. 1488.

	Name	No.	Birth
	Bertha Adelia,	1496	Manch'r., N.H., Dec.12, 1860

CHARLES IRVING AND EMMA A. (BARTON) EATON. 1490.

	Name	No.	Birth
	Anna E.,	1497	Waltham, Oct. 8, 1872

CHARLES IRVING AND ELLEN S. (BEAN) EATON. 1491.

	Name	No.	Birth
	Allie May,	1498	Waltham, Oct. 7, 1876
	Ethel Loraine,	1499	" Jan. 25, 1879
	Cora Myra,	1500	" June 26, 1881
	Charles Albert,	1501	" Nov. 16, 1884

FRANCIS HERBERT AND JENNIE (GERRISH) EATON. 1494.

	Name	No.	Birth
	Frank Elmer,	1502	Waltham, June 8, 1872
	Henry Charles,	1503	" Oct. 14, 1876
	Arthur Herbert,	1504	" Dec. 20, 1879

WILLIS DAMON AND MYRANDA (LYNCH) EATON. 1495.

	Name	No.	Birth
	Lilla Belle,	1505	Lowell, Mar. 18, 1875
	Carrie Blanche,	1506	Waltham, May 10, 1881

SYLVESTER AND URANIA LOCKE (DAMON) WOOD. 1477.

	Name	No.	Birth		Marriage	Spouse
	Earl S.,	1507	Dec. 7, 1838		Dec. 30, 1869	Fannie E. French.

WILLIAM S. AND URANIA L. (DAMON) (WOOD) HUMPHREY. 1478.

	Name	No.	Birth	Death
	George A.,	1508	Apr. 9, 1845	Aug. 12, 1848
	M. Ella,	1509	Sept. 16, 1847	Aug. 1, 1848
	Ella U.,	1510	May 27, 1864	

NATHAN AND LYDIA L. (SAWYER) BARRETT. 1370.

	Name	No.	Birth	Death
	Philander,	1511	Wrentham, May 12, 1817	Aug. 28, 1817
	Lydia Ellen,	1512	" Oct. 25, 1818	May 21, 1819

NATHAN AND HARRIET (WARE) BARRETT. 1371.

	Name	No.	Birth		Marriage	Spouse
29	Ellen Barstow,	1513	Boston, Sept. 2, 1839		Apr. 16, 1862	Gardner A. Churchill; 1839–; son Asaph and Mary.

GARDNER A. AND ELLEN BARSTOW (BARRETT) CHURCHILL. 1513.

	Name	No.	Birth
	Mary Brewer,	1514	Wrentham, Dec. 31, 1864
	Asaph,	1515	" Aug. 18, 1866
	Ellen Barrett,	1516	Dorchester, May 19, 1877

CHARLES AND LYDIA (BARRETT) RICHARDSON. 1372.

	Name	No.	Birth	Death	Marriage	Spouse
29	John Barrett,	1517	New Alstead, N.H., Oct. 24, 1815	Mar. 20, 1885	Mar. 6, 1842	Jane Eliza Larnard; 1817–.
30	Lor'zo Ham'ton {	1518	" July 29, 1817		Aug. 7, 1843	1. Abigail Taylor Bush; 1821–1852.
29		1519			Nov. 29, 1855	2. Jane E. Curtis; 1825–1869.
29	Augusta Theresa,	1520	" Aug. 24, 1819	Aug. 21, 1877	Apr. 25, 1844	Joel Bullard.
29	Franklin Locke,	1521	" Oct. 27, 1820	Apr. 12, 1867	May 21, 1851	Harriet Robinson; 1827–.
30	Lydia E. Sawyer,	1522	" Dec. 22, 1822		May 22, 1845	Joel Huntown.
	Emily O.,	1523	" Sept. 3, 1826		Feb. 1, 1860	Rev. John C. Kimball.
	Urania Barrett,	1524	" Dec. 15, 1829	Mar. 2, 1883		
	Henry M.,	1525	" Sept. 14, 1832			
	Sarah E.,	1526	" Mar. 4, 1835	Feb. 8, 1856		

JOHN BARRETT AND JANE ELIZA (LARNARD) RICHARDSON. 1517.

	Name	No.	Birth
	Gertrude Barrett,	1527	Oct. 7, 1843
	Harry,	1528	Oct. 25, 1846
	Edward,	1529	Oct. 24, 1849

LORENZO H. AND JANE E. (CURTIS) RICHARDSON. 1519.

	Name	No.	Birth
	Henry Martin,	1530	Westfield, Dec. 6, 1856
	Charles Curtis,	1531	" Aug. 24, 1859

JOEL AND AUGUSTA T. (RICHARDSON) BULLARD. 1520.

	Name	No.	Birth	Death	Marriage	Spouse
54	Charles William,	1532	May 2, 1845		Mar. 20, 1868	Emily A. Watts.
	Emily Rebecca,	1533	Aug. 25, 1847	1876		
	Edgar Henry,	1534	Aug. 15, 1850		Jan. 22, 1883	Anna C. Benjamin; dau. Charles W.

FRANKLIN LOCKE AND HARRIET (ROBINSON) RICHARDSON. 1521.

	Name	No.	Birth	Death	Marriage	Spouse
	Clinton Locke,	1535	Alstead, N.H., Mar. 15, 1852			
	Frank Aubert,	1536	" Aug. 13, 1853		June 5, 1877	Lizzie Frances Means.
29	John Edward,	1537	" Jan. 8, 1856		Nov. 16, 1883	Mamie Robb Baxter; dau. John.
29	Hattie Ann,	1538	" Mar. 16, 1858			Edwin Grapes; son George.
	Lizzie Emma,	1539	" May 3, 1861	Oct. 5, 1885		

JOHN EDWARD AND MAMIE ROBB (BAXTER) RICHARDSON. 1537.

	Name	No.	Birth
	Martyn Locke,	1540	Feb. 24, 1885

EDWIN AND HATTIE ANN (RICHARDSON) GRAPES. 1538.   (Continued page 30.)

	Name	No.	Birth
	Hattie Edna,	1541	Mar. 13, 1880

	Ida Richardson,	1542	Feb. 21, 1883			

JOEL AND LYDIA ELLEN SAWYER (RICHARDSON) HUNTOWN. 1522.

	Londean,	1543	Aug., 1846			
	Frederick Locke,	1544	Apr., 1849			

LORENZO H. AND ABIGAIL T. (BUSH) RICHARDSON. 1518.

	William Henry,	1545	Westfield, Jan. 9, 1845	Apr. 22, 1854		
	Sarah Frances,	1546	June 2, 1849		May 8, 1872	G. F. Lane.

LYMAN AND URANIA (BARRETT) GRISWOLD. 1374.

30	John Flavel,	1547	Greenfield, Feb. 12, 1825		Nov. 25, 1865	Jennie M. Bartlett; 1830–; dau. Darius and Laura.
	Theophilus Lyman,	1548	" Nov. 14, 1828	Mar., 1884		
73	Catharine Urania,	1549	" Sept. 12, 1831		Oct. 13, 1858	Oliver Proctor. No. 4130. [and Miranda A.
30	Mary Ellen, {	1550	" Jan. 31, 1835		May 3, 1860	1. Bryant Salmon Burrows; 1834–; son Salmon H.
	{	1551			Oct. 11, 1883	2. Lewis Trowbridge Covell; 1823–; s. Lewis & Dolly.
	Harriet Ware,	1552	" May 4, 1838		June 5, 1872	Edward Longley Field; 1831; s. Theodore & Deborah.

JOHN F. AND JENNIE M. (BARTLETT) GRISWOLD. 1547.

	Belle Locke,	1553	July 17, 1865	July 7, 1872		

BRYANT S. AND MARY E. (GRISWOLD) BURROWS. 1550.

	Clayton Hunt,	1554	Nov. 3, 1864	Sept. 5, 1884		
	Urania G.,	1555	Oct. 19, 1868			

DEA. THOMAS AND MARY (JONES) BARRETT. 20-4281.

30	Thomas, Capt., {	1556	Concord, Nov. 15, 1737	Mar. 31, 1816	Jan. 15, 1761	1. Dorcas P. Minott. No. 529.
30	{	1557			June 29, 1769	2. Hannah Stone; 1746–1807; dau. Dea. Jonas & Eliz.
	Ruth,	1558	" Oct. 19, 1734	Oct. 15, 1813	Mar. 3, 1759	Capt. Charles Miles; 1728–1790; son Samuel & Sarah.
32	Charles, Hon.,	1559	" Jan. 13, 1739–40	Sept 21, 1808	1764	Rebecca Minott. No. 533.
	Mary,	1560	" 1741	Oct. 30, 1755		
	Lucy,	1561	" Aug. 2, 1746	Sept. 8, 1825	Unmarried.	
34	Samuel, Dea.,	1562	" June 14, 1749	Feb. 2, 1804	1773	Sarah Farrar; –1825.
34	Amos,	1563	" Apr. 23, 1752	Jan. 25, 1829	Mar. 31, 1779	Mary Hubbard; 1755–1839; d. Ebenezer and Hannah.
35	Mary, {	1564	" Dec. 24, 1756	1834	Apr. 15, 1778	1. David Hubbard; 1754–; s. Ebenezer and Hannah.
	{	1565			1800	2. Wm. Nutting; 1752–1832; son Wm. and Jane.

CAPT. THOMAS AND DORCAS P. (MINOTT) BARRETT. 1556-529.

30	Thomas,	1566	Concord, May 24, 1762			Elizabeth Miller.
31	Timothy,	1567	" Aug. 12, 1764	June 19, 1804	Sept. 20, 1801	Sarah Dudley; 1770–1818.
31	Daniel,	1568	" Apr. 12, 1767	Dec. 1, 1850	Aug. 4, 1794	Peggy Grose; –1842.

THOMAS AND HANNAH (STONE) BARRETT. 1557.

	Submit,	1569	Concord, Sept. 8, 1770	Mar. 7, 1771		
	Hannah,	1570	" Oct. 16, 1771		July 4, 1796	Seth Brooks. Jr., of Acton.
	Dorcas,	1571	" Oct. 11, 1775	Aug. 12, 1814	Jan. 14, 1802	James Brown; 1771–1817; son Abishai and Jerusha.
	Eunice,	1572	" June 28, 1778	Apr. 5, 1801		
	Jonas Stone,	1573	" July 14, 1782	Mar. 3, 1801		
32	Nancy,	1574	" May 6, 1790	Nov. 6, 1866	Mar. 31, 1812	John Grose, Jr.; 1788–1838; son John.

THOMAS AND ELIZABETH (MILLER) BARRETT. 1566.

30	John Miller, Capt.,	1575	Baltimore, Md., Nov., 1788	Oct. 16, 1819	Jan., 1812	Mary Leahy.
30	Thomas,	1576	" Nov. 30, 1789	Aug. 15, 1832	May 14, 1812	Rachel Phillips.
31	Mary,	1577	" Nov. 30, 1793	Sept. 8, 1831	1812	Prof. Alexander Johnson; 1780–1857.

CAPT. JOHN MILLER AND MARY (LEAHY) BARRETT. 1575.

30	John Leahy,	1578	Baltimore, Md., Nov. 3, 1812		Sept. 27, 1836	Eleanor Dorry; 1818–; dau. Dr. H. G. and Eleanor.
30	Minott,	1579	" Feb., 1815	Aug. 18, 1864	Mar. 18, 1847	Margaret Morrison Babcock; 1830–; dau. John and
	William T. (no issue),	1580	" Jan. 23, 1817	Dec. 29, 1861	1855	Mary Champney. [Maria.

JOHN LEAHY AND ELEANOR (DORRY) BARRETT. 1578.

	Wm. H. Harrison,	1581	Baltimore, Md., Sept. 5, 1837	Mar. 7, 1838		
	Virginia Tyler,	1582	" Aug. 1, 1839	Jan. 24, 1863		
	Charles Carroll,	1583	" July 19, 1844	Aug. 18, 1850		
	Henry Clay,	1584	" Oct. 17, 1848	Aug. 6, 1850		
	Eleanor Dorry,	1585	" Aug. 25, 1851			
	Rebecca Morton,	1586	" July 21, 1854	June 11, 1856		
	Francis Marion,	1587	" Nov. 3, 1856			Margaret Connelly.
	Charles Carroll,	1588	" May 4, 1859			

MINOTT AND MARGARET M. (BABCOCK) BARRETT. 1579.

	John Miller,	1589	Baltimore, Md., May 1, 1848			
30	Wm. Thompson,	1590	" July 21, 1850		Nov., 1875	Mary Isabel Copper; 1855–; dau. Joshua and Eliz.
	Mary Noble,	1591	" Nov. 23, 1851	June 24, 1852		
	Maria Carr,	1592	" May 13, 1854			
	Janet Duncan,	1593	" Apr. 30, 1856		Apr. 17, 1877	Walter Reese; –1880; son Thomas M. and Martha.
	Minott,	1594	" Aug. 31, 1858			
	Alice Hope,	1595	" Mar. 8, 1861	Mar. 13, 1861		
	Harry Lee,	1596	" May 22, 1862			

WILLIAM THOMPSON AND MARY ISABEL (COPPER) BARRETT. 1590.

	William Babcock,	1597	Baltimore, Md., July 2, 1880			
	Edith Minott,	1598	Chicago, Ill., Aug. 5, 1882			
	Edward,	1599	" Jan. 11, 1884			
	Robert Miller,	1600	" Nov. 3, 1885			

THOMAS AND RACHEL (PHILLIPS) BARRETT. 1576. (Continued page 31.)

	Thomas Poe, {	1601	Baltimore, Md., June 4, 1813	July 29, 1879	1835	1. Catharine Kirk.
	{	1602				2. Elizabeth Spranburg.

	Mary Jane,	1603	Baltimore, Md., Apr.17,1815	June 15, 1885		Henry M. McKeon.
	George B.,	1604	" Jan. 5, 1816	June 23, 1884		Mary Hadley.
	William B.,	1605	" May 26, 1818	Sept. 7, 1819		
	Hiram Wiley,	1606	" Nov. 26, 1819	June 27, 1850		Cecelia Sparklia.
	Ann Elizabeth,	1607	" Aug. 7, 1821			Joseph Stallings.
	John Charles,	1608	" July 29, 1823	Sept. 29, 1824		
	Rachel Martha,	1609	" Aug. 8, 1826			Henry Schafer.
	John Latrobe,	1610	" Nov. 8, 1827			
	Caroline Hickman,	1611	" Nov. 27, 1829			Alexander Thompson.

PROF. ALEXANDER AND MARY (BARRETT) JOHNSON. 1577.

	William Henry,	1612	Wiscasset,Me., Nov.13,1813	Oct. 1, 1815		
	Alexander (no issue),	1613	" Dec. 20, 1815		Oct. 20, 1842	S. Wadsworth Neal; 1816–.
	Thomas Barrett,	1614	" Oct. 8, 1818	Nov. 25, 1881	1859	Etta Lee.
31	Ann Elizabeth,	1615	" Apr. 12, 1821	Jan. 22, 1854	Sept. 12, 1843	Daniel Stone.
	Mary,	1616	" Apr. 9, 1824	Sept. 25, 1825		
31	Susan,	1617	" May 3, 1827	Mar. 14, 1852	Nov. 19, 1849	Henry Ingalls.

DANIEL AND ANN ELIZABETH (JOHNSON) STONE. 1615.

	Alex. Johnson,	1618	Wiscasset,Me., Sept. 7, 1845			
	Louisa,	1619	" June 15, 1851			

HENRY AND SUSAN (JOHNSON) INGALLS. 1617.

	Mary Johnson,	1620	Wiscasset,Me., Aug.25,1850			

TIMOTHY AND SARAH (DUDLEY) BARRETT. 1567.

	Jonas Stone,	1621	Concord, Nov. 7, 1801	Sept. 11, 1864	1825	Mrs. Mary Brown. (Their daughter Sarah died æ. 17.)

DANIEL AND PEGGY (GROSE) BARRETT. 1568.

31	Daniel,	1622	Camden, Me., Nov. 26, 1794	May 9, 1844	Dec. 20, 1821	Bethia Jordan; son Robert and Hannah (Keating).
32	Dorcas,	1623	" Dec. 31, 1801	Mar. 17, 1872	Sept. 18, 1836	Sylvanus Russell.
32	Samuel,	1624	" Jan. 2, 1804	Mar. 6, 1875	Feb., 1831	Lovinia Ross; dau. Joseph and Mary (Jones).
32	John,	1625	" Jan. 31, 1806	Jan. 12, 1859		Adelia H. Smith; –1857; d. Benj. & Adelia (Howe).
32	Charles,	1626	" Sept. 26, 1808	Apr. 14, 1883	Nov. 3, 1838	Abby Witherspoon; 1821–; dau. Uni and Betsey.
32	William S.,	1627	" Nov. 5, 1811		Apr. 29, 1841	Martha J. Pendleton; 1814–; dau. John and Susan.
	Margaret,	1628	" Mar. 2, 1816			
32	Mary J.,	1629	" July 11, 1822		Dec. 30, 1849	Hanson Andrews; –1872; son James and Charity.
32	Amos,	1630	" Feb. 15, 1819		Feb. 19, 1851	Julia Tolman; 1826–; dau. Thomas and Lydia.

DANIEL AND BETHIA (JORDAN) BARRETT. 1622.

31	Bethia,	1631	Camden, Me., Jan. 5, 1823		June 15, 1851	William H. Frahock.
31	Daniel T.,	1632	" July, 1825			1. Louisa Rhodes; 1825–1862.
	(no issue),	1633			Apr. 19, 1863	2. Caroline M. Heal. No. 2242.
31		1634			July 28, 1864	3. Mrs. Lucy M. Cushman; 1828–.
31	Hannah J.,	1635	" Feb., 1827		Oct. 21, 1849	1. Ellis K. Cram; 1822–1854.
31		1636			Oct. 24, 1861	2. William E. Barnes; 1803–.
32	Hattie,	1637	" Apr. 25, 1833		Mar. 24, 1865	B. F. Rhodes.
32	Robert J.,	1638	" June, 1835	Sept. 8, 1873	Dec. 19, 1858	Sarah B. Gay.
31	Arethusia T.,	1639	" Oct. 30, 1837		Aug. 9, 1863	Richard R. Cram; 1832–.
	Edward H.,	1640	" Dec. 19, 1839	Dec. 29, 1876	Unmarried.	
	Nelson M.,	1641	" Mar. 10, 1842			

WILLIAM H. AND BETHIA (BARRETT) FRAHOCK. 1631.

	Herbert E., Rev.,	1642	Mar. 1, 1857		Nov. 29, 1877	Frankie Ames.

DANIEL T. AND LOUISA (RHODES) BARRETT. 1632.

	Odella L.,	1643	Rockland, Me., Mar.24,1856			
	Walter T.,	1644	" Apr. 25, 1858		June 2, 1883	Jessie Simpson.
	Laura K.,	1645	" May 2, 1860		Oct. 30, 1882	William M. Roberts.

DANIEL T. AND MRS. LUCY M. (CUSHMAN) BARRETT. 1634.

	Harry D.,	1646	Rockland, Me., July 8, 1865	Apr. 4, 1882		
	Winfred,	1647	" June 22, 1868	Apr. 21, 1871		
	Edward E.,	1648	" Oct. 12, 1870			

ELLIS K. AND HANNAH J. (BARRETT) CRAM. 1635.

31	George N.,	1649	Camden, Me., July 18, 1850		Dec. 7, 1876	Viva T. Barnes; 1856–.
31	Fannie E.,	1650	" May 28, 1853		Nov. 29, 1873	George B. Ludwig; 1850–.

WILLIAM E. AND HANNAH J. (BARRETT-CRAM) BARNES. 1636.

31	Alice C.,	1651	Camden, Me., Aug. 12, 1862	Aug. 22, 1880		William A. Fuller; 1858–.
	Effie S.,	1652	" Dec. 7, 1864.			

GEORGE N. AND VIVA T. (BARNES) CRAM. 1649.

	Ellis W.,	1653	Nov. 20, 1877			
	Gertrude,	1654	Sept. 10, 1879			

GEORGE B. AND FANNIE E. (CRAM) LUDWIG. 1650.

	Walter C.,	1655	Nov. 24, 1874	Nov. 29, 1874		
	Mabel A.,	1656	Oct. 2, 1875			
	Carrie A.,	1657	July 29, 1878			

WILLIAM A. AND ALICE C. (BARNES) FULLER. 1651.

	L. Monty,	1658	Sept. 14, 1881	Mar. 29, 1882		
	Grace V.,	1659	Mar. 22, 1884			

RICHARD N. AND ARETHUSIA T. (BARRETT) CRAM. 1639.

	Burton,	1660	Grafton, May 19, 1864			
	Fred Hudson,	1661	" Mar. 22, 1868			
	Walter Richard,	1662	" Feb. 5, 1870			

B. F. AND HATTIE (BARRETT) RHODES. 1637.

	Hattie Ellen,	1663	July 21, 1867			

ROBERT J. AND SARAH B. (GAY) BARRETT. 1638.

	Sarah Emma,	1664	Rockland, Me., July 7, 1859		Oct. 31, 1882	E. H. Burnham, M. D.

SYLVANUS AND DORCAS (BARRETT) RUSSELL. 1623.

	Amos E.,	1665	Aug. 8, 1841		Feb. 21, 1869	Mary R. Herrick; 1846–.

SAMUEL AND LOVINA (ROSS) BARRETT. 1624.

32	Samuel,	1666	Rockport, Me., Mar. 19, 1832		Apr., 1861	Sarah E. Hubbard; 1843–.
32	Charles A.,	1667	" Jan. 5, 1834		Sept. 5, 1863	Eliza Adelia Pillsbury; 1834–.

SAMUEL AND SARAH E. (HUBBARD) BARRETT. 1666.

	Fortina,	1668	Rockport, Me., Mar. 5, 1878			
	Ralph,	1669	" Dec. 15, 1881	Sept. 7, 1882		

CHARLES A. AND ELIZA A. (PILLSBURY) BARRETT. 1667.

	Jennie Adelia,	1670	Dutch Flat, Cal., Jan. 31, '65			
	Nina Ross,	1671	" Dec. 6, 1866			

JOHN AND ADELIA H. (SMITH) BARRETT. 1625.

	Addie (no issue),	1672	Camden, Me., Oct. 7, 1852		Sept. 14, 1874	Rev. Charles E. Knowlton; –1878.
32	Nancy,	1673	" Apr. 25, 1854		Oct. 19, 1873	Charles E. Eells; 1850–.
32	John F.,	1674	" Apr. 8, 1856		Jan. 1, 1879	Lizzie Belle Cousins.

CHARLES E. AND NANCY (BARRETT) EELLS. 1673.

	Joseph O.,	1675	Rockport, Me., Aug. 14, '76			

JOHN F. AND LIZZIE BELLE (COUSINS) BARRETT. 1674.

	Paul Barworth,	1676	Somerville, Nov. 18, 1885			

CHARLES AND ABBY (WETHERSPOON) BARRETT. 1626.

	George H. M.,	1677	Rockport, Me., Nov. 9, 1839			
	Adison D., Capt.,	1678	" Apr. 7, 1842		Dec. 26, 1867	Alice Holls; 1850–1868.
	Carrie A.,	1679	" Dec. 7, 1845		Nov. 10, 1870	Oliver E. Ross, M. D.; 1840–.
	Edwin N.,	1680	" Mar. 20, 1848		Nov. 9, 1881	Mary A. Brigdon; 1859–.
	Charles T.,	1681	" July, 1850	May 23, 1852		
	Randle N.,	1682	" Aug. 21, 1854			
	Hattie F.,	1683	" Nov. 28, 1858		May 14, 1883	Ernest O. Patterson; 1858–.

WILLIAM S. AND MARTHA J. (PENDLETON) BARRETT. 1627.

32	Mary,	1684	Camden, Me., Apr. 11, 1842		Apr. 26, 1868	Hanson Beverage, 1847–.
	Dorcas A.,	1685	" Jan. 22, 1844	Sept. 17, 1856		
32	Josephine M.,	1686	" Sept. 17, 1856		Dec. 21, 1869	Mark W. Calderwood; 1844–.

HANSON AND MARY (BARRETT) BEVERAGE. 1684.

	Amelia Blanche,	1687	Nov. 24, 1869			
	William Frederick,	1688	Oct. 13, 1872			
	Edith Adelia,	1689	Aug. 2, 1877			
	Herbert Ernest,	1690	Oct. 6, 1879			

MARK W. AND JOSEPHINE M. (BARRETT) CALDERWOOD. 1686.

	Walter B.,	1691	Apr. 16, 1871			
	Eben F.,	1692	May 6, 1872			
	Markie,	1693	Feb. 18, 1881	Mar. 23, 1883		
	Lottie,	1694	Oct. 15, 1882			

HANSON AND MARY J. (BARRETT) ANDREWS. 1629.

	Ada,	1695	Rockport, Me., Aug. 26, 1852		July, 1873	Ezra D. Mesnau.
	Nellie R.,	1696	" Aug. 21, 1856		July 6, 1874	Lorinton R. Morton; 1838–.

AMOS AND JULIA (TOLMAN) BARRETT. 1630.

32	Thomas T.,	1697	Rockport, Me., Jan. 22, 1852		Nov. 29, 1877	Linda Packard.
	William S.,	1698	" May 1, 1853			
	Allen A.,	1699	" Apr. 14, 1855		Aug. 15, 1883	Grace Hazleton.
	Julia E.,	1700	" Oct. 26, 1856	Mar. 22, 1862		
	Maria M.,	1701	" Jan. 10, 1859			

THOMAS T. AND LINDA (PACKARD) BARRETT. 1697.

	Maurie,	1702	Feb. 13, 1879			
	Marian II.,	1703	Feb. 5, 1881			

JOHN, JR., AND NANCY (BARRETT) GROSE. 1574.

	Thomas B.,	1704	Feb. 14, 1813		Aug. 27, 1836	Orinda Darley, 1815–.
32	Sarah W.,	1705	Oct. 13, 1815		Aug. 9, 1834	John Prince.

JOHN AND SARAH W. (GROSE) PRINCE. 1705.

	Thomas S.,	1706	Dec. 17, 1835		May 3, 1859	Hannah N. Green; 1838–.

THOMAS S. AND HANNAH N. (GREEN) PRINCE. 1706.

	Nettie,	1707	Oct. 16, 1859		Aug. 16, 1884	Benjamin H. Paul; 1862–.
	Moris,	1708	Nov. 9, 1861			
	Alice,	1709	Feb. 19, 1863	Nov. 29, 1864		
	Annie E.,	1710	July 24, 1866	Nov. 5, 1866		
	Addie R. F.,	1711	Sept. 19, 1867			

HON. CHARLES AND REBECCA (MINOTT) BARRETT. 1559–533.

(Continued page 33.)

	Charles,	1712	New Ipswich, N. H., 1765	1766		

	Name	No.	Birth place/date	Death	Marriage	Spouse
	Dorcas,	1713	New Ipswich, N.H., Apr. 20, 1767	Jan. 31, 1818	Unmarried.	[(Hall). No. 527.
33	Charles, Hon.,	1714	" Sept. 24, 1773	Sept. 3, 1836	Oct. 15, 1799	Martha Minott; 1771–1842; dau. Jonas and Mary
33	Rebecca,	1715	" Sept. 4, 1774	May 11, 1834	Dec. 5, 1795	Hon. Samuel Dana; 1767–1835; son Rev. Samuel and
	George,	1716	" Feb. 27, 1777	Aug. 14, 1812	Unmarried.	[Anna (Kendrick).
	Seth,	1717	" May 20, 1784	Jan. 9, 1792		

HON. CHARLES AND MARTHA (MINOTT) BARRETT. 1714.

	Name	No.	Birth place/date	Death	Marriage	Spouse
33	George,	1718	New Ipswich, N.H., Dec. 15, 1801	Oct. 4, 1862	Sept. 1, 1831	Frances Hall Ames; 1809–; dau. Ambrose and Han-
33	Mary Ann, {	1719	" Nov. 12, 1802	Aug., 1875	May 1, 1820	1. Silas Bullard. [nah (Allen).
33	{	1720			Sept. 13, 1838	2. Alfred C. Hersey.
	Juliet Maria,	1721	" Dec. 22, 1804	May 22, 1808		[(Lambert).
33	Charles,	1722	Boston, Jan. 11, 1807	Feb. 9, 1862	May 31, 1830	Abby Beals Harrt; –1862; d. Edmund and Mehitable
	Edw'd Augustus,	1723	" June 17, 1811	May 2, 1832		

GEORGE AND FRANCES HALL (AMES) BARRETT. 1718.

	Name	No.	Birth place/date	Death	Marriage	Spouse
33	Edward,	1724	Boston, May 18, 1834	Mar. 11, 1883	Sept. 26, 1860	Georgianna M. Chase; 1840–1883; dau. Wells and
	George R.,	1725	New Ipswich, N.H., May 17, 1844		Apr. 21, 1880	Maria (Bailey). [Eliz. (Crocker). Elizabeth M. (Lawrence) Barr; 1835; d. Daniel and

EDWARD AND GEORGIANNA M. (CHASE) BARRETT. 1724.

	Name	No.	Birth place/date	Death	Marriage	Spouse
	George Wells,	1726	Aug. 1, 1863			
	Charles Edward,	1727	Sept. 14, 1865			
	Francis Ames,	1728	Nov. 10, 1867			
	Blanche,	1729	Dec. 26, 1872	May 2, 1874		

SILAS AND MARY ANN (BARRETT) BULLARD. 1719.

	Name	No.	Birth place/date	Death	Marriage	Spouse
	Mary (no issue),	1730	New Ipswich, N.H., Nov., 1821	Sept., 1860		John S. Dwight.
	Charles Barrett,	1731	" Nov., 1823	July, 1883	May, 1848	Isabella Ames Gould.
	Martha A. (no issue),	1732	" Dec., 1825	Dec., 1857	Oct., 1853	Charles Warren Reed.
	Sarah Jane,	1733	" Sept., 1828			

ALFRED C. AND MARY ANN (BARRETT-BULLARD) HERSEY. 1720.

	Name	No.	Birth place/date	Death	Marriage	Spouse
	Alfred Henry,	1734			March, 1862	Mary Henrietta Gibson.

CHARLES AND ABBY BEALS (HARRT) BARRETT. 1722.

	Name	No.	Birth place/date	Death	Marriage	Spouse
102	Julia Maria,	1735	New Ipswich, N.H., May 11, 1832		Dec. 25, 1858	Charles Marsh; 1829–1886; son Reuben and Mary
	Mary Darracott,	1736	" Jan. 28, 1840			[(Wetherbee).
	Charles,	1737	" July 2, 1844	Aug. 31, 1845		

HON. SAMUEL AND REBECCA (BARRETT) DANA. 1715.

	Name	No.	Birth place/date	Death	Marriage	Spouse
	Charles,	1738	Groton, Apr. 7, 1799	July 31, 1819		
33	Anna,	1739	" Aug. 28, 1800	Feb. 10, 1864	Oct. 10, 1825	Col. John Sever; 1792–1855.
	George,	1740	" A●. 2, 1802	Apr. 12, 1804		
33	Rebecca,	1741	" Mar. 24, 1805	Sept. 2, 1875	Oct. 30, 1832	Kilby Page; –1868.
	Samuel,	1742	" Apr. 1, 1808	Aug. 22, 1848	Unmarried.	[Sarah R. (Greene).
33	Martha Barrett,	1743	Charlestown, Oct. 27, 1809	Dec. 15, 1883	Feb. 21, 1837	Gen. George Sears Greene; 1801–; son Caleb and
34	James, Hon., {	1744	" Nov. 8, 1811		June, 1837	1. Susan Harr't Moody; –1838; d. Paul & Susan (Mor-
	{	1745			Aug., 1841	2. Marg't Lance Tower; –1843; d. Col. Levi. [rill).
34	{	1746			June 12, 1850	3. Julia Hurd; dau. William.
34	Thesta,	1747	Groton, Dec. 19, 1816		Feb. 22, 1849	Gen. James Jackson Dana; son Dr. Samuel L.

COL. JOHN AND ANNA (DANA) SEVER. 1739.

	Name	No.	Birth place/date	Death	Marriage	Spouse
	John B.,	1748	Kingston, July 26, 1826	March, 1827		
	Anne Dana,	1749	" Apr. 23, 1828			
	Herbert,	1750		1830	1830	
	Mary (now Sister Mary Virginia), }	1751	" Sept. 5, 1832			[Mary E.
33	Ellen, {	1752	" June 14, 1835		June 3, 1857	1. Rev. Theodore Tebbets; 1831–1863; s. Noah and
33	{	1753			Nov. 25, 1868	2. Hon. Geo. Silsbee Hale; 1825–; s. Salma & Sarah.
	Martha,	1754	" Mar. 4, 1839	Nov. 13, 1864		
	Emily,	1755	", Jan. 2, 1834			

REV. THEODORE AND ELLEN (SEVER) TEBBETS. 1752.

	Name	No.	Birth place/date	Death	Marriage	Spouse
	John Sever,	1756	Medford, July 4, 1858			

HON. GEORGE S. AND ELLEN (SEVER-TEBBETS) HALE. 1753.

	Name	No.	Birth place/date	Death	Marriage	Spouse
	Robert Sever,	1757	Boston, Oct. 3, 1869	.		
	Richard Walden,	1758	" June 30, 1871			

KILBY AND REBECCA (DANA) PAGE. 1741.

	Name	No.	Birth place/date	Death	Marriage	Spouse
	Sarah Ann,	1759	Boston, May 30, 1834	May 8, 1861		
33	Kilby,	1760	" May 2, 1836		June 18, 1866	Anna Carhanie Hancock.
	Samuel Dana,	1761	" Apr. 30, 1834	Nov. 13, 1842		
	Frances,	1762	" Feb. 10, 1844	June 15, 1844		

KILBY AND ANNA CARHAINE (HANCOCK) PAGE. 1760.

	Name	No.	Birth place/date	Death	Marriage	Spouse
	Catharine Mary,	1763	Boston, Apr. 15, 1871			
	Annie Dana,	1764	" Mar. 28, 1875			
	Eliz. Hancock,	1765	" Sept. 18, 1880			

GEN. GEORGE SEARS AND MARTHA BARRETT (DANA) GREENE. 1743.

	Name	No.	Birth place/date	Death	Marriage	Spouse
33	Geo. Sears, Jr.,	1766	Lex'ton, Ky., Nov. 26, 1837		Apr. 23, 1862	Susan Moody Dana. No. 1792. [(Richmond.
34	Samuel Dana, {	1767	Cumb'l'd, Md., Feb. 11, '40	Dec. 11, 1884	Oct. 9, 1863	1. Mary Willis; 1839–1874; dau. John and Mary G.
	{	1768			Mar. 8, 1876	2. Mary Abby Babbett; dau. Jacob. [(Chandler).
34	Chas. Thruston, {	1769	Alleg'ny Co., Md., Mar. 5, '42		May 9, 1867	1. Abby Ann Hull; –1878; dau. Chas. and Emily L.
34	{	1770			Nov. 26, 1880	2. Addie Maud Suppell; 1845–; d. Henry & Clarissa.
34	Anna Mary,	1771	Cumb'l'd, Md., Feb. 19, '45		Apr. 19, 1871	Lieut. Murray Simpson Day, U. S. N.; 1845–1878; son Gen. Hannibal.
	James John,	1772	Brunswick, Me., Sept. 4, '47	Dec. 8, 1847		[Gertrude.
34	F'cis Vinton, Capt.,	1773	Prov., R. I., June 27, 1850		Feb. 25, 1879	Belle Eugenié Chevallié; 1853–; dau. Henry and

GEORGE SEARS, JR., AND SUSAN MOODY (DANA) GREENE. 1766-1792. (Continued page 34.)

	Name	No.	Birth place/date	Death	Marriage	Spouse
	Dana,	1774	New York, June 27, 1863	July 19, 1866		

	Martha,	1775	New York, Oct. 22, 1865	Apr. 6, 1884		
	Carleton,	1776	" Oct. 24, 1868			
	Mabel,	1777	" Nov. 7, 1872	Mar. 1, 1877		

SAMUEL DANA AND MARY (WILLIS) GREENE. 1767.

	Samuel Dana,	1778	Leggett's Pt., N. Y., Oct. 24, 1864			
	Mary Richmond,	1779	Annapolis, Md., Apr. 21, 1867			
	Geo. De Boketon,	1780	" Mar. 9, 1871			

CHARLES THRUSTON AND ABBY ANN (HULL) GREENE. 1769.

	Charles Wolcott,	1781	Sackett's Har., N. Y., Oct. 9, 1868			
	Anna Hull,	1782	Watertown, N. Y., Sept. 11, 1870			
	Eveline,	1783	Black River, N. Y., Mar. 12, 1873			
	Emily Dana,	1784	Newtown, Conn., Oct. 21, 1875			
	Abby Chandler,	1785	" Aug. 8, 1877			

CHARLES THRUSTON AND ADDIE MAUD (SUPPELL) GREENE. 1770.

	Clara Sturges,	1786	Warwick, R. I., Jan. 4, 1882			
	John DeBoketon,	1787	" June 29, 1883	Aug. 22, 1883		
	Martha Barrett,	1788	Hollywood, Ga., July 21, 1884			

FRANCIS VINTON AND BELLE EUGENIE (CHEVALLIÉ) GREENE. 1773.

	Warwick,	1789	Wash'n, D. C., Dec. 18, 1879			
	Donald Cameron,	1790	" Dec. 26, 1881			
	Anna Gertrude,	1791	" Mar. 26, 1884			
	Edith,		Staten Island, N. Y., Aug. 12, 1886			

HON. JAMES AND SUSAN HARRIET (MOODY) DANA. 1744..

33	Susan Moody,	1792	Charlestown, July 7, 1838	June 18, 1881	Apr. 23, 1862	George Sears Greene, Jr. No. 1766.

HON. JAMES AND JULIA (HURD) DANA. 1746.

	James, Jr.,	1793	Charlestown, Nov. 5, 1853			
	Francis,	1794	" Sept. 2, 1857			
	Julia,	1795	" Sept. 27, 1860		June 4, 1884	Harold Whiting, Ph. D.; son Hon. William.
	Mary Hurd,	1796	" Nov. 7, 1864			

GEN. JAMES JACKSON AND THESTA (DANA) DANA. 1747.

	Lucy,	1797	June 21, 1850	Apr. 29, 1853		
	Samuel,	1798	Mar. 1, 1854	June 18, 1855		
	Mary,	1799	Apr. 5, 1856	Mar., 1882		
	Richard,	1800	Dec. 4, 1860			

LIEUT. MURRAY SIMPSON AND ANNA MARY (GREENE) DAY. 1771.

| | Murray Greene, | 1801 | New York, Dec. 18, 1875 | | | |
| | Alice Lovinia, | 1802 | Florence, Italy, May 27, 1878 | | | |

DEA. SAMUEL AND SARAH (FARRAR) BARRETT. 1562.

34	Samuel (no issue), {	1803	Concord, Dec. 24, 1773	Aug. 1, 1825	Mar. 11, 1804	1. Mary Hayward; 1786–1809.
		1804			Jan. 1, 1811	2. Susan Hudson; 1783–1855.
46	Sally,	1805	" 1776	Oct., 1830	Nov. 3, 1799	Stephen Barrett. No. 2535.
47	Betsey,	1806	" Jan. 19, 1781	June 29, 1814	Oct. 18, 1810	Prescott Barrett. No. 2590.

SAMUEL AND SUSAN (HUDSON) BARRETT. 1804.

	Samuel,	1807	Concord, Feb. 3, 1812	Sept. 7, 1872	Unmarried.	
	Eliza,	1808	" Apr. 4, 1814	July 25, 1817		
	Rufus (no issue),	1809	" July 9, 1817		Jan. 13, 1846	Emeline Buttrick; 1814–1849.

AMOS AND MARY (HUBBARD) BARRETT. 1563.

34	Amos, {	1810	Concord, Jan. 6, 1780	May 18, 1862	Feb. 15, 1804	1. Susanna Blake; 1784–1834; dau. Nathan and Mary.
		1811			Nov. 10, 1836	2. Harriet Rice; 1806–; dau. Nathan D. and Deborah.
	Silas,	1812	" Aug. 11, 1782	Apr. 25, 1803		
34	Mary,	1813	" June 8, 1784	Feb. 18, 1856	Aug. 2, 1810	Rev. Henry True; 1770–1857.
35	Abigail,	1814	Union, Me., Apr. 2, 1786	Sept. 30, 1821	1816	Rufus Gilmore; 1790–1870.
	Sarah,	1815	" Nov. 16, 1788	Sept. 19, 1808		
35	Harriet,	1816	" Apr. 13, 1791	1875	July 29, 1822	Daniel Fisk Harding; 1784–1858.
	Eben'r Hubbard,	1817	" Jan. 19, 1797	1880	May 3, 1825	Joanna Vose.

AMOS AND SUSANNA (BLAKE) BARRETT. 1810.

34	Charles, {	1818	Union, Me., Nov. 19, 1806	Sept. 29, 1876	June 23, 1835	1. Marg't Jeroleman; 1810–57; d. Alex. and Frances.
		1819				2. Mrs. Jessie M. Van Evera; 1828–1876; dau. William Wells.
	Sarah,	1820	" Oct. 8, 1810	Nov., 1880	Unmarried.	
	Amos,	1821	" Aug. 6, 1818	Nov. 18, 1834		
	Henry,	1822	" Dec. 12, 1821	Sept., 1876		
	Susan,	1823	" Nov. 3, 1826	Nov. 13, 1829		

CHARLES AND MARGARET (JEROLEMAN) BARRETT. 1818.

	Elizabeth,	1824	Aug. 23, 1836	Sept. 24, 1842		
	Charles,	1825	Feb. 10, 1838	Mar. 30, 1847		
34	Elizabeth,	1826	Oct. 11, 1844		Sept. 24, 1867	Robert H. Weideman; –1883; son Frederick S. and [Natalia.

ROBERT H. AND ELIZABETH (BARRETT) WEIDEMAN. 1826.

	Charles F.,	1827	E. Saginaw, Mich., Sept. 25, 1868			
	Margaret,	1828	" Feb. 27, 1870			
	Robert M.,	1829	" Sept. 28, 1871			
	Natalia,	1830	" Sept. 17, 1873			
	Alfred W.,	1831	" June 8, 1875			
	Elizabeth,	1832	" Jan. 3, 1878			
	Mary L.,	1833	" June 28, 1879			
	Harrold F.,	1834	" Dec. 9, 1882	June 15, 1883		

REV. HENRY AND MARY (BARRETT) TRUE. 1813.

(Continued page 35.)

35	Henry Ayer, M. D.,	1835	Union, Me., Aug. 10, 1812	Dec. 12, 1876	Nov. 2, 1841	Elizabeth P. Read; –1881; dau. James.
35	Mary Barrett,	1836	" Aug. 28, 1819		May 16, 1843	Elijah Vose; 1807–1877; son David and Alice.
	Amos Barrett,	1837	" July 22, 1825	Aug. 6, 1825		

DR. HENRY AYER AND ELIZABETH P. (READ) TRUE. 1835.

35	Henry,	1838	Jan. 26, 1848		Sept. 13, 1876	Flora P. Bowen.

HENRY AND FLORA P. (BOWEN) TRUE. 1838.

Mary Alice,	1839	Sept. 25, 1877	Aug. 12, 1879		
Henry Ayer,	1840	July 26, 1879			

ELIJAH AND MARY B. (TRUE) VOSE. 1836.

Helen Ayer,	1841	Union, Me., Mar. 5, 1844		
Mary True,	1842	" Dec. 17, 1849	Mar. 8, 1853	

RUFUS AND ABIGAIL (BARRETT) GILMORE. 1814.

35	Anson B.,	1843	Nov. 12, 1817		Feb. 20, 1853	Caroline S. Packard.
35	Amos,	1844	Aug. 6, 1819	Oct. 26, 1865	1851	Esther Hagar.

ANSON B. AND CAROLINE S. (PACKARD) GILMORE. 1843.

Ella M.,	1845	Nov. 2, 1859		Dec. 25, 1885	Frank L. Whitten.

AMOS AND ESTHER (HAGAR) GILMORE. 1844.

Adella,	1846	Searsmont, Me., June 4, 1854		Nov. 25, 1878	Ellery V. Townsend.
John,	1847	" Apr. 8, 1857			
Abigail,	1848	" Nov. 22, 1858			Willis A. Meservey.
Emma,	1849	" Feb. 27, 1861		Dec. 25, 1882	Albion Jackson.
Millard,	1850	" Aug. 11, 1862			

DANIEL F. AND HARRIET (BARRETT) HARDING. 1816.

	Amos Barrett,	1851	Union, Me., Mar. 13, 1825			
35	Henry Fiske, Rev.,	1852	" Mar. 28, 1827		Sept. 21, 1856	Mary E. O'Brien.
	Daniel,	1853	" Apr. 10, 1829			
35	Harriet,	1854	" May 24, 1832		Sept. 24, 1856	Joseph W. Stickney.

REV. HENRY FISKE AND MARY E. (O'BRIEN) HARDING. 1852.

Elizabeth Pope,	1855	Machias, Me., Aug. 29, 1857			John Washburn.
Carroll E., Rev.,	1856	" Aug. 24, 1850			Alice Philbrook.
Henry O'Brien,	1857	" Mar., 1859			
Harriet O'Brien,	1858	" Nov. 2, 1864			
Florence,	1859	" Nov. 2, 1866			

JOSEPH W. AND HARRIET (HARDING) STICKNEY. 1854.

Caroline Barrett,	1860	Feb. 13, 1858			
William,	1861	Apr. 29, 1868			
Henry Harding,	1862	May 20, 1870			

DAVID AND MARY (BARRETT) HUBBARD. 1564.

	David,	1863	Concord, May 17, 1779		Unmarried.	
	Ebenezer,	1864	Hancock, N. H., Sept. 6, 1782	Oct. 3, 1871	Unmarried.	
	Charles,	1865	" Apr. 24, 1784			Susan Packard. [Susanna.
35	Mary Barrett,	1866	" Apr. 28, 1786	Sept. 6, 1847	Oct. 5, 1809	William Nutting, Jr.; 1779–1863; son William and
	Sarah Bond,	1867	" Apr. 24, 1788	Sept. 20, 1838	Unmarried.	
98	Betsey,	1868	" Mar. 4, 1790	Sept. 20, 1875	1814	Anthony Van Dorn; –1871.
	Silas,	1869	" Jan. 27, 1792		Unmarried.	

WILLIAM, JR., AND MARY BARRETT (HUBBARD) NUTTING. 1866.

	Eliza Ann (no issue),	1870	Randolph, Vt., May 23, 1810	Aug. 2, 1864	1842	Rev. S. A. Benton; } 1807–1865.
	Sarah M. (no issue),	1871	" Jan. 9, 1813	Aug. 3, 1841	1837	Rev. S. A. Benton; }
35	William,	1872	" Mar. 28, 1815	Oct. 21, 1869	Aug. 10, 1844	Mary Ann Bradshaw.
	Charles,	1873	" Mar. 6, 1817		1846	Cordelia Gilman.
35	Rufus,	1874	" June 14, 1820	May 18, 1876	1845	Sarah H. Nutting.
35	George Barrett,	1875	" Mar. 11, 1826		June 16, 1856	Susan Alice Hodges; dau. Dr. Louis and Susan D.
	David H., M. D.,	1876	" May 17, 1829		1854	Mary Elizabeth Nichols.
	Mary Olivia,	1877	" July 1, 1831			

WILLIAM AND MARY ANN (BRADSHAW) NUTTING. 1872.

Marcia Amelia,	1878	Randolph, Vt., Oct. 26, 1845		Dec. 9, 1872	Daniel A. Guptil.
George William,	1879	" Apr. 14, 1848		Sept. 11, 1872	Rosetta Jackson Stevens.
Lucy,	1880	Bellows Falls, Vt., Sept. 6, 1853			

RUFUS AND SARAH H. (NUTTING) NUTTING. 1874.

Sarah,	1881	Mar. 28, 1848	Aug. 20, 1849		
William Rufus,	1882	Sept. 1, 1851		May, 1875	Celia Frenyear.
John D., Rev.,	1883	Mar. 8, 1854		June 23, 1885	Nannie K. Miller.
Albert,	1884	July 31, 1856			
Wallace H.,	1885	Apr. 25, 1858		Oct. 18, 1884	Mary F. Waite.
Ruth Frances,	1886	July 16, 1860			
Freder'k Wheaton,	1887	Oct. 18, 1863			

GEORGE BARRETT AND SUSAN ALICE (HODGES) NUTTING. 1875.

William Whitely,	1888	Mesopotamia, Tur., Feb. 11, 1860			
Robert Boyd,	1889	" Nov. 16, 1864			
Henry Hodges,	1890	Yaman, Tur., July 27, 1867			
Susan Barrett,	1891	Oronoco, Minn., Oct. 4, 1869			
Louis Blackstone,	1892	Lansing, Minn., July 26, 1871			

COL. JAMES AND REBECCA (HUBBARD) BARRETT. 21-462. (Continued page 36.)

36	James,	1893	Concord, Jan. 4, 1733-4	Oct. 30, 1799	July 4, 1758	Miliscent Esterbrook; 1738–; dau. Jos. and Miliscent.
40	Nathan, Col.,	1894	" Dec. 30, 1735	Feb. 22, 1791	May 22, 1760	Miriam Hunt; 1741–1824, dau. Dea. Simon and Mary (Raymond).

	Lydia,	1895	Concord,	June 6, 1738	1800	Mar. 3, 1757	Josiah Melvin.
84	Rebecca,	1896	"	Nov. 19, 1741	Mar. 3, 1775	Jan. 17, 1765	Dea. George Minott. No. 530.
	Ephraim,	1897	"	Mar. 3, 1744	Mar. 3, 1771		
90	Persis,	1898	"	Sept. 25, 1747	Sept. 5, 1781	Dec. 30, 1766	Jonas Potter. No. 565.
46	Stephen,	1899	"	Jan. 29, 1750	Feb. 4, 1824	June 22, 1775	1. Sarah Barrett. No. 854. [tha (Bowman).
46		1900				Nov. 11, 1789	2. Phebe Bridge; 1756–1845; dau. Samuel and Mar-
47	Peter,	1901	"	Apr. 16, 1755	Apr. 11, 1808	July 8, 1779	Mary Prescott; 1760–1846; d. Benj. & Rebecca(Minott).
	Lucy,	1902	"	July 20, 1761	Dec. 19, 1787	Apr. 8,.1783	Noah Ripley; 1749–1835; s. Noah and Lydia (Kent).

JAMES AND MELISCENT (ESTERBROOK) BARRETT. 1893.

36	Meliscent,	1903	Concord,	Sept. 17, 1759	Aug. 1, 1838	Sept. 16, 1783	Jos. Swain; 1754–1831; s. Rev. John & Eliz.(Chipman).
37	James, Maj.,	1904	"	Aug. 8, 1761	Sept. 12, 1850	Sept. 13, 1792	Dorcas Minott. No. 4851. [(Minott).
	Rebecca,	1905	"	Aug. 30, 1763	May 4, 1795	Oct. 28, 1783	James Prescott; 1749–1842; son Benj. and Rebecca
	William,	1906	"	Dec. 17, 1765	Mar. 17, 1769		
38	Hannah,	1907	"	Feb. 5, 1768	Apr. 27, 1800	Dec. 22, 1788	Daniel Wood; 1760–1844; son Hon. Ephraim.
74	Patty,	1908	"	Dec. 12, 1770	Apr. 7, 1838	Aug. 30, 1792	Cyrus Hosmer. No. 4200.
75	Betsey,	1909	"	Sept. 28, 1773	May 11, 1810	May 25, 1797	Joshua Jones. No. 4297.
39	Phebe Bowman,	1910	"	May 25, 1776	Mar. 12, 1847	Feb. 26, 1801	Amos Dakin; –1844. [(Prescott). No. 617.
39	Joseph, Hon.,	1911	"	Mar. 15, 1778	Jan. 6, 1849	June, 1814	Sophia Fay; 1786–1848; d. Hon. Jonathan and Lucy
	Lydia,	1912	"	Apr. 14, 1780	Aug. 5, 1842	Unmarried.	

JOSEPH AND MELISCENT (BARRETT) SWAIN. 1903.

36	Meliscent,	1913	Halifax, Vt.,	Mar. 25, 1785	Aug. 6, 1851	Aug., 1817	Rev. Thomas H. Wood.
98	Betsey,	1914	"	Apr. 13, 1787	July 29, 1858	July 6, 1813	William Lyman; –1875.
	Joseph,	1915	"	Mar. 8, 1789	June, 1835		Jerusha Everts.
	Rebecca,	1916	"	Apr. 10, 1791	Oct. 31, 1871	Unmarried.	
36	William Barrett,	1917	"	May 12, 1793	May 5, 1828	1819	Tamar Brooks. [(Fox).
37	Chipman,	1918	"	Feb. 9, 1795	May 26, 1873	Jan. 1, 1822	Dency Gilbert; 1796–1867; dau. Samuel and Hannah
	Lucy Ripley,	1919	"	Nov. 11, 1796		Unmarried.	
37	James Barrett,	1920	"	Aug. 11, 1799	Dec. 6, 1834	May 11, 1828	Eunice Brigham; –1869. [and (Mary).
37	*James Prescott,	1921	"	Mar. 11, 1803	Apr. 27, 1875	Sept. 9, 1830	1. Mary Araminta Merceiux; –1839; dau. Thomas R.
37		1922				Feb. 14, 1844	2. Catharine E. Prescott; 1825–; d. James E. & Lucy.

* Name James taken after 1834.

REV. THOMAS H. AND MELISCENT (SWAIN) WOOD. 1913.

36	Meliscent Barrett,	1923	Halifax, Vt.,	Aug. 23, 1819		Apr. 10, 1843	Freeman Longley. [Lucy.
36	William Lyman,	1924	"	Oct. 29, 1826	Aug. 13, 1884	Jan. 23, 1856	Ellen Maria Prescott; 1828–1882; d. James M. and

FREEMAN AND MELISCENT BARRETT (WOOD) LONGLEY. 1923.

	Prescott Eugene,	1925	Albany, N. Y., Feb. 10, 1845
	Lawrence,	1926	Delton, Wis., Apr. 28, 1855
	Thomas H.,	1927	" Aug. 17, 1858

WILLIAM LYMAN AND ELLEN MARIA (PRESCOTT) WOOD. 1924.

	Ellen Maria,	1928	Bronxville, N. Y., Jan. 6, 1857	Mar. 19, 1872		
36	Alice Jennette,	1929	Brooklyn, N. Y., July 27, 1861		Mar. 27, 1884	Frederick Philips Washburn.
	William Prescott,	1930	" June 17, 1865	Jan. 8, 1866.		
	William Thomas,	1931	" Sept. 11, 1869			

FREDERICK P. AND ALICE JENNETTE (WOOD) WASHBURN. 1929.

	Arthur Prescott,	1932	Brooklyn, N. Y., June 22, 1885

WILLIAM BARRETT AND TAMAR (BROOKS) SWAIN. 1917.

36	Jerusha Rebecca,	1933	Athens, Pa., Apr. 8, 1820	Jan. 9, 1846	June 27, 1837	Charles Kilby Adams; 1813–1870.
36	Asa Brooks,	1934	" Mar. 2, 1822		Oct. 9, 1845	Chathame Crosse.
	Joseph Chipman,	1935	" Feb. 4, 1824		Jan., 1845	Abigail Rawson.
37	William Wisner,	1936	" Dec. 9, 1825		Dec. 23, 1852	Roxanna C. West.

CHARLES K. AND JERUSHA R. (SWAIN) ADAMS. 1933.

	Charles Edward,	1937		Apr. 21, 1838	Jan., 1883	1861	Martha Sinclair.
36	Ellen Lucebie,	1938		Sept. 1, 1840		July 3, 1856	1. Charles Andrew Rawson.
		1939					2. William B. Payne.
36	Olive Julia,	1940		July 23, 1842		Sept. 16, 1860	Elijah Lorenzo Weston.
36	Howard Brooks,	1941		Jan. 12, 1845		Nov. 13, 1867	Ruth Ann Harris.

CHARLES ANDREW AND ELLEN LUCEBIE (ADAMS) RAWSON. 1938.

36	Clara Amelia,	1942	Princeton, Wis., Mar. 8, 1858	Dec. 31, 1873	William Clark.
36	Ellen Venette,	1943	" May 20, 1860	Dec. 8, 1880	Eugene Thompson.

WILLIAM AND CLARA A. (RAWSON) CLARK. 1942.

	Charles Henry,	1944	Richmond, Mo., Oct. 2, 1874
	Daisie Payne,	1945	Gordon, Mo., Mar. 7, 1875
	Clara A.,	1946	Jeff. City, Mo., Apr. 11, 1881

EUGENE AND ELLEN V. (RAWSON) THOMPSON. 1943.

	Melinda W.,	1947	Mar. 5, 1883
	Arthur Eugene,	1948	Jan. 9, 1885

ELIJAH L. AND OLIVE J. (ADAMS) WESTON. 1940.

	Lou Mertella,	1949	Aug. 28, 1861	Mar. 24, 1881	George Andrew Shadle.
	Pearhiette,	1950	May 22, 1864		
	Howard Cyrenus,	1951	Nov. 15, 1865	Feb. 16, 1871	
	Frank Seward,	1952	July 11, 1871	May 4, 1878	
	Mira Bonnie,	1953	Oct. 20, 1879		
	Merta Blanche,	1954	Apr. 18, 1881		

HOWARD B. AND RUTH A. (HARRIS) ADAMS. 1941.

	George Irving,	1955	Aug. 17, 1870	
	Gertie May,	1956	Aug. 12, 1873	Aug. 31, 1885

ASA B. AND CHATHAME (CROSSE) SWAIN. 1934.

(Continued page 37.)

Name	No.	Born	Died	Married	Spouse
James Daniel,	1957	Sept. 29, 1846	Aug. 12, 1847		
Albert Brooks,	1958	Nov. 22, 1847	Apr. 28, 1865		
George D., M. D.,	1959	Feb. 18, 1850		Dec. 26, 1882	Harriet Steward; dau. George W. and Cynthia.
Evaline Josephine,	1960	July 20, 1853	Mar. 12, 1879		
Edith Frances,	1961	Feb. 10, 1856		Dec. 26, 1877	Augustus Le Roy Westlake.
Luella Blanche,	1962	Mar. 11, 1858			
Florence May,	1963	Feb. 12, 1860		Sept. 7, 1885	George Loudon.
Elgin Prescott,	1964	Dec. 15, 1861	Sept. 10, 1880		

WILLIAM W. AND ROXANNA C. (WEST) SWAIN. 1936.

Name	No.	Born	Died	Married	Spouse
Eva,	1965	May 5, 1854		Mar. 25, 1880	Elmer E. Hanon.
Blanche C.,	1966	Oct. 1, 1860		May 27, 1885	Allan D. Goodman.
William E.,	1967	Mar. 27, 1871			

CHIPMAN AND DENCY (GILBERT) SWAIN. 1918.

Name	No.	Born	Died	Married	Spouse
Jerusha Everts,	1968	Nov. 8, 1822	Nov. 26, 1863		Unmarried.
George Gilbert,	1969	Jan. 3, 1829		Feb. 14, 1854	Mrs. Catharine J. Welbarky.
Lucy Ann,	1970	Dec. 17, 1830			
37 William ...				June 14, 1877	Olive Edgerton Brayton.
			0, 1864		Unmarried.
				Oct. 12, 1869	Mary Ellen Warner.

...LIVE EDGERTON (BRAYTON) SWAIN. 1971.

			9, 1883		

...Y ELLEN (WARNER) SWAIN. 1973.

...E (BRIGHAM) SWAIN. 1920.

	1882	Sept. 19, 1854			Edward Todd.

...BBECCA (SWAIN) TODD. 1981.

| | 1861 | | | | |

...RY A. (MERCEUIX) SWAIN. 1921.

| | 832 | May 15, 1885 | | | David E. Smith. |

...RINE E. (PRESCOTT) SWAIN. 1922.

| | | June 20, 1882 | | | Mary Elizabeth Leggett; dau. Samuel and Ann Eliza. |

...(MINOTT) BARRETT. 1904–4851.

	75	Apr. 29, 1819	Miriam Buttrick; 1796–; dau. Samuel and Sarah.
	73	Nov. 19, 1821	Elizabeth Prescott; 1798–1882; d. James and Rebecca
	72	Aug. 29, 1825	James S. Gerrish; 1790–1883. [(Atwater).
	02		

...JTTRICK) BARRETT. 1990.

	June 2, 1844	Evelyn Pierpont; 1816–.
	Oct. 23, 1884	Abby L. Osgood.
	Nov. 16, 1864	Fanny Taylor.
	Sept. 11, 1862	Judge Walter C. Dunton.

...(BARRETT) PIERPONT. 1994.

Name	No.	Born	Died
		... 16, 1845	Sept. 30, 1877
	2005	" Nov. 15, 1848	June 5, 1870
Mary Elizabeth,	2006	" Sept. 24, 1851	June 6, 1852
Annie Evelyn,	2007	" Nov. 8, 1864	

DR. CHARLES HENRY AND FANNY (TAYLOR) BARRETT. 2000.

Name	No.	Born
Miriam,	2008	Detroit, Mich., Feb. 17, 1866
Laura,	2009	Waterloo, Ia., Nov. 30, 1868

JUDGE WALTER C. AND EMMA M. (BARRETT) DUNTON. 2002.

Name	No.	Born	Died
Agnes Ellen,	2010	Waterloo, Ia., Sept. 3, 1865	Nov. 22, 1875
Edith Kelly,	2011	" Dec. 28, 1875	
Walter Barrett,	2012	" Jan. 31, 1878	
Miriam Barrett,	2013	" Dec. 29, 1880	

GEORGE MINOTT AND ELIZABETH (PRESCOTT) BARRETT. 1991.

	Name	No.	Born	Died	Married	Spouse
	George Prescott,	2014	Concord, Oct. 15, 1822	Nov. 7, 1827		
	Rebecca Minott,	2015	" Sept. 12, 1825	June 25, 1879		Unmarried.
38	Mary Prescott,	2016	" Dec. 21, 1827	June 7, 1878	Apr. 26, 1849	Nathan H. Warren; 1827–.
	Emily Augusta,	2017	" May 14, 1829		Nov. 16, 1864	Charles Thompson; 1827–.
38	James A., Maj.,	2018	" May 7, 1832	Dec. 14, 1885	Dec. 26, 1865	Jane Farmer. No. 4262.
38	George Henry,	2019	" Aug. 17, 1836		Dec. 31, 1878	Mrs. Isabella K. Green; 1840–.

NATHAN H. AND MARY P. (BARRETT) WARREN. 2016.

Mary Elizabeth,	2020	Concord,	Aug. 12, 1850		Oct. 15, 1874	Horatio Keeler.
Ella,	2021	"	Nov. 7, 1855			
George Henry,	2022	"	May 22, 1860		1884	Maud Price.
Alice,	2023	"	Apr. 16, 1865			
Charles,	2024	Chicago, Ill., Oct. 11, 1867			

MAJ. JAMES ATWATER AND JANE (FARMER) BARRETT. 2018-4262.

Carrie Cushman,	2025	Oct. 12, 1866	Mar. 15, 1869	
George Farmer,	2026	Mar. 23, 1869		
Nellie Prescott,	2027	May 10, 1871		
Emma Jane,	2028	Nov. 2, 1873		
Charles Gerrish,	2029	Sept. 16, 1875		
Clara Hosmer,	2030	Mar. 7, 1877		

GEORGE HENRY AND ISABELLA K. (GREEN) BARRETT. 2019.

Sophronia,	2031	Georget'n, Col., Nov. 25, '81

JAMES S. AND DORCAS (BARRETT) GERRISH. 1992.

James Barrett,	2032	Concord,	June 9, 1826	Jan. 23, 1857	Unmarried.
Joseph Storey,	2033	"	June 2, 1830		

DANIEL AND HANNAH (BARRETT) WOOD. 1907.

38	Elijah,	2034	Concord,	Sept. 18, 1790	Nov. 26, 1861	Sept. 7, 1815	Eliz. Farmer; 1795-1843; d. Edw'd & Rispah (Baldwin).
38	James,	2035	"	Mar. 17, 1792	Sept. 18, 1878	Dec. 13, 1821	Rispah Farmer; 1797-1866; d. Edward and Betsey
39	Mary,	2036	"	May 4, 1794	Dec. 15, 1866	Oct. 10, 1826	Ephraim W. Russell. [(Brown).
	Milly,	2037	"	May 4, 1794	Feb. 9, 1796		
	Ephraim,	2038	"	May 24, 1796	May 4, 1801		
	William (no issue),	2039	"	Aug. 31, 1798			

ELIJAH AND ELIZABETH (FARMER) WOOD. 2034.

	Elijah,	2040	Concord,	June 2, 1816	Apr. 24, 1882	May 21, 1840	Frances W. Parker; -1882.
	John,	2041	"	Nov. 22, 1819			Charlotte P. Wood.
	Edward Farmer,	2042	"	Nov. 26, 1821			
	Augusta,	2043	"	Sept. 28, 1823	Oct. 2, 1823		
38	Henry,	2044	"	Aug. 17, 1825		Nov. 30, 1848	Lydia A. Willis; 1825-1885; d. Howard and Lydia.
	William,	2045	"	Aug. 27, 1828	Dec. 23, 1859	Unmarried.	
38	Charles,	2046	"	Oct. 11, 1830		Apr. 27, 1857	Cynthia A. Rice.
	George,	2047	"	Mar. 27, 1837			

HENRY AND LYDIA A. (WILLIS) WOOD. 2044.

Lizzie F.,	2048	Bedford,	Aug. 26, 1849	Dec. 14, 1869	A. R. Boynton.
Charles H.,	2049	"	June 20, 1851	July 28, 1870	Hattie F. March.

CHARLES AND CYNTHIA A. (RICE) WOOD. 2046.

William Louis,	2050	Maryville, Cal., Mar. 8, 1858	
Sarah Elizabeth,	2051	"	Nov. 10, 1859
Charlotte Elmere,	2052	"	Jan. 10, 1864
Charles James,	2053	"	Nov. 19, 1868

JAMES AND RISPAH (FARMER) WOOD. 2035.

103	Daniel Heald,	2054	Concord,	Jan. 8, 1823	Jan. 1, 1861	Lydia Hosmer. No. 4215.
38	James Barrett,	2055	"	Sept. 23, 1824	June 28, 1856	Ellen S. Oldham; 1836-.
38	Sarah Elizabeth,	2056	"	May 24, 1827	May 1, 1852	J. Q. A. Griffin; 1830-1866. [E. (Edwards).
38	Albert Edward,	2057	"	Mar. 13, 1830	Mar. 12, 1862	Ellen Miles Shattuck; dau. Hon. Daniel and Sarah
38	Margaret Farmer,	2058	"	Sept. 24, 1832	Sept. 9, 1858	Isaac Jones Cutter; 1830-; s. Dan'l and Sally (Jones).
	Mary Heald,	2059	"	May 8, 1835		[Sarah E. (Hurd).
39	John Farmer, {	2060	"	Oct. 2, 1838	Feb. 22, 1866	1. Ella Louisa Skinner; 1844-1882; d. John F. and
		2061			Nov. 1, 1884	2. Alice Cora Sparks; 1858-; dau. Reuben G. and
						[Sarah (Coulliard).

JAMES B. AND ELLEN S. (OLDHAM) WOOD. 2055.

Caroline Prescott,	2062	East Dorset, Vt., Oct. 2, 1860		June 2, 1886	Sherman Hoar; 1860; son Judge Ebenezer R. and
George E. Miller,	2063	"	Aug. 17, 1862	Oct. 20, 1863	[Caroline D. (Brooks).
Julia Smith,	2064	"	Sept. 19, 1864		
Richard Farmer,	2065	Concord,	June 6, 1870		
Isabel Rispah,	2066	"	Apr. 1, 1872	July 9, 1873	
Winthrop Barrett,	2067	"	Nov. 7, 1875		

JOHN Q. A. AND SARAH ELIZABETH (WOOD) GRIFFIN. 2056.

Frances Elizabeth,	2068	Charlestown, Mar. 23, 1853	Nov. 18, 1870		
Frederick Wood,	2069	"	Feb. 2, 1855		May 1, 1884	Daisy Lipman.
Edith Florence,	2070	Malden,	Apr. 29, 1857	Apr. 20, 1866	
J. Q. A., Jr.,	2071	"	Mar. 19, 1859		
Helen,	2072	Medford,	Mar. 13, 1861	May 22, 1861	
Helen Louise,	2073	"	Sept. 1, 1862	Dec. 22, 1862	
Arthur Lincoln,	2074	"	Apr. 16, 1865		

ALBERT EDWARD AND ELLEN MILES (SHATTUCK) WOOD. 2057.

Walter Shattuck,	2075	Concord,	Jan. 22, 1863		
Grace Edwards,	2076	"	Feb. 7, 1864		
Bessie Farmer,	2077	"	Aug. 10, 1865		Herbert M. Barrett.
Herbert Edward,	2078	"	Mar. 31, 1875	Sept. 1, 1875	
Gertrude Barrett,	2079	"	Nov. 17, 1876		

ISAAC JONES AND MARGARET FARMER (WOOD) CUTTER. 2058.

Rose Margarette,	2080	Concord,	May 20, 1860	Sept. 8, 1886	Henry Dingley Coolidge; 1858-; s. Henry J. and Mary
Frank Edward,	2081	"	May 20, 1861		[(Martin).

JOHN FARMER AND ELLA LOUISA (SKINNER) WOOD. 2060.

	Frederick James,	2082	London, Eng., Mar. 3, 1867			

EPHRAIM W. AND MARY (WOOD) RUSSELL. 2036.

39	Mary H.,	2083	Camden, Me., Nov. 24, 1828	Oct. 10, 1830		
	Daniel Wood,	2084	" Sept. 15, 1832		Mar. 7, 1855	1. Tirzah L. Baker.
		2085			May 8, 1861	2. Mary A. Ruggles.

DANIEL W. AND TIRZAH L. (BAKER) RUSSELL. 2084.

	Daniel Wood, Jr.,	2086	Oct. 7, 1857		Mar. 15, 1885	Emma Bourse.

AMOS AND PHEBE BOWMAN (BARRETT) DAKIN. 1910.

39	Elbridge,	2087	Concord, Oct. 19, 1802		Dec. 26, 1832	1. Mary Ann Bridge; –1835.
39		2088			Nov. 6, 1838	2. Nancy Spaulding; –1881.
	Jas. Barrett(no issue),	2089	" Mar. 21, 1804	Feb. 25, 1873	1832	1. Mary Perkins; 1708-1846.
39		2090			Oct. 2, 1855	2. Mary L. Bassett; 1832-1863.
	Phebe (no issue),	2091	" Nov. 3, 1805		Apr. 24, 1845	Jacob B. Farmer.
54	George,	2092	" Jan. 10, 1815	May 1, 1882	Aug. 25, 1841	Charlotte Caldwell Brown; 1819–; d. Jas. and Maria.
39	Charles Rufus,	2093	" Jan. 22, 1817	July 21, 1882	Sept. 5, 1839	Julia Ward; 1822–.

ELBRIDGE AND MARY ANN (BRIDGE) DAKIN. 2087.

	George B.,	2094	Geneva, N.Y., Nov. 11, 1833	Dec. 27, 1859		

ELBRIDGE AND NANCY (SPAULDING) DAKIN. 2088.

39	Sarah Phebe,	2095	Geneva, N.Y., Sept. 16, 1840		Feb. 21, 1866	Elisha C. Deane.
	William Oliver,	2096	" Nov. 23, 1842		Oct. 17, 1862	1. Hattie Wiggins; –1874.
		2097			June 27, 1876	2. Evelyn A. Sheppard.
	Mary Olivia,	2098	" June 4, 1846			

ELISHA C. AND SARAH P. (DAKIN) DEANE. 2095.

	Isabella Spalding,	2099	Buffalo, N.Y., Nov. 16, 1869			
	Elbridge Gerry,	2100	" Aug. 7, 1879			

JAMES B. AND MARY L. (BASSETT) DAKIN. 2090.

	Minnie L.,	2101	Dexter, N.Y., July 12, 1856		Sept. 22, 1875	Charles G. Gilmore.
	Kate,	2102	" Dec. 5, 1857		Sept. 2, 1881	H. J. Snook.
	James Bassett,	2103	" Aug. 15, 1859		Jan. 2, 1884	Jennie Camfield.

CHARLES RUFUS AND JULIA (WARD) DAKIN. 2093.

39	Julia Elizabeth,	2104	Waukesha, Wis., July 28, 1840		June 19, 1860	James Pettee.
	John Elbridge,	2105	" Oct. 29, 1842	Jan. 29, 1846		
	Charles Ward,	2106	" May 12, 1846	Aug. 30, 1846		
	Clara Barrett,	2107	" Dec. 6, 1847	Aug. 16, 1848		
	Harriet Sherrill,	2108	" Dec. 24, 1848		Nov. 26, 1867	John A. MacMurphy.
39	Helen Frances,	2109	" Nov. 8, 1852		Nov. 7, 1870	D. S. Liddle.
	Mary Ward,	2110	Pewarkee, Wis., May 12, 1857	May 13, 1854		
	Anna Mills,	2111	Waukesha, Wis., July 5, 1856		Feb. 14, 1882	William H. Burnison.
	Robert Ward,	2112	" July 14, 1859			
	Charles Barrett,	2113	" July 14, 1859	Apr. 28, 1863		
	Mary Phebe,	2114	Decatur, Neb., May 2, 1863			
	Talbot Donsman,	2115	" Nov. 10, 1865			

JAMES AND JULIA E. (DAKIN) PETTEE. 2104.

	Charles Joseph,	2116	Arlington, Mar. 17, 1861			
	Mary Ward,	2117	" Mar. 17, 1861			
	John Trowbridge,	2118	" Jan. 3, 1863			
	Frank Benjamin,	2119	" Nov. 1, 1869	Apr. 9, 1878		

D. S. AND HELEN F. (DAKIN) LIDDLE. 2109.

	Charles Francis,	2120	July 23, 1873			
	James Ward,	2121	July 28, 1878			
	Mary Julia,	2122	Apr. 26, 1885			

HON. JOSEPH AND SOPHIA (FAY) BARRETT. 1911.

	Lucy Prescott Fay,	2123	Concord, June 7, 1815	July 3, 1838		
39	Jonat'n Fay, Hon.,	2124	" Jan. 28, 1817	Jan. 23, 1885	Apr. 27, 1848	Lydia Ann Loring; 1827–; dau. David and Susan F.
39	Richard, Capt.,	2125	" Aug. 30, 1818	.	May 20, 1847	Lois Jane Wheeler; 1823-1875; d. Capt. Francis and
	Eliza White,	2126	" Sept. 22, 1821	Aug. 15, 1883	Unmarried.	[Susanna (Stearns).
39	William Emerson,	2127	" June 14, 1824		Apr. 25, 1847	Helen Frances Bacon; 1830–; d. Reuben and Sarah
	Ann Maria,	2128	" Apr. 13, 1827	Aug. 11, 1834		[(Clark).

HON. JONATHAN FAY AND LYDIA ANN (LORING) BARRETT. 2124.

104	Lucy Fay,	2129	Concord, Feb. 25, 1849		July 6, 1876	John H. Chapman; 1852–; s. Timothy P. and Rachel
						(Hartwell).

CAPT. RICHARD AND LOIS JANE (WHEELER) BARRETT. 2125.

39	Rich'd Fay, Capt.,	2130	Concord, Aug. 4, 1848		Dec. 26, 1872	Cora Belle Rice; 1854–; d. Reuben N. and Mary H.
	Joseph,	2131	" Sept. 10, 1850	Aug. 25, 1867		[(Hurd).
	Jeanie Susan,	2132	" Mar. 26, 1853			
	Frank Wheeler,	2133	" Mar. 10, 1855	Sept. 18, 1878		
	Annie Maria,	2134	" Apr. 10, 1857	Aug. 27, 1858		
	William,	2135	" July 5, 1859			

CAPT. RICHARD FAY AND CORA BELLE (RICE) BARRETT. 2130.

	Richard Rice,	2136	Concord, Aug. 4, 1877			

WILLIAM EMERSON AND HELEN FRANCES (BACON) BARRETT. 2127.

	Frederick Fay,	2137	Prov., R. I., 1848	Aug. 10, 1848		[Martha C.
	Clara Frances,	2138	" Aug. 2, 1850		Oct. 30, 1873	Wilbur Augustus Fiske; 1843–; son Daniel D. and
	William Fay,	2139	" Apr. 14, 1866			

COL. NATHAN AND MIRIAM (HUNT) BARRETT. 1894.

40	Nathan,	2140	Concord,	May 17, 1763	Feb. 4, 1829	Dec. 10, 1795	Mary Jones. No. 4291. [(Payson).
40	Simon,	2141	"	Sept. 24, 1764	Apr. 20, 1845	Aug. 14, 1808	Mary Hawes; 1787–1869; dau. Mathias and Sarah
41	Reuben,	2142	"	Apr. 2, 1766	Apr. 4, 1823	Feb. 6, 1794	Sarah Thorndike; 1773–1864.
	Timothy,	2143	"	Jan. 31, 1768	June 19, 1804		
	David,	2144	"	June 22, 1769	May 31, 1794	Unmarried. [Minott. No. 527.
	Miriam,	2145	"	Sept. 2, 1771	Aug. 18, 1837	Nov. 18, 1790	Jonas Minott; 1765–1809; son Jonas and Mary (Hall)
43	Ephraim,	2146	"	Aug. 22, 1772	Nov. 4, 1857	Sept., 1806	Louisa Wood; 1783–1868; dau. Thomas. [Lincoln.
67	Susanna,	2147	"	June 7, 1774	May 22, 1847	Nov., 1802	Nathan Brown; Sept. 26, 1772–Sept. 8, 1865; of
43	William,	2148	"	June 17, 1775	Nov. 15, 1834	Feb. 12, 1804	Mary K. Hall; 1783–1840; dau. Moses and Martha
	Mary,	2149	"	Apr. 18, 1777	July 23, 1833	1820	Farnham Hall. [(Sprague).
44	Francis,	2150	"	Apr. 15, 1778	Jan. 10, 1819	May 5, 1799	Maria Foster Pallisier; 1780–1868.
45	James,	2151	"	July 5, 1779	Mar. 20, 1826	1802	Jennie White; dau. Maj. George.
45	George Minott,	2152	"	Sept. 15, 1783	Apr. 17, 1838	Oct. 28, 1805	Susanna Richardson; 1787–1839; dau. Ebenezer and
	Lucy,	2153	"	Nov. 9, 1784	Jan. 26, 1826	Unmarried. [Susanna (Tufts).
45	Luther,	2154	"	Feb. 15, 1786	Dec. 4, 1835	Jan. 4, 1807	Sarah Perry; 1783–1865; d. Thos. and Mary (Wiswall).

NATHAN AND MARY (JONES) BARRETT. 2140-4291.

40	Nathan,	2155 2156	Concord,	Oct. 1, 1796	Feb. 29, 1868	Apr. 23, 1829 Jan. 24, 1855	1. Mary S. Fuller; 1805–1853; dau. Lemuel and Mary 2. Lucy A. Barrett. No. 2514. [(Shepard).
	Elisha,	2157	"	July 12, 1798	May 12, 1804		
	Mary Ann,	2158	"	Jan. 1, 1806	June 6, 1835	Unmarried.	
	Emeline Eliz.,	2159	"	June 9, 1809			

NATHAN AND MARY S. (FULLER) BARRETT. 2155.

	Nathan Henry,	2160	Concord,	Feb. 13, 1830	Sept. 2, 1873	Unmarried.	
	Maria Frances,	2161	"	Nov. 4, 1831	Dec. 16, 1850	"	[Jas. A. and Ann (Whipple).
40	Edwin Shepard,	2162	"	Oct. 31, 1833		Feb. 24, 1863	1. Maria Thomas Gilmore; 1840–1875; dau. Hon.
40		2163				Nov. 2, 1877	2. Laura Elizabeth Emerson; 1846–; dau. Henry and
	Arthur Herbert,	2164	"	Mar. 14, 1836	Jan. 10, 1880	Aug. 13, 1873	Helen Grimes. [Elizabeth (White).
	Sidney Jones,	2165	"	Oct. 21, 1841			

EDWIN SHEPARD AND MARIA T. (GILMORE) BARRETT. 2162.

	Edwin Gilmore,	2166	New York, N. Y., Dec. 17, 1863	Oct. 22, 1865	
	Nelson Macy,	2167	Fitchburg, July 8, 1865		
	Harry Edmunds,	2168	Concord, Aug. 28, 1868		
	Annie Whipple,	2169	Cambridge, Dec. 28, 1871	Dec. 29, 1871	

EDWIN SHEPARD AND LAURA E. (EMERSON) BARRETT. 2163.

	Beth Louise,	2170	Concord,	May 25, 1879
	Nathan Henry,	2172	"	Apr. 18, 1881
	Mary Shepard,	2173	"	Feb. 6, 1883
	Miriam Hunt,	2174	"	Oct. 9, 1884

SIMON AND MARY (HAWES) BARRETT. 2141.

40 40	Simon H.,	2175 2176	Hope, Me., Aug. 24, 1809	July 23, 1865	June 1, 1849	1. Mary Esther Jane Fox; 1825–. 2. Marcia Eliza Wells; 1821–1862.
40 40	Noyes Payson Hawes,	2177 2178	"	June 15, 1813	June 3, 1878	Oct. 7, 1836 Aug. 8, 1851	1. Jenette Kingsley Frary; 1817–1850; dau. Orange 2. Anna May Pembroke. [and Miriam (Kingsley).
	Mary Hunt,	2179	"	June 18, 1811	Oct. 26, 1837		
41	Maria L.,	2180	"	Mar. 20, 1818	Aug. 20, 1843	Dec. 12, 1838	Joseph Muzzy, Jr.; 1807–1868; son Jos. and Sally.
	Charles,	2181	"	Mar. 25, 1820	Apr. 28, 1848		
	Amos,	2182	"	Mar. 25, 1820	Aug. 2, 1855		
41	Fidelia F.,	2183	"	Sept. 26, 1822	Nov. 22, 1859	May, 1845	Horace Muzzy; 1813–; son Jos. and Sally.
41	Matthias,	2184	"	Apr. 6, 1825		Dec. 17, 1856	Amelia P. Hazleton; 1836–.

SIMON H. AND MARCIA ELIZA (WELLS) BARRETT. 2176.

	Simon W.,	2185		Aug. 10, 1859
	Walter H.,	2186		Oct. 4, 1861

NOYES PAYSON HAWES AND JENETTE KINGSLEY (FRARY) BARRETT. 2177.

	Amos William,	2187		Nov. 29, 1838	Feb. 15, 1862	
	Charles Spencer,	2188		Aug. 1, 1841	Dec. 26, 1842	[B. (White).
40	Franklin Noyes,	2189	W. New Brighton, N.Y., Aug. 15, 1844		Sept. 3, 1868	Mary Edith Gale; 1850–; dau. Alfred G. S. and Martha
40	Horace Frary,	2190 2191	"	Oct. 18, 1846	May 17, 1870 June 4, 1872	1. Katie May; –1871. 2. Jennie E. Nichols; 1853–.
	Jeanette,	2192	"	Mar. 10, 1850	Nov. 29, 1851	

NOYES PAYSON HAWES AND ANNA MAY (PEMBROKE) BARRETT. 2178.

	Charlie,	2193	Apr. 6, 1853	Mar. 4, 1858
	William,	2194	Apr. 26, 1857	Apr. 25, 1874
	Minnie Addie,	2195	Feb. 28, 1859	Feb. 20, 1865
	Eugene,	2196	Mar. 6, 1868	June 20, 1868
	Minnie Augusta,	2197	Oct. 31, 1870	

FRANKLIN NOYES AND MARY EDITH (GALE) BARRETT. 2189.

	Henry Root,	2198	W. New Brighton, N.Y., Oct. 26, 1870	Nov. 26, 1874
	Helen Jeanette,	2199	"	Apr. 27, 1872
	Franklin Noyes,	2200	Binghamton, N. Y., Dec. 11, 1873	Dec. 12, 1874
	Horace Frary,	2201	"	Feb. 26, 1876
	Noyes Payson Hawes,	2202	Bayone, N. J., Jan. 20, 1879	
	Mary Edith,	2203	"	May 15, 1882	June 19, 1882
	Herbert Leroy,	2204	"	July 7, 1885

HORACE FRARY AND JENNIE E. (NICHOLS) BARRETT. 2191.

	Nellie M.,	2205	Schultzville, Pa., Oct. 8, 1873	Sept. 28, 1879
	Frank Nichols,	2206	"	Mar. 31, 1876
	Abram McKinty,	2207	"	Aug. 12, 1878	Aug. 4, 1879
	Harry Hawes,	2208	"	Nov. 24, 1879

JOSEPH AND MARIA L. (BARRETT) MUZZY. 2180.

Mary Maria,	2209	Aug. 22, 1841		Feb. 28, 1866	Harlan P. Smart.

HORACE AND FIDELIA F. (BARRETT) MUZZY. 2183.

Fidelia,	2210	Apr., 1850			

MATTHIAS AND AMELIA P. (HAZLETON) BARRETT. 2184.

Amelia Hazleton,	2211	Oct. 1, 1857	Aug. 4, 1872		
Louisa,	2212	Oct. 2, 1859			
Alice,	2213	Dec. 17, 1865	Aug. 11, 1867		
Edward Kirk,	2214	Sept. 6, 1869			

REUBEN AND SARAH (THORNDIKE) BARRETT. 2142.

41	Nathan, Col.,	2215	Hope, Me., Feb. 2, 1795	Oct., 1865	Mar. 5, 1822	Sally Minott; 1798–1822; d. Jonas and Miriam (Bar-
	Sarah,	2216	" June 1, 1796	Jan. 23, 1876	Feb., 1817	Anthon Matthews; 1794–1849; son Joseph. [rett).
	David,	2217	" Feb. 8, 1798	May 9, 1819		
41	Robert T.,	2218	" Sept. 30, 1799		May 1, 1825	1. Sarah Barrett.
		2219			July 14, 1861	2. Mrs. Sarah Shattuck.
41	Eliza,	2220	" Dec. 3, 1801		Feb. 8, 1824	James Heal; 1797–1876.
42	Reuben,	2221	" Aug. 19, 1803		Jan. 20, 1828	Caroline D. Payson; 1805–.
	Irene F.,	2222	" July 23, 1806	Mar. 19, 1848	Unmarried.	
	Silas,	2223	" Mar. 9, 1808	Aug. 11, 1854		
42	John T.,	2224	" July 2, 1811		Nov. 1, 1838	Alice Tynan; 1818–.
	Caroline M.,	2225	" July 11, 1813			

COL. NATHAN AND SALLY (MINOTT) BARRETT. 2215.

	Minott T.,	2226	June 19, 1826	June 14, 1864		
	James M.,	2227	Oct. 27, 1827			
41	Mary M.,	2228	June 3, 1830	May 10, 1855	1851	Edward C. Mundy, M. D.; –1883.
	Nathan M.,	2229	Feb. 15, 1832	Mar. 24, 1843		
	Sarah A.,	2230	Dec. 8, 1834	Dec. 3, 1852		
	Franklin,	2231	June 7, 1837	Mar. 18, 1843		
	Jonas Minott,	2232				

DR. EDWARD C. AND MARY M. (BARRETT) MUNDY. 2228.

	Nathan,	2233	Aug. 20, 1852		
	Franklin,	2234	Mar. 26, 1853	Aug. 3, 1873	

ROBERT T. AND SARAH (BARRETT) BARRETT. 2218.

	Robert Thompson,	2235	July 30, 1826	Jan. 26, 1855		
	Sally,	2236	Oct. 27, 1830	Oct. 26, 1851		
	Sophia,	2237	Oct. 12, 1832	Jan. 3, 1860		
41	William,	2238	Jan. 1, 1835		Oct. 9, 1864	Bridget Gafney.

WILLIAM AND BRIDGET (GAFNEY) BARRETT. 2238.

	Sophia Annie,	2239	Nov. 18, 1865		

JAMES AND ELIZA (BARRETT) HEAL. 2220.

41	Nathan M.,	2240	Hope, Me., Nov. 3, 1824		Jan. 10, 1852	Caroline Augusta Hosmer; 1826–.
41	Joseph H.,	2241	" Nov. 3, 1824		May 20, 1850	Mary V. P. Smith.
	Caroline M. (no issue),	2242	" Feb. 25, 1826	Jan. 10, 1864	Apr. 19, 1863	Daniel T. Barrett. No. 1633.
	Louisa,	2243	" Apr. 15, 1828	Nov. 4, 1860	Unmarried.	
41	Edwin B.,	2244	" Mar. 2, 1830		Apr. 17, 1852	Patience Higgins.
	James A.,	2245	" May 10, 1832			
	Amos B.,	2246	" Dec. 30, 1833		June 28, 1859	Mary L. Ward.
41	George F.,	2247	" Dec. 16, 1836		July 1, 1869	Sarah T. Vail.
41	Peter P.,	2248	" Mar. 7, 1839		Jan. 28, 1861	Emma Swift.
	Lizzie E.,	2249	" Apr. 7, 1841			
42	Albert F.,	2250	" June 22, 1843		July 9, 1868	Susie M. Houseman.

NATHAN M. AND CAROLINE A. (HOSMER) HEAL. 2240.

Mary Augusta,	2251	Staten Island, N.Y., Jan.18, 1854		Oct. 17, 1878	Benjamin F. Adams.
Eliza Barrett,	2252	" Oct. 17, 1857			
Samuel W.,	2253	" Nov. 7, 1859	Aug. 9, 1860		
Lydia Norwood,	2254	" Aug. 29, 1861			
Caroline Hosmer,	2255	" Oct. 21, 1866			

JOSEPH H. AND MARY V. P. (SMITH) HEAL. 2241.

George H.,	2256	Carlton, N. Y., Jan. 21, 1853			
Frank J.,	2257	" May 15, 1858			
Augusta H.,	2258	" Aug. 29, 1862			
Joseph H.,	2259	" Dec. 29, 1863	Died young.		
Annie E.,	2260	" Dec. 2, 1864			
Ella B.,	2261	" Feb. 13, 1867			

EDWIN B. AND PATIENCE (HIGGINS) HEAL. 2244.

James L.,	2262	Staten Island, N.Y., Dec.20, 1854			
Charles E.,	2263	" June 26, 1858			
Harry E.,	2264	" May 29, 1864			
Clara M.,	2265	" Dec. 17, 1869			
Caroline L.,	2266	" Nov. 29, 1873			

GEORGE F. AND SARAH T. (VAIL) HEAL. 2247.

Ella Louisa,	2267	Staten Island, N.Y., May 26, 1870			
Fred Schuyler,	2268	" Jan. 1, 1877			

PETER P. AND EMMA (SWIFT) HEAL. 2248.

Lillie S.,	2269	Staten Island, N.Y., Mar. 6, 1862			
Edgar Knox,	2270	" Aug. 9, 1863			
Peter P., Jr.,	2271	" Oct. 5, 1873			

ALBERT F. AND SUSIE M. (HOUSEMAN) HEAL. 2250.

	Hattie M.,	2272	Staten Island, N. Y., Apr. 21,'74			

REUBEN AND CAROLINE D. (PAYSON) BARRETT. 2221.

42	John Tilston,	2273	Hope, Me., Sept. 1, 1828	Mar. 4, 1884	Mar. 30, 1855	Elizabeth Bartlett.
42	Augusta M.,	2274	" Sept. 25, 1830		Sept. 25, 1857	Thomas Nichols; 1820–; son Thomas and Deborah.
42	Amanda M.,	2275	" Sept. 22, 1831		Jan. 9, 1866	Gideon M. Yates; 1822–; son William.
42	Mary Cordelia	2276	" Mar. 4, 1833		Sept. 7, 1856	Ferdinand Hanson; 1830–.
	Sarah Thorndyke,	2277	" Apr. 6, 1835			
42	Reuben N.,	2278	" Apr. 10, 1837		June 23, 1859	Sophia Burbank; 1837–.
42	William H., {	2279	" Apr. 5, 1840		Apr. 21, 1863	1. Fannie Houghrant; 1839–1867; d. Peter N. & Ann.
	{	2280			Feb. 1, 1883	2. Mary G. Agnew; 1851–.
42	Carrie Miriam,	2281	" May 6, 1841	Dec. 2, 1883	Jan. 29, 1871	Charles F. Curtis; 1840–1883.
42	Annie Minott,	2282	" Sept. 17, 1842	Oct. 14, 1881	June 27, 1869	James E. Nichols; 1842–; son James and Lois.
42	Nathan M.,	2283	" Jan. 17, 1844		Feb. 12, 1870	Sarah Carman; 1851–1885; d. Frederick and Jane.
42	Robert Franklin,	2284	" Nov. 17, 1846		Aug. 5, 1874	Mary E. Fowler; 1851–.
	Louise Ellen,	2285	" Jan. 1, 1848	May 25, 1871	Unmarried.	

JOHN TILSTON AND ELIZABETH (BARRETT) BARRETT. 2273.

	Minnie C.,	2286	Hope, Me., June 9, 1856			
	Edward S.,	2287	" May 9, 1860	May 22, 1864		
	Sophia,	2288	" June 6, 1862	Aug. 18, 1864		
	Nathan F.,	2289	" Oct. 22, 1865			

THOMAS AND AUGUSTA M. (BARRETT) NICHOLS. 2274.

	Charles B.,	2290	Hope, Me., June 26, 1858			
	Wilder F.,	2291	Bristol, Me., Apr. 12, 1861	Sept. 10, 1861		
	Thomas B.,	2292	" July 24, 1862	Aug. 7, 1862		
	Thomas W.,	2293	" July 14, 1864			
	Frank B.,	2294	" Feb. 2, 1868			

GIDEON M. AND AMANDA M. (BARRETT) YATES. 2275.

	Augusta,	2295	Jan. 13, 1868			

FERDINAND AND MARY C. (BARRETT) HANSON. 2276.

	Ralph G.,	2296	Rockport, Me., July 3, 1861	July 4, 1861		
	Reuben A.,	2297	" Mar. 27, 1864			
	Kate W.,	2298	" Dec. 19, 1865	Oct. 27, 1872		
	Emily A.,	2299	" Apr. 20, 1875	Oct. 13, 1875		

REUBEN N. AND SOPHIA (BURBANK) BARRETT. 2278.

	William N.,	2300	Staten Island, N. Y., Jan. 13,'62			
	John B.,	2301	" Nov. 1, 1863			
	Frank J.,	2302	Englew'd, N. J., July 14, '66			
	Reuben E.,	2303	" Apr. 15, 1870	July 17, 1870		
	Annie Louise,	2304	" Aug. 19, 1871			
	Reuben E.,	2305	" Sept. 20, 1875			

WILLIAM H. AND FANNIE (HOUGHRANT) BARRETT. 2279.

	William Pierce,	2306	Port Richmond, July 21, '64			

CHARLES F. AND CARRIE MERIAM (BARRETT) CURTIS. 2281.

	Edith B.,	2307	Feb. 15, 1874	May 12, 1874		
	Everett N.,	2308	May 24, 1875			

JAMES E. AND ANNIE M. (BARRETT) NICHOLS. 2282.

	Carrie Louise,	2309	Round Pond, Me., Apr. 5,'72			
	Mary Hinds,	2310	" Nov. 2, 1875			
	Everett Augusta,	2311	" Jan. 11, 1880			

NATHAN M. AND SARAH (CARMAN) BARRETT. 2283.

	Fredelia,	2312	Sept. 9, 1870			
	Cordelia M.,	2313	June 19, 1872	July 28, 1873		
	Emma A.,	2314	July 25, 1874	Oct. 8, 1874		
	Charles N.,	2315	Jan. 8, 1876			
	Nathan M.,	2316	Dec. 23, 1879			
	Ralph,	2317	Feb. 27, 1881			
	Wash't'n Lafay'te,	2318	Feb. 22, 1883	July 22, 1883		

ROBERT F. AND MARY E. (FOWLER) BARRETT. 2284.

	Louisa R.,	2319	July 15, 1875			
	Susie G.,	2320	Oct. 23, 1876			
	Robert F.,	2321	Jan. 8, 1880	Mar. 30, 1881		
	Ethel C.,	2322	Feb. 18, 1883			

JOHN T. AND ALICE (TYNAN) BARRETT. 2224.

	Clarence Tynan,	2323	Aug. 19, 1840		Jan. 13, 1871	Anna E. Hutchins; dau. Wm. D. and Elizabeth.
	Laura Ann,	2324	Apr. 22, 1842			
	Arabella Caroline,	2325	May 22, 1844	Nov. 14, 1877	Nov. 2, 1865	Orville D. Jewett; 1837–1877; son John.
43	Nathan Franklin,	2326	Nov. 19, 1845		June 6, 1870	Lucy Mildred Lampkin; d. America F. and Terrell M.
42	Sarah Irene,	2327	July 11, 1848		Apr. 9, 1819	John P. Truesdell, 1846–; s. Edw'd D. and Henrietta J.
43	John David,	2328	Aug. 17, 1852		Sept. 4, 1878	Amelia L. Higgins; 1853–; dau. A. Foster and Sarah
	Harriet,	2329	Aug. 15, 1854			[H.
	Charles M.,	2380	May 30, 1861			

JOHN P. AND SARAH IRENE (BARRETT) TRUESDELL. 2327.

	Edward Delavan,	2331	Feb. 4, 1880			
	Thorndyke,	2332	Sept. 18, 1881	June 6, 1883		
	John Phillips,	2333	July 13, 1883	Nov. 22, 1884		

JOHN DAVID AND AMELIA L. (HIGGINS) BARRETT. 2328.

	Sadie Cornell,	2334	Dec. 16, 1879			
	Foster Higgins,	2335	Feb. 5, 1882			
	Alice,	2336	July 6, 1884			

NATHAN F. AND LUCY MILDRED (LAMPKIN) BARRETT. 2326.

	Mildred F.,	2337	July 7, 1870	June 15, 1871		
	Alice Irene,	2338	Oct. 8, 1871			
	Nathan,	2339	Mar. 24, 1874	Sept. 8, 1874		
	Arabella,	2340	Aug. 6, 1875	Apr. 8, 1876		
	Hesse Laura,	2341	Dec. 13, 1877	June 10, 1878		
	John Terrell,	2342	Feb. 13, 1879			
	Nathan,	2343	Mar. 20, 1882	Aug. 21, 1882		
	Lamar Thorndyke,	2344	July 26, 1883	Sept. 30, 1884		

EPHRAIM AND LOUISA (WOOD) BARRETT. 2146.

	Lucy,	2345	Camden, Me., Mar. 29, 1807	May 11, 1814		
	Ephraim A.,	2346	" Dec. 17, 1808	Feb. 8, 1809		
43	Mary E.,	2347	" Aug. 15, 1810		Oct. 4, 1833	Alex. J. Sweet; 1811–1884.
	Louisa E.,	2348	" June 26, 1812		Dec. 3, 1846	Ezra Meriam; 1808–1883.
	William George,	2349	" Aug. 7, 1814			
43	Caroline M.,	2350	" Nov. 29, 1816		Dec. 12, 1837	George W. Kimball; 1805–1879.
	Harriet B.,	2351	" June 30, 1819	May 8, 1851	Aug. 2, 1849	William E. Lawrence; 1811–1882.
	Charles Henry, {	2352	" Feb. 4, 1821		Apr. 6, 1861	1. Elizabeth G. Barber; 1827–1863; dau. John W.
43	{	2353			Sept. 12, 1871	2. Ella Josephine McCanon; 1838–.
43	Theresa,	2354	" Sept. 20, 1822		July 1, 1846	Capt. George W. Thorndyke; 1816–1883.
	Sarah A. (no issue),	2355	" July 29, 1824	Nov. 22, 1882	June 28, 1861	Thomas N. Hosmer; 1823–.
43	Susan A.,	2356	" July 29, 1824		Sept. 22, 1851	Austin N. Parkhurst; 1823–; son Ziba and Sophronia.
43	Francis A.,	2357	" June 16, 1827		Oct. 28, 1851	Agnes Berry; dau. Nicholas and Sally Ann.

ALEX. J. AND MARY E. (BARRETT) SWEET. 2347.

	Ellen,	2358	Oct. 24, 1834			
	Joseph B.,	2359	June 24, 1836			
	Ann L.,	2360	May 24, 1839			
	George A.,	2361	Sept. 21, 1843	Sept., 1852		
	Susan J.,	2362	Aug. 7, 1748	Aug. 17, 1849		
	Harriet B.,	2363	May 14, 1851			

GEORGE W. AND CAROLINE M. (BARRETT) KIMBALL. 2350.

	Adelia Barrett,	2364	Camden, Me., Feb. 9, 1839		Sept. 28, 1863	John Schott.
	Louisa W.,	2365	" Aug. 6, 1843	June 17, 1847		
	Edgar H.,	2366	Winterproof, Me., May 7, 1845			

CAPT. CHARLES HENRY AND ELLA JOSEPHINE (McCANON) BARRETT. 2353.

| | Daisy Vivian, | 2367 | Orange, N. J., Jan. 26, 1873 | | | |

CAPT. GEORGE W. AND THERESA (BARRETT) THORNDYKE. 2354.

	William H.,	2368	July 11, 1847			
	Theresa L.,	2369	Apr. 18, 1849			
	Emeline,	2370	Mar. 23, 1852	Feb. 5, 1854		
	Ephraim B.,	2371	Aug. 19, 1855		June 24, 1885	Helen G. Kinsley.

AUSTIN N. AND SUSAN A. (BARRETT) PARKHURST. 2356.

	Fred A.,	2372	Charl'st'wn, June 26, 1853		Sept. 25, 1884	Laura B. Noyes.
	Ellen Louise,	2373	Winchend'n, Feb. 15, 1855		Dec. 4, 1884	Henry Ackerman.
	Henry Francis,	2374	Charl'st'wn, Jan. 23, 1860			
	Georgianna A.,	2375	" June 1, 1863			
	Eunice Theresa,	2376	" June 24, 1866	Aug. 10, 1876		

FRANCIS A. AND AGNES (BERRY) BARRETT. 2357.

	Sarah L.,	2377	Camden, Me., Oct. 11, 1852	Oct. 26, 1859		
	Mary E.,	2376	" Apr. 16, 1855	June 9, 1857		
	Charles W.,	2377	" May 11, 1859		Feb. 18, 1855	Minnie Thomas; dau. John C. and Catharine B.
	Mary Frances,	2378	" Dec. 13, 1863			
	Susan Agnes,	2379	" Feb. 9, 1865			

WILLIAM AND MARY K. (HALL) BARRETT. 2148.

	Caroline,	2380	Malden, Oct. 27, 1804	Aug. 31, 1805		
	William,	2381	" Jan. 20, 1806	Dec. 5, 1838		
	Henry (no issue), {	2382	" Oct. 19, 1807		Sept., 1835	1. Louisa Brown. No. 3803.
43	{	2383			Feb. 25, 1841	2. Hannah R. Hudson; –1844. [A. (St. Agnau).
43	{	2384			Jan. 19, 1848	3. Lucy T. G. Stearns; 1824–; d. Richard S. and Mary
	Caroline,	2385	" July 14, 1809	Oct. 28, 1836	Mar. 25, 1833	Caleb S. Winslow.
44	Simon Hall,	2386	" Feb. 11, 1811		Dec. 16, 1836	Mary Ann Pratt; 1807–; d. Daniel and Mary (Hall).
44	Augustus Ludlow,	2387	" Jan. 31, 1813		July 31, 1845	Helen Maria Whitman; 1827–.
44	Aaron,	2388	" Aug. 13, 1814	Oct. 2, 1878	Oct. 28, 1841	Lucinda W. Bean. [and Sally (Hodgon).
44	Mary Hall,	2389	" Sept. 14, 1816	Dec. 5, 1860	Nov. 3, 1839	Rev. John Greenleaf Adams, D. D.; 1810–; son John
	Louisa B.,	2390	" June 8, 1818		Mar. 25, 1841	Edwin H. Hall; 1810–; son Capt. John and Sally.
	Elizabeth (no issue),	2391	" May 2, 1820	May 17, 1883	Mar. 30, 1884	Charles Eastham; 1813–; son Henry L. and Martha.
	Charles,	2392	" May 3, 1822	Sept. 14, 1822		[and Lydia (Hill).
67	Augusta Maria,	2393	" Dec. 28, 1823		Dec. 25, 1844	William Henry Richardson; 1823–1874; son Wm. H.

HENRY AND HANNAH R. (HUDSON) BARRETT. 2383.

| | Henry Hudson, | 2394 | Malden, Nov. 16, 1841 | Dec. 1, 1843 | | |

HENRY AND LUCY T. G. (STEARNS) BARRETT. 2384   (Continued page 44.)

44	Lucy St. Agnau,	2395	Malden, Dec. 21, 1848		Apr. 16, 1874	Rev. Geo. P. Huntington; s. Bishop F. D. & Hannah.
	Harry Hudson,	2396	" Mar. 10, 1851			[(Penniman).
44	Richard Stearns,	2397	" May 2, 1854		June 30, 1879	Ella Martha Devens; dau. George A. and Martha S.

	Caroline Stearns,	2398	Malden,	Mar. 14, 1859	Sept. 14, 1859		
	Caroline Stearns,	2399	"	July 24, 1860			

REV. GEORGE P. AND LUCY ST. AGNAU (BARRETT) HUNTINGTON. 2395.

	Henry Barrett,	2400	Malden,	Jan. 17, 1875			
	Constant Davis,	2401	"	Sept. 20, 1876			
	James Lincoln,	2402	"	Mar. 30, 1880			
	Paul St. Agnau,	2403	"	Aug. 26, 1882			

RICHARD S. AND ELLA M. (DEVENS) BARRETT. 2397.

	Richard Devens,	2404	Malden,	Dec. 26, 1880			
	Th'resa St. Agnau,	2405	"	July 29, 1885			

SIMON HALL AND MARY ANN (PRATT) BARRETT. 2386.

	Franklin H.,	2406	Malden,	Jan. 24, 1838	Aug. 19, 1839		
	May H.,	2407	"	Apr. 15, 1839	Aug. 6, 1867		
	William H.,	2408	"	Nov. 4, 1840			
	Ellen A.,	2409	"	June 27, 1842		Dec. 8, 1867	D. F. Jackson; 1831-; son Morrison and Hannah E.
	Elizabeth E.,	2410	"	Sept. 12, 1843	Oct. 10, 1844		

AUGUSTUS L. AND HELEN M. (WHITMAN) BARRETT. 2387.

	Caroline Louise,	2411	Malden,	July 16, 1846		Jan. 20, 1869	Frank H. Nevens.
	Emma Maria,	2412	"	July 10, 1849			
	Helen Augusta,	2413	"	Aug. 9, 1853	Jan. 30, 1855		
	Augustus Ludlow,	2414	"	Aug. 26, 1855	Jan. 27, 1877		
	Louise Gardner,	2415	"	Jan. 21, 1858			
	Eliz. Eastham,	2416	"	Sept. 30, 1862			

AARON AND LUCINDA W. (BEAN) BARRETT. 2388.

44	Lucinda Hooper,	2417	Malden,	Sept. 14, 1842	Mar. 29, 1866	July 29, 1863	Henry E. Turner; 1842-; s. Henry E. and Sophronia (Burns). [(Burns).
44	Mary Helen,	2418	"	Sept. 1, 1844		May 15, 1867	Joseph F. Turner; 1839-; s. Henry E. and Sophronia
44	George W.,	2419	"	Sept. 11, 1846		June 3, 1869	Eliz. B. Crocker; 1846-; d. Matthias and Esther R.
44	Charles A.,	2420	"	Aug. 22, 1848		June 1, 1871	Mary E. Herrick; 1849-.
	James H.,	2421	"	Dec. 4, 1850		Mar. 20, 1881	Ida L. Davis.
44	Anna Webster,	2422	"	Oct. 1, 1852		May 30, 1872	Edward E. Currier; 1847-.
	Georgianna,	2423	"	May 22, 1854	Jan. 26, 1855		
	Georgianna,	2424	"	Oct. 28, 1855		July 10, 1877	Edwin C. Clark; son Dudley.
	Minnie Franklin,	2425	"	Mar. 12, 1857		Dec. 25, 1879	John C. Russell; 1860-.
	Jennie Livingst'n,	2426	"	Oct. 12, 1861			
	Horace W.,	2427	"	July 1, 1863	Mar. 20, 1864		

HENRY E. AND LUCINDA H. (BARRETT) TURNER. 2417.

	Anabel,	2428		March, 1864			
	Henry Hudson,	2429		Mar. 25, 1866			

JOSEPH F. AND MARY H. (BARRETT) TURNER. 2418.

	Bessie Barrett,	2430		May 11, 1868			
	Herbert S.,	2431		Nov. 5, 1869			

GEORGE W. AND ELIZABETH B. (CROCKER) BARRETT. 2419.

	Eliz. Boylston,	2432		Jan. 25, 1871	Jan. 25, 1871		
	Jessie Gertrude,	2433		Nov. 22, 1872			
	Edward Bell,	2434		Dec. 16, 1876	June 26, 1877		
	Laura Whitman,	2435		Sept. 13, 1879			

CHARLES A. AND MARY E. (HERRICK) BARRETT. 2420.

	Ethel,	2436		June 30, 1873			

EDWARD E. AND ANNA W. (BARRETT) CURRIER. 2422.

	Agnes,	2437		Nov. 30, 1874			

REV. JOHN G. AND MARY HALL (BARRETT) ADAMS. 2389.

98	George Wallace,	2438	Malden,	June 1, 1841		June 1, 1870	Charlotte Eliza'th Bedlow; 1844-; dau. Cornelius, Jr., and Harriette (Pond). [Georgiana (Priest).
	Myra Greenleaf,	2439	"	Aug. 6, 1847	Sept. 8, 1847		
98	John Coleman, Rev.,	2440	"	Oct. 25, 1849		July 18, 1883	Miriam Priest Hovey; 1864-; dau. Charles A. and
	Mary Alice,	2441	"	July 4, 1854			

EDWIN H. AND LOUISA B. (BARRETT) HALL. 2390.

	Dexter A.,	2442		Jan. 25, 1843		Jan. 18, 1877	Augusta W. Hayes.
	Edwin Harris,	2443		Feb. 14, 1846	July 5, 1852		

FRANCIS AND MARIA F. (PALLISIER) BARRETT. 2150.

	Maria Foster,	2444	Concord,	June 9, 1800	Aug. 7, 1801		
	Maria Foster,	2445	"	Dec. 7, 1801	Nov. 15, 1803		
	Francis,	2446	"	Aug. 25, 1803	Sept. 25, 1847		Matilda Smith.
	Charles Minott,	2447	"	Aug. 8, 1805	June 29, 1834		
44	Ann Maria,	2448	"	Feb. 1, 1807		Nov. 23, 1831	Horatio Nelson Hewett; 1809-1856.
45	Emeline Augusta,	2449	"	Nov. 19, 1809		Aug. 23, 1829	Herman Atwell; 1804-1863; s. Ebenezer and Sarah.
	George Henry,	2450	"	Oct. 30, 1811	July 30, 1866	July 19, 1853	Harriet F. Shovey.
	Catharine P.,	2451	"	Jan. 1, 1814		June 6, 1844	Lemuel Fuller; 1812-1864.
	The'dore A., Capt.,	2452	"	Dec. 28, 1816		Apr. 10, 1864	Mary D. Davis; 1827-; dau. Daniel and Mary.
	Benj. Franklin,	2453	"	May 21, 1819	July 24, 1868	Unmarried.	

HORATIO N. AND ANN M. (BARRETT) HEWETT. 2448.

44	James Pomeroy,	2454		Sept. 29, 1836		Nov. 13, 1861	Eliza Jane Vermilyea.
45	Maria Augusta,	2455		June 15, 1839		Jan. 14, 1866	Robert Taylor Sherman.
45	Sophia Estelle,	2456		July 20, 1842		Dec. 14, 1864	Josiah Otis Ward.

JAMES POMEROY AND ELIZA JANE (VERMILYEA) HEWETT. 2454.

	James Dalton,	2457		Apr. 7, 1877			
	George Mitchell,	2458		May 10, 1880			

ROBERT TAYLOR AND MARIA AUGUSTA (HEWETT) SHERMAN. 2455.

	Cora Pallesier,	2459	Oct. 16, 1866			
	Ada,	2460	Apr. 11, 1868			
	Eugene King,	2461	Aug. 25, 1871			

JOSIAH OTIS AND SOPHIA ESTELLE (HEWETT) WARD. 2456.

	Josiah Otis, Jr.,	2462	Aug. 24, 1868			
	Edith,	2463	Oct. 7, 1871			
	Estelle Adelaide,	2464	Aug. 3, 1874			
	Mabel,	2465	Nov. 16, 1877			

HERMAN AND AMELIA A. (BARRETT) ATWELL. 2449.

	Herman,	2466	New York, N. Y.,Mar. 3, '43		Mar. 21, 1871	Emma O. Marriner.
45	Paul Ralph George,	2467	" Nov. 25, 1844		Oct. 14, 1871	Addie Northrop; d. Jay Lord and Martha Letitia.

PAUL R. G. AND ADDIE (NORTHROP) ATWELL. 2467.

	George F.,	2468	June 4, 1883			

JAMES AND JENNIE (WHITE) BARRETT. 2151.

	Myrick,	2469	Nov., 1802		1829	Sarah Crosby.
45	George W.,	2470	Camden, Me., Sept. 15, 1804	June 14, 1839	Oct. 22, 1829	Paulina Osgood; 1808–; dau. Jacob and Susanna.
	Lucy,	2471	" June, 1806	June, 1836	1828	John Downing.
45	John,	2472	" July 5, 1808	Jan. 12, 1871	Oct. 3, 1841	Dorcas S. Osgood; 1821–; dau. Jacob and Susanna.
45	Ephraim,	2473	No. Haven,Me.,Sept. 27,'10	Feb. 21, 1874	Oct. 16, 1842	Charlotte Augusta Holt; 1820–1857.
	Silas,	2474	May, 1813	Dec., 1815		
	Louisa,	2475	Aug., 1820	Nov., 1843		

GEORGE W. AND PAULINE (OSGOOD) BARRETT. 2470.

45	Augusta,	2476	Surry, Me., July 6, 1830		Dec. 22, 1846	James O. Jarvis.
	Julia Ann,	2477	" Oct. 22, 1832	Aug., 1866		
	Henry,	2478	" July 13, 1836	Aug. 7, 1836		
	Ellen M.,	2479	" Feb. 11, 1838	Nov. 28, 1855		

JAMES O. AND AUGUSTA (BARRETT) JARVIS. 2476.

45	James Edward,	2480	Feb. 13, 1849		May 16, 1874	L. C. Brown.
	Lizzie Maria,	2481	Mar. 28, 1854	Mar. 31, 1867		
	Howard Barrett,	2482	Mar. 20, 1858		May 13, 1886	E. R. Gale.

JAMES E. AND L. C. (BROWN) JARVIS. 2480.

	James Henry,	2483	Brooklyn, N.Y., May 29,'76			
	Eddie Barrett,	2484	" Feb. 8, 1878			
	Susan M.,	2485	" Jan. 4, 1880			

JOHN AND DORCAS S. (OSGOOD) BARRETT. 2472.

45	Emeline T.,	2486	Bluehill, Me., June 7, 1844	Sept. 1, 1869	Dec. 10, 1862	John H. Jarvis.
45	Myra E.,	2487	" Dec. 18, 1846		Nov. 17, 1867	Seth R. Lord.
	Albert A.,	2488	" Aug. 26, 1853	Dec. 19, 1872		

JOHN H. AND EMELINE T. (BARRETT) JARVIS. 2486.

	Ida F.,	2489	Surry, Me., Sept. 7, 1863		Aug. 22, 1885	Robert Newcomb.

SETH R. AND MYRA E. (BARRETT) LORD. 2487.

	Lizzie J.,	2490	Surry, Me., Jan. 11, 1869			
	Lulu F.,	2491	" Aug. 10, 1871			

EPHRAIM AND CHARLOTTE A. (HOLT) BARRETT. 2473.

	Frederick M.,	2492	Sept. 1, 1843	Sept. 28, 1843		
	Frances Augustus	2493	Oct., 1845	Aug. 14, 1858		
	Charles Ephraim,	2494	Feb., 1848	Aug. 31, 1852		
	Louise Adelia,	2495	June 1, 1852	Jan. 12, 1854		
	Emily Augusta,	2496	Jan. 23, 1857			

GEORGE MINOTT AND SUSANNA (RICHMOND) BARRETT. 2152

45	Susan,	2497	Malden, Sept. 19, 1806	Dec. 2, 1842	Mar. 26, 1829	John H. Jones; 1805–1843.
	George,	2498	" Oct. 31, 1807	Dec. 10, 1869	Unmarried.	
	Varnum,	2499	" Feb. 7, 1809	June 22, 1840	"	
	Adaline,	2500	" Apr. 7, 1811	Feb. 18, 1879	"	
45	Ellen Miriam,	2501	" Oct. 25, 1815		Apr. 6, 1834	George Washington Matsell; 1811–1877; son George [and Elizabeth (Constable).
	Lucretia Richardson,	2502	" Feb. 10, 1818			Joshua Mersereau.
	Isabella,	2503	" Jan. 26, 1820		Apr. 2, 1846	Isaac Davis; 1811–1864; son Isaac and Lucretia.
	Frances Ann,	2504	Staten Island, N. Y., Dec. 27,'31			Luke B. French.

JOHN H. AND SUSAN (BARRETT) JONES. 2497.

	John,	2505	Nov. 2, 1833	Sept. 20, 1834		
	Susan Barrett,	2506	Sept. 16, 1840		Oct. 25, 1882	Joseph W. Sillsby; 1846–.

GEORGE W. AND ELLEN M. (BARRETT) MATSELL. 2501.

	Geo. Washington,	2507	Feb. 14, 1835			
	Susan Jane,	2508	Sept. 5, 1837			
	Augustus Barrett,	2509	Aug. 6, 1841			
	Henry Charles,	2510	Apr. 8, 1847			

LUTHER AND SARAH (PERRY) BARRETT. 2154.

46	Luther Gustavus,	2511	Sept. 10, 1808	Oct. 22, 1859	Mar. 6, 1834	Margaret Ridley; 1811–; dau. Thomas and Caroline. [(Fiske).
	Sarah W.,	2512	Aug. 3, 1810			
46	Mary Adaline,	2513	July 18, 1813		Oct. 29, 1833	Rufus Fiske Brooks; 1808–; s. Benjamin and Esther
	Lucy A.,	2514	Dec. 4, 1816		Jan. 24, 1855	Nathan Barrett. No. 2156.
	Francis H. (no issue),	2515	Oct. 20, 1818		Sept. 14, 1841	Abby Pierce; 1842–1883.
	Charles H.,	2516	Oct. 12, 1823	June 28, 1837		

LUTHER G. AND MARGARET (RIDLEY) BARRETT. 2511.

46	Margaret Ridley,	2517	Watertown, Jan. 4, 1835		June 8, 1859	Rich'd Benj. Thayer; 1830–; s. Thos. A. & Eliz. (Wales).
46	Luth'r Gustavus, Rev.,	2518 2519	" Dec. 5, 1838		June 9, 1869 Sept. 15, 1885	1. Mary Annette Hawks; 1843–1877; d. Ezra&MaryAnn. 2. Ella Maria Short; 1860–; d. Herbert D. and Mary.
46	John Perry, Rev.,	2520	" Feb. 19, 1841		May 11, 1868	Lizzie Aiken Wheeler; dau. Wm. H. and Sarah W.
	Caroline Augusta,	2521	" June 7, 1845			

RICHARD BENJAMIN AND MARGARET RIDLEY (BARRETT) THAYER. 2517.

	Frank Oliver,	2522	Boston, May 8, 1861	Mar. 8, 1863		
	Herbert Applet'n,	2523	" Apr. 10, 1864			
	Mary Caroline,	2524	" Feb. 6, 1868			

REV. LUTHER G. AND MARY A. (HAWKS) BARRETT. 2518.

	Florence Hawks,	2525	Worcester, Mar. 26, 1870		
	George Ridley,	2526	New York, N. Y., Feb., 1876	July, 1876	
	Helen Jeannette,	2527	" 1877	June, 1877	

REV. JOHN P. AND LIZZIE A. (WHEELER) BARRETT. 2520.

	Frank Perry,	2528	Boston, Apr. 16, 1869	Aug. 19, 1875
	George Edson,	2529	" Nov. 9, 1871	Aug. 15, 1875
	Mabel Winslow,	2530	" Feb. 8, 1874	

RUFUS F. AND MARY A. (BARRETT) BROOKS. 2513.

	Esther Maria,	2531	Watertown, Mar. 28, 1837	Oct. 10, 1839		
46	Sarah Adaline,	2532	Boston, Dec. 26, 1838	Apr. 12, 1866	Dec. 25, 1861	F. Hiram Rice; son Augustus and Esther.

F. HIRAM AND SARAH A. (BROOKS) RICE. 2532.

	Jessie Maria,	2533	Oct. 13, 1862	
	Lucy Addie,	2534	June 3, 1864	

STEPHEN AND SARAH (BARRETT) BARRETT. 1899–854.

46	Stephen,	2535	Concord, Apr. 30, 1776	June 9, 1856	Nov. 3, 1799	Sally Barrett. No. 1805.
47	Emerson,	2536 2537	" Apr. 30, 1777	Feb. 12, 1854	Feb. 10, 1810 May 4, 1837	1. Martha Jones; 1785–1824. No. 4297. 2. Abigail Stow; 1781–1852.
	Sally (no issue), (no issue),	2538 2539	" July 31, 1779	Sept. 18, 1839	Jan. 3, 1805 Feb. 13, 1812	1. Capt. Nathan Wood; 1766–1810. 2. Stephen Wood; 1764–1820.
	Nancy,	2540	" Apr. 19, 1781	Dec. 7, 1810	Jan. 16, 1806	Capt. James Farrar. No. 4154.
	Rebecca,	2541	" Aug. 9, 1782	Nov. 26, 1807		Nehemiah Davis; 1768–1808; s. Nehemiah & Dorothy.

STEPHEN AND PHEBE (BRIDGE) BARRETT. 1900.

	Cyrus,	2542	Concord, Sept. 2, 1792	Aug. 28, 1820	Unmarried.

STEPHEN AND SALLY (BARRETT) BARRETT. 2535–1805.

	Sally,	2543	Concord, Apr. 19, 1801	Apr. 30, 1868	Oct. 10, 1822	Thos. Whitney; 1800–1865; s. Thos. & Henrietta (Parker).
46	Varnum,	2544	Shirley, Dec. 10, 1801	Feb. 14, 1875	Nov. 12, 1827	Susan Willard Longley; 1803–1857; dau. Joseph and [Mary (Pratt).
	Rebecca,	2545	"	Feb. 5, 1837	Unmarried.	
46	Stephen,	2546	" Jan. 14, 1804		Oct. 25, 1835	Catharine Hodgin; 1808–.
	Emerson,	2547	" 1807	Feb. 7, 1852	Unmarried.	
	Samuel,	2548	" June 10, 1810	Oct. 13, 1849	Apr. 29, 1838	Susan Treadwell; 1812–. [Mary (Flagg).
46	Harriet,	2549	" Jan. 20, 1812		May 29, 1837	John Kendall Gowing; 1810–1866; son John K. and
	George,	2550	" 1815	Jan. 31, 1852	Unmarried.	[(Hartwell).
46	Elizabeth,	2551	" Nov. 28, 1818		May 18, 1845	Artemas Longley; 1815–1876; s. Artemas and Desire
	Phebe (no issue),	2552	" Jan. 10, 1823	Oct. 27, 1861		E. Dana Bancroft; 1821–.
	Charles,	2553	" 1826	Sept. 30, 1851		

VARNUM AND SUSAN WILLARD (LONGLEY) BARRETT. 2544.

	George Varnum,	2554	Shirley, July 10, 1837		Aug. 9, 1876	Ella A. Johnson. No. 1231.
46	Mary E.,	2555	" Nov. 12, 1840	Aug. 30, 1869	Nov. 18, 1858	Orrin M. Bennett; 1831–.
	Josephine,	2556	" July 12, 1843	July 9, 1876	Unmarried.	

ORRIN M. AND MARY E. (BARRETT) BENNETT. 2555.

	Minnie Augusta,	2557	Ashburnham, June 10, 1861		May 27, 1885	Frank S. Keith.
	Alice Maria,	2558	Shirley, Sept. 27, 1864	July 24, 1876	
	Charles,	2559	" Sept. 17, 1866	Apr. 17, 1870	

STEPHEN AND CATHARINE (HODGIN) BARRETT. 2546.

46	Charles Stephen,	2560	Feb. 5, 1837		Oct. 18, 1866	Nancy Maria Farmer; 1847–.
	Samuel,	2561	Aug. 26, 1847		Unmarried.	

CHARLES S. AND NANCY M. (FARMER) BARRETT. 2560.

	Nelly Gertrude,	2562	July 22, 1870	Nov. 22, 1870
	Josephine,	2563	Oct. 24, 1871	Oct. 26, 1871
	Ada Louise,	2564	Dec. 8, 1872	
	Hattie Mabel,	2565	Oct. 20, 1874	Dec. 21, 1875
	Charles Albert,	2566	Oct. 4, 1877	

JOHN KENDALL AND HARRIET (BARRETT) GOWING. 2549.

46	Henry Barrett,	2567	May 7, 1839		Oct. 28, 1867	Nellie M. Chambers; 1846–.

HENRY B. AND NELLIE M. (CHAMBERS) GOWING. 2567.

	Mabel,	2568	Boston, Dec. 21, 1868
	Gertrude,	2569	" Jan. 2, 1870
	John Kendall,	2570	" Oct. 29, 1872

ARTEMAS AND ELIZABETH (BARRETT) LONGLEY. 2551.

(Continued page 47.)

	Elizabeth,	2571	Shirley, July 12, 1847		
	Harriet Gowing,	2572	" Aug. 19, 1849	Oct. 17, 1866	Aug. 27, 1885	George S. Prescott.
	Emily,	2573	" Jan. 21, 1852		
	Sarah Frances,	2574	Groton, Sept. 12, 1854		

	Jennie,	2575	Groton,	Aug. 11, 1857		
	George Artemas,	2576	"	Sept. 29, 1860		

EMERSON AND MARTHA (JONES) BARRETT. 2536–4297.

	Nancy Farrar,	2577	Concord,	May 15, 1811	May 17, 1834		
	William Emerson,	2578	"	May 30, 1814	Nov. 30, 1815		
	Elizabeth Jones,	2579	"	Dec. 6, 1815		Oct. 22, 1835	Hildreth P. Dutton.
47	Abel Jones,	2580	"	Mar. 17, 1817	Feb. 4, 1841	Sybil Spaulding.
	Sarah Wood,	2581	"	Nov. 22, 1818	Jan. 11, 1847	Sept. 23, 1841	A. C. Wright.
	Humphrey,	2582	"	Apr. 8, 1821	Sept. 11, 1822		
	Humphrey,	2583	"	June 13, 1823	Sept. 9, 1823		

ABEL JONES AND SYBIL (SPAULDING) BARRETT. 2580.

	James Waldo,	2584		June 3, 1842	Feb. 5, 1871	Unmarried.	
	George Edwin,	2585		May 5, 1844			
	Martha Ellen,	2586		Nov. 23, 1848		Oct. 28, 1875	John F. Quigley.

PETER AND MARY (PRESCOTT) BARRETT. 1901.

	Mary,	2587	Concord,	Aug. 2, 1781	Mar. 12, 1841	Mar. 23, 1802	Jonathan Heywood; 1775–1807.
47	Mercy,	2588	"	Sept. 13, 1783	Feb. 7, 1837	Sept. 24, 1811	Wm. Gibbs; 1785–; son Henry and Mercy (Prescott).
	Rebecca,	2589	"	Jan. 8, 1786	Oct. 30, 1846	Unmarried.	
47	Prescott, {	2590	"	Feb. 27, 1788	Oct. 15, 1861	Oct. 18, 1810	1. Betsey Barrett. No. 1806.
47		2591				Jan. 15, 1818	2. Olive Hayward; 1790–1873.
	Henry,	2592	"	July 17, 1790	Feb. 5, 1815	Unmarried.	
47	Sherman, Col.,	2593	"	Sept. 18, 1793	Feb. 27, 1863		Mary Hopper Worthington; 1801–1864.
47	Benjamin, M. D.,	2594	"	Feb. 2, 1796	June 14, 1869	Aug., 1826	Mary Wright; 1796–1867; dau. Seth.

WILLIAM AND MERCY (BARRETT) GIBBS. 2588.

	William Prescott,	2595	Salem,	Aug. 5, 1812	1852		

PRESCOTT AND BETSEY (BARRETT) BARRETT. 2590–1806.

	Henry Prescott,	2596	Concord,	Apr. 14, 1811	Mar. 22, 1854	Unmarried.	
	Jonathan Heywood,	2597	"	Feb. 6, 1813	Mar. 1, 1816		

PRESCOTT AND OLIVE (HAYWARD) BARRETT. 2591.

	Mary Elizabeth,	2598	Concord,	Apr. 17, 1819			
47	George Hayward,	2599	"	Jan. 20, 1821		Apr. 25, 1858	Mary Whitcomb; –1885; dau. John and Anna.
47	William Gibbs,	2600	"	June 16, 1823		June 17, 1846	Sophia Barrett Dodge; 1823–.
	Martha Sherman,	2601	"	Nov. 11, 1824			
	Augusta Hayward,	2602	"	Nov. 11, 1824			
47	Charles Mason, {	2603	"	Nov. 4, 1827		Dec. 9, 1852	1. Sarah P. Conant. No. 3910.
		2604				Dec. 3, 1861	2. Adaline A. Conant. No. 3920.
	Hayward,	2605	"	June 13, 1830	Nov. 26, 1869	Mar. 30, 1868	Rebecca M. Tidd; 1841–; d. Chas. and Rebecca M.
	Frank,	2606	"	Sept. 18, 1837		Nov. 27, 1871	Laura Stone.

GEORGE HAYWARD AND MARY (WHITCOMB) BARRETT. 2599.

	Maud Blanche,	2607	Concord,	Jan. 10, 1864	1865		
	Maria Nagle,	2608	"	Mar. 11, 1867			

WILLIAM GIBBS AND SOPHIA B. (DODGE) BARRETT. 2600.

	Henry Herbert,	2609	Concord,	Apr. 7, 1847	Jan. 12, 1863		
	George Prescott,	2610	"	Aug. 9, 1851			Arvilla Wright.
	Charles Otis,	2611	"	Mar. 18, 1857		Nov. 5, 1884	Lilla Park.
47	Herbert Malcolm,	2612	"	Jan. 14, 1863			Bessie Wood; 1865; dau. Albert E. and Ellen M.
	Edwin C.,	2613	"	Aug. 19, 1868			

HERBERT MALCOLM AND BESSIE (WOOD) BARRETT. 2612.

	Miliscent Sophia,	2614		Jan. 5, 1885			

CHARLES MASON AND SARAH P. (CONANT) BARRETT. 2603–3910.

	Mary Conant,	2615	So. Acton,	Sept. 16, 1854		Dec. 22, 1881	Thomas H. Ellison.

COL. SHERMAN AND MARY H. (WORTHINGTON) BARRETT. 2593.

104	Henry Aug., M.D.,	2616	Norfolk, Va.,	May 29, 1818		Sept. 30, 1863	Eliza Leighton; 1840–; dau. Wm. and Mary (Need- [ham).
	William Gibbs,	2617	"	Aug. 27, 1820			
47	Edward Sherman,	2618	Concord,	Nov. 14, 1824	Nov. 27, 1876	Sept. 19, 1850	Martha Blanchard; 1833–1867.
104	Mary H.,	2619	"	Oct. 16, 1827		Nov. 9, 1847	Henry Livingston Shattuck; 1822–; s. Hon. Daniel & [Sarah E. (Edwards).
	Benj. Franklin,	2620	"	Oct. 19, 1830			
	David Prescott, {	2621	"	Nov. 1, 1833	June 5, 1876	Nov. 10, 1860	1. Jennie E. Cutter.
		2622				Aug. 23, 1865	2. Ellen T. Wilson.

EDWARD S. AND MARTHA (BLANCHARD) BARRETT. 2618.

47	Jennie May,	2623	Concord,	Oct. 26, 1850		Jan. 14, 1872	Arthur Mills; 1850–.
	Frederick,	2624	"	June 21, 1853	Oct. 1, 1858		
47	Jessie F.,	2625	"	May 22, 1856		Mar. 31, 1875	Frederick M. Dennie.
	Edw'd Benjamin,	2626	"	May 25, 1862			

ARTHUR AND JENNIE MAY (BARRETT) MILLS. 2623.

	Charles Henry,	2627	Plattsmouth, Neb.,	Sept. 25, 1872			
	Elsie Barrett,	2628	"	Dec. 12, 1873			

FREDERICK M. AND JESSIE F. (BARRETT) DENNIE. 2625.

	Harrold Barrett,	2629	Concord,	Oct. 4, 1875			
	Eliz. Colburn,	2630	"	Nov. 27, 1879			
	Ruth May,	2631	"	Nov. 14, 1882			
	Frank Edward,	2632	"	Mar. 30, 1885			

DR. BENJAMIN AND MARY (WRIGHT) BARRETT. 2594.

	Edw'd Benj., M.D.,	2633	Northampton,	Oct. 1, 1836	Nov. 24, 1865	Unmarried.	
48	Mary Wright,	2634	"	Jan. 18, 1838		June 2, 1866	Henry R. Hinckley; 1838–; s. Sam'l and Henrietta E.

47

HENRY R. AND MARY W. (BARRETT) HINCKLEY. 2634.

Ref	Name	No.	Birth	Death	Married	Spouse
	Edward Barrett,	2635	Northampton, June 6, 1868			
	Donald Rose,	2636	" Sept. 18, 1869			
	Henry Barrett,	2637	" Mar. 1, 1871			
	Rose,	2638	" Feb. 23, 1874			
	Benjamin Barrett,	2639	" Aug. 4, 1875			
	George Lyman,	2640	" July 6, 1879			

DEA. TIMOTHY AND MRS. DINAH (WITT) BARRETT. 24.

Ref	Name	No.	Birth	Death	Married	Spouse
	Persis,	2641	Feb. 3, 1752	Feb. 28, 1849	Feb. 16, 1769	Ithener Bigelow; 1745–1807; son Samuel.

STEPHEN AND ELIZABETH (HUBBARD-HOW) BARRETT. 28.

Ref	Name	No.	Birth	Death	Married	Spouse
	Lydia,	2642	Paxton, Mar. 28, 1751		July 12, 1768	Israel Stone; 1749–; son John and Eliz. [mond].
48	Stephen (no issue), {	2643	" Feb. 8, 1753	May 21, 1832	Apr. 20, 1774	1. Ruth Stearns; –1777; dau. Nath'l and Grace (Ham-
		2644				2. Molly Barrett; 1757–1838; d. Oliver & Anna (Fiske).
49	Israel,	2645	" Mar. 21, 1756			Lucy Mower; –1838; d. Sam'l and Comfort (Larned).
50	Benjamin,	2646	" Sept. 19, 1759	Feb. 8, 1845	1766	Clarinda Barnes; –1839.

STEPHEN AND MOLLY (BARRETT) BARRETT. 2644.

Ref	Name	No.	Birth	Death	Married	Spouse
48	Mary,	2647	Winchendon, Nov. 2, 1783	Mar. 31, 1845	Nov. 17, 1805	Maj. Jotham Tower; 1776–1845. [(Knight).
48	Betsey,	2648	" May 16, 1788	Jan. 28, 1815	Dec. 20, 1809	Calvin Reed; 1779–1818; son Luther and Sarah
49	Stephen,	2649	Paris, N. Y., Mar. 1, 1793	Apr. 22, 1866	Dec. 11, 1817	Lois Day; 1796–1870.

JOTHAM AND MARY (BARRETT) TOWER. 2647.

Ref	Name	No.	Birth	Death	Married	Spouse
48	Mary Ann,	2650	Waterville, N.Y., Nov. 2, '08		Feb. 17, 1830	William Phelps Cleveland, M. D.; 1800–.
48	Ursula,	2651	" Jan. 4, 1811	Apr. 3, 1881	Jan., 1832	Bradford C. Montgomery; 1803–1868.
	Fidelia A.,	2652	" July 4, 1813	Apr. 26, 1828		
	Sherman B.,	2653	" Aug. 30, 1815	Oct. 25, 1838		
	James M.,	2654	" Aug. 30, 1817	May 17, 1818		
	Marcus Barrett,	2655	" Mar. 30, 1819	Apr. 19, 1847		
	Julius C.,	2656	" Nov. 23, 1821	June 8, 1882	July 6, 1841	Harriet N. Willis.
48	Alonzo B.,	2657	" May 6, 1824	Nov. 24, 1874	Mar. 15, 1852	Eliza Winchell.
48	Harriet Elizabeth,	2658	" Dec. 14, 1826		July 17, 1844	Ira L. Reed.
	George C.,	2659	" Feb. 24, 1829	July 26, 1832		

DR. WILLIAM PHELPS AND MARY ANN (BARRETT) CLEVELAND. 2650.

Ref	Name	No.	Birth	Death	Married	Spouse
48	Ellen Cornelia,	2660	Waterville, N.Y., Aug. 2, '31		Aug. 8, 1855	Wallace W. Osborn; 1832–1865.
48	Albert William,	2661	" May 6, 1834		Oct. 28, 1862	Catharine Carter; 1838–.
48	Mary Jane,	2662	" Jan. 21, 1836	Mar. 29, 1884	June, 1862	Rev. Willliam H. Moffett.
	Emery Bissell,	2663	" Mar. 29, 1839	June 24, 1848		
	Emma Celina,	2664	" Dec. 30, 1842		Sept. 6, 1865	Clark P. Washburn.
	Herbert Coburn,	2665	" Jan. 21, 1847	July 17, 1851		
48	Anna Caroline,	2666	" Nov. 1, 1849		June 13, 1877	George E. Westcott.
	Hattie Reed,	2667	" Nov. 21, 1851		Dec. 1, 1881	Fred H. Coggeshall.

WALLACE W. AND ELLEN CORNELIA (CLEVELAND) OSBORN. 2660.

Ref	Name	No.	Birth	Death	Married	Spouse
	Mary Amelia,	2668	St. Jo., Mo., Nov. 12, 1859			
	Ada Caroline,	2669	" Dec. 14, 1861			
	Emma Cleveland,	2670	" Dec. 7, 1863	Nov. 7, 1870		

ALBERT WILLIAM AND CATHARINE (CARTER) CLEVELAND. 2661.

Ref	Name	No.	Birth	Death	Married	Spouse
	Mary Cate,	2671	Oct. 19, 1863			
	William Phelps,	2672	Jan. 16, 1867			
	Grace Carter,	2673	Sept. 27, 1872	Apr. 7, 1875		
	Frances S.,	2674	Feb. 27, 1875			

REV. WILLIAM H. AND MARY JANE (CLEVELAND) MOFFETT. 2662.

Ref	Name	No.	Birth	Death	Married	Spouse
	Clevel'd Langston,	2675	Apr. 27, 1863			
	Charles William,	2676	Apr. 27, 1867			
	Emma Goshee,	2677	Oct. 21, 1869	Mar. 16, 1870		
	Mabel,	2678	Apr. 21, 1876			

GEORGE E. AND ANNA CAROLINE (CLEVELAND) WESTCOTT. 2666.

Ref	Name	No.	Birth	Death	Married	Spouse
	Hattie Cleveland,	2679	Mar. 27, 1878			
	George Edwin,	2680	Apr. 13, 1881			

BRADFORD C. AND URSULA (TOWER) MONTGOMERY. 2651.

Ref	Name	No.	Birth	Death	Married	Spouse
	Charles M.,	2681	Aug. 12, 1832			
	Edward T.,	2682	Apr. 25, 1835	Sept. 17, 1880		
48	Julius H.,	2683	Nov. 6, 1839		Dec. 16, 1863	Maryette Benedict.

JULIUS H. AND MARYETTE (BENEDICT) MONTGOMERY. 2683.

Ref	Name	No.	Birth	Death	Married	Spouse
	Florence T.,	2684	May 1, 1865		Feb. 24, 1886	George H. Greenman.

ALONZO B. AND ELIZA (WINCHELL) TOWER. 2657.

Ref	Name	No.	Birth	Death	Married	Spouse
	George W.,	2685	Mar. 19, 1853			

IRA L. AND HARRIET E. (TOWER) REED. 2658.

Ref	Name	No.	Birth	Death	Married	Spouse
48	Mary,	2686	Oct. 12, 1845		Dec. 17, 1868	Henry W. Emmons.

HENRY W. AND MARY (REED) EMMONS. 2686.

Ref	Name	No.	Birth	Death	Married	Spouse
	Walter,	2687	Aug. 29, 1876			
	Harry,	2688	Mar. 27, 1878			
	Arthur W.,	2689	Dec. 23, 1882			

CALVIN AND BETSEY (BARRETT) REED. 2648.

Ref	Name	No.	Birth	Death	Married	Spouse
49	Harriet Barrett,	2690	Sept. 20, 1809		Mar. 13, 1833	Rev. John Davis Pierce; 1789–1882; s. Gad and Sarah.
49	William B.,	2691	Jan. 3, 1813	Dec. 5, 1846	Jan. 3, 1843	Elizabeth S. Hawks; 1816–.

REV. JOHN DAVIS AND HARRIET BARRETT (REED) PIERCE. 2690.

49	Augusta M.,	2692	Marshall, Mich., Mar. 7, 1841	Aug. 17, 1865		
49	Sarah E.,	2693	" Aug. 5, 1843	Sept. 17, 1878	June 6, 1872	John E. Graham.
49	Mary A.,	2694	" May 11, 1846		Oct. 11, 1876	Edward D. Emerson.

JOHN E. AND SARAH E. (PIERCE) GRAHAM. 2693.

	Irma Pierce,	2695	Mar. 14, 1873
	Zada,	2696	Mar. 14, 1873
	Irving Augustus,	2697	Oct. 21, 1874
	Florence P.,	2698	Nov. 22, 1876

EDWARD D. AND MARY A. (PIERCE) EMERSON. 2694.

	Joseph Bulkeley,	2699	June 25, 1868

WILLIAM B. AND ELIZABETH S. (HAWKS) REED. 2691.

	Harriet,	2700	Feb. 6, 1844	Mar. 21, 1876	—— Messinger.

STEPHEN AND LOIS (DAY) BARRETT. 2649.

49	Mary Elizabeth,	2701	Sangerfield, N. Y., Sept. 30, 1818	May 10, 1881	Sept. 18, 1837	Denton G. Shuart; 1805–; son Abraham and Betsey.
	Juliet,	2702	" May 6, 1821			
	Miranda K.,	2703	" Sept. 27, 1824			
49	Emily Sophia,	2704	" Jan. 7, 1828		Oct. 15, 1855	W. C. Hanford.

DENTON G. AND MARY E. (BARRETT) SHUART. 2701.

49	Denton B.,	2705	Honeoye Falls, N. Y., 1842	1866	Unmarried.	
	William Herbert,	2706	" Sept. 21, 1852		Feb. 7, 1884	Nella Summer Phillips.
	Clarence Allison,	2707	" 1857		Sept. 27, 1883	Frances A. Park.
	Irving J.,	2708	" July 7, 1860			

WILLIAM HERBERT AND NELLA SUMMER (PHILLIPS) SHUART. 2706.

	Christine,	2709	Dec. 11, 1884

WILLIAM C. AND EMILY SOPHIA (BARRETT) HANFORD. 2704.

	Emogene D.,	2710	Emer'ld G've, Wis., Oct. 20, 1858
	Lincoln Barrett,	2711	Rockf'rd, Ill., June 12, 1860
	Anna Lois,	2712	" Oct. 21, 1865

ISRAEL AND LUCY (MOWER) BARRETT. 2645.

	Israel,	2713	Paris, N. Y., Feb. 20, 1778	Apr. 9, 1803		
	Phila (no issue),	2714	" Feb. 20, 1779	Nov. 1, 1851		1. Eli Crosley.
	(no issue),	2715				2. Newman Allen.
49	Lucy,	2716	Winchend'n, Jan. 5, 1786	Apr. 27, 1862	Sept., 1807	Isaac Crosby; 1782–1851; son Miller and Rebecca.
49	Samuel, Maj.,	2717	Paris, N. Y., June 29, 1792	July 23, 1862	Feb. 15, 1818	Betsey Hunt; 1794–1879.
50	Henry,	2718	" Apr. 20, 1798	Jan. 9, 1836	Nov. 18, 1823	Lucy Lawrence; 1805–1876; dau. Artemas and Lucy.

ISAAC AND LUCY (BARRETT) CROSBY. 2716.

	Israel,	2719	Brattleboro', Vt., June 3, 1810	Dec. 19, 1813		
49	Eunice Newton,	2720	" June 5, 1812		Sept. 1, 1837	Septimus Perkins.
49	Samuel Cobb,	2721	" Dec. 20, 1814	May 17, 1881	Dec. 15, 1841	Mary Ann Foote; 1823–; dau. Judge Ellad.
49	Lucy Moore,	2722	" Feb. 17, 1817		Sept. 1, 1839	Obed Hyatt Foote.
49	Joanna Borden,	2723	" Mar. 1, 1819		Jan. 22, 1840	Zalmon G. Keeler; 1810–.
	Israel Mower,	2724	" Feb. 2, 1821			Laura Chamberlain.
	William Henry,	2725	" Feb. 12, 1823			
	Jonas Mann,	2726	" Oct. 13, 1826			Cornelia Cunningham.
49	Danford Miller,	2727	" Jan. 19, 1828		June 14, 1849	Mary Elizabeth Gray.

SEPTIMUS AND EUNICE NEWTON (CROSBY) PERKINS. 2720.

	Ella J.,	2728	Jamestown, N. Y., Feb. 20, 1850	Oct. 20, 1868	George Washington Thomas.

SAMUEL C. AND MARY ANN (FOOTE) CROSBY. 2721.

	Florence Ellen,	2729	Jamestown, N. Y., Nov. 11, 1842		
	Emmett Lawrence,	2730	" Jan. 26, 1843	Aug. 28, 1873	Ruth Iowa Pickering; 1842–1881.
	Samuel Foote,	2731	" Oct. 25, 1845	Jan. 19, 1872	Ruth Cheeney; 1853.

OBED HYATT AND LUCY MOORE (CROSBY) FOOTE. 2722.

49	Lucy Elizabeth,	2732	Jamestown, N. Y., June 13, 1840		Nov. 25, 1865	James Martin Barrett; 1832–; s. Geo. and Catharine.
	Ellen Eunice,	2733	" Nov. 16, 1848		Oct. 25, 1877	John R. Smith; 1850–; son Thomas and Alice R.
	Dora Mary,	2734	" May 19, 1860		May 31, 1882	Joseph Bruff Ware; 1860–.

JAMES MARTIN AND LUCY ELIZABETH (FOOTE) BARRETT. 2732.

	James Foote,	2735	Battle Cr'k, Mich., June 17, 1869
	Bessie Catharine,	2736	" Nov. 22, 1874
	Lucy,	2737	" June 30, 1877
	Laura Ellen,	2738	" Aug. 24, 1881

ZALMON G. AND JOANNA BORDEN (CROSBY) KEELER. 2723.

	Isadore Rebecca,	2739	Jamestown, N. Y., Aug. 17, 1841		Jan. 20, 1863	Charles W. Winslow.
	Consanda,	2740	" Feb. 28, 1846			
	Zalmon R.,	2741	" Nov. 23, 1849	Sept. 1, 1850		
	Lucy Adelaide,	2742	" Sept. 30, 1852		Sept. 9, 1875	David H. Allen.
	Kate Barrett,	2743	" May 24, 1856		Unmarried.	

DANFORD M. AND MARY ELIZABETH (GRAY) CROSBY. 2727.

	Alfred William,	2744	Jamestown, N. Y., Apr. 3, 1850		
	Hattie Valeria,	2745	" Jan. 12, 1857	Oct. 10, 1877	Amos D. Greene.

MAJ. SAMUEL AND BETSEY (HUNT) BARRETT. 2717.

(Continued page 50.)

50	Henry W., M. D.,	2746	Jamestown, N. Y., Aug. 8, 1819	Feb. 13, 1844	May 18, 1853	Electa M. Horton; 1830–1857.

	Name	No.	Born	Died	Married	Spouse
50	Samuel Hunt, {	2747	Jamestown, N.Y., Feb. 5, 1822		Sept. 16, 1844	1. Maria Spencer; 1825–1864; dau. Rev. Eliphalet.
50		2748			Nov. 23, 1866	2. Lucy Adelia Lake; 1829–.
50	William Elliott,	2749	" Sept. 19, 1824	Oct., 1884	May 29, 1845	Laura A. Wescott.
	Florinda Maria,	2750	" June 23, 1826		June 24, 1846	Levant W. Brown; –1875; son Samuel A.
50	Lucy Elizabeth,	2751	" Aug. 9, 1829		July 25, 1851	John H. White; 1821–1877.
	Evelyn Mary,	2752	" June 17, 1831	May 8, 1880	Aug. 21, 1862	Elial F. Hall; 1827–; son James and Polly (Cheeney).
50	Sarah Philander,	2753	" Nov. 14, 1833	Oct. 18, 1871		Willard Harvey; 1829–1872; son Charles.

DR. HENRY WARREN AND ELECTA M. (HORTON) BARRETT. 2746.

	Name	No.	Born	Died	Married	Spouse
50	Corrine,	2754	Apr. 10, 1854		Aug. 19, 1879	Maj. George Rodney Smith; 1850–; son Hiram.
	Electa,	2755	Mar. 12, 1857		July 21, 1880	Dwight B. Breed; son Joshua.
	Henry,	2756	Mar. 12, 1857		Sept. 10, 1881	Lora Newton.

MAJ. GEORGE RODNEY AND CORRINE (BARRETT) SMITH 2754.

	Name	No.	Born	Died	Married	Spouse
	Barrett,	2757	Sept. 22, 1880			
	Rodney,	2758	Nov. 28, 1884			

SAMUEL HUNT AND MARIA (SPENCER) BARRETT. 2747.

	Name	No.	Born	Died	Married	Spouse
	Theo. Spencer,	2759	Jamestown, N.Y., Mar. 21, 1848	Feb. 28, 1870		
50	Eva Electa,	2760	Randolph, N.Y., Apr. 11, 1850		Oct. 11, 1877	Prof. David Dusenbury.
50	Samuel Eliphalet,	2761	" Sept. 8, 1853		June 18, 1878	Lillian Stryker.

SAMUEL HUNT AND LUCY ADELIA (LAKE) BARRETT. 2748.

	Name	No.	Born	Died	Married	Spouse
	Jessie Maud,	2762	Randolph, N.Y., Sept. 27, 1867			
	Frederick Lake,	2763	Cold Spring, N.Y., June 22, 1870	Feb. 13, 1871		

PROF. DAVID AND EVA ELECTA (BARRETT) DUSENBURY. 2760.

	Name	No.	Born	Died	Married	Spouse
	Winona A.,	2764	Hebron, Neb., Nov. 9, 1878			
	Barrett Hall,	2765	" July 12, 1880	Sept. 20, 1880		
	Evelyn A.,	2766	" May 15, 1882	Oct. 15, 1883		
	Roy,	2767	" Aug. 28, 1883	Aug. 1, 1884		
	Lucile,	2768	Wahoo, Neb., Nov. 12, 1884			

SAMUEL E. AND LILLIAN (STRYKER) BARRETT. 2761.

	Name	No.	Born	Died	Married	Spouse
	Samuel Alfred,	2769	Nov. 12, 1880			

WILLIAM ELLIOTT AND LAURA A. (WESCOTT) BARRETT. 2749.

	Name	No.	Born	Died	Married	Spouse
50	Virginia,	2770	Feb. 19, 1846		Jan. 1, 1870	Alvin Chadwick; son Francis.
50	Laura Elizabeth,	2771	Jan. 27, 1847		May 24, 1865	John W. Oddie; son Walter M.
50	E. Pauline A.,	2772	Jan. 22, 1853		Nov. 15, 1880	William Andrew Mansfield; son Andrew.
	William Lowry,	2773	Sept. 22, 1854			
	John Keith,	2774	Jan. 23, 1861	Jan. 30, 1861		
	Lucy White,	2775	Aug. 9, 1864			
	Edith May,	2776	July 9, 1866	Jan. 13, 1867		

ALVIN AND VIRGINIA (BARRETT) CHADWICK. 2770.

	Name	No.	Born	Died	Married	Spouse
	Maggie,	2777	Red Bank, N.J., May 11, 1871			
	Pauline,	2778	" Sept. 25, 1872			
	Edith,	2779	" Jan. 1, 1874			
	Alvin,	2780	" Dec. 21, 1875			
	Maud,	2781	" Aug. 3, 1877	Jan. 13, 1879		

JOHN W. AND LAURA E. (BARRETT) ODDIE. 2771.

	Name	No.	Born	Died	Married	Spouse
	John Barrett,	2782	Mar. 17, 1866	Mar. 18, 1866		
	Daisy Rosalie,	2783	May 19, 1867			
	William Elliott,	2784	Nov. 27, 1869			
	John White,	2785	Dec. 18, 1871			
	Charles Fisher,	2786	May 23, 1873			

WILLIAM ANDREW AND E. PAULINE A. (BARRETT) MANSFIELD. 2772.

	Name	No.	Born	Died	Married	Spouse
	Early,	2787	June 13, 1882			

JOHN H. AND LUCY ELIZABETH (BARRETT) WHITE. 2751.

	Name	No.	Born	Died	Married	Spouse
	George Barrett,	2788	New York, Jan. 25, 1853			
	John Henry,	2789	" Jan. 1, 1857	Mar. 16, 1858		
	Eva King,	2790	" Mar. 1, 1860	Aug. 11, 1860		
	Isabella Hunt,	2791	Bergen Point, N. J., July 4, 1861		June 30, 1885	Charles Gordon Fuller, M. D.; 1856–; son F. A.
	Lillian King,	2792	New York, Jan. 6, 1865			
	Lucy Elizabeth,	2793	" Sept. 20, 1870			

WILLIAM AND SARAH PILANDER (BARRETT) HARVEY. 2753.

	Name	No.	Born	Died	Married	Spouse
	Willard Barrett,	2794	Jan. 15, 1861	Aug. 27, 1861		
	Elizabeth,	2795	Mar. 5, 1863			
	Evelyn,	2796	Oct. 7, 1865			
	Mary Augusta,	2797	July 13, 1868	July 15, 1876		
	Samuel Barrett,	2798	Nov. 9, 1870	June 19, 1871		

HENRY AND LUCY (LAWRENCE) BARRETT. 2718.

	Name	No.	Born	Died	Married	Spouse
	Henry Lawrence,	2799	Nov. 23, 1824	Aug. 3, 1850	Unmarried.	
	Ann Elizabeth,	2800	May 20, 1826	Sept., 1876	Unmarried.	
	Frederick Clay,	2801	Apr. 13, 1829	Oct. 15, 1867	Unmarried.	
	Cons. Mower (no iss.),	2802	July 16, 1833	Aug. 28, 1859	Apr. 30, 1856	Alexander Lowry.

BENJAMIN AND CLARINDA (BARNES) BARRETT. 2646.

(Continued page 51.)

	Name	No.	Born	Died	Married	Spouse
51	Stephen, Dea.,	2803	Paris, N. Y., Nov. 15, 1791	Oct. 26, 1877	May 14, 1816	Lucia Smith; 1797–1878.
	Benjamin,	2804	" Jan. 17, 1793			Dolly Beckwith.
52	Clarinda,	2805	" Mar., 1795	1816	Mar. 9, 1815	Amos Atkins.
52	Oliver, {	2806	" June 22, 1798	Jan. 10, 1873	Aug. 14, 1823	1. Eliza Brown; 1801–1849.
52		2807				2. Susan (Osborne) Hubbell.
52	Charles,	2808	" Sept. 22, 1799	May 21, 1864	1824	Sarah Benson; 1800–1864.

53	George,	2809 / 2810 / 2811	Paris, N. Y., Nov. 1, 1801	Mar. 10, 1884	Mar., 1825 / Mar., 1840 / Sept. 10, 1853	1. Maria Bennett; –1838; dau. Abraham and Maria. / 2. Mrs. Eliza Clark. / 3. Mrs. Phebe Hubbell.
53	Amos,	2812	" Dec. 8, 1803	Mar. 30, 1886	Mar. 20, 1827	Annis Maria Brown.
53	Jotham,	2813	Chautauqua, N. Y., 1807	1882		Caroline ——.
54	Alonzo,	2814 / 2815	Jan. 21, 1810	Aug. 21, 1876	Dec. 1, 1834 / Mar. 8, 1870	1. Mrs. Elizabeth Root; –1867. / 2. Mrs. Louisa K. Atwood.

DEA. STEPHEN AND LUCIA (SMITH) BARRETT. 2803.

51	Lucretia C.,	2816	Chautauqua, N. Y., June 19, '17	Oct. 22, 1883	Feb. 28, 1841	Albert Tuttle; 1816–.
51	Betsey L.,	2817	Kingsville, Ohio, Mar. 29, 1819		Apr. 19, 1841	Edward F. Lewis; –1885.
51	Martha Eliza,	2818	" Feb. 2, 1821		July 19, 1840	Hiram Washington Wood; –1885.
51	Am'da Euphemia,	2819	" Sept. 26, 1823		Feb. 28, 1843	Hiram Nash; 1819–.
52	Cornelia Ch'tianna,	2820	" July 24, 1825	Feb. 5, 1869	Oct. 16, 1850	Lemuel S. Stowe.
52	Emeline Mary,	2821	" Aug. 7, 1827	Oct. 7, 1859	Feb. 19, 1849	Nathaniel Wolcott; –1872.
52	Harriet P.,	2822	" Apr. 10, 1829		Feb. 19, 1849	Norman A. Robbins.
52	Octavia Lucinda,	2823	" Dec. 29, 1830		Feb. 16, 1858	Rev. Jackson Van Vorris.
	Adaline M.,	2824	" Aug. 20, 1833	Aug. 20, 1838		

ALBERT AND LUCRETIA C. (BARRETT) TUTTLE. 2816.

	Leslie S.,	2825	Clinton, Wis., Jan. 11, 1842	1881	Bell Hame.
	Alfred L.,	2826	Tuttle, Wis., July 26, 1844	1885	Elizabeth Williams.
	Alice C.,	2827	" Dec. 19, 1853		

EDWARD F. AND BETSEY L. (BARRETT) LEWIS. 2817.

	Judson Adoniram,	2828	Tuttlev'e, Wis., Aug. 25, '43	May 22, 1863		
	Charles LeRoy,	2829	" Sept. 15, 1846	Died infancy.		
51	Stephen Barrett,	2830	" July 12, 1848		July, 1878	Elizabeth Church.
51	Franklin Filmore,	2831	Lewiston, Wis., Sept. 28, '50		Nov. 29, 1877	Victorine Rockwell.
	Edward Barrett,	2832	" Dec. 28, 1852	June 4, 1872		
	Geo. Washington,	2833	" Jan. 20, 1856	Died infancy.		
51	William Lincoln.	2834	Portage, Wis., Aug. 13, 1857		Oct. 15, 1883	Priscilla Harrigan.

STEPHEN B. AND ELIZABETH (CHURCH) LEWIS. 2830.

	Rollin Church,	2835	Portage, Wis., Aug. 29, 1884

FRANKLIN F. AND VICTORINE (ROCKWELL) LEWIS. 2831.

	Mabel Barrett,	2836	Portage, Wis., Aug. 24, 1879
	Edward Rockwell,	2837	" Apr. 19, 1881	Died infancy.

WILLIAM LINCOLN AND PRISCILLA (HARRIGAN) LEWIS. 2834.

	Guy Edward,	2838	Portage, Wis., Jan. 11, 1885

HIRAM W. AND MARTHA ELIZA (BARRETT) WOOD. 2818.

51	Charles Morton,	2839	Beloit, Wis., July 26, 1842		Aug. 6, 1872	Alice A. Bartlett.
	Mary Ella,	2840	" May 5, 1847		Dec. 22, 1870	P. R. Turneaure; s. John and Maria (Mabie).
51	Clara Maria,	2841	" June 11, 1852	Jan. 23, 1881	Dec. 12, 1872	Samuel H. Ladd; son John and Sarah (Willmarth).
51	Herbert Chalmer,	2842	Clinton, Wis., Nov. 12, 1855		Jan., 1878	Mary Louisa Putnam; dau. Capt. James S. and Mary Ann.
	Olive,	2843	" Nov., 1862	Jan., 1864		

CHARLES M. AND ALICE A. (BARTLETT) WOOD. 2839.

	Bertie,	2844	Sept. 12, 1873	Aug. 12, 1874
	Herbert Hiram,	2845	1876	
	Ernest,	2846	1872	
	Adella Louisa,	2847	1883	

SAMUEL H. AND CLARA M. (WOOD) LADD. 2841.

	Arthur Wilmarth,	2848	Clinton, Wis., May 26, 1874	
	Scott Herbert,	2849	Sheldon, Ia., Dec. 8, 1880	Apr. 21, 1881

HERBERT C. AND MARY L. (PUTNAM) WOOD. 2842.

	Herbert J.,	2850	July 29, 1881	Aug. 30, 1881
	Louise B.,	2851	Apr. 9, 1883	Sept. 13, 1883

HIRAM AND AMANDA E. (BARRETT) NASH. 2819.

51	Adaline A.,	2850	Beloit, Wis., Dec. 22, 1843	Oct. 18, 1863	Horatio W. Tiel.
	Adison Barrett,	2851	" Nov. 27, 1845	Aug. 23, 1874	Mrs. Mary A. Childs.
51	Stephen Chalmer,	2852	Clinton, Wis., May 26, 1848	Sept., 1877	Anna Butterfield.
51	Ella R.,	2853	" Aug. 21, 1851	Mar. 24, 1871	Amariah Worden.
51	Frank Herbert,	2854	Lancaster, Wis., Jan. 22, '58	May 23, 1881	Emma M. Ward.
	Mattie L.,	2855	Grant Co., Wis., May 6, 1865	Oct. 20, 1884	Frank H. Zander.
	Charles Barrett,	2856	Lancaster, Wis., Jan. 10, '68		

HORATIO W. AND ADALINE A. (NASH) TIEL. 2850.

	Maud Emily,	2857	Lancaster, Wis., Aug. 14, '66
	Louie Leroy,	2858	" May 23, 1867

STEPHEN C. AND ANNA (BUTTERFIELD) NASH. 2852.

	Maud Mary,	2859	Sheldon, Ia., Oct. 14, 1878
	Chalmer Stephen,	2860	" Nov. 17, 1880

AMARIAH AND ELLA R. (NASH) WORDEN. 2853.

	Alfred,	2861	Mar., 1872	Sept. 29, 1879
	Frank,	2862	Feb., 1878	
	Mable,	2863	June 6, 1880	Dec. 26, 1884
	Mattie,	2864	Sept. 27, 1885	

FRANK H. AND EMMA R. (WARD) NASH. 2854.

	Jay Edward,	2865	Cherokee, Ia., Oct. 23, '83
	Frank Howard,	2866	Sheldon, Ia., May 26, 1885

LEMUEL S. AND CORNELIA C. (BARRETT) STOWE. 2820.

	Name	No.	Birth	Death	Marriage	Spouse
	Lois Cornelia,	2867	Burr Oak, Wis., Dec. 2, 1852			
	Kitty,	2868	Tafton, Wis., May 30, 1855	Feb. 28, 1857	Dec. 25, 1882	John H. Pelham.
	Edmund,	2869	Brownville, Mo., May 6, 1859		Mar. 17, 1886	Annie Newton.

NATHANIEL AND EMELINE M. (BARRETT) WOLCOTT. 2821.

	Name	No.	Birth	Marriage	Spouse
52	Harriet Abigail,	2870	July 14, 1853	Nov. 25, 1875	Horace Kenyon Hamblin.
52	Mary Celestia,	2871	Oct. 7, 1856	Sept. 26, 1880	Elbert Burton Zimmerman.

HORACE KENYON AND HARRIET A. (WOLCOTT) HAMBLIN. 2870.

	Name	No.	Birth	Death
	Grace May,	2872	Conway, Ia., Dec. 24, 1877	
	Maud Lillian,	2873	" July 16, 1883	Aug. 23, 1885

ELBERT B. AND MARY CELESTIA (WOLCOTT) ZIMMERMAN. 2871.

	Name	No.	Birth
	Edna Verlie,	2874	Bedford, Ia., Sept. 12, 1881
	Bessie May,	2875	" Aug. 20, 1883
	Ralph Elbert,	2876	Ulysses, Neb., Aug. 9, 1885

NORMAN A. AND HARRIET P. (BARRETT) ROBBINS. 2822.

	Name	No.	Birth	Marriage	Spouse
52	Clara Bell,	2877	Clinton, Wis., Jan. 16, 1852	July 10, 1872	Frank Williams.
52	Emma Octavia,	2878	" July 27, 1855	Nov. 25, 1875	Abraham G. Huston.
52	Elmer L.,	2879	Magnolia, Wis., Apr. 28, 1860	Dec. 24, 1881	A. K. Barnes.

FRANK AND CLARA BELL (ROBBINS) WILLIAMS. 2877.

	Name	No.	Birth
	Jessie E.,	2880	Apr. 23, 1873
	Myrtle B.,	2881	Nov. 6, 1877

ABRAM G. AND EMMA O. (ROBBINS) HUSTON. 2878.

	Name	No.	Birth
	Nellie A.,	2882	Apr. 22, 1877
	Raymond B.,	2883	June 4, 1884

ELMER L. AND A. K. (BARNES) ROBBINS. 2879.

	Name	No.	Birth
	Bertha M.,	2884	Nov. 19, 1882
	Clara B.,	2885	Mar. 15, 1884

REV. JACKSON AND OCTAVIA L. (BARRETT) VAN VORRIS. 2823.

	Name	No.	Birth
	Lulu A.,	2886	Nov. 24, 1858
	Mary Luella,	2887	July 14, 1861
	William Arthur,	2888	Mar. 26, 1867
	Emma Belle,	2889	Oct. 7, 1871
	Charles J.,	2890	June 22, 1873

AMOS AND CLARINDA (BARRETT) ATKINS. 2805.

	Name	No.	Birth	Marriage	Spouse
52	Horatio Barrett,	2891	Gerry, N.Y., Dec. 15, 1815	Sept. 12, 1847	Rosantha Majors; 1828–1884; d. Adolphus & Lydia.

HORATIO B. AND ROSANTHA (MAJORS) ATKINS. 2891.

	Name	No.	Birth	Death	Marriage	Spouse
	Dudley Horatio,	2892	Toledo, Ohio, Apr. 30, 1849	July 30, 1849		
	Myron Barrett,	2893	Wash., " June 30, 1850	Aug. 23, 1868		
52	Alice Rosantha,	2894	Toledo, " Oct. 3, 1855		June 2, 1882	Clinton Wyatt Hickok; 1853–; s. Wyatt and Fanny.

CLINTON WYATT AND ALICE ROSANTHA (ATKINS) HICKOK. 2894.

	Name	No.	Birth
	Myron Wellington,	2895	Toledo, Ohio, Sept. 29, 1883

OLIVER AND ELIZA (BROWN) BARRETT. 2806.

	Name	No.	Birth	Death	Marriage	Spouse
52	Samantha,	2896	Kingsville, O., May 11, 1825	Aug. 6, 1879	Nov. 27, 1846	Rev. Isaac Bloomer; 1812–1883.
52	Mary Eliza,	2897	" Sept. 10, 1826		Aug. 30, 1853	Benjamin Newell; 1819–; son Arnold and Rachel.
52	Dorliska,	2898	" Nov. 16, 1829		Mar. 23, 1854	Orlando Luce; 1830–.
52	Oliver W.,	2899	" Nov. 20, 1832		Dec. 13, 1861	1. Phila Amelia Delaplaine; –1866.
52		2900				2. Frances Marie Osborn; dau. Salmon S. & Mary L.
	Clinton,	2901	" Aug. 27, 1835	Feb. 15, 1836		

REV. ISAAC AND SAMANTHA (BARRETT) BLOOMER. 2896.

	Name	No.	Birth
	Frank W.,	2902	Jan. 17, 1849
	Edgar R.,	2901	Apr. 17, 1855

BENJAMIN AND MARY ELIZA (BARRETT) NEWELL. 2897.

	Name	No.	Birth	Death	Marriage	Spouse
	George Arnold,	2902	Beaver Dam, Wis., Nov. 21, 1858		Mar. 22, 1882	Mary Elizabeth Mowry.
	Mary Amelia,	2903	" Sept. 15, 1860	Oct. 10, 1863		
	Alice Rosetta,	2904	" Jan. 26, 1862			
	Benjamin Oliver,	2905	" Jan. 16, 1866			

ORLANDO AND DORLISKA (BARRETT) LUCE. 2898.

	Name	No.	Birth	Death
	Carey Barrett,	2906	June 7, 1860	July 28, 1864
	Artemus Barrett,	2907	June 27, 1863	

OLIVER W. AND PHILA A. (DELAPLAINE) BARRETT. 2899.

	Name	No.	Birth	Marriage	Spouse
	Phila Delaplaine,	2908	Oct. 5, 1862	Oct. 5, 1883	Harry Raymond.
	Oliver Samuel,	2909	Aug. 4, 1866		

OLIVER W. AND FRANCES M. (OSBORN) BARRETT. 2900.

	Name	No.	Birth	Death
	Edith Osborn,	2910	May 18, 1876	Feb. 10, 1880

CHARLES AND SARAH (BENSON) BARRETT. 2808.

	Name	No.	Birth	Death	Marriage	Spouse
	Syloice,	2911	Feb. 11, 1825	Mar. 4, 1883	Unmarried.	
53	Orpha M.,	2912	June 5, 1826	Mar. 2, 1879	July 25, 1844	Ephraim Capron; 1818–1884; son Abijah and Mary.
53	Mary E.,	2913	June 15, 1828	Apr. 29, 1880		Lucius F. Curtis.
	Charles S.,	2914	Nov. 3, 1831			
	Elsie,	2915	June 23, 1836	Mar. 14, 1837		
	Sarah E.,	2916	Dec. 6, 1838	Mar. 4, 1856		
53	Benson S.,	2917	May 6, 1840		Dec. 25, 1874	Louisa S. Parker.

EPHRAIM AND ORPHA M. (BARRETT) CAPRON. 2912.

	Name	No.	Birth	Death	Married	Spouse
53	Mary M.,	2918	Conneaut, O., Aug. 28, 1846		Aug. 11, 1883	Thomas H. Johnson.
	Dudley S.,	2919	" Mar. 25, 1848		Apr. 4, 1872	Malvina Armstrong.
53	Adoniram,	2920	" Aug. 21, 1849		Dec. 10, 1872	Elizabeth Shultz.
53	Charles B.,	2921	" Apr. 6, 1851		Mar. 6, 1883	Kate Rogers.
	Edwin E.,	2922	" Oct. 12, 1854		Oct. 8, 1884	Lottie E. Irwin.
	Marshall F.,	2923	" Sept. 13, 1856			
	Albert J.,	2924	" June 21, 1858		Aug. 28, 1883	Eliza Chambers.
	Clarence E.,	2925	" Apr. 7, 1861			
	Clara L.,	2926	" Apr. 7, 1861			

THOMAS H. AND MARY M. (CAPRON) JOHNSON. 2918.

	Name	No.	Birth	Death	Married	Spouse
	Marshall C.,	2927	May 30, 1884			

ADONIRAM AND ELIZABETH (SHULTZ) CAPRON. 2920.

	Name	No.	Birth	Death	Married	Spouse
	Carlton Irving,	2928	May 15, 1876			
	Calla May,	2929	Feb. 4, 1878			
	Jay E.,	2930	June 2, 1883			

CHARLES B. AND KATE (ROGERS) CAPRON. 2921.

	Name	No.	Birth	Death	Married	Spouse
	Hazel Baxter,	2931	Feb. 11, 1885			

LUCIUS F. AND MARY E. (BARRETT) CURTIS. 2913.

	Name	No.	Birth	Death	Married	Spouse
	Andrew,	2932				
	Addie May,	2933				

BENSON S. AND LOUISA S. (PARKER) BARRETT. 2917.

	Name	No.	Birth	Death	Married	Spouse
	Fanny Andrews,	2934	Dec. 23, 1884			

GEORGE AND MARIA (BENNETT) BARRETT. 2809.

	Name	No.	Birth	Death	Married	Spouse
53	Clarinda,	2935	1826	Died infancy.		
	Emma Calista,	2936	May 2, 1827		Sept. 11, 1845	Truman Dixon Palmer.
	George Hubbell,	2937	Oct. 10, 1829		Apr. 25, 1859	Annette P. Southard.
	Dudley,	2938	1832	1838		

GEORGE AND MRS. PHEBE (HUBBELL) BARRETT. 2811.

	Name	No.	Birth	Death	Married	Spouse
	Hulburt,	2939	Sept. 10, 1855	Feb. 18, 1867		

TRUMAN D. AND EMMA C. (BARRETT) PALMER. 2936.

	Name	No.	Birth	Death	Married	Spouse
	Amelia,	2940	Jan. 4, 1847		May 22, 1864	John Ware.
	Eugene C.,	2941	Aug. 18, 1849			
	George E.,	2942	Jan. 12, 1853	Died young.		
	Frank Lee,	2943	Dec. 5, 1856			
	Mary A.,	2944	Mar. 3, 1858		Feb. 29, 1880	Conrad Smith.
	Clara A.,	2945	Sept. 9, 1860	1875		
	Leland H.,	2946	Sept. 27, 1862			
	Jennie A.,	2947	Oct. 27, 1864		Feb. 6, 1884	William J. Duffy.
	Albert Carlton,	2948	Apr. 7, 1868	July 18, 1885		
	Emma Evelyn,	2949	Dec. 6, 1870			

AMOS AND ANIS MARIA (BROWN) BARRETT. 2812.

	Name	No.	Birth	Death	Married	Spouse
53	Myron Erastus,	2950	Kingsville, O., Dec. 28, 1827		May 9, 1855	Angeline Tuttle; 1831-; dau. Timothy.
	Perry G., M. D., {	2951	" July 27, 1830		Aug. 20, 1856	1. Nellie O. Fiske; -1860.
53	{	2951			Jan. 20, 1866	2. Almeda Hodge; dau. Veloms and Emeline.
53	Amos J., Rev.,	2952	" Apr. 1, 1832		June 14, 1860	Emily Julia Barrows; 1830-; Capt. Storrs and Sylvia.
53	Stephen P., Prof.,	2953	" June 7, 1834		July 16, 1862	Mary J. Hovey; 1837-; dau. Alfred and Mary.
	Clarinda,	2954	" July 7, 1835	Aug. 1, 1836		
53	Clinton S., Capt.,	2955	" Dec. 12, 1836		June 22, 1859	Mary Melissa Banister; 1837-; dau. Wm. and Eliza.
53	Emily Lucinda,	2956	" July 27, 1839		Dec. 1, 1856	Rush Warner; 1832-; dau. John and Maria.
	Susie Eliza,	2957	" Oct. 8, 1841			
	Adelaide,	2958	" Apr. 12, 1847	Mar. 25, 1851		
	Albert T., Prof.,	2959	" Apr. 12, 1847		Oct. 2, 1871	Kate C. Stanton; 1847-; dau. Warner and Mary E.

MYRON ERASTUS AND ANGELINE (TUTTLE) BARRETT. 2950.

	Name	No.	Birth	Death	Married	Spouse
	Judson S.,	2960	June 18, 1856	Aug. 19, 1881		
	Lelia,	2961	Oct. 29, 1858			
	Bertha,	2962	July 30, 1869			

DR. PERRY GORDON AND ALMEDA (HODGE) BARRETT. 2951.

	Name	No.	Birth	Death	Married	Spouse
	Julia,	2963	Erie, Pa., Sept. 10, 1869			

REV. AMOS JUDSON AND EMILY JULIA (BARROWS) BARRETT. 2952.

	Name	No.	Birth	Death	Married	Spouse
	Helen Maria,	2964	July 31, 1861			
	Anne Louise,	2965	Feb. 27, 1863			
	Storrs B.,	2966	Aug. 12, 1864			

PROF. STEPHEN PALEY AND MARY J. (HOVEY) BARRETT. 2953.

	Name	No.	Birth	Death	Married	Spouse
	Harvey Paine,	2967	Buchanan, Mich., July 12, 1863			
	Jay Antos,	2968	Nunda, N.Y., Jan. 25, 1865			
	Grace Mary,	2969	Buchanan, Mich., Sept. 15, 1868			
	Edith Annis,	2970	Niles, Mich., Aug. 1, 1871			
	Inez Delyra,	2971	The Dalles, Ore., July 25, 1876			

CAPT. CLINTON SAMUEL AND MARY MELISSA (BANISTER) BARRETT. 2955.

	Name	No.	Birth	Death	Married	Spouse
	Jay Clinton,	2972	Feb. 22, 1860	Feb. 23, 1860		
	Florence May,	2973	May 27, 1864			
	Clinton Webster,	2974	Feb. 22, 1868	Aug. 11, 1868		

RUSH AND EMILY LUCINDA (BARRETT) WARNER. 2956.

	Name	No.	Birth	Death	Married	Spouse
	John Harley,	2975	Jan. 19, 1864			

ALONZO AND MRS. ELIZABETH (ROOT) BARRETT. 2814.

54	Clarinda M.,	2976	Feb. 11, 1835		Aug. 16, 1849	James R. Sweet; 1825-; son Willard H. and Susanna.
54	Anna Maria,	2977	Apr. 13, 1840	Dec. 26, 1876	Apr. 13, 1860	Thomas A. Freeman.
54	Alice S.,	2978	Sept. 13, 1845		Oct. 25, 1863	Bryant H. Fiske; 1836-1883; son Abraham and Sarah.

ALONZO AND MRS. LOUISA K. (ATWOOD) BARRETT. 2815.

Mary Eliza,	2979	Mar. 10, 1871		
Myron Alonzo,	2980	Jan. 18, 1874	Feb. 5, 1874	

JAMES R. AND CLARINDA M. (BARRETT) SWEET. 2976.

William Marion,	2981	Linesville, Pa., Dec. 28, 1851			
Mary Evaline,	2982	" Dec. 18, 1856		Jan. 1, 1875	Russell M. Knapp; 1853-.
James Alfred,	2983	" Mar. 14, 1857			
Julia Anice,	2984	" May 24, 1858			
Horatio Alvin,	2985	Union City, Pa., July 26, 1860	Sept., 1861		
Frank Riley,	2986	Waterford, Pa., Dec. 1, 1863			
Alice Elizabeth,	2987	" Apr. 27, 1868			
Perry Barrett,	2988	" Oct. 23, 1869			
Clinton Edward,	2989	" May 22, 1874	Dec. 26, 1874		

THOMAS A. AND ANNA MARIA (BARRETT) FREEMAN. 2977.

Mary Frances,	2990	June 16, 1861	Mar. 9, 1865
Charles Barrett,	2991	Jan. 16, 1863	Feb. 13, 1863
William James,	2992	Jan. 16, 1863	Apr. 1, 1865
Clarinda Julia,	2993	Jan. 29, 1865	
Thomas Alonzo,	2994	June 30, 1868	
Peter Edward,	2995	June 27, 1870	Mar. 27, 1873

BRYANT H. AND ALICE S. (BARRETT) FISKE. 2978.

Elmar Bryant,	2996	Linesville, Pa., Sept. 9, 1864
Vincent Barrett,	2997	Girard, Pa., Oct. 14, 1868

GEORGE AND CHARLOTTE CALDWELL (BROWN) DAKIN. 2092.

Robert Boyda,	2998			Nov. 26, 1883	Anna M. Boss.
Georgi'na Natalie,	2999			Feb. 10, 1870	Edward L. Lawrence.
James Brown,	3000		July 2, 1847		
Anna Maria,	3001				
Charlotte Brown,	3002		Jan. 19, 1853		
Emma Durant,	3003				
Hannah Louise,	3004				
Charles Sumner,	3005			Oct. 6, 1885	Mary Winslow Ives.
George, Jr.,	3006				
Julia Lizzie,	3007		Oct. 2, 1866		

CHARLES WILLIAM AND EMILY A. (WATTS) BULLARD. 1532.

Joel E.,	3008	Jan. 25, 1868
Auburt S.,	3009	Oct. 12, 1870
Wallace E.,	3010	Jan., 1872
Dexter H.,	3011	June, 1879
Edgar H.,	3012	Aug., 1882
Harry W.,	3013	Aug., 1882

JOHN AND ELIZABETH (POTTER) BROWN. 158-555.

	John,	3014	Concord, Dec. 1, 1715	July 21, 1718			
	Elizabeth,	3015	" Sept. 4, 1718				
	Grace,	3016	" Feb. 5, 1720-1	Sept. 6, 1762	Nov. 10, 1740	John Wheat; -1784.	
54	John,	3017	" July 1, 1724	1803	Jan. 26, 1751	Elizabeth Bateman; -1804.	
	Hannah,	3018	" Mar. 25, 1727				
	Josiah,	3019	" Dec. 30, 1729	Died infancy.			
	Joseph,	3020	"	Feb. 11, 1731-2			
	Joseph,	3021	" Nov. 12, 1733				
	Rebecca,	3022	" Oct. 4, 1736				
59	Josiah, Capt.,	3023	" Jan. 30, 1742	Mar. 18, 1831	Oct. 31, 1765	Sarah Wright; 1744-1821.	

JOHN AND ELIZABETH (BATEMAN) BROWN. 3017.

64	Elizabeth,	3024	Concord, Jan. 30, 1753	Feb. 24, 1812		Lieut. Samuel Brown. No. 3641.
54	John, Rev.,	3025	" Dec. 5, 1755	Nov. 17, 1830	About 1780	Abigail Wright.
	Thadeus,	3026	" Mar., 1758			
	Asa,	3027	" Apr. 10, 1759	Feb. 25, 1834		
	Anna,	3028	" May 8, 1761	Apr. 28, 1825	Dec. 6, 1785	Willard Spaulding; 1761-1822.
56	Rebecca,	3029	" Mar. 17, 1763	Mar. 13, 1813		Josiah French; -1840.
57 / 57	Joseph, Rev.,	3030 / 3031	" Feb. 21, 1765	Dec. 16, 1840	Sept., 1795 / Nov. 5, 1811	1. Rebecca Walker; 1770-1811. / 2. Lucy Proctor.
61	Hannah,	3032	" Apr. 28, 1767	Feb. 15, 1852	Apr. 16, 1795	Aaron Brown. No. 3327.
57	Reuben,	3033	" Mar. 15, 1769	July 17, 1853	July 1, 1793	Sarah Brown. No. 3326.
	Hepzabah,	3034	" Aug. 27, 1771	1834	1796	Stephen Davis; 1775-.
	Thomas,	3035	" June 25, 1774			
58	Polly,	3036	New Ipswich, N.H., Aug. 24, 1779	Feb. 24, 1832	About 1798	Samuel Wyman; -1855.

REV. JOHN AND ABIGAIL (WRIGHT) BROWN. 3025.

55	Patty,	3037	New Ipswich, N. H., 1781	June 21, 1803	Apr. 19, 1801	David Nay; 1781-1803.
	Abigail,	3038	" 1783	About 1803	Unmarried..	
55	Cyrus,	3039	" May 20, 1785	Oct. 30, 1846	Dec., 1810	Milla Lawrence; -1849; dau. Benj. and Rebecca.
56	John,	3040	" Mar. 5, 1787	Dec. 22, 1852	Oct. 12, 1817	Mary Skeldon; -1884.
	Edward,	3041	" 1789	May 2, 1863	1818	Almira Jones; -1868.
	Sally,	3042	" 1791		1818	George Adams.

DAVID AND PATTY (BROWN) NAY. 3037.

55	David, Jr.,	3043	Petersburg, N. H., Feb. 28, 1802	Sept. 17, 1864	Oct. 16, 1825	Thetis C. North; 1806–1871.

DAVID AND THETIS C. (NORTH) NAY. 3043.

	Oliver Wright (no issue),	3044	Darien, N. Y., Aug. 1, 1826	Oct. 21, 1875	1852	1. Elizabeth Worthington; 1832–1859.
	(no issue),	3045				2. Sabina Gibson.
55	Helen Mar, {	3046	" Apr. 15, 1828		June 19, 1850	1. Lewis Bardolf; 1827–1854.
55	{	3047			Apr. 13, 1857	2. Henry I. Lincoln; 1822–.
	Robert Bruce,	3048	" June 16, 1834			
55	Geo. Manning,	3049	" Aug. 25, 1831	Mar. 30, 1862	Aug. 25, 1858	Sarah A. Ware.
55	James Agard,	3050	" Apr. 9, 1836		Feb. 28, 1867	Laura A. Tyler; 1836–.
55	David DeWitt,	3051	" June 30, 1838		Apr. 30, 1869	Carrie May Rowley; 1843–.
55	Olive Hungerford,	3052	" Mar. 27, 1840	Apr. 30, 1869	Jan. 1, 1867	Sherman A. Griswold, M. D.; 1839–1884.
55	Noah North,	3053	" May 30, 1844		Sept. 13, 1873	Carrie S. Ames; 1853–.

LEWIS AND HELEN MAR (NAY) BARDOLF. 3046.

	Henry Charles,	3054	Darien, N. Y., Aug. 10, 1852			

HENRY I. AND HELEN MAR (NAY-BARDOLF) LINCOLN. 3047.

	Hattie Mar,	3055	Oct. 21, 1858			
	Abe,	3056	May 26, 1860			
	James Henry,	3057	Dec. 12, 1862			

GEORGE MANNING AND SARAH A. (WARE) NAY. 3049.

	Charles David,	3058	Mar. 23, 1860	1862		

JAMES A. AND LAURA A. (TYLER) NAY. 3050.

	Leonard Agard,	3059	Nov. 22, 1867	Oct. 3, 1870		
	Henry Wilbur,	3060	Apr. 16, 1869	Feb. 29, 1876		

DAVID DeWITT AND CARRIE MAY (ROWLEY) NAY. 3051.

	David Norton,	3061	Detroit, Mich., May 23, 1873			

DR. SHEMAN A. AND OLIVE H. (NAY) GRISWOLD. 3052.

	DeWitt Elliott,	3062	Franklin Grove, Ill., Apr. 30, 1869			

NOAH N. AND CARRIE S. (AMES) NAY. 3053.

	Edwin North,	3063	Detroit, Mich., Sept. 6, 1874	Sept. 25, 1875		
	Henry North,	3064	" Nov. 5, 1875			
	Everett Ames,	3065	Chicago, Ill., Sept. 13, 1878			
	Helen Louisa,	3066	" June 12, 1884			

CYRUS AND MILLA (LAWRENCE) BROWN. 3039.

55	Joshua L., {	3067	Sharon, N. H., Aug. 12, 1812	June 20, 1860	Nov., 1835	1. Eliza A. Colby; –1836.
	{	3068			Dec. 1, 1842	2. Dianna Osborne.
55	Abigail W.,	3069	" Dec. 8, 1815	Jan. 4, 1836	Feb., 1835	Daniel W. Noble.
	John W.,	3070	" May 7, 1817		Jan. 1, 1838	Lorette R. Noble; 1818–.
	Harriet M.,	3071	Pembroke, N. Y., Aug. 2, 1819	Aug. 4, 1880	Dec., 1841	Joseph M. Gowing.
	Martha W., {	3072	" Apr. 3, 1822		Oct., 1842	1. Robert Denham.
	{	3073			Jan. 3, 1865	2. Mark Kidder; –1884.
	Cyrus J.,	3074	" Dec. 12, 1824	Jan. 19, 1849	Unmarried.	
56	Sarah Theressa,	3075	" Sept. 23, 1827	Jan. 4, 1863	Nov. 20, 1850	Nathaniel W. Stowell.
	Edward Dana,	3076	" Oct., 1829	July 12, 1850	Unmarried.	
56	Levant R., {	3077	" Mar. 3, 1832		Mar. 28, 1854	1. Laura A. Warner; –1877.
56	{	3078			June 2, 1882	2. Emma L. Sweeney.

JOSHUA L. AND DIANNA (OSBORN) BROWN. 3068.

55	Allan D., {	3079	Batavia, N. Y., Sept. 2, 1843		Dec. 29, 1863	1. Gertrude Tyler.
	{	3080			Oct., 1880	2. Adaline Pierce.
55	Guy A., Capt.,	3081	" Dec. 8, 1846		July 22, 1869	Mary E. Holmes.
55	Florence,	3082	" Mar. 26, 1848		Apr. 9, 1872	George W. Tyler, U. S. N.

ALLAN D. AND GERTRUDE (TYLER) BROWN. 3079.

	Helen Tyler,	3083	Brattleboro', Vt., Oct. 14, 1864			
	Ethel Ruth,	3084	Annapolis, Md., Apr. 1, 1870			

CAPT. GUY A. AND MARY E. (HOLMES) BROWN. 3081.

	Edward Provest,	3085	Lincoln, Neb., May 18, 1870			
	Eugene Wayburn,	3086	" Oct. 1, 1872			
	Allan LaRue,	3087	" Jan. 19, 1874			
	Lawrence Ashton,	3088	" Oct. 19, 1880	May 30, 1880		

GEORGE W. AND FLORENCE (BROWN) TYLER. 3082.

	Faith,	3089	Valejo, Cal., Feb. 5, 1875			
	Royall,	3090	Brattleboro', Vt., Dec. 3, 1876	Apr. 3, 1877		

JOHN W. AND LORETTE R. (NOBLE) BROWN. 3070.

	Julia M. (no issue),	3091	Pembroke, N. Y., Nov. 7, '38	July 23, 1860	Nov. 9, 1859	Charles H. Wells.
	Daniel W.,	3092	" Aug. 26, 1840	May 5, 1841		
56	Adalaide R.,	3093	" Mar. 6, 1842		Sept. 8, 1868	John D. Shiller.
56	Cyrus W., Lieut.,	3094	" July 20, 1844		Dec. 25, 1872	Ada Robinson.
	Theresa C.,	3095	" Mar. 26, 1847			
56	Arthur Hudson,	3096	" Feb. 7, 1849		Dec. 24, 1874	Alice M. Brown. No. 3137.
56	Anthon Herman,	3097	" Feb. 7, 1849		Aug. 17, 1870	Maria Vedder.
	DeForest,	3098	" Jan. 20, 1851	June 15, 1851		
	Estelle L.,	3099	" Aug. 4, 1852			
	Harl'w Jacks'n, M.D.,	3100	" Oct. 2, 1854			
	Sarah Elizabeth,	3101	" Nov. 5, 1856		Nov. 17, 1880	Fred L. Sanons.

JOHN D. AND ADALAIDE R. (BROWN) SHILLER. 3093.

	Guy Burton,	3102	Jackson, Mich., Oct. 5, '78		

LIEUT. CYRUS W. AND ADA (ROBINSON) BROWN. 3094.

	Harlan Rexwold,	3103	Joliet, Ill., May 8, 1878		
	Julia Estelle,	3104	" Jan. 26, 1880		
	Cyrus Winfield,	3105	" July 25, 1881		

ARTHUR HUDSON AND ALICE M. (BROWN) BROWN. '3096-3137.

	Bertha Estelle,	3106	Pembroke, N.Y., July 1, '76		

ANTHON AND MARIA (VEDDER) BROWN. 3097.

	Ina May,	3107	Aug. 8, 1878		
	Bessie Loretta,	3108	Oct. 30, 1881		

NATHANIEL W. AND SARAH THERESSA (BROWN) STOWELL. 3075.

	Milla Abigail,	3109	Elma, N. Y., Mar. 29, 1852	June 3, 1885	Unmarried.
	Bethia Theressa,	3110	" Aug. 17, 1862		
	Dana,	3111	" Nov. 4, 1855		

LEVANT R. AND LAURA A. (WARNER) BROWN. 3077.

	Frank C.,	3112	Feb., 1856	Died infancy.	
	Guy W.,	3113	Mar. 30, 1858		
	Susan,	3114	Apr., 1877		

LEVANT R. AND EMMA L. (SWEENEY) BROWN. 3078.

	Levant R., Jr.,	3115	Nov. 27, 1884		

JOHN AND MARY (SKELDON) BROWN. 3040.

56	John J., M. D.,	3116 3117	Toronto, Can., Jan. 29, 1819	Feb. 23, 1845 July 12, 1871	1. Rebecca A. Hadley; 1820–1868. 2. Harriet J. Gallup.
56	Mary Ann,	3118	Buffalo, N.Y., Nov. 10, 1820	May, 1856	David Flint; –1872.
	George,	3119	" Apr. 3, 1822	Mar. 22, 1833	
	Thomas,	3120	" Aug. 11, 1825	Aug. 17, 1834	
56	Sarah J.,	3121	" Mar. 24, 1827	Dec., 1854	James Coalsworth.
56	Edward,	3122	" Aug. 10, 1830	June 7, 1864 Sept. 5, 1853	Sarah Winans.
	Cyrus, Lieut.,	3123	" July 8, 1832	Aug. 13, 1863 July 7, 1855	Sabrina Hutchinson.
56	George, 2d,	3124	" Apr. 10, 1834	Apr. 5, 1860	Carrie Garlock.
56	Abigail,	3125	Darien, N. Y., Feb. 28, 1836	Apr. 5, 1860	Charles Davis.
56	Millie,	3126	" May 24, 1839	Apr. 3, 1861	Hon. Henry M. Rich.
56	Daniel C.,	3127	" Apr. 15, 1841	Sept. 18, 1878	Louisa Brown.

DR. JOHN J. AND REBECCA A. (HADLEY) BROWN. 3116.

	Sarah W.,	3128	June 22, 1846		
56	Frank H.,	3129	July 10, 1850	Feb. 6, 1878	Martha Rhodes.
	John R.,	3130	Apr. 4, 1852	Apr. 30, 1882	Jennie Wilcox.
	Mary E.,	3131	May 8, 1853		
	Addah L.,	3132	June 29, 1859		

FRANK H. AND MARTHA (RHODES) BROWN. 3129.

	Willie Goodhue,	3133	Feb. 3, 1882		

DAVID AND MARY ANN (BROWN) FLINT. 3118.

	Bettie,	3134	May, 1857	Sept. 19, 1882	William L. Turner.

JAMES AND SARAH J. (BROWN) COALSWORTH. 3121.

	Nettie,	3135	May, 1856		
	Eugene,	3136	July, 1857		

EDWARD AND SARAH (WINANS) BROWN. 3122.

56	Alice M.,	3137	May 27, 1854	Dec. 24, 1874	Arthur Hudson Brown. No. 3096.
	Adison,	3138	Jan. 26, 1856		
	Cyrus,	3139	May 21, 1863		

GEORGE AND CARRIE (GARLOCK) BROWN. 3124.

	Eddie,	3140	May, 1861		
	Mattie,	3141	Aug. 13, 1863		

CHARLES AND ABIGAIL (BROWN) DAVIS. 3125.

	Amanda,	3142	Pembroke, N.Y., July 22, '63		
	Loretta,	3143	" Oct. 24, 1868		

HON. HENRY M. AND MILLIE (BROWN) RICH. 3126.

	Libbie D.,	3144	Corfu, N. Y., May 13, 1862		
	Daniel H.,	3145	Postville, Ia., Jan. 29, 1873		

DANIEL C. AND LOUISA (BROWN) BROWN. 3127.

	Edith M.,	3146	No. Collins, N. Y., Dec. 16, 1879		
	Mabel K.,	3147	" Feb. 20, 1882	Nov. 26, 1884	
	Fred. W.,	3148	" Nov. 26, 1884		

JOSIAH AND REBECCA (BROWN) FRENCH. 3029.

	Josiah,	3149	Cavendish, Vt.		Betsey Adams.
56	Calista,	3150	" Nov. 24, 1794	Feb. 13, 1875	Sept. 19, 1819	Samuel Adams; 1789–1875.
57	Calvin,	3151	" Aug. 28, 1799	May 15, 1879	Dec. 30, 1830	Valeria Blood; 1810–.
57	Rebecca,	3152	"	May 9, 1871	June 8, 1836	Hiram Giddings.
57	Luther,	3153	" Apr. 23, 1802	Apr. 28, 1865	Mar. 8, 1829	Lydia Brown; 1808–1846.

SAMUEL AND CALISTA (FRENCH) ADAMS. 3150.

(Continued page 57.)

	Samuel L.,	3154	Cavendish, Vt., June 16, 1820	July 2, 1848	Betsey M. Parker.

	Name	No.	Birthplace & Date				Married / Notes
	Charles P.,	3155	Cavendish, Vt., Aug. 22, 1822	Dec. 21, 1823			
	Maryett A.,	3156	" June 18, 1824			Jan. 3, 1855	Friend Weeks.
	Marcella,	3157	" Aug. 4, 1827			Apr. 14, 1852	Ira H. Adams.
	Josiah Q.,	3158	" May 2, 1830			Mar. 12, 1874	E. E. Hemenway.
	Jerusha J.,	3159	" Dec. 19, 1832	Apr. 7, 1872		Oct. 14, 1863	Moses Marston.
	Ellen M.,	3160	" Nov. 24, 1835	June 17, 1862		Sept. 12, 1859	Moses Marston.
	Betsey M.,	3161	" Aug. 7, 1838	Sept. 27, 1865		Sept. 3, 1863	John M. Foster.

CALVIN AND VALERIA (BLOOD) FRENCH. 3151.

	Name	No.	Birthplace & Date				Married / Notes
	George B.,	3162	Cavendish, Vt., Apr. 14, 1836			Sept. 30, 1874	Belle T. Martin.
	Mary Kate,	3163	" Mar. 5, 1850			Jan. 1, 1877	Henry P. Gammon.
	John Quincy,	3164	" June 9, 1844	May 5, 1864			
	Jerusha,	3165	" Sept. 16, 1842			Jan. 26, 1870	Hezron G. Day.

LUTHER AND LYDIA (BROWN) FRENCH. 3153.

	Name	No.	Birthplace & Date				Married / Notes
	Martin Luther,	3166	Cavendish, Vt., Sept. 2, 1830	July 11, 1851			
57	Windsor Brown,	3167	" July 28, 1832			June 2, 1868	Emma Pitcher; –1875.
	Lydia Ann,	3168	" Apr. 9, 1834	Oct. 19, 1834			
57	Walton W., M. D.,	3169	" Sept. 2, 1835			Oct. 6, 1864	Mary Elizabeth Deyoe.
	Rosamanda,	3170	Wilton, N.Y., Aug. 6, 1837	Jan. 11, 1838			
	Cortland,	3171	" Sept. 2, 1839	Dec. 12, 1846			
57	Antoinette,	3172	" Dec. 22, 1841			Feb. 28, 1882	Frank C. Osborn.
57	Mariette,	3173	" Oct. 26, 1843			Sept. 12, 1872	Howard William Aldrich.
	Charles Byron,	3174	" Nov. 20, 1845	May 29, 1847			

WINDSOR B. AND EMMA (PITCHER) FRENCH. 3167.

	Name	No.	Birthplace & Date				Married / Notes
	Georgianna,	3175	Saratoga, N. Y., July 30, 1870				
	Emma Winsor,	3176	" July 4, 1873	Apr. 9, 1885			
	Winsor Pitcher,	3177	" Aug. 23, 1875				

DR. WALTON W. AND MARY E. (DEYOE) FRENCH. 3169.

	Name	No.	Birthplace & Date				Married / Notes
	Lora,	3178	Dec. 13, 1865				
	Martin Luther,	3179	May 11, 1869				
	Howard Walton,	3180	Oct. 27, 1872				
	Mary Lydia,	3181	Oct. 1, 1878				

FRANK C. AND ANTOINETTE (FRENCH) OSBORN. 3172.

	Name	No.	Birthplace & Date				Married / Notes
	Emily,	3182	Jan. 24, 1883				
		3183	Apr. 19, 1886				

HOWARD W. AND MARYETTE (FRENCH) ALDRICH. 3173.

	Name	No.	Birthplace & Date				Married / Notes
	William Howard,	3184	Chicago, Ill., Dec. 18, 1873				
	Windsor French,	3185	" May, 1876				
	Marian,	3186	" Jan., 1878				

HIRAM AND REBECCA (FRENCH) GIDDINGS. 3152.

	Name	No.	Birthplace & Date				Married / Notes
	Calista Maria,	3187	June 23, 1838			Feb. 25, 1867	Gilbert Hart.
	Benjamin Henry,	3188	May 2, 1841	Jan. 14, 1843			
	Benj. Franklin,	3189	July 5, 1843			June 2, 1884	Rose Latham.
	Aurilla Lucetta,	3190	Apr. 8, 1846			Jan. 1, 1868	Henry Wheldon.

REV. JOSEPH AND REBECCA (WALKER) BROWN. 3030.

	Name	No.	Birthplace & Date				Married / Notes
57	Mary,	3191	Cavendish, Vt., Oct. 8, 1796	Mar. 7, 1866	Dec. 31, 1819		Israel Moore.
57	John, M. D., {	3192	" July 5, 1801	Feb. 22, 1843	Nov. 10, 1829		1. Clarissa B. Whipple; –1832.
		3193					2. Harriet Doolittle.

REV. JOSEPH AND LUCY (PROCTOR) BROWN. 3031.

	Name	No.	Birthplace & Date				Married / Notes
57	Lucy Amelia,	3194	Cavendish, Vt., Feb. 15, 1813			Apr. 11, 1839	Anson Spaulding.
	Geo. Wellington, {	3195	" Oct. 4, 1814			Dec. 2, 1841	1. Sophia Soper; –1843.
57		3196				Mar. 7, 1845	2. Irene Woodbury.

ISRAEL AND MARY (BROWN) MOORE. 3191.

	Name	No.	Birthplace & Date				Married / Notes
	Rebecca E.,	3197	Cavendish, Vt., Sept. 30, 1820				
	John Newton,	3198	" Nov. 29, 1823				
	Clara B.,	3199	" Dec. 1, 1831				

DR. JOHN AND CLARISSA B. (WHIPPLE) BROWN. 3192.

	Name	No.	Birthplace & Date				Married / Notes
	John Henry,	3200	Aug. 15, 1830				

ANSON AND LUCY A. (BROWN) SPAULDING. 3194.

	Name	No.	Birthplace & Date				Married / Notes
	Amelia Brown,	3201	Sept. 17, 1841	Sept. 4, 1868		Jan. 24, 1866	Harry A. Salmon.
	Julia Ann,	3202	Sept. 3, 1850			Feb. 18, 1875	H. G. Kittridge.

GEORGE W. AND IRENE (WOODBURY) BROWN. 3196.

	Name	No.	Birthplace & Date				Married / Notes
	George Edward,	3203	Aug. 22, 1847	Mar. 25, 1864			
57	Byron L.,	3204	Apr. 5, 1850			Oct. 7, 1875	Emma M. Adams; 1851–.
	Frank Henry,	3205	Nov. 26, 1851			June 12, 1878	Henrietta E. Farnim; 1851–.

BYRON L. AND HENRIETTA E. (FARNIM) BROWN. 3204.

	Name	No.	Birthplace & Date				Married / Notes
	Ernest Raymond,	3206	Sept. 9, 1876				
	Harrold Lincoln,	3207	Apr. 20, 1879				
	Leslie Adams,	3208	Feb. 2, 1881				
	Rachel Emily,	3209	Nov. 8, 1882				

REUBEN AND SARAH (BROWN) BROWN. 3033–3326. (Continued page 58.)

	Name	No.	Birthplace & Date				Married / Notes
	Charles B., Rev.,	3210	New Ipsw'h, N. H., May 10, 1796			Nov. 14, 1816	Sophia Stone.
	George,	3211	" Aug. 24, 1797				
	Reuben,	3212	" 1798				
58	Olive,	3213	Whitingham, Vt., May 11, 1801	July 6, 1883		Jan. 21, 1819	Zenas Carey; 1792–.
	Jesse,	3214	" Oct. 22, 1802				

	Name	No.	Born	Died	Married	Married to
	Betsey,	3215	Whitingham, Vt., Mar.4,1804			
58	Abner,	3216	" July 27, 1805	Sept. 12, 1877	Sept. 27, 1829	Lucy French; 1805–1882.
	Hannah,	3217	" July 27, 1805			
	Sarah,	3218	" Mar. 13, 1807			
58	John Bateman,	3219	" Mar. 10, 1811		Sept. 13, 1837	Lucy Herrick.
	Lyman Lockwood,	3220	" Mar. 18, 1815			

ZENAS AND OLIVE (BROWN) CASEY. 3213.

	Name	No.	Born	Died	Married	Married to
58	Morris John,	3221	Pamelia, N.Y., May 31,1826		Sept. 2, 1850	Editha Warner.
	Sarah Louisa,	3222	Richland, N.Y., Aug.4,1836		Oct. 31, 1862	William H. Winch; 1864–.
	Adalaide Rosalthe,	3223	" Sept. 17, 1841			
58	Caroline Matilda,	3224	Pamelia, N.Y., Oct.8,1820		Feb. 15, 1859	David H. Lindsley.
	Judson Newell,	3225	" Oct. 13, 1822			
	Eveline Melissa,	3226	" Dec. 29, 1831			
58	Charles Byron,	3227	Richland, N.Y.		Feb. 3, 1859	Lydia Tarbell.

MORRIS J. AND EDITHA (WARNER) CASEY. 3221.

	Name	No.	Born	Died	Married	Married to
	Elsie Adelle,	3228	Felts Mills, N.Y., Feb. 13, 1853		Feb. 15, 1882	Charles Wesley Nims.
	Gilbert Allan,	3229	" Mar. 14, 1858			

DAVID H. AND CAROLINE MATILDA (CASEY) LINDSLEY. 3224.

	Name	No.	Born	Died	Married	Married to
	Frances Adella,	3230	Alto, Wis., Feb. 25, 1851			
	George Henry,	3231	Lyme, N.Y., Sept. 6, 1853	Sept. 16, 1867		
	Alice M.,	3232	" Sept. 27, 1854			
	Charles Edward,	3233	" May 16, 1857	Dec. 4, 1860		
	Newel Arthur,	3234	" June 7, 1858	Dec. 10, 1860		
	Charles Arthur,	3235	" Apr. 1, 1860			

CHARLES B. AND LYDIA (TARBELL) CASEY. 3227.

	Name	No.	Born	Died	Married	Married to
	Olive Harriet,	3236	Lyme, N.Y., Nov. 23, 1861		Apr. 10, 1883	Fred A. Miller.
	Laura M.,	3237	" Feb. 20, 1864		Jan. 23, 1884	George H. Patchin.
	Lydia Tarbell,	3238	" Apr. 13, 1867			
	Emma Louisa,	3239	" Jan. 18, 1870			
	Florence Matilda,	3240	Cape Vincent, N.Y., July 5,1874			

ABNER AND LUCY (FRENCH) BROWN. 3216.

	Name	No.	Born	Died	Married	Married to
	Bateman A.,	3241	July 15, 1830		June 27, 1874	Nancy Horten; 1837–.
	Sarah J.,	3242	Mar. 20, 1832	Feb. 16, 1858	May 1, 1856	William A. Sampson; –1859.
58	Lyman M.,	3243	May 1, 1834		Dec. 1, 1867	Emma A. Buell; 1845–.
	Charles A.,	3244	Apr. 21, 1836	Nov. 22, 1869		
	Mahala L.,	3245	Mar. 23, 1838			
	Susan C.,	3246	Dec. 3, 1840	July 14, 1841		
	Olive A.,	3247	July 30, 1842	Nov. 14, 1860		
	Newel C.,	3248	Dec. 6, 1844	Feb. 21, 1873		
58	Hiram E.,	3249	July 7, 1849	Aug. 26, 1882	Nov. 21, 1875	Minnie Hendrickson; 1857–.

LYMAN M. AND EMMA A. (BUELL) BROWN. 3243.

	Name	No.	Born	Died	Married	Married to
	Sarah A.,	3250	Nov. 8, 1873			
	Charles M.,	3251	Mar. 8, 1877			
	George A.,	3252	Aug. 22, 1878			

HIRAM E. AND MINNIE (HENDRICKSON) BROWN. 3249.

	Name	No.	Born	Died	Married	Married to
	Lena O.,	3253	Sept. 3, 1876			
	Lillian I.,	3254	Jan. 11, 1878			
	Belle M.,	3255	Dec. 12, 1879			
	Blanche M.,	3256	Mar. 20, 1882			

JOHN BATEMAN AND LUCY (HERRICK) BROWN. 3219.

	Name	No.	Born	Died	Married	Married to
	George M.,	3257	June 13, 1838	Aug. 22, 1846		
	Marvin H., Rev.,	3258	Dec. 30, 1844		Oct. 28, 1868	Martha A. Porter.
	Mary E.,	3259	July 10, 1849		June 3, 1869	Daniel N. Middlekauff.

REV. MARVIN H. AND MARTHA A. (PORTER) BROWN. 3258.

	Name	No.	Born	Died	Married	Married to
	George M.,	3260	Aug. 13, 1869			
	Lucy E.,	3261	Sept. 16, 1870			
	Mary E.,	3262	Aug. 8, 1873			

SAMUEL AND POLLY (BROWN) WYMAN. 3036.

	Name	No.	Born	Died	Married	Married to
58	Frederick,	3263	Cavendish.Vt., Oct.12,1800	Jan. 17, 1879	Apr. 13, 1828	Melinda Hall; 1802–1880.
	Stedman,	3264	" Aug. 24, 1802	Jan. 16, 1824	Unmarried.	
	John,	3265	" Sept. 4, 1804	May 15, 1807		
59	Mary,	3266	" Oct. 26, 1806	Nov. 15, 1876	Dec. 6, 1826	Benjamin Persons; –1879.
59	Franklin,	3267, 3268	" Jan. 26, 1808		Aug. 30, 1840 / 1872	1. Ruth King Darrow; 1809–1863. [Otis. 2. Mrs. Charity (Otis) Winnegar; 1828–; d. Sardis
59	Alfred,	3269	" Jan. 11, 1811	Dec. 29, 1853	July 22, 1841	Hepsabeth Gregory.
	Samuel,	3270	" June 15, 1815		Mar., 1854	Mrs. Elsie Sherman.
59	Charles,	3271	" Sept. 15, 1816	Mar. 21, 1875	Mar. 14, 1849	Mrs. Matilda Streter; 1825–.
59	Philesta,	3272, 3273	" June 29, 1818		1838	1. Cyrus B. Collins. 2. —— Eddy.
59	Eliza B.,	3274	" July 29, 1820	Apr. 17, 1844	Feb. 14, 1841	Franklin Farnsworth; 1845–.
	Roxane,	3275	" Nov. 17, 1835	Sept. 6, 1848		

FREDERICK AND MELINDA (HALL) WYMAN. 3263.

	Name	No.	Born	Died	Married	Married to
59	Melinda S.,	3276	Granville, N.Y., Feb.18,1829	Aug. 1, 1851	June 7, 1848	Adison Willett; –1886.
	Frederick S.,	3277	" July 13, 1830	Aug. 22, 1831		
	Mary Brown,	3278	" Nov. 26, 1835	Dec. 17, 1864		
	Marcella,	3279	" Mar. 26, 1837		July 27, 1884	J. Hamilton Kincaid.
	Merel,	3280	" Oct. 22, 1839	Aug. 22, 1841		
	Martha H. J.,	3281	" Dec. 21, 1842	Dec. 23, 1880		

ADISON AND MELINDA S. (WYMAN) WILLETT. 3276.

100	Harriet Melinda,	3282	Aug. 1, 1851		Sept. 18, 1872	Calvin B. Orcutt.

BENJAMIN AND MARY (WYMAN) PERSONS. 3266.

	Adeline,	3283	Reading,Vt., May 28, 1830	May 26, 1835		
59	Eliza W.,	3284	Windsor,Vt., May 10, 1832		June 17, 1849	Horace F. Sherwin.
59	Maria,	3285	" Mar. 10, 1834		Oct. 3, 1853	Norman A. Smith.
59	Prudence M.,	3286	" Aug. 1, 1837	Feb. 10, 1873	Aug. 9, 1861	Adin T. Reed.
	Ellen M.,	3287	" Feb. 10, 1847	Mar. 16, 1858		

HORACE F. AND ELIZA W. (PERSONS) SHERWIN. 3284.

	Ada Eliza,	3288	Woodstock,Vt.,May 10,1852		Feb. 25, 1886	Fillmore A. Persons.
	Elmer H.,	3289	" Sept. 29, 1856		Feb. 21, 1878	Irene D. Rockwood.

NORMAN A. AND MARIA (PERSONS) SMITH. 3285.

	Ella M.,	3290	Oct. 18, 1858		Oct. 18, 1884	Fred J. Dorand.

ADIN T. AND PRUDENCE M. (PERSONS) REED. 3286.

	Alice P.,	3291	Mar. 18, 1864			

FRANKLIN AND RUTH R. (BARROWS) WYMAN. 3267.

59	Mary Frances,	3292	Boston, June 9, 1841		Nov. 26, 1841	Atwood Sargeant.
	Benj. Franklin,	3293	" June 9, 1841		June 23, 1869	Amanda Woodbury.
	Samuel Brown,	3294	Charlestown, Nov. 6, 1843			
	Eliza Anne,	3295	Granville,N.Y.,Mar.21,1846			[(Fillebrown).
	Rebecca Fidelia,	3296	" June 9, 1848		Feb. 22, 1867	Chas. Miller Charters; 1837-; s. James and Mary B.

ATWOOD AND MARY F. (WYMAN) SARGEANT. 3292.

	Ruth Wyman,	3297	Chester, Vt., Aug. 29, 1872			
	Alice Agie,	3298	" June 15, 1875			
	Mary Genevieve,	3299	" Dec. 23, 1877			
	Julia,	3300	" Oct. 21, 1880			

ALFRED AND HEPZABAH (GREGORY) WYMAN. 3269.

	Emily,	3301	Caledonia, Ill., Apr. 22, 1842		Feb. 14, 1857	Caleb C. Vance.
59	Mary E.,	3302	" Jan. 19, 1844	May 30, 1877	Nov. 17, 1863	J. K. Ormsby.
59	Eliza B.,	3303	" July 12, 1846		Dec. 21, 1870	Andrew Lovejoy.
59	Susie,	3304	" July 21, 1850		Dec. 21, 1871	Leslie Lovejoy.

J. K. AND MARY E. (WYMAN) ORMSBY. 3303.

	James K.,	3305	Nov. 21, 1866			
	George N.,	3306	Aug. 10, 1876			

ANDREW AND ELIZA B. (WYMAN) LOVEJOY. 330¾.

	Wyman N.,	3307	Mar. 6, 1871			

LESLIE AND SUSIE (WYMAN) LOVEJOY. 3304.

	Clara,	3308	Feb. 29, 1872	Sept. 20, 1873		
	Mark,	3309	July 17, 1874	Aug 3, 1877		
	Leonard,	3310	Sept. 6, 1876			
	Grace,	3311	July 31, 1879			

CHARLES AND MRS. MATILDA (STREETER) WYMAN. 3271.

59	Maria M.,	3312	Caledonia, Ill., Aug. 9, 1850		Sept. 27, 1870	W. T. Ball; 1847-.
	Edwin C.,	3313	" Jan. 21, 1853			
	Mary E.,	3314	" Apr. 29, 1856			
	Edwin L.,	3315	" Nov. 27, 1857		Dec. 9, 1882	Bryant R. Bennett.
	Justin J.,	3316	" Apr. 18, 1866			

W. T. AND MARIA M. (WYMAN) BALL. 3312.

	Charles T.,	3317	Oct. 30, 1873			
	George,	3318	Mar. 3, 1876	Apr. 16, 1879		
	Mabel M.,	3319	Dec. 20, 1879			

CYRUS B. AND PHILESTA (WYMAN) COLLINS. 3272.

	Rollin,	3320	Granville,N.Y.,Nov. 21,1841	1863		
	Emma,	3321	" Dec. 7, 1842		1870	Jacob Wells.

FRANKLIN AND ELIZA B. (WYMAN) FARNSWORTH. 3274.

	Adelaide M.,	3322				—— Wolcott.

CAPT. JOSIAH AND SARAH (WRIGHT) BROWN. 3023.

59	Josiah,	3323	New Ipswich, N. H.,Oct. 1, 1766	Jan. 20, 1858	Apr. 19, 1792	Meliscent Wright; 1767-1849; d. Edw'd & Thankful.
60	Joseph,	3324	" Oct. 10, 1767	Mar. 2, 1827		Sophronia Preston.
60	Jonas,	3325	" Mar. 4, 1769	Feb. 23, 1836	Feb. 20, 1796	Lois Russell; dau. Samuel and Abigail.
57	Sarah,	3326	" Nov. 22, 1770	Apr. 20, 1822	July 1, 1793	Reuben Brown. No. 3033.
61	Aaron,	3327	" Dec. 8, 1772	Feb. 15, 1828	Apr. 16, 1795	Hannah Brown. No. 3032.
62	Amos,	3328	" Sept. 11, 1774	May 10, 1863	Apr. 5, 1803	Sarah Tarbell; 1782-.
62	Abner,	3329	" July 27, 1776	Apr. 4, 1824	Dec. 10, 1805	1. Polly Jaquith.
62		3330				2. Polly Ayer.
	Rebecca,	3331	" July 5, 1778	June 9, 1853		Nathan Perry.
	Levi,	3332	" Aug. 6, 1780	Sept. 10, 1840	May 15, 1803	Betsey Temple.
62	Nathan,	3333	" July 25, 1782	Jan. 21, 1862	June 3, 1806	Betsey Goldsmith.
63	Heywood,	3334	" July 2, 1784	Mar. 2, 1867	Feb. 5, 1809	Sally Wolcott; 1788-1876.
	Betsey,	3335	" Feb. 7, 1787	July 11, 1793		
	Abigail,	3336	" June 22, 1790	Apr. 24, 1864		Asa Farnsworth.

JOSIAH AND MILISCENT (WRIGHT) BROWN. 3323. (Continued page 60.)

	Josiah,	3337	Whitingham, Vt., Sept. 24, 1793	July 19, 1794		

	Name	No.	Born	Died	Married	Spouse / Notes
60	Rufus,	3338	Whitingham, Vt., Jan. 12, 1797	Aug. 9, 1875	May 1, 1820	1. Polly Smead; 1802–1839.
	(no issue),	3339			1841	2. Ruth (Greenwood) Belknap; –1847. [Betsey.
60		3340			Dec. 13, 1848	3. Eliza M. (Winn) Edwards; 1818–; d. Abiatha and
	Cyrus,	3341	" Apr. 20, 1795	Sept. 21, 1797		
	Peter,	3342	" July 28, 1798	July 30, 1798		
	Clement (no issue),	3343	" May 23, 1800	Aug. 7, 1849	1823	Polly Eames; 1800–1856.
	Meliscent,	3344	" July 3, 1802	Feb. 24, 1803		
	Abram,	3345	" Dec. 10, 1803	Dec. 19, 1803		
60	Edmund,	3346	" July 13, 1805	Oct. 11, 1866	May 5, 1831	Elizabeth Prescott. No. 5412.
	George Witherell,	3347	" Mar. 18, 1810		Oct. 4, 1832	Frances E. Bemis.

RUFUS AND POLLY (SMEAD) BROWN. 3338.

	Name	No.	Born	Died	Married	Spouse / Notes
60	Rufus Albert,	3348	Whitingham, Vt., Feb. 2, 1828		Sept. 22, 1885	Martha Hare; 1825–1881.
60	Mary Almeda,	3349	" Dec. 19, 1824	Mar. 19, 1866	Oct., 1854	Horace Pease Dewey; 1818–1871.
	Miliscent Almira,	3350	" Mar. 25, 1827			Francis E. Brigham.
	Ann Eliza,	3350	" Jan. 18, 1832	Nov. 20, 1832		

RUFUS AND ELIZA M. (WINN-EDWARDS) BROWN. 3340.

	Name	No.	Born	Died	Married	Spouse / Notes
60	Marcia Sophia,	3351	Whitingham, Vt., Oct. 2, 1849		Oct. 2, 1869	Abner Augustine Butterfield; 1844–; son Ezra T. and
	Charles Francis,	3352	" Mar. 20, 1860		Sept. 13, 1885	Alice Luella Abbey; 1862–. [Mary (Leonard).

RUFUS ALBERT AND MARTHA (HARE) BROWN. 3348.

Name	No.	Born	Died	Married	Spouse / Notes
Lewis Albert,	3353	July 27, 1859			
Edward Rufus,	3354	July 20, 1862			

HORACE PEASE AND MARY A. (BROWN) DEWEY. 3349.

Name	No.	Born	Died	Married	Spouse / Notes
Jessie May,	3355	Aug. 10, 1855		June 29, 1874	Prof. Alembert W. Brayton.
Jennie Brown,	3356	Apr. 5, 1859			

ABNER A. AND MARCIA S. (BROWN) BUTTERFIELD. 3351

Name	No.	Born	Died	Married	Spouse / Notes
Marcius August'e,	3357	Whitingham, Vt., July 12, 1870			
Ossian Rufus,	3358	" May 3, 1872			
Alice Adele,	3359	" Oct. 13, 1874			
Mary Blanche,	3360	" May 27, 1881			
Marcia Amelia,	3361	" Jan. 1, 1883			

EDMUND AND ELIZABETH (PRESCOTT) BROWN. 3346–5412.

	Name	No.	Born	Died	Married	Spouse / Notes
	Edm'd Prescott,	3362	Whitingham, Vt., June 9, 1832		Apr. 23, 1861	1. Lois Ellen Robinson; 1842–1865.
60		3363			July 29, 1868	2. Lottie A. Morrison.
60	Elizabeth Jane,	3364	" Aug. 1, 1834	May 22, 1879	Apr. 11, 1867	Numan Harrington.
60	Sophronia Almira,	3365	" Sept. 4, 1836		Sept. 24, 1861	Henry Ellis Winslow; 1832–.
	Amherst Lamb,	3366	" Nov. 15, 1839	Oct. 24, 1844		
60	Ruth Ann,	3367	" Apr. 30, 1842	Sept. 13, 1871	Sept. 24, 1867	Myron E. Lampman.
	Martha Eliza,	3368	" Feb. 12, 1848			

EDMUND PRESCOTT AND LOTTIE A. (MORRISON) BROWN. 3363.

Name	No.	Born	Died	Married	Spouse / Notes
Edmund C.,	3369	May 16, 1871			

NUMAN AND ELIZABETH JANE (BROWN) HARRINGTON. 3364.

Name	No.	Born	Died	Married	Spouse / Notes
Nellie,	3370	Mar. 11, 1868			
Jennie Elizabeth,	3371	Aug. 24, 1870			
Freddie Brown,	3372	Mar. 28, 1874			
Clarence Numan,	3373	Feb. 8, 1876			

HENRY E. AND SOPHRONIA A. (BROWN) WINSLOW. 3365.

Name	No.	Born	Died	Married	Spouse / Notes
Fanny Elizabeth,	3374	1863			

MYRON E. AND RUTH A. (BROWN) LAMPMAN. 3367.

Name	No.	Born	Died	Married	Spouse / Notes
Flora Elizabeth,	3375	Nov. 7, 1868			

JOSEPH AND SOPHRONIA (PRESTON) BROWN. 3324.

Name	No.	Born	Died	Married	Spouse / Notes
Joseph Wright,	3376		July 18, 1855		
James Preston,	3377				
Jemmima,	3378				

JONAS AND LOIS (RUSSELL) BROWN. 3325.

	Name	No.	Born	Died	Married	Spouse / Notes
	Jeremiah,	3379	Nov. 29, 1796	Mar. 4, 1849		Clarissa Fowler.
	Nancy,	3380	Mar. 16, 1798			James Peebles.
	Gratis,	3381	Apr. 16, 1800	Apr. 22, 1868		Joseph Eames.
	Harvey,	3382	Dec. 15, 1801	Feb. 13, 1874		Lucena Fuller.
	Abigail,	3383	June 25, 1803	Mar. 3, 1873	1823	Joseph Peebles; 1799–1879.
60	Leonard,	3384	Sept. 24, 1806		Feb. 9, 1834	Lucinda Martin.
60	Lois,	3385	Aug. 25, 1808		Jan. 29, 1829	Daniel Fowler.
	Jonas,	3386	Apr. 8, 1810	Apr. 20, 1856		Emeline Aldrich.
	Russell,	3387	Feb. 21, 1812	May 7, 1835	Unmarried.	
	Martin,	3388	Nov. 7, 1813	July 11, 1861		Mary A. Stacey.
	Abel W.,	3389	Nov. 2, 1817			Lucy Horsley.

LEONARD AND LUCINDA (MARTIN) BROWN. 3384.

Name	No.	Born	Died	Married	Spouse / Notes
Sarah M.,	3390	Dec. 22, 1834	May 24, 1864		David E. Hutchins.
William R.,	3391	Nov. 3, 1838			Cretia Marshall.
George H.,	3392	Jan. 13, 1841	May 12, 1864	Unmarried.	
Anna L.,	3393	May 10, 1843			Daniel G. Taylor.
Ella E.,	3394	Jan. 19, 1850			William G. Marshall.

DANIEL AND LOIS (BROWN) FOWLER. 3385.

Name	No.	Born	Died	Married	Spouse / Notes
Anson C.,	3395	Whitingham, Vt., Aug. 19, 1829	July 4, 1879	Apr. 5, 1855	Kate Bassett.
Caroline M.,	3396	" Apr. 13, 1831		Nov. 28, 1853	S. E. Peck.
Oscar A.,	3397	" Sept. 19, 1833	Aug. 4, 1877	Jan. 22, 1859	Sarah Allen.
Lanah J.,	3398	" Sept. 19, 1835			
Olive F.,	3399	" Feb. 9, 1840		Mar. 4, 1861	Frank E. Ward.

AARON AND HANNAH (BROWN) BROWN. 3327-3032.

	Name	No.	Birth		Death	Notes
	Betsey,	3400	New Ipsw'h, N. H., Jan. 23, 1796	Jan. 26, 1804		
	Aaron, Jr.,	3401	" Sept. 28, 1797	May 22, 1798		
61	Adison, Rev.,	3402	" Mar. 11, 1799	May 11, 1872	Dec. 13, 1832	Ann Elizabeth Wetherbee; 1807–; d. Abijah and Eliz.
61	Hermon, Dea.,	3403	" Dec. 28, 1800	Aug. 23, 1876	Apr. 13, 1828	Sophronia Prescott. No. 5410.
	Mary (no issue),	3404	" Feb. 14, 1803	Dec. 1, 1837	1836	William Billings.
61	John S., Rev.,	3405	" Apr. 26, 1806		Aug. 16, 1836	Mary Ripley; 1806–1878; dau. David and Orra (Bliss).

REV. ADISON AND ANN ELIZABETH (WETHERBEE) BROWN. 3402.

	Name	No.	Birth		Death	Notes
	Frances Allen,	3406	Brattleboro', Vt., June 15, 1834	Aug. 27, 1870	Unmarried.	
61	Ann Elizabeth,	3407	" June 26, 1836	Feb. 9, 1862	May 30, 1853	Christian Frederick Schuster.
	Adison, Jr., Lt.-Col.	3408	" June 6, 1838	Mar. 3, 1865	Feb. 7, 1863	Florida S. Starr.
61	Chas. Wetherbee,	3409	" Nov. 7, 1840		Aug. 20, 1867	Elizabeth Starr; 1846–; dau. Nehemiah and Lucretia.
	Mary Hannah,	3410	" July 5, 1842		July 31, 1863	1 Capt. Dennis W. Farr; –1864.
61		3411			Feb. 7, 1867	2. Col. Augustus T. Dunton.

CHRISTIAN FREDERICK AND ANN ELIZABETH (BROWN) SCHUSTER. 3407.

	Name	No.	Birth		Death	Notes
	Elanora Louisa,	3412	Brattleboro', Vt., May 14, 1854	Jan. 24, 1867		
	Anna Mary,	3413	" Feb. 2, 1856	Jan. 4, 1867		
61	Paul Frederick,	3414	" Apr. 15, 1858		Apr. 15, 1879	Lizzie Butterworth.
	Lizzie Frances,	3415	" June 6, 1860			

PAUL FREDERICK AND LIZZIE (BUTTERWORTH) SCHUSTER. 3414.

	Name	No.	Birth			
	Paul Butterworth,	3416	Rockf'd, Ill., Mar. 18, 1883			
	Adison Brown,	3417	" Nov. 29, 1884			

CHARLES WETHERBEE AND ELIZABETH (STARR) BROWN. 3409.

	Name	No.	Birth			
	Melanchton Starr,	3418	Rockf'd, Ill., Sept. 19, 1868			
	Elizabeth,	3419	" Apr. 4, 1870			
	Frances Agnes,	3420	" Mar. 10, 1880			
	Alice,	3421	" July 16, 1882			

COL. AUGUSTUS T. AND MARY H. (FARR-BROWN) DUNTON. 3411.

	Name	No.	Birth			
	Flora Starr,	3422	Rockf'd, Ill., May 10, 1868			

DEA. HERMON AND SOPHRONIA (PRESCOTT) BROWN. 3403-5410.

	Name	No.	Birth		Death	Notes
61	Adison Prescott,	3423	New Ipswich, N.H., Aug. 2, 1827		Dec. 26, 1850	Frances Louisa Chase; 1829–.
	Hann'h Elizab'th,	3424	" May 21, 1829	Sept. 14, 1831		
61	Joseph Aaron,	3425	" May 8, 1831		Feb. 8, 1854	Lucy A. Davis; 1836–1879; d. Benj. F. and Mary E.
	John Humphrey,	3426	" Mar. 22, 1834	Feb. 23, 1845		
61	Mary Elizabeth,	3427	" Mar. 16, 1836		May 21, 1857	Charles Henry Burroughs; 1832–.
61	Alfred Hermon,	3428	" July 14, 1838		Jan. 20, 1872	Margaret E. Gale; 1851–.
	George Stillman,	3429	" Nov. 12, 1840	Dec. 11, 1840		
	Sophronia Eliza,	3430	" Aug. 20, 1842	Sept. 16, 1842		
	Hannah Eliza,	3431	" Nov. 19, 1843	Sept. 13, 1845		

ADISON PRESCOTT AND FRANCES LOUISA (CHASE) BROWN. 3423.

	Name	No.	Birth		Death	Notes
61	Carrie Louisa,	3432	Bellows Falls, Vt., Mar. 11, 1852		Oct. 26, 1874	Trophimers Kain Page.
61	Mary Sophronia,	3433	Brattleboro', Vt., Nov. 19, 1853		Nov. 19, 1874	Joel Gilman Willard.
	Homer John,	3434	Worcester, June 8, 1866			

TROPHIMERS KAIN AND CARRIE LOUISA (BROWN) PAGE. 3432.

	Name	No.	Birth			
	Lora May,	3435	June 18, 1877			
	Amy Louisa,	3436	May 15, 1881			

JOEL GILMAN AND MARY SOPHRONIA (BROWN) WILLARD. 3433.

	Name	No.	Birth			
	Edna May,	3437	Brooklyn, N. Y., Jan. 18, 1877	Feb. 11, 1885		
	Walter Clifton,	3438	New York, N. Y., Oct. 8, 1879			
	Carrie Goodrich,	3439	" July 23, 1882			

JOSEPH AARON AND LUCY A. (DAVIS) BROWN. 3425.

	Name	No.	Birth		Death	Notes
	Frank Hermon,	3440	Concord, N. H., Sept. 3, 1855		Mar. 18, 1875	Ira M. Blaisdell; 1855–.
	Aura Anna,	3441	" Sept. 27, 1857	June 7, 1863		
	Ella Gertrude,	3442	Nashua, N. H., July 22, 1860			
	Joseph Edwin,	3443	Canterbury, N. H., Sept. 20, 1863			
	J. Alfred,	3444	" May 10, 1869			
	Grace Maud,	3445	Manchester, N. H., Oct. 10, 1875			

CHARLES H. AND MARY ELIZABETH (BROWN) BURROUGHS. 3427.

	Name	No.	Birth			
	Willie H.,	3446	Boxboro', Apr. 19, 1858	May 27, 1858		
	Mary Louisa,	3447	" Nov. 17, 1861			
	Lizzie Sophronia,	3448	" Oct. 11, 1863	May 21, 1881		
	George Wayland,	3449	" Sept. 29, 1865			
	Charles Hermon,	3450	" June 5, 1869			
	Marion E.,	3451	" June 1, 1873			

ALFRED HERMON AND MARGARET E. (GALE) BROWN. 3428.

	Name	No.	Birth			
	Josie Maud,	3452	Canterbury, N. H., Jan. 1, 1873			
	Fred Hermon,	3453	" Mar. 19, 1874			
	Mary Prescott,	3454	" May 2, 1877			

REV. JOHN STILLMAN AND MARY (RIPLEY) BROWN. 3405.

	Name	No.	Birth		Death	Notes
61	Sarah Alvord,	3455	Buffalo, N. Y., Jan. 23, 1838		Oct. 28, 1868	Lizzie E. Balcom; 1845–1884.
61	William Ripley,	3456	" July 16, 1840		Aug. 16, 1871	Harriet Bell; 1839–; dau. William and Sarah.
62	Charles Edward,	3457	Greenfield, Sept. 15, 1842	June 15, 1880	Apr. 4, 1867	Alfred Whitman; 1842–; s. Col. Edw'd B. and Nancy.
62	Mary Whiton,	3458	Fitzwilliam, N.H., Jan. 15, 1845			

WILLIAM RIPLEY AND LIZZIE E. (BALCOM) BROWN. 3456. (Continued page 62.)

	Name	No.	Birth			
	Marg't Lombard,	3459	Cot'nW'd F'ls, Kan., Jan. 24, '70			

	Adison,	3460	Lawrence,Kan.,Sep.16,1872	Mar. 22, 1876	
	William Ernest,	3461	Hutchinson, Kan., Nov. 21, 1877		

CHARLES EDWARD AND HARRIET (BELL) BROWN. 3457.

	Hermon,	3462	Wakarusa,Kan.,Jun.10,1872		
	Lola Bell,	3463	" July 24, 1874		
	Mary Ripley,	3464	" June 28, 1878		

ALFRED AND MARY WHITON (BROWN) WHITMAN. 3458.

	Russell Ripley,	3465	Louisville, Ky., Oct. 31, 1868		
	John Pratt,	3466	" Mar. 21, 1871		
	Henry Pirtle,	3467	" July 6, 1872	Died infancy.	
	Ruth Heywood,	3468	" Feb. 19, 1874		
	Alfred Edmund,	3469	" June 8, 1876	Mar. 27, 1877	
	Waldo,	3470	Lawrence, Kan., Apr. 25, 1882		
	Merrill,	3471	" Aug. 24, 1884		

AMOS AND SARAH (TARBELL) BROWN. 3328.

62	Elliott, M. D.,	3472	Aug. 15, 1804		June 7, 1826	Polly Kingsbury.
	Aldis, {	3473	Dec. 1, 1805			1. Mary Goodenough.
		3474				2. Phila F. Tenney.
	Amos,	3475	July 9, 1807	Apr. 2, 1810		
	Sally,	3476	Aug. 13, 1809	Dec. 4, 1849		T. G. Davis.
	Clarissa,	3477	Oct. 11, 1811	July 24, 1855	June 6, 1841	Dr. Allen Carkins.
	Hannah,	3478	Jan. 5, 1816	June 13, 1817		
	Amos A.,	3479	Oct. 18, 1817	Jan. 2, 1869	Nov. 28, 1839	Mary R. Temple.

DR. ELLIOTT AND POLLY (KINGSBURY) BROWN. 3472.

	Mary Minerva,	3480	Apr. 5, 1827		
	Sarah Sophronia,	3481	July 19, 1830		
	Henry Bradley,	3482	Mar. 27, 1832	Apr. 23, 1832	
	Love Letitia,	3483	July 28, 1833		
	Elliott Kingsbury,	3484	Apr. 20, 1835		
	Hannah Helen,	3485	Sept., 1837		
	Harriet Herman,	3486	Oct. 21, 1840		

ABNER AND POLLY (JAQUITH) BROWN. 3329.

	Mary,	3487	New Ipswich,N.H.,June23,1807	Nov. 6, 1835		
62	Almira,	3488	" Apr. 30, 1809	Jan. 23, 1857	June 9, 1833	John G. Wilson.
62	Lebanon,	3489	" Jan. 23, 1811	July 21, 1846	Dec. 24, 1835	Marinda Blanchard.
	Lurena,	3490	" Dec. 19, 1812	July 6, 1833		

ABNER AND POLLY (AYER) BROWN. 3330.

62	AbnerHartwell,M.D.,	3491	New Ipswich, N. H., July6,1816	Apr. 21, 1851	Apr. 13, 1847	Susan Augusta Shurtleff.
	Marshall H.,	3492	" Mar. 1, 1817	Apr. 16, 1835		
62	Fidelia O.,	3493	" Dec. 13, 1820		1840	David M. Dodge.
	Sophronia P.,	3494	" Nov. 4, 1822	Oct. 18, 1826		

JOHN G. AND ALMIRA (BROWN) WILSON. 3488.

	Anna Maria,	3494	Mason Village,N.H.,July31,1834		
62	Horace M.,	3495	" Jan. 16, 1866		Harriet A. Putnam.

HORACE M. AND HARRIET A. (PUTNAM) WILSON. 3495.

	Nettie A.,	3496	Feb. 13, 1860

LEBANON AND MIRANDA (BLANCHARD) BROWN. 3489.

62	Marsh'l Leb'non,M.D.,	3497	New Ipswich,N.H.,Apr.14,1837		Nov. 10, 1869	Helen (Adams) Child.
	Millen Howard,	3498	" Nov. 11, 1839	July 16, 1840		
62	Mary Miranda,	3499	Keene, N. H., May 21, 1841		Feb. 9, 1865	William D. Parlin. [line E. (Cowles)
62	George Abner,	3500	" June 8, 1845		June 22, 1867	Ida Lavine Stewart; 1847–; dau. Reuben and Caro_

DR. MARSHALL L. AND HELEN (ADAMS-CHILD) BROWN. 3497.

	Mary Fr'ces Adams,	3501	Winchendon, Nov. 2, 1871

WILLIAM D. AND MARY M. (BROWN) PARLIN. 3499.

	Mary Winifred,	3502	May 11, 1875
	Marion Louise,	3503	Sept. 21, 1879

GEORGE ABNER AND IDA L. (STEWART) BROWN. 3500.

	Robert Forbes,	3504	Keene, N. H.,Dec. 18, 1868
	Marshall Stewart,	3505	" Nov. 6, 1870
	Lloyd,	3506	Somerville, Jan. 24, 1876
	Caroline,	3507	Keene, N. H., Jan. 28, 1880
	Ida May,	3508	" Apr. 28, 1883
	Ray,	3509	" Jan. 13, 1886

DR. ABNER H. AND SUSAN A. (SHURTLEFF) BROWN. 3491.

	Abn'r Hartwell,Jr.,	3510	Hanover, N.H., Dec., 1848	Sept. 20, 1849	
	Susan Anna,	3511	" Aug. 19, 1850	May 16, 1885	

DAVID M. AND FIDELIA O. (BROWN) DODGE. 3493.

	Adelaide E.,	3512	Lowell, 1845		June, 1870	Rev. Sylvester Jones.
	Lucius H.,	3513	" Dec., 1847			

NATHAN AND BETSEY (GOLDSMITH) BROWN. 3333.

63	Nathan, Rev., {	3514	New Ipswich,N.H.,June 22,1807	Jan. 1, 1886	May 6, 1830	1. Eliza Whitney Ballard; –1871.
63		3515			July 24, 1872	2. Mrs. Charlotte A. Marlett.
63	Sophia Burnham,	3516	Whitingham, Vt., Oct. 27, 1809		May 23, 1833	Jonathan Ballard; 1798–1862.
63	William G.,	3517	" Mar. 3, 1812		Oct. 10, 1839	Eunice Fisher.
	Josiah W.,	3518	" June 15, 1815	July 5, 1816		
	Mary E.,	3519	" Sept. 9, 1818	Sept. 9, 1872	Unmarried.	

REV. NATHAN AND ELIZA WHITNEY (BALLARD) BROWN. 3514.

Dorothy Sophia,	3520	Charlemont, May 6, 1832	Sept. 29, 1838		
William Ballard,	3521	Maulmain, Burmah, June 7, 1835	Aug. 10, 1835		
Nathan Ballard,	3522	Sadiga, Assam, Sept. 8, 1836	Feb. 11, 1841		
Eliz. Whitney,	3523	" Sept. 30, 1838			
William Pearce,	3524	Sibsagor, Assam, Dec. 12, 1842			

REV. NATHAN AND MRS. CHARLOTTE A. (MARLETT) BROWN. 3515.

Nathan Worth,	3525	Yokohama, Japan, Oct. 22, 1877			

JONATHAN AND SOPHIA B. (BROWN) BALLARD. 3516.

63	Nathan Brown, {	3526	Charlemont, Mar. 29, 1834		Nov. 26, 1857	1. Adelia Rice; –1880.
63		3527			June 9, 1882	2. Mrs. Ellen N. Sherman.
	Eliza Brown,	3528	" Aug. 9, 1839			
63	Dorothy Sophia,	3529	" Aug. 23, 1843		Nov. 25, 1869	Alonzo Tower; 1839-.
63	Mary Adelaide,	3530	" Apr. 16, 1848		Nov. 25, 1869	Russell Judson Waters; 1843-.
	Frances Whitney,	3531	" Sept. 13, 1851			

NATHAN B. AND ADELIA (RICE) BALLARD. 3526.

63	Adelia Emeline,	3532	Charlemont, Sept. 30, 1858		Jan. 15, 1879	Francis Hillman; 1852–1884.
63	Maria Idaline,	3533	Rowe, Oct. 1, 1859		Jan. 17, 1883	Edgar Roberts; 1853-.
	Ellen Zervia,	3534	Charlemont, July 9, 1862			
	Julia Rice,	3535	" Dec. 21, 1868			

NATHAN B. AND ELLEN M. (SHERMAN) BALLARD. 3527.

Susan May,	3536	Charlemont, June 26, 1885			

FRANCIS AND ADELIA E. (BALLARD) HILLMAN. 3533.

Mabel Adelia,	3537	Charlemont, Aug. 12, 1881			

EDGAR AND MARIA IDALINE (BALLARD) ROBERTS. 3533.

Clarence Ballard,	3538	Pittsfield, July 20, 1884			
Edgar,	3539	" Jan. 12, 1886			

ALONZO AND DOROTHY S. (BALLARD) TOWER. 3529.

John Ballard,	3540	Hoosac Tunnel, July 28, 1873			

RUSSELL J. AND MARY A. (BALLARD) WATERS. 3530.

Arthur J.,	3541	Chicago, Ill., Mar. 4, 1871			
Effie Ballard,	3542	" June 28, 1873	Feb. 19, 1874		
Albert Judson,	3543	" Mar. 16, 1876	July 7, 1876		
Mabel C.,	3544	" Nov. 27, 1877			

WILLIAM G. AND EUNICE (FISHER) BROWN. 3517.

63	Ann Judson, {	3545	Wolford, Vt., Aug. 8, 1840		Dec. 11, 1869	1. Capt. Frank Preston; –1880.
		3546			Oct., 1881	2. James A. Durfee.
63	Adison W.,	3547	" Nov. 25, 1841		Nov., 1864	Julia M. Barr.
63	Francis Fisher,	3548	Halifax, Vt., Dec. 1, 1843		June 26, 1867	Susie Seaman Brooks.
	Mary Elizabeth,	3549	Wilmington, Vt., May 10, '49		Oct. 9, 1875	Moses W. Lyman.
63	Frederick C.,	3550	Holyoke, Sept. 21, 1854		March, 1878	Ada I. Slyter.

CAPT. FRANK AND ANNA JUDSON (BROWN) PRESTON. 3545.

Willie Goldsmith,	3551	Farmington, Wis., Apr. 14, 1871			
Mary Elizabeth,	3552	Kankakee, Wis., May 27, 1875			

ADISON W. AND JULIA M. (BARR) BROWN. 3547.

Alice M.,	3553	Springfield, May 8, 1867			

FRANCIS F. AND SUSIE S. (BROOKS) BROWN. 3548.

Frank Granger,	3554	Chicago, Ill., July 2, 1868			
Carrie Eunice,	3555	" May 5, 1870			
Minnie,	3556	" Apr. 10, 1872	Aug. 23, 1873		
Edna,	3557	" Aug. 28, 1873			
Walter,	3558	St. Josephs, Mich., Feb. 9, 1876			
Herbert,	3559	Chicago, Ill., Aug. 14, 1878			
Goldsmith,	3560	" Feb. 4, 1880			
Susie,	3561	" Mar. 18, 1881			
Florence,	3562	" Feb. 6, 1883			
Robert,	3563	" May 5, 1885			

FREDERICK C. AND ADA I. (SLYTER) BROWN. 3550.

Eunice,	3564	Chicago, March, 1881			

HEYWOOD AND SALLY (WOLCOTT) BROWN. 3334.

	Jas. Madison, Dea., {	3565	Lewis, N. J., Feb. 8, 1810		Aug. 17, 1839	1. Laura Keyes; 1802–1848.
63		3566			Dec. 26, 1848	2. Amanda Pingrey; 1826-.
64	Josiah Wolcott, Rev.,	3567	Concord, May 18, 1812		Oct. 23, 1842	Harriet Newell Parker; 1821-.
64	Louise Sacharissa,	3568	Acton, Apr. 3, 1815		June 1, 1835	John Wetherbee; 1807–1867.
	Jane Ann,	3569	" Apr. 9, 1817		June 17, 1860	George Baker Oxley; 1807-.
64	Samuel Heywood,	3570	" Aug. 3, 1819	Dec. 14, 1880	Apr. 30, 1850	Elethina Burnham; 1822–1863.
64	Sarah Wright,	3571	" Jan. 8, 1822		Nov. 29, 1849	S. Augustus Child; 1822-.
64	August's Winslow,	3572	" Aug. 29, 1824		Apr. 4, 1848	Lovey Blodget; 1827-.
64	Mary Baker,	3573	" Mar. 4, 1827		Nov. 28, 1848	Moses F. Greenwood; 1827-.
64	Harvey Darkman,	3574	" Aug. 14, 1831		July 4, 1855	Jerusha C. Little; 1834-.

JAMES M. AND AMANDA (PINGREY) BROWN. 3565. (Continued page 64.)

James Heywood,	3575	Littleton, Jan. 28, 1850		May 3, 1882	Mary Amelia Taylor.
Laura Amanda,	3576	" Feb. 14, 1852			
John Pingrey,	3577	" Dec. 15, 1854		Feb. 23, 1882	Clara Emma Richardson; 1861-.

Name	No.	Birthplace and Date	Death	Married	Spouse
Adams Franklin,	3578	Littleton, Feb. 4, 1857			
Charles Henry,	3579	" June 18, 1859	Nov. 26, 1859		
Mary Eliza,	3580	" Jan. 31, 1861	Sept. 23, 1863		
Alice Sophia,	3581	" Apr. 7, 1863			
Samuel Walker,	3582	" July 9, 1865			
Jennie Louise,	3583	" May 24, 1868			
Ulrick Freeman,	3584	" Sept. 25, 1870			

REV. JOSIAH WOLCOTT AND HARRIET N. (PARKER) BROWN. 3567.

Name	No.	Birthplace and Date	Death	Married	Spouse
Frencina Harriet,	3585	Concord, May 8, 1845	July 21, 1860		
Ella Eliza,	3586	" Nov. 5, 1848	Nov. 5, 1860		
Wolcott Josiah,	3587	Derry, N. H., Dec. 7, 1850	July 14, 1860		
Abby Elwood,	3588	Manchester, Vt., Jan. 24, '57	June 20, 1860		
Charles Ellsworth,	3589	" Jan. 4, 1860	July 23, 1860		

JOHN AND LOUISA S. (BROWN) WETHERBEE. 3568.

Name	No.	Birthplace and Date	Death	Married	Spouse
Francis Winslow,	3590	Apr. 4, 1837	Apr. 18, 1839		
Augustus Winslow, Hon.,	3591	Sept. 1, 1839		Jan. 1, 1870	Hattie Lane; 1844–1884.

SAMUEL H. AND ELETHINA (BURNHAM) BROWN. 3570.

Name	No.	Birthplace and Date	Death	Married	Spouse
Sarah Emily,	3592	Acton, Apr. 3, 1851		May 29, 1872	William Henry Cooper; 1844–.
Willie Chalmers,	3593	Littleton, July 13, 1857		June 21, 1883	Annie E. Horman; 1860–.
Clarence Wolcott,	3594	" May 19, 1860			

S. AUGUSTUS AND SARAH W. (BROWN) CHILD. 3571.

Name	No.	Birthplace and Date	Death	Married	Spouse
Melvine Aug'tus,	3595	West Acton, Oct. 21, 1850		Feb. 1, 1874	Eveline Cochran.
Arabelle Louisa,	3596	" Jan. 5, 1852	Nov. 8, 1864		
Alice May,	3597	Littleton, May 5, 1854			
Florence Emma,	3598	Manchester, Vt., Oct. 5, 1855			

AUGUSTUS W. AND LAURA (BLODGETT) BROWN. 3572.

Name	No.	Birthplace and Date	Death	Married	Spouse
Francina A.,	3599	Jan. 25, 1849		Oct. 21, 1868	Henry B. Littlefield; 1842–.
Josephine Adelia,	3600	May 3, 1851		Dec. 12, 1871	Albert E. Richardson; 1844–.
Marietta Estelle,	3601	Jan. 13, 1853	Sept. 2, 1877	Nov. 25, 1873	Cecil J. Howard; 1850–1881.
Louisa Jane,	3602	Sept. 18, 1854			Charles Pollard.
Edwin Augustus,	3603	Mar. 14, 1856			
Hattie Lorie,	3604	Oct. 13, 1857			
Lydia Emma,	3605	Apr. 25, 1859	Mar. 13, 1862		
George Winslow,	3606	Sept. 1, 1861	Dec. 13, 1861		
Carrie Eliza,	3607	Mar. 18, 1863			
Winslow Wolcott,	3608	Apr. 8, 1865	Feb. 26, 1867		

MOSES F. AND MARY B. (BROWN) GREENWOOD. 3573.

Name	No.	Birthplace and Date	Death	Married	Spouse
Emily F.,	3609	Sept. 1, 1849	Jan. 15, 1873		Hattie M. Rogers; 1848–.
May Effie,	3610	Sept. 1, 1851		Nov. 16, 1870	Thomas E. Jackson; 1849–.
Agnes W.,	3611	May 28, 1854			
Lizzie Jane,	3612	Feb. 5, 1860	Feb. 2, 1863		
Charles Hiram,	3613	July 11, 1862			
Clifton Grant,	3614	Feb. 27, 1868			

HARVEY D. AND JERUSHA C. (LITTLE) BROWN. 3574.

Name	No.	Birthplace and Date	Death	Married	Spouse
William Wolcott,	3615	Apr. 2, 1856			
Mary Ann,	3616	Oct. 23, 1857			
Cora Sally,	3617	June 15, 1859			
Myrta A.,	3618	Dec. 30, 1860			E. Herbert Hayden.
Francis Harvey,	3619	Sept. 20, 1871			

EPHRAIM AND HANNAH (WILSON) BROWN. 154.

Name	No.	Birthplace and Date	Death	Married	Spouse
Thomas,	3620	Concord, Dec. 26, 1720	1784	May 26, 1748	Mary Flint.
William,	3621	" Jan. 9, 1722–3			
Hannah,	3622	" Feb. 14, 1724–5	Jan. 16, 1749		Unmarried.
Elias,	3623	" Mar. 7, 1726–7	Oct. 31, 1794		"
Mary,	3624	" Jan. 21, 1728–9		July 14, 1756	Capt. Jonathan Buttrick. No. 212.
Sarah,	3625	" Jan. 29, 1730–1	June 6, 1815	July 23, 1751	Joseph Buttrick. No. 213.
David, Capt.,	3626	" Mar. 12, 1732–3	May 22, 1802	Sept. 30, 1756	Abigail Monroe; –1832.
Ruth,	3627	" Oct. 26, 1739			

THOMAS AND HANNAH (POTTER) BROWN. 153–551.

	Name	No.	Birthplace and Date	Death	Married	Spouse
64	Ephraim, Dea.,	3628	Concord, Nov. 7, 1710	Oct. 9, 1788	June 20, 1732	Abigail Wheeler.
	Timothy,	3629	" Aug. 17, 1712			Rebecca Farrar. No. 304.
	Luke,	3630	" Nov. 3, 1714			
	Hannah,	3631	" Dec. 6, 1716			

DEA. EPHRAIM AND ABIGAIL (WHEELER) BROWN. 3628.

	Name	No.	Birthplace and Date	Death	Married	Spouse
	Abigail,	3632	Concord, Apr. 9, 1733		Nov. 1, 1753	Thomas Hubbard.
	Ephraim,	3633	" Apr. 7, 1735	Feb. 6, 1736–7		
	Edward, {	3634	" Feb. 15, 1736–7	1781	Jan. 15, 1761	1. Mary Brown; 1740–1778.
		3635			1780	2. Beulah Hosmer.
	Thankful,	3636	" Dec. 16, 1740	Sept. 9, 1776	July 6, 1758	Edward Wright.
	Ephraim,	3637	" Dec. 20, 1742	Jan. 18, 1812		
	Hannah,	3638	" Apr. 1, 1745	June 8, 1745		
	Sarah,	3639	" Sept. 25, 1746			
	Thomas,	3640	" Mar. 25, 1749	Apr. 25, 1774	Unmarried.	
64	Samuel, Lieut.,	3641	" Feb. 18, 1752	Oct. 29, 1819		Elizabeth Brown. No. 3024.

LIEUT. SAMUEL AND ELIZABETH (BROWN) BROWN. 3641–3024. (Continued page 65.)

	Name	No.	Birthplace and Date	Death	Married	Spouse
	Lucy,	3642	Concord, July 2, 1773	Feb. 18, 1786		
	Thomas,	3643	" Mar. 9, 1775	Feb. 11, 1834		[(Baker).
65	Samuel,	3644	" Mar. 7, 1777	May 29, 1843	June 5, 1800	Betsey Tuttle; 1783–1843; dau. Sam'l and Elizabeth
94	Elizabeth,	3645	" Feb. 28, 1779	Apr. 6, 1863	June 7, 1798	Samuel Potter Prescott. No. 5403.

	Hannah,	3646	Concord,	June 2, 1781	Oct. 16, 1845		
	Abigail Wheeler,	3647	"	Mar. 29, 1783	Mar. 9, 1806		
65	Joshua,	3648	"	June 20, 1787	Dec. 11, 1855	Oct. 11, 1807	1. Sally Potter. No. 5175.
65		3649				Jan. 27, 1811	2. Rebecca Derby; –1816.
	Edward,	3650	"	Mar. 25, 1785	Mar. 11, 1813		
	Ephraim,	3651	"	Apr. 9, 1789	Oct. 2, 1844		
66	John,	3652	"	Jan. 10, 1792	Feb. 28, 1852	July 2, 1820	1. Clarissa Harmon; –1845.
66		3653					2. Olive S. Green; –1867.
66	Joel,	3654	"	Feb. 20, 1793	Sept. 22, 1851	Dec. 28, 1818	Lucy Whitney; 1800–1863; dau. David and Betsey.

SAMUEL AND BETSEY (TUTTLE) BROWN. 3644.

65	Almira,	3655		Nov. 23, 1801	Sept. 14, 1877	Feb. 3, 1820	1. Samuel Handley; 1792–1827.
65		3656				Nov. 4, 1832	2. Horace Tuttle; –1859.
	Horace Tuttle,	3657		Oct. 15, 1803	Sept. 24, 1805		
65	Caleb Sumner,	3658		July 6, 1806	July 9, 1877		Isannah Page.
	Samuel,	3659		June 27, 1808			1. Rebecca Russell.
		3660					2. Jane O. Gay.
	Aaron,	3661		Aug. 12, 1810	July 24, 1819		
	Abigail Wheeler,	3662		Aug. 12, 1812	June 2, 1822		
	Eri Edward,	3663		Nov. 23, 1814	Oct. 3, 1817		
65	Hiram,	3664		Sept. 4, 1817			Susan Nitham.
65	Elizabeth,	3665	Carlisle,	Feb. 6, 1820		Mar. 21, 1844	Samuel Sewell; 1819–; son Rev. Samuel and Martha.
	Olive S.,	3666	"	Mar. 7, 1822		Sept. 3, 1843	Charles Butters; 1819–; son Josiah and Sally.
	Ephraim,	3667	"	Aug. 23, 1824	Mar. 26, 1827		

SAMUEL AND ALMIRA (BROWN) HANDLEY. 3655.

	Otis H.,	3668	Carlisle,	Mar. 14, 1821	Apr. 25, 1871		
	Samuel W.,	3669	"	Dec. 22, 1822			
65	Andrew,	3670	"	Oct. 5, 1825		Apr. 29, 1852	Hannah E. Cutler.

HORACE AND ALMIRA (BROWN-HANDLEY) TUTTLE. 3656.

	Almira E.,	3671		Oct. 18, 1833	Apr. 1, 1877		
65	Mary Jane,	3672		Feb. 28, 1835		Aug. 21, 1860	E. G. Hastings.
	Lucy Ann,	3673		Aug. 22, 1837	June 20, 1870	Jan. 1, 1865	George L. Herrick.
	Horace B.,	3674		Mar. 1, 1842		Oct. 28, 1870	Martha J. Shattuck.
	Henry W.,	3675		Apr. 29, 1846	June 28, 1870		Sarah Travis; –1871.

ANDREW AND HANNAH E. (CUTLER) HANDLEY. 3670.

	Herbert L.,	3676	N. Camb'ge,	July 19, 1860			
	Carrie E.,	3677	Billerica,	May 17, 1866			
	M. Gertrude,	3678	"	Oct. 25, 1868			

E. G. AND MARY JANE (TUTTLE) HASTINGS. 3672.

	Julia Alfreda,	3679		Jan. 7, 1864		Aug. 6, 1885	Leander Emery.
	Minnie Arabel,	3680		Mar. 3, 1867			

CALEB SUMNER AND ISANNAH (PAGE) BROWN. 3658.

	Isannah,	3681		Aug. 8, 1833		July 31, 1853	Ward B. Frothingham; 1828–.
65	Harriet,	3682		July 13, 1835		May 25, 1856	Cyrus H. Haynes.
	Emma,	3683		Aug. 22, 1837			
	Vivian,	3684		Feb. 24, 1840			Charles Adams.
	Aradine,	3685		Aug. 27, 1841			
	Eugenia,	3686		Nov. 29, 1843		Mar. 22, 1869	Charles Fletcher.
	Otis Sumner,	3687		Feb. 20, 1845		Sept. 13, 1870	Ella Lawrence.
	Elizabeth,	3688		Feb. 14, 1847		Apr. 7, 1870	Hiram Hutchinson.
	Thomas P.,	3689		June 29, 1853			

CYRUS H. AND HARRIET (BROWN) HAYNES. 3682.

	Clifford C.,	3690		Aug. 10, 1859			
	Nathaniel L.,	3691		June 7, 1868			
	Philip L.,	3692		Feb. 28, 1872			
	Caleb S.,	3693		Oct. 5, 1875			
	Otis B.,	3694		Oct. 8, 1877			

HIRAM AND SUSAN (NITHAM) BROWN. 3664.

	Lafayette,	3695		Oct. 13, 1844			
	George H.,	3696		Apr. 23, 1846			
	Lilly Addie,	3697		Apr. 9, 1853			

SAMUEL AND ELIZABETH (BROWN) SEWELL. 3665.

	Samuel Brown,	3698	Burlington,	Aug. 17, 1846	July 5, 1883	June 11, 1872	Louisa Elizabeth Farrington.
	Martha Elizabeth,	3699	"	May 18, 1858		July 3, 1879	T. S. Curtis.

JOSHUA AND SALLY (POTTER) BROWN. 3648–5175.

65	Amasa,	3700	Concord,	Apr. 16, 1808	Mar. 10, 1883	Sept. 3, 1833	Maria Wilkins; 1808–.
66	James Potter,	3701	"	Mar. 1, 1810	Apr. 22, 1873	Nov. 27, 1834	Susanna Baker; 1808–.

JOSHUA AND REBECCA (DERBY) BROWN. 3649.

	William (no issue),	3701	Concord,	June 7, 1812	Feb. 3, 1866	Oct. 22, 1835	Sarah C. Reed; 1815–.
	John,	3702	"	June 15, 1814	Oct. 16, 1815		
66	Joseph Derby,	3703	"	Oct. 31, 1816		Feb. 13, 1840	Lucy Reed; 1813–1886.
66	Joshua Warren,	3704	"	Mar. 30, 1819	Sept. 7, 1869	1846	Catharine Shaw.

AMASA AND MARIA (WILKINS) BROWN 3700. *(Continued page 66.)*

	Joshua,	3705		June 29, 1834	Aug. 11, 1853		
66	Rebecca D.,	3706		Mar. 6, 1836	Feb. 12, 1881	Nov. 10, 1839	Lorenzo A. Lane.
66	James A.,	3707		Nov. 7, 1837		May, 1856	1. Adaline L. Small; 1838–1863.
66		3708				Mar. 24, 1865	2. Adaline A. Davis; 1850–.
	Sarah P.,	3709		May 25, 1840			
	Susan B.,	3710		May 25, 1840	May 26, 1840		

	Name	No.	Birth	Death	Marriage	Spouse / Notes
	George W.,	3711	Feb. 11, 1842	May 25, 1863		
	Hiram W.,	3712	July 7, 1844			
	Charles D.,	3713	Dec. 6, 1850			

JAMES A. AND ADALINE L. (SMALL) BROWN. 3707.

	Name	No.	Birth	Death		
	James I.,	3714	Mt. Vernon, N.H., Mar., 1858	Apr., 1858		
	Clara M.,	3715	" May 18, 1860	Feb. 25, 1879		
	Sarah Jane,	3716	" June, 1863	Dec. 27, 1863		

JAMES A. AND ADALINE A. (DAVIS) BROWN. 3708.

	Name	No.	Birth
	Susan Emma,	3717	Mt. Vernon, N.H., July 17, 1866
	James William,	3718	" Dec. 19, 1868
	Albert I.,	3719	" June 23, 1870
	Joseph D.,	3720	" July 8, 1873
	Charles R.,	3721	" Jan. 22, 1876
	George A.,	3722	" Nov. 8, 1878
	Sarah E.,	3723	" Oct. 16, 1881
		3724	" Apr. 16, 1884

LORENZO A. AND REBECCA D. (BROWN) LANE. 3706.

	Name	No.	Birth
	Elmer Clifford,	3725	Ashburnham, Oct. 15, 1867

JAMES POTTER AND SUSANNA (BAKER) BROWN. 3701.

	Name	No.	Birth	Death	Marriage	Spouse / Notes
66	James Baker,	3726	Concord, Sept. 30, 1835	May 28, 1870	June 29, 1868	Annie E. Kimball; 1839–.
	John, 2d,	3727	" Oct. 21, 1836			
66	William, Rev.,	3728	" Sept. 10, 1838		June 15, 1865	Salone S. Williams; 1837–.
	Susan Amanda,	3729	" Oct. 3, 1840			
	Henry Taylor,	3730	" Nov. 18, 1843	June 2, 1881		
66	Hersey,	3731	" Aug. 28, 1846		Oct. 21, 1884	Bertha Temple Lenox; 1859–; dau. Chas. S. S. and [Louisa A. H.

JAMES BAKER AND ANNIE E. (KIMBALL) BROWN. 3726.

	Name	No.	Birth
	Alice F.,	3732	Nov. 5, 1868
	Edith B.,	3733	July 28, 1870

REV. WILLIAM AND SALONE S. (WILLIAMS) BROWN. 3728.

	Name	No.	Birth
	Corella,	3734	July 15, 1866
	William C.,	3735	May 17, 1868
	Ophelia S.,	3736	Sept. 20, 1870

HERSEY AND BERTHA TEMPLE (LENOX) BROWN. 3731.

	Name	No.	Birth
	Richmond Lenox,	3737	Brooklyn, N.Y., Aug. 1, 1885

JOSEPH DERBY AND LUCY (REED) BROWN. 3703.

	Name	No.	Birth	Death	Marriage	Spouse / Notes
	Lucy Rebecca,	3738	Concord, Jan. 12, 1841		Dec. 16, 1868	George Vialle; 1845–; son Samuel.
	Sarah,	3739	" Sept. 24, 1842	Oct. 2, 1866		
	Ellen Augusta,	3740	" 1844	Jan. 19, 1869	Apr. 22, 1868	Caleb H. Wheeler; son Henry.
	Abby,	3741	" Nov. 10, 1845			
	Elizabeth,	3742	" Aug. 23, 1848		Nov. 12, 1870	Hiram Worthley; 1844–. [(Hosmer).
66	Joseph D., Jr.,	3743	" Feb. 23, 1850		Oct. 9, 1873	Martha Walcott; 1851–; dau. Joel W. and Martha P.
	Daniel,	3744	" Nov. 18, 1851	1851		
	Mary,	3745	" 1853			

JOSEPH D., JR., AND MARTHA (WALCOTT) BROWN. 3743.

	Name	No.	Birth
	Clark Osmer,	3746	Concord, Apr. 16, 1875
	Horace Reed,	3747	" July 10, 1879

JOSHUA WARREN AND CATHARINE (SHAW) BROWN. 3704.

	Name	No.	Birth	Death	Marriage	Spouse / Notes
66	Benjamin W.,	3748	Concord, 1847		June 17, 1879	L. Cora Myrick.
	Ella C.,	3749	" Oct. 6, 1848	Aug. 26, 1849		
	Amelia,	3750	" Dec. 29, 1849			
	Charlotte A.,	3751	" Apr. 12, 1852			
	Martha J.,	3752	" Mar. 16, 1854	Aug. 4, 1855		
66	Wm. Francis,	3753	" Dec. 5, 1856		Dec. 27, 1883	Eugenia Bennett Van Derberg.

BENJAMIN W. AND L. CORA (MYRICK) BROWN. 3748.

	Name	No.	Birth
	Roger W.,	3754	Concord, Jan. 10, 1883
		3755	Apr. 5, 1885

WILLIAM FRANCIS AND EUGENIA B. (VAN DERBERG) BROWN. 3753.

	Name	No.	Birth
	Geo. Van Derberg,	3756	Nov. 1, 1884

JOHN AND CLARISSA (HARMON) BROWN. 3652.

	Name	No.	Birth	Death	Marriage	Spouse / Notes
	Stark Edward,	3757	Lancaster, N.Y., Mar. 17, 1822	Oct. 15, 1832		
	Quincy Harmon,	3758	" Nov. 24, 1823	1875	Sept. 4, 1844	Bethema R. Robinson.

JOHN AND ALICE S. (GREEN) BROWN. 3653.

	Name	No.	Birth	Death	Marriage	Spouse / Notes
	Clarissa Ann,	3759	Lancaster, N.Y., Dec. 17, 1846		Oct. 11, 1869	1. Julius A. Carmer.
		3760			Apr., 1880	2. S. D. Damon.
	Martha Jane,	3761	" Dec. 18, 1849		Dec. 24, 1873	John H. Kline.

JOEL AND LUCY (WHITNEY) BROWN. 3654.

(Continued page 67.)

	Name	No.	Birth	Death	Marriage	Spouse / Notes
67	David Whitney,	3762	Concord, Dec. 29, 1819		May 30, 1844	Mary M. Stiles.
	Alzirus,	3763	" Oct. 16, 1821		Nov. 16, 1843	Harriet D. Proctor.
	Lucy Alzina,	3764	" Apr. 14, 1824	Apr. 10, 1831		
	Sarah Ann Eliza,	3765	" Apr. 18, 1826		Nov. 15, 1847	Asa J. Hersey.
	Eunice Andrews,	3766	" Apr. 25, 1828	May 2, 1831		
	Ezra Ripley,	3767	" Feb. 5, 1830	Apr. 29, 1845		

67	Mary Celestia, {	3768	Concord,	Mar. 13, 1832		Jan. 12, 1851	1. Edward H. Parker; 1827–1874.
		3769	"			July 21, 1875	2. John F. Landers.
	Juliette Patterson,	3770	"	Mar. 23, 1834	1870	Nov. 15, 1853	George J. Hobbs.
67	Lucy Sophia,	3771	"	May 25, 1836		Apr. 7, 1852	George Philo Slocomb.
	Betsey Whitney,	3772	"	Jan. 31, 1839	Mar. 18, 1842		
	Eunice Elizabeth,	3773	"	Mar. 10, 1842		May 10, 1866	Paul Tibbits.

DAVID WHITNEY AND MARY M. (STILES) BROWN. 3762.

	John Emerson,	3774	June 22, 1853			
	Josiah,	3775	May 28, 1855			
	Charles Jerome,	3776	Dec. 16, 1858			
	Mary Eugenia,	3777	July 9, 1861			

EDWARD H. AND MARY C. (BROWN) PARKER. 3768.

	Arthur A.,	3778	Apr. 5, 1855	
	Clarence E.,	3779	Apr. 4, 1860	
	Eddie H.,	3780	Jan. 4, 1867	
	Theodore,	3781	Sept. 8, 1869	

GEORGE P. AND LUCY S. (BROWN) SLOCOMB. 3771.

	Mary Parker,	3782	Sept. 3, 1853	Apr. 6, 1876	Amos V. James.
	Lillie Maria,	3783	Oct. 30, 1861		
	Alzirus,	3784	Dec. 24, 1866		
	George Whitney,	3785	Oct. 24, 1868		
	Lance Brown,	3786	June 10, 1877		

STEPHEN AND MELISCENT (WOOD) HOSMER. 441.

	Mary,	3787	Concord,	May 23, 1773			—— Wyman.
	Stephen,	3788	"	Apr. 19, 1736			Elizabeth ——.
	Silas,	3789	"	Sept. 13, 1738	Jan. 30, 1741		[(Davis). No. 439.
104	Nathan,	3790	"	Mar. 2, 1740	Dec. 25, 1777	Aug. 16, 1763	Buelah Hosmer; 1742–1778; dau. James and Eliz.
	Meliscent,	3791	"	May 16, 1744			Daniel Holden.
	Silas,	3792	"	Mar. 26, 1747	May 19, 1753		
	Oliver,		"	July 19, 1751			

WILLIAM H. AND AUGUSTA M. (BARRETT) RICHARDSON. 2393.

	William Shelley,	3793	Malden, Dec. 13, 1850	Feb. 2, 1852

NATHAN AND SUSANNA (BARRETT) BROWN. 2147.

67	Harriet (no issue),	3800	Camden, Me., Aug. 8, 1803	Jan. 5, 1879	Oct. 22, 1835	Joseph C. Stetson.
	Mary Ann,	3801	" Apr. 8, 1805	Feb. 12, 1847	Sept. 25, 1823	Joseph Jones; 1797–1859.
	Susan,	3802	" Oct. 8, 1807	June, 1847	Unmarried.	
	Louisa (no issue),	3803	" Nov. 22, 1809	July, 1838	Sept., 1835	Henry Barrett. No. 2382.

JOSEPH AND MARY ANN (BROWN) JONES. 3801.

67	Eliz. Eldridge,	3804	Dec. 2, 1824		June 2, 1852	John Phynas; 1822–.
	Nathan Brown,	3805	Apr. 23, 1827	April, 1861	Unmarried.	
	Joseph Henry,	3806	July 4, 1829			
67	Frances Louisa,	3807	Apr. 30, 1832		July 12, 1854	Charles Bellows Hazeltine; 1828–.
67	Sidney Augustus,	3808	May, 1835			Ellen Furber.
	Marianna,	3809	Nov. 18, 1837	June 6, 1850		
	Oscar Rockwood,	3810	July 31, 1840			
67	Susan Ford,	3811	Feb. 20, 1843		1870	José R. de Casanova; 1841–.
	Sophia Morris,	3812	Oct. 26, 1845	Apr. 13, 1880	Unmarried.	

JOHN AND ELIZABETH ELDRIDGE (JONES) PHYNAS. 3804.

	Harriet Stetson,	3813	May 28, 1853	
	Jessie,	3814	Apr. 2, 1855	
	Mary Jones,	3815	Feb. 14, 1857	
	Francis Hazleton,	3816	Mar. 6, 1859	Feb., 1862
	Amelia Tudor,	3817	Sept. 30, 1862	
	John Simpson,	3818	Jan. 17, 1864	

CHARLES B. AND FRANCES L. (JONES) HAZELTINE. 3807.

	Grace,	3819	Belfast, Me., Apr. 28, 1855	Mar. 4, 1861
	Benjamin,	3820	Boston, Mar. 24, 1857	
	Mary,	3821	Belfast, Me., July 9, 1861	
	Frances,	3822	Nice, France, Feb. 2, 1868	Feb. 8, 1868
	Louisa,	3823	Belfast, Me., Nov. 21, 1873	

SIDNEY A. AND ELLEN (FURBER) JONES. 3808.

	Marianna,	3824	1864
	John Phynas,	3825	1868
	Joseph,	3826	1870
	James,	3827	1870

JOSÉ R. AND SUSAN F. (JONES) DE CASANOVA. 3811.

	Joseph Stetson,	3828	Sept. 22, 1871
	Charles Francis,	3829	Apr. 21, 1873
	Louisa Lorne Lee,	3830	Nov. 28, 1878

SAMUEL POTTER AND REBECCA (TUTTLE) CONANT. 245.

101	Samuel,	3831	Acton,	Jan. 21, 1790		Aug. 2, 1812	Mehitable Piper.
99	Nathan,	3832	"	Oct. 30, 1791		Sept. 26, 1816	Sukey Davis; 1793–1860.
68	Paul,	3833	"	Jan. 23, 1793	July 7, 1843	Apr. 8, 1817	Matilda Jewett.
101	Rebecca,	3834	"	Jan. 1, 1798		May 24, 1821	Nathan Brooks.
	Susanna C. (no issue),	3835	"	Jan. 5, 1800	Nov. 26, 1878	Nov. 7, 1819	Robert Chaffin; 1797–.
68	Silas,	3836	"	May 4, 1803		Feb. 22, 1824	Eliza Wheeler; 1804–1870.
	Charles (no issue),	3837	"				
	Simon (no issue),	3838	"				
99	Nahum,	3839	"			Jan. 21, 1832	Eliza A. Gibson.

PAUL AND MATILDA (JEWETT) CONANT. 3833.

Samuel,	3840		Apr. 11, 1818	Apr. 11, 1839		[(Hayward).
Emeline,	3841		June 4, 1820	Dec. 7, 1884	Apr. 23, 1839	William H. Conant; 1815–; son Joel and Hannah
Sophia,	3842		Jan. 27, 1822	Dec. 30, 1847	May 5, 1842	Phinneas Harrington.
John,	3843		Oct. 11, 1824	Aug. 16, 1828		
Francis (no issue),	3844		Sept. 3, 1827		May 10, 1849	1. Martha Ann Jones.
					Apr. 14, 1880	2. Mrs. Ella J. Marshall; 1836–.
Maria,	3845		Oct. 14, 1830	Sept. 6, 1845		
Henry S.,	3846		May 27, 1835	Oct. 5, 1885	Oct. 26, 1854	Hannah F. Tolles.

SILAS AND ELIZA (WHEELER) CONANT. 3836.

Silas,	3847		Oct. 15, 1825			
Nathan,	3848		Sept. 16, 1827		Jan. 31, 1849	George Lawrence.
Eliza,	3849		Sept. 10, 1829			
Susan Chaffin,	3850		July 28, 1832			Maria Dooney.
George,	3851		Apr. 28, 1835			
Simon Tuttle,	3852		Dec. 15, 1837			
Elbridge,	3853		Jan. 22, 1841	Feb. 9, 1863	Jan. 2, 1864	Nelson Holman; 1843–.
Charlotte Aug'ta,	3854		Nov. 3, 1843		Oct. 10, 1863	George M. Kendall; 1841–.
Henrietta C.,	3855		July 16, 1846			

CAPT. REUBEN AND LOIS (CONANT) HAYWARD. 248.

	William Conant,	3856	Concord, Mar. 30, 1796	July 9, 1847	Unmarried.	[(Whitcomb).
68	Reuben, Jr.,	3857	" Apr. 30, 1797	Feb. 3, 1866	May 26, 1825	Lucy W. Houghton; 1805–1881; dau. Jacob and Sarah
68	James.	3858	" Aug. 7, 1798	Mar. 8, 1877	Dec. 15, 1830	Nancy Hayward; 1808–1874; dau. Cyrus and Sarah
	Daniel,	3859	" June 6, 1802	Apr. 18, 1803		[(Pierce).
90	Mary,	3860	" May 19, 1810		Dec. 7, 1828	Francis Potter. No. 5185.

REUBEN, JR., AND LUCY W. (HOUGHTON) HAYWARD. 3857.

68	Mary Jane,	3861	Concord, Apr. 27, 1826		Dec. 15, 1848	1. William G. Priest.
68		3862			May 29, 1867	2. Lewis C. Puffer.
68	Reuben, 2d,	3863	" June 22, 1828		June 8, 1851	Mary Jane Fletcher. No. 4501.
68	Lois Conant,	3864	" Apr. 15, 1836		May 17, 1849	George Washington Robbins, Jr., 1827–; son George
68	Lucy W.,	3865	" June 18, 1839		Feb. 26, 1862	David Dow; 1839–. [W., Jr., and Rebecca (Robbins).
	Russell S.,	3866	" June 6, 1842		Jan. 7, 1869	Mary Hunt.
68	Elizabeth M.,	3867	" Dec. 30, 1846		Mar. 14, 1867	Francis Cassidy; 1844–.
68	Laura,	3868	" Feb. 17, 1849		Dec. 25, 1869	Stephen W. Page; 1839–.

WILLIAM G. AND MARY JANE (HAYWARD) PRIEST. 3861.

	William H.,	3869	Concord, Oct. 5, 1849	July 26, 1875		
	Henri L.,	3870	" Feb. 4, 1851	Oct. 27, 1867		
	Mary J.,	3871	" Dec. 5, 1855			
68	Georgie,	3872	" Jan. 14, 1856		Aug., 1879	Jonathan P. Blodgett.

LEWIS C. AND MARY J. (HAYWARD–PRIEST) PUFFER. 3862.

Lewis H.,	3873		July, 1868
Eddie E.,	3874		Aug. 26, 1871

JONATHAN P. AND GEORGIE (PRIEST) BLODGETT. 3872.

William H.,	3875		June 17, 1878
Walter P.,	3876		June 29, 1880
Raymond P.,	3877		July 21, 1884

REUBEN, 2D, AND MARY JANE (FLETCHER) HAYWARD. 3863–4501.

68	Emma,	3878	Acton, Sept. 29, 1853		Dec. 22, 1876	Sam'l Jones; 1851–; s. Sam. and Martha A. (Handley).

SAMUEL AND EMMA (HAYWARD) JONES. 3878.

Jessie H.,	3879	Acton,	Dec. 7, 1877
Howard L.,	3880	"	May 19, 1881

GEORGE WASHINGTON, JR. AND LOIS CONANT (HAYWARD) ROBBINS. 3864.

Geo. Wash'ton, Jr.,	3881	Concord,	Aug. 16, 1850
Clarence Aug'tus,	3882	Nashua, N. H.,	Jan. 30, '56

DAVID AND LUCY W. (HAYWARD) DOW. 3865.

Elvietta,	3883		Dec. 26, 1866

FRANCIS AND ELIZABETH M. (HAYWARD) CASSIDY. 3867.

Martha A.,	3884	Concord,	Apr. 17, 1869
Edward F.,	3885	"	Aug. 24, 1872

STEPHEN W. AND LAURA (HAYWARD) PAGE. 3868.

Abby J.,	3886		Dec. 19, 1871
Willie R.,	3887		Jan. 25, 1873
Walter S.,	3888		Feb. 9, 1877
Mary E.,	3889		Feb. 23, 1884

JAMES AND NANCY (HAYWARD) HAYWARD. 3858.

James Edwin,	3890	Concord, Apr. 19, 1832		Nov. 2, 1867	Mary Ann Hanscom; 1837–; dau. John M. and Ann
Eliza Ann (no issue),	3891	" June 26, 1833	Dec. 18, 1863	Oct. 25, 1857	Horace R. Hosmer. [(Woodman).
Harriet Ruth (no iss.),	3892	" Apr. 20, 1837	Jan. 15, 1863	Aug. 29, 1858	George Conant.
William Adolphus,	3893	" Feb. 28, 1838	May 28, 1838		
Nancy,	3894	" June 10, 1843	Oct. 12, 1861	Unmarried.	
Sarah Piece,	3895	" Apr. 15, 1847	June 16, 1849		

SILAS AND ABIGAIL (LAWRENCE) CONANT. 249.

(Continued page 69.)

	Abigail,	3896	Concord, Feb. 11, 1797	Nov. 29, 1815		
69	Silas,	3897	" Dec. 24, 1798	Sept. 4, 1865	Apr. 1, 1824	Sally Hayw'd; d. Cyrus and Sally (Pierce). [(French).
69	Joshua Lawrence,	3898	" Oct. 3, 1801	June 19, 1860	Apr. 29, 1828	Adaline Aug'ta Merriam; 1808–1865; d. Sam. and Ruth
69	Lois Potter,	3899	" Mar. 5, 1803	Oct. 15, 1840	Nov. 27, 1828	Jos. Haynes; 1799–1870; s. Luke and Lydia (Carr).
69	Sarah Fiske,	3900	" Sept. 25, 1805		May 3, 1827	Nathaniel Farmer; 1803–1880; s. Thomas and Harriet
						(Blodgett).

68

SILAS AND MARY (HAYWARD) CONANT. 250.

	Andrew,	3901	Concord,	Feb. 3, 1808		Sept. 8, 1831	Eliza Sawyer; dau. Leander and Cynthia.
	Nancy,	3902	"	May 3, 1810	Jan. 12, 1812		[ward).
69	Mary Ann	3903	"	Dec. 5, 1811		Sept. 6, 1836	Orville Giles; 1807–1878; son Luther and Eliz. (Hay-
	Nancy Hayward,	3904	"	Jan. 23, 1814	Sept. 28, 1814		[(Pierce).
69	Lucy Abigail,	3905	"	Mar. 23, 1816		Nov. 25, 1837	Sylvester Hayward; 1812–1883; son Cyrus and Sallie
	Elizabeth,	3906	"	Apr. 29, 1821	July 19, 1837		

SILAS AND SALLY (HAYWARD) CONANT. 3896.

69	Cyrus Hayward, {	3907	Concord,	July 30, 1825		Mar. 7, 1851	1. L. Frances Dunlap; 1833–1855.
		3908				May 1, 1857	2. Betsey M. Dox.
		3909				Nov. 13, 1861	3. Electa W. Russell.
47	Sarah Pierce,	3910	"	June 17, 1827	Nov. 26, 1858	Dec. 9, 1852	Charles Mason Barrett. No. 2603. [(Woodman).
69	George Henry,	3911	"	July 30, 1829		Nov. 29, 1856	Emma Frances Hanscom; 1833–; d. John M. and Ann
69	Ellen Ruth,	3912	"	June 4, 1833	Jan. 18, 1864	Oct. 26, 1856	Dwight Leverett Dimock; 1828–.
	Mary Ann,	3913	"	Oct. 13, 1835	Feb. 13, 1854		
	Silas,	3914	"	Aug. 22, 1839		Sept. 2, 1860	Angeronia S. Tarbell.
	Andrew,	3915	"	June 16, 1841			

CYRUS HAYWARD AND L. FRANCES (DUNLAP) CONANT. 3907.

	Francis H.,	3916	Concord,	July 6, 1853	Sept. 21, 1853

GEORGE HENRY AND EMMA FRANCES (HANSCOM) CONANT. 3911.

	Dwight Henry,	3917	Concord,	May 28, 1857	Oct. 18, 1866
	Charles H.,	3918	"	Nov. 11, 1860	

DWIGHT L. AND ELLEN R. (CONANT) DIMOCK. 3912.

	Dwight Hersey,	3919	Lowell,	Oct. 16, 1862

JOSHUA L. AND ADALINE A. (MERRIAM) CONANT. 3898.

	Adaline Augusta,	3920	Lowell,	Aug. 4, 1829		Dec. 3, 1861	Charles Mason Barrett. No. 2604.
69	William Andrew,	3921	"	July 28, 1831	Jan. 9, 1880	Apr. 15, 1855	Euseba Fowle Vinton.
69	Martha Ann,	3922	"	May 11, 1835		Nov. 26, 1857	Zemira Chase.
	John Merriam,	3923	"	June 7, 1844			Rebecca Vans.

WILLIAM ANDREW AND EUSEBA FOWLE (VINTON) CONANT. 3921.

	Nellie Euseba,	3924	Boston,	Mar. 25, 1858		Frank Zindle.

ZEMIRA AND MARTHA ANN (CONANT) CHASE. 3922.

	Mira Conant,	3925		Dec. 11, 1858		Sept. 23, 1883	John H. Wiley.

JOSEPH AND LOIS POTTER (CONANT) HAYNES. 3899.

69	Louise Conant,	3926	Sudbury,	Dec. 7, 1829	Sept. 30, 1870	Dec. 12, 1854	C. N. Davenport; 1830–1882; s. C. N. & Lucy (White).

CHARLES NEWTON AND LOUISA C. (HAYNES) DAVENPORT. 3926.

69	Charles Haynes,	3927	Wilmington, Vt., Mar. 25, 1856		June 17, 1884	Anna Potter Laughton; d. Eben O. and Cyrene M.
	Herbert Joseph,	3928	" Aug. 10, 1861			[(Potter).

CHARLES HAYNES AND ANNA POTTER (LAUGHTON) DAVENPORT. 3927.

	Louise Haynes,	3929	Brattleboro', Vt., Apr. 11, 1885	

NATHANIEL AND SARAH FISKE (CONANT) FARMER. 3900.

	John,	3930	Lowell,	Sept. 13, 1829	Oct. 4, 1829		
	Sarah Jane,	3931	"	Dec. 31, 1831	Dec. 23, 1845		
	Sar'h Jane (by adoption),	3932	"	Jan. 18, 1840		June 3, 1860	William Leonard Rugg; 1837–; son Reuben and Sarah
							[Ann (Leonard).

ORVILLE AND MARY ANN (CONANT) GILES. 3903.

69	Eliza Ann,	3933	Newfi'ld, Me., Dec. 22, 1837		Apr. 15, 1856	Charles Kinney Ball; 1829–1878; son Ebenezer and
	Andrew Conant,	3934	", Dec. 16, 1839	May 20, 1865		[Sally (Kinney).
	James Edwin,	3935	" Oct. 16, 1842	May 12, 1845		
	Albert Henry,	3936	" Feb. 14, 1845	Feb. 22, 1845		
	Mary Louise,	3937	Tewksb'ry, Aug. 5, 1846	Dec. 21, 1865		
	Frank Leander,	3938	Bedford, N. H., June 8, 1849	Aug. 28, 1849		

CHARLES KINNEY AND ELIZA ANN (GILES) BALL. 3933.

	Rena Emogene,	3939	Bedford, N. H., Aug. 11, 1858	Apr. 7, 1878
	George Eugene,	3940	" Sept. 22, 1862	

SYLVESTER AND LUCY ABIGAIL (CONANT) HAYWARD. 3905.

	Elizabeth Conant,	3941	Concord,	Dec. 5, 1838	Apr. 9, 1854		
	Ada Jane (no issue),	3942	"	Apr. 5, 1845	Sept. 6, 1866		Francis Chamberlin; son Joseph. [(Ward).
69	Lillian Lander,	3943	Bedford, N. H., Apr. 3, 1850		Nov. 30, 1882	Jewett Newton Darling; 1851–; s. Elisha and Tamison
69	Henry Walden,	3944	Concord, Dec. 30, 1855		Nov. 4, 1879	Susan B. Barnes; 1860–; d. W. B. & S. A. (Carpenter).

JEWETT N. AND LILLIAN L. (HAYWARD) DARLING. 3943.

	Roger Conant,	3945	Charlton, Feb. 4, 1884	

HENRY W. AND SUSAN B. (BARNES) HAYWARD. 3944.

	Ralph Waldo,	3946	Charlton, Feb. 8, 1881	
	Wm. Bradbury,	3947	" Aug. 8, 1884	

JAMES AND SEBA (DAVIS) CONANT. 252.

	Suseba Wright,	3948		Apr. 14, 1811
	Louisa,	3949		Sept. 26, 1812
	James Franklin,	3950		Nov. 23, 1814
	Jesse Davis,	3951		Oct. 22, 1818

SIMON AND HANNAH (POTTER-BROWN) DAVIS. 272–552. (Continued page 70.)

	Elizabeth,	3952	Concord, Mar. 8, 1719–20	

	Name	No.	Birthplace & Date	Death	Marriage	Spouse
	Simon,	3953	Concord, Apr. 21, 1722			
	Hannah,	3954	" June 9, 1724			
	Lucy,	3955	" June 26, 1726			
70	Nehemiah,	3956	" Apr. 23, 1728	Mar. 10, 1782		Dorothy ——; 1730–1805.
	Mary,	3957	" Dec. 9, 1730			
	Elenor,	3958	" Nov. 25, 1733	Aug. 19, 1739		
	Moses,	3959	" Jan. 23, 1736	Nov. 8, 1736		

NEHEMIAH AND DOROTHY (   ) DAVIS. 3956.

	Name	No.	Birthplace & Date	Death	Marriage	Spouse
	Elizabeth Lydia,	3960	Concord, Nov. 22, 1757			
	Sarah,	3961	" Dec. 10, 1759			
	Asa,	3962	" Aug. 13, 1770			

ELEAZER AND EUNICE (POTTER) DAVIS. 284–549.

	Name	No.	Birthplace & Date	Death	Marriage	Spouse
70	Eleazer,	3963	Concord, Mar. 5, 1705-6	Sept. 12, 1748	June 17, 1731	Rebecca Chandler; 1711-.
	Hannah,	3964	" Oct. 18, 1707		Apr. 12, 1765	Benjamin Wheeler.
72	Timothy,	3965	" Dec. 8, 1709	1800	Feb. 9, 1737	Hannah Smith; 1716–1787.
	Sarah,	3966	" Mar. 23, 1711-12		Sept. 1, 1736	Isaac Merriam.
	Eunice,	3967	" Dec. 18, 1716		Nov. 22, 1748	William Marshall.
	Rebecca,	3968	" May 13, 1719		Feb. 3, 1749	Ezra Wheeler; 1717–1798.
	Abigail,	3969	" May 16, 1721		May 17, 1741	Ezekiel Davis.

ELEAZER AND REBECCA (CHANDLER) DAVIS. 3963.

	Name	No.	Birthplace & Date	Death	Marriage	Spouse
70	Eleazer,	3970	Concord, May 30, 1734		Sept. 3, 1756	1. Mary Davis.
70		3971			Feb. 23, 1764	2. Rebecca Putnam.
	Rebecca,	3972	" Aug. 2, 1736		Oct. 14, 1755	Zachariah Fitch.
	Elizabeth,	3973	" July 2, 1739	Feb. 6, 1750		
	Abigail,	3974	" Oct. 23, 1741		Aug. 9, 1759	Solomon Hartwell.
	Sarah,	3975	" Oct. 13, 1743		Oct. 27, 1761	Jonathan Fassett.
	Samuel,	3976	" Aug. 2, 1747	Feb. 17, 1750		

ELEAZER AND MARY (DAVIS) DAVIS. 3970.

	Name	No.	Birthplace & Date	Death	Marriage	Spouse
	Mary,	3977	Concord, Aug. 19, 1760			
	Rebecca,	3978	" June 18,	Oct. 16, 1844	Unmarried.	

ELEAZER AND REBECCA (PUTNAM) DAVIS. 3971.

	Name	No.	Birthplace & Date	Death	Marriage	Spouse
70	Betsey,	3979	Bedford, Feb. 16, 1765	Aug. 13, 1799	Aug. 14, 1793	Joseph Adams; 1757–1830; son John and Abigail.
101	Lucy,	3980	" July 11, 1766	Aug. 16, 1852	Oct. 7, 1790	Timothy Hartwell; 1765–1830; son Joseph.
71	Eleazer,	3981	" Jan. 13, 1768	Aug. 22, 1841	Jan. 1, 1799	Martha Skinner; 1774–1865.
98	Joanna,	3982	" Aug. 19, 1769	Oct. 30, 1808	Oct. 13, 1796	William Hartwell; 1770–1819; son Joseph.
71	Sarah,	3983	" Aug. 19, 1769	Jan. 31, 1861	June 21, 1796	Job Webber; 1769–1838. [Lot and Martha. 227.
72	Abigail,	3984	" Aug. 8, 1774	Apr. 6, 1843	June 26, 1794	Levi Conant; 1767–1842; s. Wm. and great-grandson of
	Hannah,	3985	" Aug. 26, 1775		Aug. 7, 1804	James Webber.

JOSEPH AND BETSEY (DAVIS) ADAMS. 3979.

	Name	No.	Birthplace & Date	Death	Marriage	Spouse
70	Mary,	3986	Littleton, May 3, 1794	Mar. 12, 1872	Unmarried.	
70	James,	3987	" May 2, 1796	June 1, 1863	Oct. 17, 1822	1. Roxalana Hoar; 1802–1838. [Mary (McNeil).
70		3988				2. Jane Thomas Robinson; 1803–; dau. David and
84	Betsey,	3989	" Apr. 18, 1797		Sept. 25, 1817	David Heard; 1793–1881; s. David & Sibyl (Sherman).
	Lovey,	3990	" June 22, 1798			[(Gates).
71	Benjamin,	3991	" Aug. 9, 1799	July 12, 1876	Aug. 7, 1824	Charlotte Hudson; 1799–; dau. Melzar and Catharine

JAMES AND ROXALANA (HOAR) ADAMS. 3987.

	Name	No.	Birthplace & Date	Death	Marriage	Spouse
	Daniel Hoar,	3992	Concord, Aug. 21, 1823		Nov. 24, 1842	Sarah Ann Pratt; 1824–1848; dau. Alvan and Sarah
	Roxalana,	3993	" Nov. 1, 1824	Nov. 11, 1824		[Ann (Marble).
70	Henry William,	3994	" Nov. 17, 1825		Aug. 31, 1848	Nancy Jackson Wright; 1828–; dau. Abel and Vara-
	William Henry,	3995	" Nov. 17, 1825	June 25, 1826		[zina (Tower).
	Mary Jane,	3996	" June 8,-1828	Mar. 13, 1830		
	Joseph Nelson,	3997	" Apr. 2, 1830	June 28, 1831		
	Lucy Ann,	3998	" Apr. 17, 1832	Nov. 23, 1832		
	Simon Rogers,	3999	" Aug. 11, 1833	Sept. 17, 1833		
	Georgianna,	4000	" Oct. 17, 1834	Sept. 1, 1853		[oline R. (Kimball).
70	James, Jr.,	4001	" Aug. 8, 1836		May 2, 1865	Sarah Serena Tash; 1837–; dau. Nathan B. and Car-

JAMES AND JANE T. (ROBINSON) ADAMS. 3988.

	Name	No.	Birthplace & Date	Death	Marriage	Spouse
70	Caroline,	4002	Concord, Oct. 1, 1843		Feb. 17, 1861	Charles Adison Hemingway; 1838–; son Daniel and
	Jennie May,	4003	" Sept. 15, 1845	Aug. 6, 1866		[Tabitha P. (Wiley).

HENRY WILLIAM AND NANCY JACKSON (WRIGHT) ADAMS. 3994.

	Name	No.	Birthplace & Date	Death	Marriage	Spouse
70	Flora Louise,	4004	Cooperstown, N. Y., July 6, 1851		Jan. 4, 1871	Oscar Cutler Hatch; 1848–; s. Geo. & Hannah (Vance)
70	George Henry,	4005	Wells River, Vt., Mar. 9, 1857		June 12, 1878	Martha Frances Sherman; 1853–; dau. Ashael and
	Nellie Roxalana,	4006	" June 1, 1861	Oct. 20, 1864		[Elizabeth (Newton).
	Mary Josie,	4007	" May 4, 1869	Nov. 5, 1871		

OSCAR C. AND FLORA L. (ADAMS) HATCH. 4004.

	Name	No.	Birthplace & Date	Death	Marriage	Spouse
	Leslie Adams,	4008	Littleton, N. H., Jan. 17, 1876			
	Henry Oscar,	4009	" May 11, 1877			
	George Arthur,	4010	" May 12, 1882	Nov. 30, 1883		
	Margaret Eliz.,	4011	" Dec. 19, 1885			

GEORGE HENRY AND MARTHA FRANCES (SHERMAN) ADAMS. 4005.

	Name	No.	Birthplace & Date	Death	Marriage	Spouse
	George Harold,	4012	Waltham, Oct. 31, 1879			
	Roxalana,	4013	" Aug. 2, 1883			

JAMES, JR., AND SARAH S. (TASH) ADAMS. 4001.

	Name	No.	Birthplace & Date	Death	Marriage	Spouse
	Forest Nathan,	4014	Natick, Sept. 27, 1866			

CHARLES A. AND CAROLINE (ADAMS) HEMINGWAY. 4002.

	Name	No.	Birthplace & Date	Death	Marriage	Spouse
	Jennie Adams,	4015	Framingham, Oct., 1861		Dec. 30, 1885	Albert Littlefield.
	Charles Freddie,	4016	" Dec. 24, 1866	July 6, 1873		
	Charles Bertie,	4017	" Jan. 23, 1882	Jan. 26, 1882		

BENJAMIN AND CHARLOTTE (HUDSON) ADAMS. 3991.

	Name	No.	Birth	Death	Married	Spouse
81	Chas. Kingman,	4018	Concord, Dec. 3, 1825		Oct. 21, 1851	Mary Elizabeth Bayley; 1829–; dau. Edward H. and
	Charlotte Cath'ine,	4019	Bangor, Me., Aug. 2, 1828	Aug. 31, 1828		[Mary (Jones).
	Henry Hudson,	4020	" July 30, 1829	Aug. 5, 1829		
	Winslow Chase,	4021	" June 2, 1831	Nov. 29, 1831		
	Ellen Jane,	4022	" Apr. 12, 1834			[Betsey (Williams).
84	Mary Catharine,	4023	" Apr. 29, 1841		Apr. 30, 1860	William Henry Kirkpatrick; 1836–; son James and

ELEAZER AND MARTHA (SKINNER) DAVIS. 3981.

	Name	No.	Birth	Death	Married	Spouse
	Betsey,	4024	Bedford, Dec. 26, 1799	Aug. 14, 1879	Unmarried.	[(Spofford).
71	John Skinner,	4025	" May 6, 1801	Nov. 26, 1875	Oct. 1, 1839	Lucy Chaplin; 1803–1878; d. Eliphalet and Martha
	Mary,	4026	" May 22, 1803	Jan. 9, 1843	Unmarried.	[Anna (Harrington) Winship.
71	Eleazer Page, }	4027	" Jan. 30, 1805		Mar. 15, 1831	1. Emily (Winship) Reed; 1797–1831; d. Thos. and
71	{	4028			Apr. 7, 1842	2. Susan Maria Sayles; 1816–1876; d. Ezekiel and
	Susan (no issue),	4029	" Jan. 7, 1807	June 17, 1869	Oct. 20, 1846	Lewis P. Gleason; 1799–1885. [Lydia (Wilbur).
	Martha Joanna,	4030	" Oct. 5, 1808	Feb. 10, 1817		
	Benjamin Josiah,	4031	" Dec. 20, 1810			
	Hannah Skinner,	4032	" May 25, 1813	July 22, 1831	Unmarried.	
	Samuel,	4033	" Aug. 15, 1815			
	Martha Maria,	4034	" Sept. 7, 1817	May 24, 1884	Unmarried.	
	George E.,	4035	" Sept. 7, 1819	Jan. 20, 1851		

JOHN SKINNER AND LUCY (CHAPLIN) DAVIS. 4025.

	Name	No.	Birth	Death	Married	Spouse
	John Chaplin,	4036	Lexington, Mar. 15, 1841	Sept. 15, 1841		
	Martha Chaplin,	4037	" June 18, 1845			

ELEAZER PAGE AND EMILY (WINSHIP-REED) DAVIS. 4027.

	Name	No.	Birth	Death	Married	Spouse
	Emily Maria,	4038	Bedford, June 13, 1831			

ELEAZER PAGE AND SUSAN M. (SAYLES) DAVIS. 4028.

	Name	No.	Birth	Death	Married	Spouse
71	Ellen Amelia,	4039	Bedford, Mar. 10, 1845		Mar. 30, 1865	Abel P. Fitch; 1838–; son Abel and Nancy (Bacon).
71	Abby Caroline,	4040	" Sept. 14, 1846		July 22, 1869	Chas. H. Clark; 1837–; s. Joseph & Lucinda (Davis).
	Mary Susan,	4041	" Jan. 15, 1852	May 6, 1875		
	George Page,	4042	" Mar. 11, 1858			

ABEL P. AND ELLEN AMELIA (DAVIS) FITCH. 4039.

	Name	No.	Birth	Death	Married	Spouse
	Winfred Porter,	4043	Aug. 3, 1870			
	Alice Maria,	4044	Jan. 5, 1872			
	Horace Wilbur,	4045	Apr. 6, 1874	Aug. 8, 1874		

CHARLES H. AND ABBY C. (DAVIS) CLARK. 4040.

	Name	No.	Birth	Death	Married	Spouse
	Eugene,	4046	Apr. 17, 1870			
	Herbert Leslie,	4047	Jan. 31, 1880			
	Myron Henry,	4048	July 25, 1881			

JOB AND SARAH (DAVIS) WEBBER. 3983.

	Name	No.	Birth	Death	Married	Spouse
	John,	4049	Littleton, Apr. 25, 1797	Sept. 24, 1879		Lydia Stevens.
71	Sally,	4050	" June 9, 1798	Dec. 27, 1857	Jan. 1, 1834	Jas. Park; 1795–1882; son Alex. & Martha (Betton).
	Nancy,	4051	" June 9, 1798	Mar. 6, 1879	Unmarried.	
71	Artemus, Dea.,	4052	" May 3, 1800	Dec. 19, 1846	May 20, 1827	Sarah Wyman Richardson; 1804–1874.
85	Job Page,	4053	" Nov. 23, 1801	Feb. 19, 1875	Feb. 1, 1823	Tabitha Abraham Jones; 1803–; dau. Timothy and
	Eliza Farley,	4054	" June 12, 1805	Jan. 21, 1839	Unmarried.	[Betsey (Abraham).
84	Benj. Newton,	4055	" Aug. 24, 1812		Sept. 12, 1837	Ann Hill; 1816–1883; d. John & Mary (Cunningham).

JAMES AND SALLY (WEBBER) PARK. 4050.

	Name	No.	Birth	Death	Married	Spouse
	Eliza Farley,	4056	Windham, Vt., Dec. 21, 1838			

ARTEMUS AND SARAH WYMAN (RICHARDSON) WEBBER. 4052.

	Name	No.	Birth	Death	Married	Spouse
71	Marcus Bruce,	4057	Bedford, Mar. 9, 1828	Feb. 12, 1886	Nov. 22, 1852	Eliz. Frances Gleason; d. Lewis P. & Lucy (Butler).
71	Sarah Abigail,	4058	" Jan. 23, 1830	Dec. 23, 1876	Mar. 11, 1852	Henry Augustus Gleason; 1829–; son Lewis P. and
	Ruth Adelaide,	4059	" Feb. 16, 1834			[Lucy (Butler).
72	Maria Cordelia,	4060	" Dec. 4, 1837		May 1, 1861	Alvah Cotton; –1882.

MARCUS BRUCE AND ELIZABETH FRANCES (GLEASON) WEBBER. 4057.

	Name	No.	Birth	Death	Married	Spouse
	Kate Putnam,	4061	Bedford, Jan. 21, 1855	Aug. 12, 1864		[A. (Smith).
71	Wallace Gleason,	4062	" Aug. 13, 1856		June 22, 1881	Mary Augusta Putnam; 1860–; d. Wm. A. and Mary
	Carrie Maria,	4063	" Aug. 9, 1858	May 23, 1881		
	Arthur Wyman,	4064	" Sept. 9, 1860	May 15, 1883		
	Henry Francis,	4065	" Dec. 7, 1862	Oct. 22, 1864		
	Warren Putnam,	4066	" May 12, 1864	Feb. 28, 1866		
	Marion Waldo,	4067	" Oct. 21, 1865			
	Alfred Augustus,	4068	" Nov. 28, 1868			
	Alden Brown,	4069	" Nov. 28, 1868			
	Lizzie Frances,	4070	" Jan. 15, 1871			
	Olive Putnam,	4071	" Nov. 19, 1872			
	Lewis Butler,	4072	" June 4, 1875	Oct. 4, 1875		
	Marcus Howard,	4073	" Aug. 10, 1876	Nov. 2, 1876		

WALLACE GLEASON AND MARY AUGUSTA (PUTNAM) WEBBER. 4062.

	Name	No.	Birth	Death	Married	Spouse
	Carrie Putnam,	4074	Bedford, June 3, 1882			
	Paul Barron,	4075	" Apr. 27, 1884			

HENRY AUGUSTUS AND SARAH ABIGAIL (WEBBER) GLEASON. 4058.

	Name	No.	Birth	Death	Married	Spouse
	Frank Waldo,	4076	Bedford, Mar. 25, 1853		June 3, 1885	Mary Isabella Wood.
	Alfred Webber,	4077	" Nov. 30, 1855			
72	Mary Wilder,	4078	" Jan. 25, 1857		June 1, 1886	Edward Gardner Pierce.
	Herbert Lewis,	4079	" Sept. 15, 1861			
	Henry Walter,	4080	Woburn, Jan. 29, 1866		Sept. 25, 1886	Eda M. Titus.
	Herman Page,	4081	" Jan. 9, 1871			

EDWARD G. AND MARY W. (GLEASON) PIERCE. 4078.

	Lewis Edward,	4082	Woburn, May 16, 1882			

ALVAH AND MARIA CORDELIA (WEBBER) COTTON. 4060.

	Arthur Edgerly,	4083	Woburn, July 26, 1864			
	Marcus Howard,	4084	" Feb. 4, 1867			
	Alvah Chester,	4085	" Jan. 26, 1869			
	Edwin Clark,	4086	" June 11, 1872			

LEVI AND ABIGAIL (DAVIS) CONANT. 3984.

97	Benjamin,	4087	Harvard, July 13, 1795	July 25, 1834	Feb. 14, 1826	Cynthia Lewis; 1800–; d. Jesse and Azubah (Hallett).
98	Rebekah,	4088	" Jan. 23, 1797	Aug. 1, 1870	1820	Robert Gardner Wilson; 1782–1858.
	Sewall,	4089	" Oct. 13, 1798	1850	Unmarried.	
	Abigail,	4090	" Mar. 31, 1800	1826	"	
	Eliza,	4091	" Aug. 6, 1801	1828		Otis Jefferson.
98	Lucinda,	4092	" Apr. 28, 1803	Mar. 13, 1844	Oct. 19, 1827	Samuel Mead; –1856.
97	Geo. Washington,	4093	" Apr. 10, 1805	Dec. 1, 1884	Apr. 16, 1829	Anna Stevens; 1809–; d. Wm. and Anna (Mead).
97	Levi, Jr.,	4094	" Feb. 6, 1810		May 4, 1836	Anna Whitney Mead; 1809–1873; d Abraham and Lucy (Kimball). [(Whitaker).
97	Henry,	4095	" Sept. 18, 1815		Sept. 18, 1838	Harriet Ann Blood; 1817–; dau. Jonathan and Eliza

TIMOTHY AND HANNAH (SMITH) DAVIS. 3966.

	Timothy,	4096	Townsend, May 16, 1738	Died young.		
	Joseph,	4097	" Feb. 20, 1739–40		Feb. 14, 1769	Sarah Campbell.
	Joshua,	4098	" May 8, 1744			
	Lucy,	4099	" May 22, 1746	1747		
	Lucy,	4100	July 10, 1748		Sept. 24, 1771	Thomas Eaton.
	Eleazer,	4101	May 3, 1751		Mar. 4, 1779	Martha Stevens.
	Josiah,	4102	May 24, 1753		Mar. 4, 1779	Sarah Sawtelle.
	Joel,	4103	July 31, 1755			—— Chary.
	Reuben,	4104	1757	1767		
72	Timothy,	4105	Feb. 2, 1760	Feb. 7, 1826	Oct. 3, 1782	Betty Flagg; 1759–; d. Wm. and Lydia (Child).
	Mary,	4106	Feb. 2, 1760			

TIMOTHY AND BETTY (FLAGG) DAVIS. 4105.

72	Seth, Hon.,	4107	Ashby, Sept. 3, 1787		Oct. 27, 1810	1. Mary Durell, 1789–1867; d. John & Mary(Winch'ter).
		4108			July 1, 1868	2. Mary J. Glidden; d. John and Eliza (Braun).
72	Asa,	4109	" Feb. 14, 1793	May 7, 1847		Alice (Williams) McLay; 1790–1862; d. Wm. and Ab-
72	Betsey,	4110	" June 28, 1796		June 25, 1818	Abner Proctor; 1785–1868. [igail (Harris) Williams.
	Timothy,	4111	" Apr. 26, 1798			Abigail Wellington.
	William,	4112	" Nov. 17, 1803	1839		Eunice Turner.

HON. SETH AND MARY (DURELL) DAVIS. 4107.

	Mary W.,	4113	Nov. 27, 1813	Nov. 12, 1842	May 7, 1835	Rev. Augustus W. Willard.
	Harris L.,	4114	Feb. 24, 1829	Mar. 12, 1853		

ASA AND ALICE (WILLIAMS-McLAY) DAVIS. 4109.

	Asa,	4115	Townsend,	Died young.		
	Matilda,	4116	East Cambridge,	"		
72	Watson H.,	4117	" Oct., 1825			1. Julia Gove; –1851.
		4118				2. Mrs. Charlotte Daniels.
72	Granville C.,	4119	" Aug. 23, 1828		July 1, 1851	Ann H. Kendall.
	Emily,	4120	" May, 1834			Josiah Bartlett.

WATSON H. AND JULIA (GOVE) DAVIS. 4117.

	Julia,	4121	1847			
	Alice,	4122	1849			

GRANVILLE C. AND ANN H. (KENDALL) DAVIS. 4119.

	Frank G., Rev.,	4123	Shirley, Dec. 8, 1852		Oct. 28, 1880	Lillian F. Crow.
	Herbert G.,	4124	Pepcrell, Dec. 10, 1855	Apr. 20, 1856		
	Julia E.,	4125	Shirley, Dec. 5, 1856		Apr. 7, 1872	Lawrence Benningham.
	Nellie J.,	4126	" Dec. 15, 1866			
	Evelena,	4127	" Sept. 3, 1870			

ABNER AND BETSEY (DAVIS) PROCTOR. 4110.

72	Mary E.,	4128	Dec. 14, 1819		Feb., 1843	Albert Turner.
72	Abner, Jr.,	4129	June 9, 1821		July 17, 1845	Emeline Brown; 1832–; d. John and Hepzabah.
73	Oliver,	4130	July 2, 1823		Oct. 13, 1858	Catharine U. Griswold. No. 1549.
	Sarah M.,	4131	Apr. 12, 1825		Sept. 10, 1878	Ralph Ball.
73	Abigail,	4132	Jan. 6, 1827		Nov. 26, 1853	Charles Hastings; 1823–.
73	Malvina,	4133	Oct. 12, 1829		July 21, 1863	John Selden Angus; 1830–.
	Lydia C.,	4134	Feb. 26, 1832		Nov. 1, 1877	James Phillips Farley; 1816–1884.
	Emily,	4135	Apr. 1, 1834	Dec. 16, 1839		
	Clementine,	4136	Dec. 24, 1838	Oct. 18, 1840		

ALBERT AND MARY E. (PROCTOR) TURNER. 4128.

	Albert Davis,	4137	Dec. 4, 1843		June 1, 1871	Abbie Spaulding.
72	Abbie Clementine,	4138	Aug. 19, 1847		Oct. 13, 1881	Eugene R. Kilburn.

EUGENE R. AND ABBIE C. (TURNER) KILBURN. 4138.

	Albert Sidney,	4139	Aug. 24, 1882			
	Farley Eugene,	4140	Apr. 19, 1884			

ABNER, JR., AND EMELINE (BROWN) PROCTOR. 4129.

	Laura Emma,	4141	Sept. 21, 1848	Aug. 30, 1849		
72	Mary Ada,	4142	Dec. 29, 1850		Sept. 29, 1866	Wm. Franklin Merritt; 1846–; s. Wm. and Mary A.

WILLIAM F. AND MARY ADA (PROCTOR) MERRITT. 4142.

	Mabel Louise,	4143	Dec. 17, 1867	Oct. 1, 1880		

OLIVER AND CATHARINE U. (GRISWOLD) PROCTOR. 4130-1549.

Milo Griswold,	4144		Apr. 4, 1861		
Edward Oliver,	4145		Mar. 21, 1869		
Galen Abner,	4146		Sept. 19, 1871		

CHARLES AND ABIGAIL (PROCTOR) HASTINGS. 4132.

George Herbert,	4147		Aug. 14, 1854		
Emily Proctor,	4148		June 29, 1856		
Percy Wellington,	4149		Feb. 8, 1861		
Nellie Elizabeth,	4150		Aug. 4, 1865	Nov. 13, 1883	
Charles Alfred,	4151		June 7, 1870		

JOHN S. AND MALVINA (PROCTOR) ANGUS. 4133.

Marshall Proctor,	4152		Sept. 4, 1864	Sept. 9, 1869	

SAMUEL AND MERCY (HOAR) FARRAR. 314.

73	Samuel,	4153	Lincoln,	Dec. 13, 1773	Jan. 22, 1848	Oct. 30, 1814	Phebe (Edwards) Hooker.
	James,	4154	"	Oct. 12, 1776	Oct. 9, 1867	Jan. 16, 1806	1. Nancy Barrett. No. 2540.
		4155				Feb. 20, 1812	2. Mary Fiske Hoar; –1813.
		4156				Jan. 16, 1815	3. Dorcas Chapin.
	John, Prof.,	4157	"	May 1, 1779			1. Lucy Maria Buckminster.
		4158					2. Eliza Rotch.
	Rebecca,	4159	"	Nov. 21, 1782	July 5, 1784		
	Rebecca,	4160	"	Dec. 21, 1785		Dec. 5, 1804	Rev. Jonathan French.

JAMES AND DORCAS (CHAPIN) FARRAR. 4156.

	Samuel,	4161	Lincoln,	1816	1838		
	George,	4162	"	1818	Jan. 18, 1851	1848	Julia Carlton.
73	James,	4163	"	Sept. 22, 1820		Mar. 19, 1845	Adeline Hyde.
73	John Williams,	4164	"	Jan. 20, 1823		Oct. 25, 1848	Elizabeth D. French.

JAMES AND ADELINE (HYDE) FARRAR. 4163.

George,	4165	Lincoln,	Dec. 4, 1849		
Samuel,	4166	"	Aug. 4, 1851		
Mary Bradley,	4167	"	Oct. 6, 1853		
Abbie Chapin,	4168	"	Nov. 30, 1855	Aug. 31, 1876	
James Hyde,	4169	"	July 19, 1858		
Edward Rogers,	4170	"	Mar. 17, 1863		

JOHN W. AND ELIZABETH D. (FRENCH) FARRAR. 4164.

73	Julia Carlton,	4171	Lincoln,	Jan. 22, 1851		Oct. 17, 1872	1. Amos Prescott Sherman; –1882.
		4172				Sept. 2, 1884	2. Horace Winslow Warren.
73	Eliza Rotch,	4173	"	Dec. 10, 1853		Oct. 24, 1878	Charles Stearns Wheeler.
73	John French,	4174	"	Aug. 31, 1856		Oct. 27, 1881	Susan A. Giles.
	Herbert Williams,	4175	"	Nov. 28, 1858			
	Rebecca Dora,	4176	"	Oct. 30, 1860			
	Lizzie French,	4177	"	Oct. 5. 1862	Mar. 19, 1873		
	Anna Hazen,	4178	"	Aug. 21, 1865			
	Grace,	4179	"	Mar. 6, 1868			

AMOS P. AND JULIA C. (FARRAR) SHERMAN. 4171.

Annie Prescott,	4180		Jan. 9, 1874		
Carlton Farrar,	4181		Oct. 23, 1877		

CHARLES S. AND ELIZABETH R. (FARRAR) WHEELER. 4173.

Julia,	4182		1879	1880	
Mary Louise,	4183		Nov. 27, 1880		
Elizabeth French,	4184		May 19, 1884		

JOHN F. AND SUSAN A. (GILES) FARRAR. 4174.

Herbert G.,	4185		Jan. 29, 1883		

TIMOTHY AND ANNA (BANCROFT) FARRAR. 319.

73	Timothy,	4186		Mar. 17, 1788		Sept. 14, 1817	Sarah Adams; 1789–.

TIMOTHY AND SARAH (ADAMS) FARRAR. 4186.

73	Anna Bancroft,	4187		Mar. 20, 1819		Jan. 25, 1842	Edward Crane; 1816–.
	Sarah Elizabeth,	4188		Sept. 5, 1820		May 16, 1848	William Craige Burke, M. D.; 1812–.

EDWARD AND ANNA (BANCROFT) CRANE. 4187.

Timothy Farrar,	4189		Feb. 8, 1843		
Mary Ospah,	4190		Oct. 27, 1844		
Edward Barrows,	4191		May 8, 1849		

THOMAS AND PRUDENCE (HOSMER) HOSMER. 437-440.

	Lucy,	4192	Concord,				
73	Joseph, Maj.,	4193	"	Dec. 25, 1735	Jan. 31, 1821		Lucy Barnes.
	Persis,	4194	"				
	Dinah,	4195	"				
	Lydia,	4196	"				
	Benjamin,	4197	"				

MAJ. JOSEPH AND LUCY (BARNES) HOSMER. 4193.

	Lucy,	4198	Concord,		Died young.		
	Lavinia,	4199	"				Abel Davis.
74	Cyrus,	4200	"	Feb. 28, 1865	May 3, 1818	Aug. 30, 1792	Patty Barrett. No. 1908.
	Lucinda,	4201	"				Timothy Brooks.
	Rufus,	4202	"	1779	1832		

CYRUS AND PATTY (BARRETT) HOSMER. 4200–1908.

	Patty,	4203	Concord, Sept. 2, 1793	Feb. 23, 1814		
74	Cyrus,	4204	" Sept. 15, 1795	Dec. 19, 1833	Jan. 23, 1823	Lydia Parkman Wheeler; 1800–1884; dau. Ephraim.
74	Rebecca Prescott,	4205	" Nov. 28, 1797	Apr. 17, 1882	Sept. 14, 1818	Henry Francis Cogswell; 1796–1881.
	Washington,	4206	" Aug. 1, 1800	Jan. 5, 1803		[(Poor).
74	Geo. Wash., Rev.,	4207	" Nov. 27, 1803	July 5, 1881	Apr. 25, 1831	Hannah P. Kendall; 1805–; d. Rev. John and Sarah
74	Meliscent,	4208	" Feb. 6, 1806	May, 1843	Sept. 16, 1828	Jacob B. Farmer.
	Elizabeth,	4209	" Nov. 8, 1810	1840	Jan. 19, 1832	Joshua Buttrick; –1851.

CYRUS AND LYDIA P. (WHEELER) HOSMER. 4204.

	Sarah Parkman,	4210	Concord, June 7, 1824	Feb. 1, 1885	Unmarried.	
	Joseph Henry,	4211	" Sept. 19, 1826	July 10, 1831		[(Holden).
99	Martha,	4212	" June 17, 1829		June 15, 1848	Andrew Jackson Harlow; 1824–; s. Ellis and Miriam
99	Henry Joseph,	4213	" Feb. 2, 1832		Dec. 3, 1874	Laura Anna (Ballou) Whiting; 1833–; d. Hosea, 3d, [and Lydia (Hines).
99	Cyrus, 3d,	4214	" Nov. 17, 1833	Apr. 9, 1885	June 17, 1873	Anna Eliza Prescott; 1839–; d. Phineas G. and Sarah
103	Lydia,	4215	" Nov. 17, 1833		Jan. 1, 1861	Daniel Heald Wood. No. 2054. [(Salisbury).

REV. GEORGE WASHINGTON AND HANNAH P. (KENDALL) HOSMER. 4207.

	Edward Jarvis,	4216	May 29, 1832	July 29, 1834		
74	Jas. Kendall, Prof., {	4217	Northfield, Mass., Jan. 29, 1834		Oct. 15, 1863	1. Elizabeth Adelaide Cutler; –1877.
74	{	4218			Nov. 27, 1878	2. Jenny Persis Garland.
74	William Rufus,	4219	July 31, 1835		June 20, 1871	Josephine Louisa Grant.
74	Geo. Herbert, Rev.,	4220	May 14, 1839		Dec. 10, 1868	Julia W. Sheldon.
	Anna H.,	4221	Oct. 21, 1841		Oct. 21, 1862	Rev. William H. Savary.
	Ella,	4222	Oct. 21, 1841	Oct. 27, 1842		
	Edward Jarvis,	4223	July 12, 1843	Jan. 24, 1863		

PROF. JAMES KENDALL AND ELIZABETH ADELAIDE (CUTLER) HOSMER. 4217.

Edward Stebbins,	4224	Deerfield, June 2, 1866		
Eliot Norton,	4225	Y'llow Springs, Ohio, Dec. 28, 1868	June 24, 1869	
Ernest Cutler,	4226	" July 1, 1870		
Josephine,	4227	Columbia, Mo., Mar. 31, 1874		

PROF. JAMES KENDALL AND JENNIE PERSIS (GARLAND) HOSMER. 4218.

Ruth,	4228	St. Louis, Mo., Oct. 18, 1879		
Herbert Garland,	4229	" Jan. 22, 1881	May 27, 1882	
Meliscent,	4230	" Jan. 16, 1884		

WILLIAM RUFUS AND JOSEPHINE LOUISA (GRANT) HOSMER. 4219.

Mary Louise,	4231	Apr. 22, 1878	

REV. GEORGE HERBERT AND JULIA W. (SHELDON) HOSMER. 4220.

Ralph Sheldon,	4232	Mar. 4, 1874	

HENRY FRANCIS AND REBECCA PRESCOTT (HOSMER) COGSWELL. 4205.

	Martha Rebecca,	4233	Peterboro, N. H., May 26, 1820	June 23, 1836		
74	Caroline Hosmer,	4234	" May 26, 1823		Sept. 1, 1846	Ethan H. Howard. [(Wilkins).
74	William Henry,	4235	" June 10, 1826	Mar. 28, 1858	Aug. 22, 1848	Catharine Hayes; 1831–; dau. Thomas and Abigail
	Albert Smith,	4236	" Nov. 23, 1827	Sept. 13, 1848		
	Geo. Washington,	4237	" July 1, 1830	Apr. 22, 1854	Sept. 3, 1851	Sarah Hall.
	Eliza,	4238	" Feb. 17, 1832	Jan. 3, 1855		
74	Sarah,	4239	" Feb. 10, 1834		June 2, 1852	J. Mortimer Whitcomb.

ETHAN H. AND CAROLINE HOSMER (COGSWELL) HOWARD. 4234.

Henry Cogswell,	4240	Buffalo, N. Y., Sept. 20, 1847		Jan. 4, 1869	Jennie M. Jewett.

WILLIAM HENRY AND CAROLINE (HAYES) COGSWELL. 4235.

	Albert Smith,	4241	Peterboro, N. H., Nov. 10, 1849		July 8, 1874	Julia Rich Holmes; 1853–.
74	Abbie Rebecca,	4242	" Jan. 11, 1851		May 12, 1875	Cyrus A. Veatch; 1846–; son Decalin and Matilda A.
74	Sarah Hayes,	4243	Springville, N. Y., Sept. 21, 1852		May 12, 1875	Lemuel James Morse; 1844–; son Chas. and Sarah.
74	Henry Francis,	4244	Hudson, Mich., Oct. 30, 1854		Sept. 17, 1872	Lettie E. Garlinghouse; 1848–; d. David & Margaret.
74	Geo. Washington,	4245	" Oct. 25, 1856		Dec. 23, 1877	Debbie Parkhill; 1859–.

CYRUS A. AND ABBIE R. (COGSWELL) VEATCH. 4242.

Irene Gertrude,	4246	Chicago, Ill., July 10, 1876		
Cora Edna,	4247	Streator, Ill., Oct. 26, 1877		
Oscar Howard,	4248	" Apr. 5, 1879		
Dana V.,	4249	Forest, Ill., Aug. 24, 1881		
Sarah,	4250	Pontiac, Ill., Nov. 5, 1885		

LEMUEL J. AND SARAH H. (COGSWELL) MORSE. 4243.

Jennie Howard,	4251	Apr. 4, 1876	

HENRY F. AND LETTIE E. (GARLINGHOUSE) COGSWELL. 4244.

Carrie Lulu,	4252	Dec. 22, 1883	
Jennie Vialettie,	4253	Sept. 5, 1885	

GEORGE W. AND DEBBIE (PARKHILL) COGSWELL. 4245.

Carrie Maud,	4254	Sept. 13, 1878	
Abbie Rebecca,	4255	Dec. 23, 1879	

J. MORTIMER AND SARAH (COGSWELL) WHITCOMB. 4239.

Elizabeth,	4256	Buffalo, N. Y., June 18, 1856		
Harriet Rebecca,	4257	" July 30, 1858	Nov. 3, 1879	
Mortimer Osgood,	4258	" Jan. 4, 1861	Sept. 26, 1861	
Sarah,	4259	" Aug. 12, 1862		

JACOB B. AND MELISCENT (HOSMER) FARMER. 4208. (Continued page 75.)

75	Elizabeth,	4260	Concord, July 1, 1829		Apr. 18, 1848	George A. Leete; 1817–1884.

38	Martha,	4261	Concord,	July 16, 1831		Nov. 25, 1873	Charles L. Leete; 1823–.
	Jennie,	4262	"	Feb. 14, 1836		Dec. 26, 1865	James A. Barrett. No. 2018.
	Nellie,	4263	"	Dec. 19, 1839			
	Edwin,	4264	"	Dec. 6, 1842			
	Henry,	4265	"				

GEORGE A. AND ELIZABETH (FARMER) LEETE. 4260.

	George F.,	4266	Rochester, N. Y., Jan. 23, 1849			Apr. 26, 1871	Mary Harriet Remington; dau. Daniel and Betsey R.
	Elizabeth J.,	4267	Providence, R. I., July 31, 1851			Apr. 23, 1874	Edward W. Foster; son John and Lucretia.
	William A.,	4268	" Aug. 28, 1853			Nov. 25, 1879	Sophia E. Rawson; dau. Henry M. and Sophia E.
	Charles H.,	4269	Brooklyn, N. Y., Apr. 26, 1855	Died young.			
	Meliscent,	4270	" May 31, 1856				
	Edward M.,	4271	" July 20, 1857	Died young.			
	S. Louise,	4272	" Oct. 24, 1858				
	Alexander D.,	4273	" Nov. 3, 1861				

SAMUEL AND RUTH (BROWN) JONES. 483-150.

	Elizabeth,	4274	Concord,	Oct. 7, 1700			—— Wright.
75	Thomas,	4275	"	Nov. 30, 1702	Aug. 3, 1774	July 20, 1727	Mary Miles; 1709–1782.
	Ruth,	4276	"	Mar. 16, 1704	June 29, 1734	Sept. 16, 1733	Capt. Malachi Foot; 1711–.
76	Samuel,	4277	"	Oct. 17, 1707	June 7, 1802	Dec. 21, 1732	Sarah Hubbard; 1716–1802.
23	Rebecca, {	4278	"	Apr. 15, 1810		1730	1. Benjamin Barrett. No. 19. [ful (Wheeler).
		4279				Dec. 23, 1740	2. Jonas Prescott; 1703–1784; son Jonas and Thank-
	Joseph,	4280	"	Nov. 4, 1712		Oct. 7, 1756	Mary Carter.
30	Mary,	4281	"	Mar. 23, 1715	Jan. 30, 1804	1730	Dea. Thomas Barrett. No. 20.
	Lucy,	4282	"	Jan. 11, 1717	Jan. 10, 1808	1739	Joseph Lee, M. D.; 1715–1797.

THOMAS AND MARY (MILES) JONES. 4275.

	Thomas,	4283	Concord,	May 28, 1728	Aug. 28, 1799	Feb. 28, 1754	Martha Brooks; 1731–1795.
96	John, Capt.,	4284	"	Dec. 7, 1730	Dec. 18, 1811	Oct. 24, 1754	Phebe Brewer; 1734–; d. Daniel and Phebe (Locke).
	Mary,	4285	"	Mar. 1, 1734		Nov. 16, 1769	Daniel Jones; 1728–.
	Elizabeth,	4286	"	June 2, 1737	July 18, 1831	Feb. 16, 1762	Timothy Brooks; 1732–1803. [(Cutler).
	Samuel, Capt.,	4287	"	May 21, 1741	May 6, 1812	Apr. 25, 1771	Hepzabah Jones; 1753–1839; dau. Ephraim and Alice
75	Elisha, Lieut.,	4288	"	May 23, 1744	Feb. 1, 1810	Feb. 22, 1770	Elizabeth Farrar; 1750–1826.
	Ruth,	4289	"	May 11, 1747			
	James,	4290	"	Apr. 22, 1751	Feb. 13, 1754		

LIEUT. ELISHA AND ELIZABETH (FARRAR) JONES. 4288.

40	Molly,	4291	Concord,	Mar. 17, 1771	July 5, 1853	Dec. 10, 1795	Nathan Barrett. No. 2140.
75	Elisha, {	4292	"	Mar. 31, 1773	Aug. 23, 1829	1803	1. Betsey Thayer.
75		4293					2. Leah Thayer. [No. 2150.
	James (no issue),	4294	"	Sept. 28, 1776	Mar. 16, 1838	Dec. 2, 1819	Maria F. (Palisier) Barrett; wid. of Francis Barrett.
	Abel,	4295	"	Mar. 17, 1779	Oct. 1, 1815	Unmarried.	
	Betsey,	4296	"	Apr. 5, 1782	Apr. 20, 1849	1801	John Dakin; 1780–1830.
47	Patty,	4297	"	Nov. 25, 1785	May 31, 1824	Feb. 10, 1809	Emerson Barrett. No. 2536.

ELISHA AND BETSEY (THAYER) JONES. 4292.

75	Henry Elisha,	4298	Boston,	Aug. 3, 1804	Dec. 2, 1874	May 12, 1829	Lydia Hannah Hunstable; 1809–1884.
76	James Sullivan,	4299	"	Feb. 7, 1806		May 11, 1835	Almira Chever.

ELISHA AND LEAH (THAYER) JONES. 4293.

76	George W.,	4300		May 7, 1808	Mar. 7, 1879	May 25, 1833	Deborah Mann.
	Henry,	4301		Feb. 13, 1810	Apr. 15, 1815		
	Elizabeth,	4302		Apr. 15, 1812	Apr. 17, 1831		

HENRY ELISHA AND LYDIA HANNAH (HUNSTABLE) JONES. 4298.

75	Henry L., {	4303	Holliston,	Mar. 22, 1830		Oct. 5, 1853	1. Ellen Maria Cartwright; 1834–1857.
75		4304				May 1, 1880	2. May Josephine McMahon; 1850–.
75	Starr Southmayd,	4305	"	Oct. 10, 1831		Dec. 20, 1859	Nancy Elizabeth Hollenbuck; 1839–1882.
	Chas. Hunstable,	4306	"	Jan. 12, 1834	Aug. 13, 1842		
	Wm. Parkman,	4307	"	Jan. 25, 1836	Mar. 26, 1836		
	Caroline Evarts,	4308	"	Dec. 19, 1836	Feb. 26, 1837		
	Sam'l Parkman,	4309	"	Aug. 23, 1838			
	James Augustus,	4310	"	Jan. 7, 1841		Oct. 4, 1870	Clara Elizabeth Parsons; 1840–.
	Wilberforce R.,	4311	"	Sept. 3, 1843	Sept. 8, 1844		
75	Robert Morrison,	4312	"	Jan. 2, 1846		Jan. 27, 1881	Emma Julia Cushing; 1855–.
	Hannah Amelia,	4313	"	May 13, 1848			

HENRY LIVINGSTON AND ELLEN M. (CARTWRIGHT) JONES. 4303.

	Henry L., Jr.,	4314	Holliston,	July 18, 1854	Aug. 3, 1858
	Daniel William,	4315	Chelsea,	June 3, 1856	Oct. 10, 1856

HENRY L. AND MAY J. (McMAHON) JONES. 4304.

	Gertrude May F.,	4316	New York, N. Y., Dec. 29, 1883	June 19, 1884
	Florence Henry,	4317	" Jan. 5, 1886	June 25, 1886

STARR S. AND NANCY E. (HOLLENBUCK) JONES. 4305.

	Stella Louise,	4318	Galveston, Tex., Mar. 11, 1861	
	Lottie Blessings,	4319	" Dec. 31, 1863	
	Frank Henry,	4320	" Sept. 21, 1866	
	Charles Fowler,	4321	" Dec. 4, 1869	
	Alice May,	4322	" May 7, 1872	
	Nettie Starr,	4323	" Dec. 9, 1874	Mar. 29, 1876
	Ethel Pearl,	4324	" Feb. 4, 1877	
	Katie Gilbert,	4325	" Sept. 2, 1879	Feb. 28, 1880

ROBERT M. AND EMMA J. (CUSHING) JONES. 4312.

	Alice Amelia,	4326	Dec. 23, 1881	
	Robert Cushing,	4327	Nov. 18, 1883	
	Marion Emma,	4328	Dec. 7, 1885	

JAMES SULLIVAN AND ALMIRA (CHEVER) JONES. 4299.

	Sarah Everett,	4329	Wrentham, Feb. 19, 1836	Feb. 13, 1883		
	Francis Edward,	4330	" Nov. 5, 1838	Nov. 1, 1839		
	Martha Elmira,	4331	" Sept. 30, 1840	Apr. 2, 1848		
76	Mary Elizabeth,	4332	" Feb. 15, 1845		Jan. 28, 1868	Owen Bearse, Jr.
	Alice Emily,	4333	" May 27, 1853			

OWEN, JR., AND MARY ELIZABETH (JONES) BEARSE. 4332.

Fanny Cheever,	4334	Dorchester, Mar. 28, 1869			
Lellah Alice,	4335	" June 16, 1872	June 1, 1873		
Mary Palmer,	4336	" Oct. 11, 1874			
Mark Livingston,	4337	" Feb. 9, 1879	July 1, 1884		
Alice Howland,	4338	Wrentham, May 12, 1881			

GEORGE W. AND DEBORAH (MANN) JONES. 4300.

76	Eliza A.,	4339	Randolph, Dec. 31, 1833		Mar. 6, 1859	John Bigelow.
76	Lorianna Metcalf,	4340	" Feb. 20, 1836		Feb. 1, 1876	Mary Orcutt.

JOHN AND ELIZA A. (JONES) BIGELOW. 4339.

Charles F.,	4341	Brookfield,Vt., Jan. 21, 1861		Aug. 9, 1884	Amanda E. Bacon.
George Elmer,	4342	" Mar. 21, 1863			
Edward P.,	4343	" May 21, 1866			
Arthur, Jr.,	4344	" Jan. 28, 1869			
Ernest C.,	4345	" June 29, 1877			

LORIANNA M. AND MARY (ORCUTT) JONES. 4340.

George S.,	4346	Aug. 29, 1876	
Willie P.,	4347	Apr. 24, 1878	
Herbert,	4348	May 29, 1880	
Mary Lizzie,	4349	Mar. 16, 1883	

SAMUEL AND SARAH (HUBBARD) JONES. 4277.

	Sarah,	4350	Concord, Jan. 5, 1734	Nov. 3, 1793		John Merriam; 1720–1775.
76	Samuel, Jr.,	4351	Acton, Sept. 30, 1775	Nov. 29, 1796	July 30, 1782	Hannah (Brown) Davis; wid. Capt. Isaac Davis.
	Ruth,	4352	" May 16, 1737		Sept. 5, 1765	Jonas Allen.
	Oliver,	4353	" Feb. 5, 1739	Aug. 11, 1820	Dec. 29, 1763	Hannah Woolley; 1741–1822.
	Amos,	4354	" July 20, 1741		Oct. 11, 1770	Lydia Woolley.
	Joseph,	4355	" Sept. 3, 1743	Feb., 1827	Mar. 3, 1774	Sarah French.
	Silas,	4356	" Nov. 12, 1744	Oct. 9, 1756		
	Charles,	4357	" Feb. 28, 1748	Nov. 29, 1748		
	Rebecca,	4358	" Dec. 28, 1748	Aug. 16, 1802		
78	Peter,	4359	" Mar. 24, 1751	Oct. 12, 1826	Dec. 24, 1782	Hepzabah Farrar; 1757–1824.
78	Aaron,	4360	" Dec. 4, 1754	June 11, 1836	Apr. 8, 1779	Abigail Billings; 1757–1832.
	Eunice,	4361	" Nov. 13, 1757	Aug. 26, 1792		

SAMUEL AND HANNAH (BROWN-DAVIS) JONES. 4351.

76	Samuel,	4362	Acton, Mar. 11, 1783	Oct. 21, 1811	Oct. 20, 1806	Anna Tuttle; –1828; dau. John.
76	James,	4363	" July 10, 1784	July 30, 1820	Oct. 20, 1807	Dorothy Jones. No. 4479.
77	Betsey,	4364	" May 25, 1786	Oct. 15, 1866	Apr. 1, 1807	Levi Wait; 1780–1823; s. Phinehas & Eddie (Fassett).

SAMUEL AND ANNA (TUTTLE) JONES. 4362.

76	Anna Tuttle,	4365	Acton, Jan. 31, 1808		June 2, 1829	Rev. Artemus Bullard, D.D.; –1855; s. Dr. Artemus.
	Sarah Susanna,	4366	" Jan. 15, 1810	Dec. 27, 1815		

REV. ARTEMUS AND ANNA TUTTLE (JONES) BULLARD. 4365.

	Artemus Everett,	4367	Charlestown, July 19, 1830	Apr. 13, 1836		
	Anna Maria,	4368	Boston, July 9, 1832	Apr. 28, 1833		
	Thos. Green Fessenden,	4369	Walnut Hills, O., Mar. 25, 1834	Nov. 12, 1838		
	Robert Leighton,	4370	" Mar. 21, 1837	Jan. 25, 1848		
76	Henry, Rev. & D. D.,	4371	St. Louis, Mo., Sept. 23, 1839		Aug. 30, 1871	Maria Nelson; dau. Rev. Henry A. Nelson, D. D.
	Ann Elizabeth,	4372	" Sept. 29, 1842	Jan. 13, 1848		
	Edward Payson,	4373	" Jan. 19, 1845	Jan. 12, 1848		

REV. HENRY, D. D., AND MARIA (NELSON) BULLARD. 4371.

Annie Leighton,	4374	Feb. 19, 1873	July 16, 1873
Henry Nelson,	4375	Nov. 19, 1874	
Alice,	4376	Oct. 4, 1876	
Arthur,	4377	Dec. 8, 1879	

JAMES AND DOROTHY (JONES) JONES. 4363-4479.

76	James Madison,	4378	Acton, Dec. 9, 1808	Apr. 25, 1827		[abeth (Hunt).
77	Henrietta,	4379	" Aug. 16, 1810		Apr. 3, 1828	Joseph Warren Tuttle; 1805–; son Simon and Eliz-
	Samuel,	4380	" Aug. 24, 1812		Apr. 8, 1838	Martha Ann Handley; 1817–; dau. John and Lucy
	Charles Henry,	4381	" Sept. 24, 1815	June 30, 1821		[(Proctor).
	Hiram A.,	4382	" June 12, 1818	Dec. 11, 1881		

JOSEPH WARREN AND HENRIETTA (JONES) TUTTLE. 4379.

76	Henrietta,	4383	Acton, June 2, 1829		Nov. 24, 1846	Geo. Wash. Todd; 1822–1880; s. Levi & Nancy (Corey).
77	George Warren,	4384	" June 9, 1831		Jan. 1, 1854	Anna Tuttle; 1834–; d. Dan'l & Emeline E. (Handley).
	Albert Jones,	4385	" Sept. 7, 1833	May 8, 1834		[(Tenney).
84	Jones,	4386	" Apr. 2, 1835	Feb. 3, 1868	Nov. 29, 1855	Nancy Maria Wright; 1836–; dau. George and Mary
77	Angelia,	4387	" May 30, 1838		Nov. 12, 1857	Edward Nelson Robbins; 1836–; son Tilley & Joanna
						(Noyes). [(Handley).
77	Charles Henry,	4388	Leominster, Sept. 17, 1841		Dec. 8, 1861	Loretta Tuttle; 1844–; dau. Daniel and Emeline E.
77	Aaron,	4389	Acton, Mar. 11, 1844		Aug. 19, 1862	Naomi Grover Wheeler; 1841; dau. Joel and Sarah.
	Herbert Alfonso,	4390	" June 16, 1851		Sept. 25, 1872	Ida Isabel Moore; 1853–; d. Chas. H. & Nancy (Turk).

GEORGE WASHINGTON AND HENRIETTA (TUTTLE) TODD. 4383.

(Continued page 77.)

Mary Ann,	4391	Acton, Sept. 19, 1847	Dec. 30, 1883	Unmarried.
Emma Augusta,	4392	" Nov. 28, 1849		

	Name	No.	Place & Born	Died	Married	Spouse / Notes
	Jennette Estelle,	4393	Acton, Aug. 20, 1851	Feb. 18, 1856		[(Miller)
77	Ella Angelia,	4394	" Nov. 5, 1853		Dec. 1, 1875	Frank Miller Davis; 1854–; son Wm. L. and Sarah N.
77	Nellie Luella,	4395	Concord, Dec. 25, 1856		June 2, 1880	Christopher Fairbanks Whitney; 1856–; son Reuben
	Willie,	4396	" Mar. 5, 1863	Mar. 10, 1863		[F. and Jane L. (Tubbs).
	Winnie,	4397	" Mar. 5, 1863	Mar. 5, 1863		
	George Walter,	4398	" Sept. 19, 1864			

FRANK M. AND ELLA A. (TODD) DAVIS. 4394.

	Name	No.	Place & Born
	Marion Estelle,	4399	Burlington, Vt., Aug. 30, 1878
	Frank Leonard,	4400	" May 2, 1880

CHRISTOPHER F. AND NELLIE L. (TODD) WHITNEY. 4395.

	Name	No.	Place & Born
	Helen Mary,	4401	Hartford, Conn., Sept. 6, '85

GEORGE W. AND ANNA (TUTTLE) TUTTLE. 4384.

	Name	No.	Place & Born	Married	Spouse
77	Willie Warren,	4402	Boston, Oct. 15, 1854	Oct. 4, 1877	Nellie C. Jourdain.
	Lizzie Handley,	4403	" May 20, 1861		
	George Herman,	4404	" Feb. 28, 1866		

WILLIE W. AND NELLIE C. (JOURDAIN) TUTTLE. 4402.

	Name	No.	Place & Born
	George Raymond,	4405	Chicago, Ill., Sept. 5, 1878
	Fred LeRoy,	4406	Chelsea, June 8, 1880

EDWARD NELSON AND ANGELIA (TUTTLE) ROBBINS. 4387.

	Name	No.	Place & Born	Married	Spouse
77	Nettie Flora,	4407	Acton, Jan. 25, 1859	June 3, 1879	Walter Edwards Hayward; 1856–; son Cyrus and Mary
	Clifford Warren,	4408	" Mar. 25, 1877		[P. (Edwards)

WALTER E. AND NETTIE F. (ROBBINS) HAYWARD. 4407.

	Name	No.	Place & Born
	Grace Alice,	4409	Acton, Aug. 3, 1880

CHARLES H. AND LORETTA (TUTTLE) TUTTLE. 4388.

	Name	No.	Place & Born	Married	Spouse
77	Flora Belle,	4410	Concord, Sept. 22, 1862	Oct. 18, 1882	Charles Howard Campbell; 1860–; son Uriah B. and
	Albert Henry,	4411	Boston, June 25, 1871		[Evelyn M. (Hall).
	Freddie Warren,	4412	" June 25, 1871		

CHARLES H. AND FLORA B. (TUTTLE) CAMPBELL. 4410.

	Name	No.	Place & Born
	Howard Tuttle,	4413	Chelsea, July 25, 1883

AARON AND NAOMI G. (WHEELER) TUTTLE. 4389.

	Name	No.	Place & Born
	Edith Gertrude,	4414	Boston, Apr. 15, 1866
	Walter Aaron,	4415	" June 26, 1876

SAMUEL AND MARTHA A. (HANDLEY) JONES. 4380.

	Name	No.	Place & Born	Died	Married	Spouse / Notes
77	Charles,	4416	Acton, Jan. 6, 1839		Sept. 16, 1863	Marilla H. Finney; dau. Dea. Lyman.
	George,	4417	" Nov. 30, 1840			
	Samuel,	4418	" Feb. 9, 1842	July 31, 1845		
	Martha,	4419	" Sept. 27, 1843			
103	Laura Ann,	4420	" 1845		Dec. 25, 1882	James Perry Brown. No. 5932. [(Fletcher).
	Samuel, Jr.,	4421	" Apr. 24, 1851		Dec. 22, 1875	Emma E. Hayward; 1853–; dau. Reuben and Mary J.
	Ellen Louisa,	4422	" Oct. 29, 1854		Jan. 28, 1880	Anson C. Piper; 1851 .
	Lucle Amelia,	4423	" June 9, 1858			

CHARLES AND MARILLA H. (FINNEY) JONES. 4416.

	Name	No.	Place & Born
	Susan Mabel,	4424	Burke, Vt., June 16, 1866
	Martha Maud,	4425	Chelsea, Mar. 31, 1868
	Helen,	4426	" Aug. 22, 1870
	Walter Finney,	4427	" Aug. 6, 1875

LEVI AND BETSEY (JONES) WAIT. 4364.

	Name	No.	Place & Born	Died	Married	Spouse / Notes
77	Wm. Boynton, {	4428	Groton, Jan. 10, 1808		Dec. 11, 1838	1. M'tha Lavinia Reardon; 1809–1863; d. L'mb't & Ann-
77		4429			May 20, 1867	2. Fannie (Easton) Tyler; 1833–; d. Thos. and Lucin-
77	George, {	4430	" June 10, 1809	Jan. 9, 1881	July 30, 1835	1. Minerva Hinckley; 1860–1840. [da (Gayle).
77		4431			July 28, 1843	2. Mary H. Fox; 1819–; dau. Alanson and Maria
99	Sarah Maria,	4432	" May 20, 1811	May 23, 1885	July, 1832	Anthony M. Strong. [(Cheesborough).
	Elizabeth,	4433	" Apr. 14, 1813			
99	Anna,	4434	" Jan. 9, 1815	June 1, 1847	May 7, 1835	Charles Scovel; –1868.
77	Mary,	4435	Albany, N. Y., Nov. 9, 1816		Nov. 7, 1843	Hezekiah Gould Scovel.
	Charlotte,	4436	" Apr. 5, 1819			[and Submit (Dickinson).
78	Hannah Jones,	4437	" Apr. 6, 1821		June 3, 1846	Rev. Philander Dickinson Young; 1817–; son Horace

WILLIAM B. AND MARTHA L. (REARDON) WAIT. 4428.

	Name	No.	Place & Born	Died
	Lambert Reardon,	4438	Little Rock, Ark., Sept. 27, 1839	Oct. 27, 1851
	William Boynton,	4439	" Aug. 30, 1842	Jan. 3, 1843
	George Herbert,	4440	" Oct. 6, 1844	Aug. 2, 1863
	Charles Edward,	4441	" Nov. 3, 1849	

WILLIAM B. AND FANNIE (EASTON-TYLER) WAIT. 4429.

	Name	No.	Place & Born
	Robert Easton,	4442	Little Rock, Ark., July 24, 1869

GEORGE AND MINERVA (HINCKLEY) WAIT. 4430.

	Name	No.	Place & Born	Died
	Edward Dunn,	4443	Albany, N. Y., May 31, 1837	July 30, 1869

GEORGE AND MARY H. (FOX) WAIT. 4431.

	Name	No.	Place & Born
	Sheridan Fox,	4444	Albany, N. Y., May 19, 1844
	Maria Fox,	4445	" Oct. 16, 1852
	Helen Louise,	4446	" Sept. 21, 1854

HEZEKIAH G. AND MARY (WAIT) SCOVEL. 4435. *(Continued page 78.)*

	Name	No.	Place & Born	Married	Spouse
	Mary Louisa,	4447	Nashville, Tenn., Dec. 7, '46	Sept. 21, 1869	Charles W. Calkins.
	Anna Wait,	4448	" July 27, 1849	Sept. 21, 1870	Chauncy Butler.

	Spencer Gould,	4449	Nashville, Tenn., Aug. 30, 1851			
	Betsey Jones,	4450	" Mar. 14, 1854			
	Effie Lapsley,	4451	" Apr. 25, 1857			
	William Wait,	4452	" Sept. 4, 1859			

REV. PHILANDER D. AND HANNAH J. (WAIT) YOUNG. 4437.

	Sarah Maria,	4453	Edwardsville, Ill., Nov. 30, 1847	Apr. 24, 1854		
	Horace Dickinson,	4454	" July 19, 1849			
	Charlotte Eliz.,	4455	" June 23, 1851	Nov. 9, 1852		
	Mary Eunice,	4456	" Apr. 18, 1853	Aug. 29, 1854		
	William Wait,	4457	" July 20, 1855			
	Francis Leighton,	4458	" Nov. 6, 1856	Dec. 30, 1864		

PETER AND HEPZABAH (FARRAR) JONES. 4359.

78	Peter,	4459	Acton, Apr. 1, 1784	Jan. 20, 1845	Oct. 1, 1855	Nancy Wilkins; 1794–1879.
	Hepzabah,	4460	" Nov. 25, 1785	Mar. 1, 1856	Unmarried.	
	Sybil,	4461	" Feb. 28, 1791	Sept. 10, 1861	Unmarried.	
	Rebecca,	4462	" Aug. 8, 1793	Mar. 19, 1865	Apr. 14, 1825	John Le Gross.
	Edward,	4463	" July 15, 1795	Mar. 14, 1864	Unmarried.	

PETER AND NANCY (WILKINS) JONES. 4459.

	Nancy,	4464	Feb. 28, 1816	Aug. 1, 1823		
	Maria,	4465	Mar. 30, 1823			Amos Adams.
78	Hiram, {	4466	Dec. 11, 1825		Sept., 1853	1. Mary J. Heald; 1833–1863.
78	{	4467			Aug., 1865	2. Mrs. Emily J. Scott.

HIRAM AND MARY J. (HEALD) JONES. 4466.

	James W.,	4468	Aug. 6, 1854		Dec. 14, 1882	Ellen M. Stuart; 1858–.
	Alice W.,	4469	Feb. 26, 1856			
	Arthur C. H.,	4470	Sept. 5, 1859		Nov. 14, 1883	Martha O. Sargent; 1864–.

HIRAM AND EMILY J. (SCOTT) JONES. 4467.

	George C.,	4471	May 17, 1866			

AARON AND ABIGAIL (BILLINGS) JONES. 4360.

78	Lucinda,	4472	Acton, June 22, 1780	Aug. 14, 1803	Jan. 5, 1802	Ebenezer White; 1777–1807.
78	Aaron, Jr., {	4473	" Dec. 13, 1781	Aug. 1, 1837	Oct. 11, 1803	1. Lydia Jones; 1784–.
78	{	4474			June 23, 1818	2. Ruth Rand; –1854. [(Wright).
79	Abel,	4475	" Aug. 26, 1783	Jan. 18, 1872	Jan. 3, 1805	Lucy Hapgood; 1783–1844; dau. Abraham and Mary
	Abigail,	4476	" May 26, 1785		Mar. 29, 1803	Archibald McFarlin.
81	Silas,	4477	" Feb. 26, 1787	Apr. 23, 1861	Oct. 12, 1809	Lucinda Wetherbee; 1787–1871.
81	Luther Blanch'rd,	4478	" Feb. 1, 1789	Dec. 27, 1855	June 28, 1821	Charlotte Billings; –1857.
76	Dorothy, {	4479	" June 3, 1791	Aug. 25, 1833	Oct. 20, 1807	1. James Jones. No. 4363.
81	{	4480			June 27, 1825	2. Dennis Putnam; 1795–1877.
82	Elnathan,	4481	" Apr. 7, 1795	July 5, 1873	Mar. 4, 1821	Eliza Tuttle; 1797–1876; d. Simon and Eliz. (Hunt).
	Luke,	4482	" Oct. 2, 1797	May 25, 1807		[(White).
82	Clarissa,	4483	" Aug. 16, 1799	Feb. 8, 1875	Apr. 25, 1822	Hon. John Fletcher; 1791–1879; s. James and Lydia
	Eunice,	4484	" Aug. 26, 1793	June 2, 1861	May 6, 1813	Abraham Conant; 1783–1861.

AARON, JR., AND LYDIA (JONES) JONES. 4473.

78	Lydia Lucinda,	4485	Acton, Nov. 8, 1804	Feb. 8, 1883	Mar. 31, 1825	Aaron Fletcher; 1801–1881; son John Swift and Lucy (Forbush).
	Hepzabah,	4486	" May 1, 1808		Sept. 8, 1831	Jonathan Augustus Piper; 1808–1881; son Silas and Mehitable (Barker).
79	Elizab'th Hannah,	4487	" Mar. 18, 1810		Apr. 10, 1834	Reuben Dole; 1808–; s. Lemuel and Ruth (Barker).
102	Mary Stratton,	4488	" July 30, 1816	Mar., 1849	Apr. 21, 1830	John Mead; 1799–1868; son Stephen.

AARON, JR., AND RUTH (RAND) JONES. 4474.

	Abigail Billings,	4489	Acton, Mar. 13, 1819		Dec. 11, 1836	Benjamin Marshall Herrick. [(Kneeland).
101	Nancy Robbins,	4490	" Dec. 22, 1820		Nov. 25, 1842	John Hinckley Sanders; 1817–; son Richard and Sally
	Aaron Marshall,	4491	" Apr. 14, 1823			Augusta Tarbell. [(Gipson).
103	Charlotte Louisa,	4492	" Mar 26, 1825		Jan. 12, 1842	Francis Brown; 1817–1881; dau. Nath'l and Betsey
101	Francis,	4493	Stowe, Jan. 3, 1828		Aug. 31, 1851	Ann Elizabeth Robbins; 1828–; dau. Tilly and Joan—
	Ebenezer White,	4494	" Dec. 29, 1831			—— Sanborn. [na H. (Noyes).
	Henrietta Jane,	4495	" Sept. 27, 1834	Mar. 11, 1866	June 5, 1851	Geo. Henry Harris; 1830–; s. John & Mary (White).
101	Edwin Augustine,	4496	" Sept. 29, 1837		Feb. 20, 1863	Miranda Butler; 1841–; dau. Charles and Nancy L. Farnsworth.

AARON AND LYDIA L. (JONES) FLETCHER. 4485.

78	Hersina Kni'ht, {	4497	Acton, Sept. 10, 1825		Oct. 8, 1846	1. Augustus Dole; 1818–1849; s. Lemuel and Ruth (Barker).
78	{	4498			Nov. 11, 1855	2. Wm. Jones Paul; 1810–; s. Stephen & Mary G. (Spinney).
	Eliza,	4499	" Aug. 29, 1827		Feb. 11, 1862	John Murray Sprague; 1830–; s. John and Lydia (Sanderson).
78	Aaron Swift,	4500	" Mar. 7, 1830		Jan. 14, 1866	Sarah Townsend Kidd; 1838–; d. Andrew and Sarah P. (Ring).
68	Mary Jane,	4501	" Oct. 13, 1833		June 8, 1851	Reuben Hayward. No. 3663. [bah (Jones).
78	Weltha Taylor,	4502	" Mar. 27, 1835		Apr. 27, 1854	Jonathan Newell Gates; 1830–1876; son Edward and Hepza—
79	Martha Farrar,	4503	" Apr. 30, 1838		Jan. 1, 1860	Wm. Albert Lydston; 1836–; s. Dan'l and Almira (Freeman).
79	Aaron Jones,	4504	" Apr. 28, 1841		Nov. 18, 1866	Mary Eliza Burner; 1845–; d. Levi and Rebecca E. (Jones).
79	Hepsa Augusta,	4505	" Mar. 17, 1845		May 29, 1866	Joseph Wm. Wherren; 1838–; s. Dan'l & Mary Eliz. (Briggs).
79	Jonathan Piper,	4506	" Dec. 12, 1848		Dec. 22, 1875	Lizzie Roth; 1856–; dau. John and Fanny (Howard).

AUGUSTUS AND HERSINA K. (FLETCHER) DOLE. 4497.

	Emma,	4507	Acton, Sept. 4, 1847	Sept. 21, 1848		

WILLIAM J. AND HERSINA K. (FLETCHER-DOLE) PAUL. 4498.

	Ada Fletcher,	4508	Eliot, Me., Dec. 22, 1857			
	Lizzie Mead,	4509	" Nov. 12, 1860			

AARON SWIFT AND SARAH TOWNSEND (KIDD) FLETCHER. 4500.

	Charles Andrew,	4510	Acton, Aug. 21, 1869	June 11, 1870		
	Willie Swift,	4511	" Mar. 10, 1871			
	Evie Blanche,	4512	" Dec. 12, 1874			

JONATHAN NEWELL AND WELTHA TAYLOR (FLETCHER) GATES. 4502.

(Continued page 79.)

79	George Newell,	4513	Acton,	Mar. 1, 1855		May 25, 1882	Lizzie Alma Brown; 1861–; d. David L. & Maria (Bell).
79	Addie Jones,	4514	Sudbury,	June 17, 1857		Mar. 27, 1879	William Eli Harrington; 1849–; son Eli and Eunice
	Fred Kirk,	4515	Shrewsbury, Feb. 6, 1859				[G. (Stow).
	Hattie Eliza,	4516	"	Oct. 25, 1861			
	Carrie Leora,	4517	"	Apr. 29, 1864			
	Lewis Eddy,	4518	"	Sept. 19, 1866			
	Walter Hartwell,	4519	"	Jan. 12, 1871			
	Lottie Peaslee,	4520	"	June 13, 1874			

GEORGE NEWELL AND LIZZIE ALMA (BROWN) GATES. 4513.

	Estella Maria,	4521	Shrewsbury, July 4, 1884			

WILLIAM ELI AND ADDIE JONES (GATES) HARRINGTON. 4514.

	Carrie Eunice,	4522	Shrewsbury, Aug. 2, 1880			
	Frank Newell,	4523	" Feb. 9, 1885			

WILLIAM ALBERT AND MARTHA FARRAR (FLETCHER) LYDSTON. 4503.

	Nettie Cora,	4524	Eliot, Me., Apr. 2, 1861	·	Nov. 11, 1883	Linville Scott Remick; 1860–; son John W. and
	Albert Willie,	4525	" July 28, 1874			[Emily (Hammond).

AARON JONES AND MAY ELIZA (PURNER) FLETCHER. 4504.

	Harry Atwood,	4526	Buckmertingham, Md., May 29, 1867			
	Mary Florence,	4527	Acton, Oct. 20, 1869			
	Charles Jones,	4528	" Oct. 1, 1871			
	Jennie Purner,	4529	" Jan. 19, 1881			

JOSEPH WILLIAM AND HEPZABAH AUGUSTA (FLETCHER) WHERREN. 4505.

	Charles Fletcher,	4530	Eliot, Me., Mar. 14, 1869			
	Frank Milton,	4531	" Feb. 12, 1874			
	Lizzie Lucinda,	4532	" Sept. 4, 1879			

JONATHAN PIPER AND LIZZIE (ROTH) FLETCHER. 4506.

	Jennie Evelyn,	4533	Acton, Mar. 23, 1882			

REUBEN AND ELIZABETH HANNAH (JONES) DOLE. 4487.

79	Elizabeth,	4534	Marlboro, Mar. 23, 1835	Sept. 24, 1857	Sept. 14, 1851	John Bennett.	[(Jones).
	Elizaette,	4535	" Sept. 21, 1838		May 3, 1863	John Hale Howe; 1838–; s. Ephraim, Jr., and Susan
79	Ellen,	4536	" Sept. 12, 1845		Dec. 15, 1873	Lorenzo Augustus Pratt; 1836–; s. Geo. W. and Jane
						(Kimball).

JOHN AND ELIZABETH (DOLE) BENNETT. 4534.

	Loretta,	4537	Marlboro, Sept. 9, 1852	Nov. 9, 1854		

LORENZO AUGUSTUS AND ELLEN (DOLE) PRATT. 4536.

	Reuben Clifford,	4538	California, Jan. 28, 1875			
	Blanche Emily,	4539	" June 18, 1878			

ABEL AND LUCY (HAPGOOD) JONES. 4475.

	Lucinda White,	4540	Acton,	Aug. 24, 1805	July 6, 1864	Nov. 23, 1826	Luther Robbins.
79	Lucy Jane,	4541	"	Sept. 17, 1807	Aug. 5, 1845	Mar. 15, 1827	Horace Tuttle; 1800–; s. Simon and Eliz. (Hunt).
79	Abigail Merriam,	4542	"	Apr. 24, 1809		Sept. 10, 1827	Lewis Wood; 1802–; s. Jonas & Rebecca (Norcross).
80	Char'te Hapgood, {	4543	"	Nov. 24, 1810		July 19, 1827	1. Geo. Wash. Tuttle; 1803–1831; s. Simon & Eliz (Hunt).
80		4544				Dec. 31, 1840	2. Theo. Ames; 1813–1885; s. Dan'l & Mary (Barker).
80	Abel White,	4545	"	Jan. 20, 1812	Feb. 5, 1882	Aug. 30, 1843	Ann Maria Johnson; 1823–; dau. John and Eunice
	Clarissa,	4546	"	Sept. 16, 1814	Jan. 1, 1815		[(Pierce).
80	Luke, {	4547	"	Nov. 16, 1815	Aug. 28, 1849	Jan. 23, 1842	1. Lucy K. Brigham; 1819–1842.
80		4548				Apr. 10, 1845	2. Hannah Geer; 1825–; d. Asa and Esther (Smith).
80	Clarissa,	4549	"	Oct. 26, 1817		July 19, 1836	Dan. Weth'bee; 1814–1883; s. Edw. & Sus'na (Hapg'd).
80	Abrah'm Hapgood,	4550	"	Aug. 22, 1819		Jan. 17, 1844	Harriet Esterbrook Hosmer; 1826–1883; dau. Simon
	Winth'p Emers'n,	4551	"	Nov. 25, 1821			[and Harriet (Esterbrook).
80	James Francis,	4552	"	Jan. 26, 1830		Nov. 23, 1851	Elizabeth Whitney; 1834–; d. Chris. & Dolly (Brooks).

HORACE AND LUCY JANE (JONES) TUTTLE. 4541.

	Horace, Jr.,	4553	Acton,	Jan. 1, 1828	Feb. 13, 1828	
	Luke,	4554	"	Apr. 20, 1829	·	S. Sophia Harris.
	George,	4555	"	Nov. 2, 1832	Nov. 6, 1832	
	Adison,	4556	"	Sept. 17, 1834	June 14, 1835	
	Abram,	4557	"	Feb. 5, 1841		Martha A. Putnam.
	Horace, Jr.,	4558	"	Nov. 27, 1842	Mar. 20, 1843	
	Lucy Jane,	4559	"	Sept. 12, 1846	July 23, 1848	

LEWIS AND ABIGAIL MERRIAM (JONES) WOOD. 4542.

79	Lewis, Jr.,	4560	Acton,	Dec. 11, 1827			Laura Ann Hanscom; 1832–; d. Jere. & Eliz. (Dunn).
80	Rebecca Wheeler,	4561	"	Dec. 7, 1829	Aug. 23, 1854	Aug. 7, 1851	Henry Orville Lothrop; 1823–; son Charles and Mary
	Georgianna,	4562	"	Feb. 12, 1832	Aug. 22, 1845		[(Johnson).
	Geo. Wash'gton, {	4563	"	Feb. 14, 1834			1. Elzina Fenno.
		4564					2. Eluzia S. Fenno.
	Susan Broadwell,	4565	"	Mar. 21, 1836			John Cram.
	Winth'p Emers'n,	4566	"	May 6, 1838			Lydia Bruce.
	Abel Jones,	4567	"	Sept. 29, 1840			Miriam Bickley.
	Jonas,	4568	"	Feb. 27, 1843			Ella Rogers.
	William Henry,	4569	"	Aug. 6, 1845			Hattie Tuttle; dau. Edward.
	Ira Fayette,	4570	"	Aug. 28, 1848			Lizzie Crowley.
	Ida Jeanette,	4571	"	Aug. 28, 1848	Aug. 13, 1883		
	Walter W.,	4572	"	Aug. 10, 1851			Alice Bickley.

LEWIS, JR., AND LAURA ANN (HANSCOM) WOOD. 4560.

	Lewis Elcestine,	4573	Boston,	May 26, 1852		[(Mercer).
80	Laura Estelle,	4574	"	June 14, 1857	July 28, 1874	Luther Winthrop Puffer; 1855–; s. Alvin D. and Sarah
	William Norcross,	4575	Malden,	Apr. 25, 1867		

LUTHER WINTHROP AND LAURA ESTELLE (WOOD) PUFFER. 4574.

	Luther Winthrop, Jr.,	4576	Medford,	Aug. 12, 1876			
	Alvin Wood,	4577	"	Aug. 11, 1878			
	Leon Hanscom,	4578	"	July 26, 1880			

HENRY ORVILLE AND REBECCA WHEELER (WOOD) LOTHROP. 4561.

	Orville Henry,	4579	Acton,	Apr. 11, 1848	Aug. 22, 1848		[Almira (Whittridge).
80	William Henry,	4580	Milford,	Sept. 8, 1851		Nov. 9, 1874	Lelia Antoinette Sanborn; 1853–; d. Edward R. and
80	George Jenks,	4581	"	Jan. 26, 1853		Jan. 26, 1882	Mary Louisa O'Neill; 1856–; d. John & Eliz. (Rogers).
	Rebecca Wheeler,	4582	"	Aug. 14, 1854	Oct. 6, 1854		

WILLIAM HENRY AND LELIA ANTOINETTE (SANBORN) LOTHROP. 4580.

Clara Velma,	4583	Boston,	Mar. 9, 1877		

GEORGE JENKS AND MARY LOUISA (O'NEIL) LOTHROP. 4581.

Jennie Louisa,	4584	Boston,	Feb. 3, 1883	Oct. 14, 1883	

GEORGE WASHINGTON AND CHARLOTTE HAPGOOD (JONES) TUTTLE. 4543.

Charlotte Ann,	4585	Lowell,	Jan. 23, 1831		

THEODORE AND CHARLOTTE HAPGOOD (JONES-TUTTLE) AMES. 4544.

80	Ellen Maria,	4586	Lowell,	Sept. 7, 1842	Sept. 24, 1875	Feb. 13, 1862	Elbridge Jones Robbins; 1834–; son Elbridge and
	George Theodore,	4587	"	Aug. 1, 1844			[Charlotte (White).
80	Frank Waldo Fisher,	4588	"	Apr. 5, 1847		Oct. 13, 1866	Georgianna Eaton Bryant; 1846–; d. John and Caro-
	Algernon LaForest,	4589	"	Sept. 22, 1850	July 12, 1852		[line G. (Burgess).

ELBRIDGE JONES AND ELLEN MARIA (AMES) ROBBINS. 4586.

George Laforest,	4590	Acton,	Jan. 18, 1867		
Grace Evelyn,	4591	"	Oct. 28, 1872	Sept. 24, 1874	
Fred Linwood,	4592	"	Oct. 24, 1874		

FRANK WALDO FISHER AND GEORGIANNA EATON (BRYANT) AMES. 4588.

Stella May,	4593	Charlestown,	Sept. 21, 1867		
Frank Eugene,	4594	"	Dec. 19, 1868		
Georgia Edith,	4595	"	June 27, 1873		

ABEL WHITE AND ANN MARIA (JOHNSON) JONES. 4545.

	Clara Maria,	4596	Acton,	July 5, 1844	May 17, 1865	Unmarried.	[Eliza C. (Nichols).
80	George Abel,	4597	"	Aug. 1, 1845		Sept. 1, 1869	Hannah Amanda Messinger; 1849–; d. Daniel E. and

GEORGE ABEL AND HANNAH AMANDA (MESSINGER) JONES. 4597.

George Herman,	4598	Hopedale,	June 1, 1870		
Ernest Wellrose,	4599	"	Mar. 7, 1873		

LUKE AND LUCY K. (BRIGHAM) JONES. 4547.

Charles Brigham,	4600	Worcester,	Nov., 1842	Nov., 1842	

LUKE AND HANNAH (GEER) JONES. 4548.

Charles Luke,	4601	Worcester,	Oct. 18, 1846	Oct. 25, 1846	

DANIEL AND CLARISSA (JONES) WETHERBEE. 4549.

	Daniel,	4602	Acton,	Mar. 25, 1838	Aug. 12, 1838		
80	Clara,	4603	"	Sept. 16, 1840		Sept. 11, 1866	J. R. Bassett. [Phebe (Flagg).
80	Daniel James,	4604	"	Jan. 23, 1844		Jan. 23, 1867	Augusta Adelaide Putney; 1843–; s. Jonas K. and
	Rosella,	4605	"	Apr. 8, 1846	Mar. 17, 1854		[M. (Weston).
80	Emma,	4606	"	July 17, 1848		Apr. 20, 1870	Isaac Warren Flagg; 1848–; s. Isaac T. and Eunice
	Charles Carroll,	4607	"	Jan. 20, 1852		Dec. 13, 1875	Mary Emma Perkins; 1851–; d. Israel B. and Mary
	Frank,	4608	"	Aug. 14, 1854	Apr. 14, 1862		[Esther (Davis).
	Roswell, M. D.,	4609	"	Aug. 30, 1857		June 3, 1885	Harriet Maud Raymond; 1858–; d. Francis & Susan
	Susan Adelaide,	4610	"	May 24, 1860			[L. (Smith).
	Frank Ellsworth,	4611	"	Nov. 14, 1862			

J. R. AND CLARA (WETHERBEE) BASSETT. 4603.

Minnie Gertrude,	4612	Acton,	Aug. 16, 1868		
Blanche Madie,	4613	"	May 2, 1871		
Eva,	4614	"	Feb. 3, 1873	Jan. 9, 1878	
Eva Clarissa,	4615	"	Dec. 29, 1877		

DANIEL JAMES AND AUGUSTA ADELAIDE (PUTNEY) WETHERBEE. 4604.

James Roland,	4616	Acton,	June, 1869		
Ernest Elwood,	4617	"	Sept. 26, 1870		
Mabel Frances,	4618	"	July 9, 1880		

ISAAC WARREN AND EMMA (WETHERBEE) FLAGG. 4606.

Irving Warren,	4619	Acton,	Dec. 17, 1872	Mar. 19, 1874	
Florence Hersom,	4620	"	Mar. 15, 1875		

ABRAM HAPGOOD AND HARRIET ESTERBROOK (HOSMER) JONES. 4550.

103	Oscar Abram,	4621	Acton,	Apr. 20, 1845		May 16, 1870	Eliz. Freelove Brown; 1848–; d. James & Dorcas E.
103	Lowell Atwood,	4622	"	Sept. 23, 1847		Nov. 21, 1869	Sarah Ann Parmenter; 1837–; d. Charles and Fanny
							(Goodnow). [Minerva R. (Danforth).
104	Charles Luke,	4623	"	Jan. 21, 1850		Nov. 24, 1874	Estella May Phillips; 1854–1886; dau. George and
	Clarence Harvey,	4624	"	Mar. 3, 1851			Emma Corson.
	Harriet Emma,	4625	"	July 12, 1853			
103	Ada Isabell,	4626	"	May 17, 1856		Sept. 8, 1878	Frank Marshall.

JAMES F. AND ELIZABETH (WHITNEY) JONES. 4552.

(Continued page 81.)

Lizzie Sophia,	4627	Stowe,	Oct. 2, 1854	July 3, 1855	
Florence Kate,	4628	Acton,	Sept. 16, 1856	July 5, 1880	
Herbert Whitney,	4629	"	June 7, 1860		

	Warren Henry,	4630	Acton,	July 15, 1865			
	Bertha May,	4631	Hudson,	May 1, 1871			

SILAS AND LUCINDA (WETHERBEE) JONES. 4477.

	Silas Wetherbee,	4633	Acton,	June 26, 1810	Mar. 13, 1834	May 12, 1833	Ann E. W. Piper.
81	Lucinda Eleanor,	4634	"	July 10, 1811	Feb. 8, 1850	June 19, 1828	Timothy Hartwell. No. 5860. [well).
81	Daniel, {	4635	"	Mar. 23, 1813	June 16, 1879	June 14, 1840	1. Mary E. Wheeler; dau. Alfred and Mary W. (Hart.
81	{	4636				Jan. 27, 1855	2. Maria T. Hildreth. [(Kelley).
101	Luther,	4638	"	Aug. 21, 1817	Nov. 17, 1862	Dec. 30, 1847	Susanna Kelley; 1824–1885; dau. Jonathan and Eliz-
81	Thos. G. Fes'nd'n,	4639	"	Jan. 12, 1822	Oct. 19, 1874	May 6, 1846	Louisa O. Tuttle; 1828–'74; d. Jeddediah and Louisa (Osborn).

TIMOTHY AND LUCINDA ELEANOR (JONES) HARTWELL. 4634.

81	Ellen, {	4640	Acton,	Apr. 9, 1830		Mar. 22, 1849	1. J. B. Hildreth; 1823–'64; s. Jos. & Pamelia (Read).
	{	4641				Nov. 21, 1877	2. M. D. Smith; 1827–; s. Josh'a & Eunice (Towns'nd).
	Lucinda,	4642	"	Aug. 24, 1832	Aug. 25, 1832		[R. (Hale).
81	Henry,	4643	"	Aug. 20, 1835		Apr. 1, 1863	Augusta H. Penniman; 1846–; dau. Otis H. and Eliz.
81	Chauncey,	4644	"	Oct. 2, 1841	June 19, 1885	Oct. 29, 1866	Emma F. Spear; 1847–; dau. Jos. and Syrena (Hoyt).

JOSEPH BARNARD AND ELLEN (HARTWELL) HILDRETH. 4640.

81	Mary Eleanor,	4645	Acton,	Dec. 12, 1849	May 26, 1881	Dec. 13, 1871	John Henry Farrington; 1851–1883; son. Alvin and
	Ella Maria,	4646	Westford,	May 11, 1851	Dec. 21, 1851		[Agnes (Maxwell).
	William Eugene,	4647	"	Feb. 19, 1856			
	Julia Victor,	4648	"	Nov. 4, 1857			

JOHN HENRY AND MARY ELEANOR (HILDRETH) FARRINGTON. 4645.

	Frederick Ernest,	4649	Waltham,	Dec. 15, 1872			

HENRY AND AUGUSTA HUTCHINSON (PENNIMAN) HARTWELL. 4643.

	Herman Otis,	4650	Acton,	May 2, 1864			[(Haynes).
	Bertha May,	4651	"	June 29, 1867			
	Emma Augusta,	4652	"	Dec. 23, 1869		Sept. 27, 1885	Herbert Nealey; 1866–; son Edward F. and Helen P.
	Herbert Henry,	4653	Concord,	Jan. 9, 1877	Jan. 15, 1878		
	Nettie Elizabeth,	4654	"	Jan. 1, 1879			

CHAUNCEY AND EMMA FRANCES (SPEAR) HARTWELL. 4644.

	Mabel Eleanor,	4655	Waltham,	Aug. 7, 1867			
	Arthur Spear,	4656	"	Nov. 14, 1869			

DANIEL AND MARY E. (WHEELER) JONES. 4635.

	George V.,	4657	Acton,	Oct. 9, 1841	July 20, 1842		
81	Anna Elizabeth,	4658	"	Mar. 24, 1844		Apr. 21, 1864	Silas P. Blodgett; 1836–; s. Jonas and Ann E. (Piper).

DANIEL AND MARIA T. (HILDRETH) JONES. 4636.

	Willie Clifton,	4659	Acton,	Dec. 24, 1855			
	Maria Theressa,	4660	"	Aug. 24, 1857	Aug. 25, 1857		
	Rosalie Hildreth,	4661	"	Aug. 8, 1858			
	Daniel Edward,	4662	"	Mar. 27, 1871			

SILAS PIPER AND ANNA ELIZABETH (JONES) BLODGETT. 4658.

	Perry Hartwell,	4663	Hyde Park,	Aug. 12, 1873			
	Helen Louise,	4664	"	July 19, 1877	Apr. 3, 1879		
	Amy Clifton,	4665	"	Oct. 12, 1880			

THOMAS GREEN FESSENDEN AND LOUISA OSBORN (TUTTLE) JONES. 4639.

	Ora Louisa,	4666	Acton,	Mar. 16, 1848	Sept. 30, 1870	Sept. 5, 1868	Henry H. Hanscomb; 1847–.
	Rosenna Tuttle,	4667	"	Oct. 10, 1851	June 20, 1867		[H. (Wales).
103	Lizzie Edna,	4668	"	Apr. 21, 1856		July 5, 1874	Charles Henry Martin; 1841–; son Geo. H. and Eliz.
	Carrie Josephine,	4669	"	Apr. 5, 1862			

LUTHER BLANCHARD AND CHARLOTTE (BILLINGS) JONES. 4478.

	Luther B.,	4670	Acton,	1822	May 2, 1827		
	Henry,	4671	"	1824	May 20, 1827		
	Clarinda B.,	4672	"	July 7, 1829	June 12, 1861	Nov. 30, 1856	Bradford Pickins, 1831–.
	Luther H.,	4673	"	1832	Sept. 6, 1881		
	Sarah Frances,	4674	"	1835	Aug. 24, 1836		

DENNIS AND DOROTHY (JONES) PUTNAM. 4480.

81	Harriet,	4675	Acton,	Oct. 8, 1825	June 17, 1865	June 1, 1848	Capt. A. C. Handley; 1823–; son John and Lucy (Proctor).
81	Susan, {	4676	"	Jan. 24, 1828		Sept. 14, 1849	1. Wm. R. Lothrop; 1820–'53; s. Chas. and Mary (Johnson).
	{	4677	"			Mar. 6, 1856	2. Henry O. Lothrop; 1823–; son Chas. and Mary (Johnson).
81	James Henry, {	4678	"	May 9, 1833		Oct. 29, 1856	1. Harriet A. Butler; 1830–'71; d. Sam'l and Nancy (Pollard).
	{	4679	"			Apr. 12, 1876	2. Jane A. Colburn; 1832–; d. Dwi't and Aurilla (Underw'd).

CAPT. AARON CHAFFIN AND HARRIET (PUTNAM) HANDLEY. 4675.

81	Harriet Elizabeth,	4680	Acton,	Jan. 27, 1852		June 1, 1877	Augustus Tuttle; 1846–; son Uriel H. and Lucy
	Emma Jane,	4681	"	Nov. 21, 1857			[(Burpee).
	Carrie Etta,	4682	"	Jan. 9, 1861	June 19, 1865		

AUGUSTUS AND HARRIET ELIZABETH (HANDLEY) TUTTLE. 4680.

	Alice Handley,	4683	Sterling,	June 26, 1881			

WILLIAM REED AND SUSAN (PUTNAM) LOTHROP. 4676.

81	Clara Jane,	4684	Acton,	Aug. 22, 1850		Nov. 5, 1873	James E. Walker; 1849–; s. Horace and Elmira A. (Chapin).

JAMES EUGENE AND CLARA JANE (LOTHROP) WALKER. 4684.

	Lelia Amy,	4685	Milford,	Mar. 14, 1880			
	Percy Lothrop,	4686	"	Dec. 23, 1884			

JAMES HENRY AND HARRIET AUGUSTA (BUTLER) PUTNAM. 4678.

(Continued page 82.)

	Name	No.	Birthplace	Birth	Death	Marriage	Spouse
	Louis Butler,	4687	Milford,	Sept. 4, 1859			
	Carrie Viola,	4688	"	Feb. 18, 1863	Apr. 9, 1863		

ELNATHAN AND ELIZA (TUTTLE) JONES. 4481.

	Name	No.	Birthplace	Birth	Death	Marriage	Spouse
82	Eliza,	4689	Acton,	Apr. 1, 1822		May 12, 1841	J. Tuttle; 1818–; s. Hon. Francis & Harriet (Wetherbee).
82	Evalina Tuttle,	4690	"	Apr. 12, 1826		Apr. 12, 1846	Henry Shapley; 1823–; s. Henry C. & Abigail (Parker).
	Geo. Elnathan,	4691	"	Sept. 25, 1828	Dec. 17, 1828		[riet (Wetherbee).
82	Elnathan,	4692	"	Dec. 11, 1829		Dec. 30, 1851	Elizabeth Tuttle; 1829–; dau. Hon. Francis and Har-
	Martha Ann (no issue),	4693	"	Dec. 15, 1831	Sept. 17, 1878	May 10, 1849	Francis Conant; 1827–; s. Paul and Matilda (Jewett).
	Caroline,	4694	"	Oct. 17, 1834	Apr. 15, 1835		
	George T.,	4695	"	Nov. 8, 1836	Aug. 21, 1839		
	Augusta,	4696	"	Aug. 13, 1838	Sept. 19, 1838		

JAMES AND ELIZA (JONES) TUTTLE. 4689.

	Name	No.	Birthplace	Birth	Death	Marriage	Spouse
	Laurietta,	4697	Acton,	Sept. 28, 1841	Feb. 25, 1842		
	James Herbert,	4698	"	Apr. 2, 1843	Apr. 11, 1844		
	James Adison,	4699	"	Mar. 30, 1845	Mar. 8, 1847		
82	Henry Waldo,	4700	"	Oct. 20, 1847		June 4, 1873	Lizzie Piper.
82	Ella F.,	4701	"	Feb. 9, 1850		Jan. 5, 1870	Lucius Hosmer.
82	Anna Ardella,	4702	"	July 10, 1853		Dec. 11, 1872	Theron F. Norton. [Lucretia P.
101	Nellie Louise,	4703	"	Mar. 11, 1856		Dec. 11, 1884	Chas. Henry Fairbanks; 1851–; son Madison and
	Arlettie J.,	4704	"	Jan. 4, 1859	Aug. 14, 1860		

HENRY WALDO AND LIZZIE (PIPER) TUTTLE. 4700.

	Name	No.	Birthplace	Birth	Death	Marriage	Spouse
	Howard Knowlton,	4705	Acton,	Aug. 22, 1880			
	Florence Piper,	4706	"	Sept. 21, 1883			

LUCIUS AND ELLA F. (TUTTLE) HOSMER. 4701.

	Name	No.	Birthplace	Birth	Death	Marriage	Spouse
	Lucius E.,	4707	Acton,	Aug. 14, 1870			

THERON F. AND ANNA A. (TUTTLE) NORTON. 4702.

	Name	No.	Birthplace	Birth	Death	Marriage	Spouse
	Bertha May,	4708	Acton,	Mar. 15, 1878			

HENRY AND EVALINE TUTTLE (JONES) SHAPLEY. 4690.

	Name	No.	Birthplace	Birth	Death	Marriage	Spouse
	Emma Augusta,	4709	Acton,	Aug. 20, 1846	Sept. 19, 1847		
	George Henry,	4710	"	July 5, 1848		Sept., 1877	Sadie C. Bromade.
82	Charles Herbert,	4711	"	Oct. 2, 1850			Lizzie M. Tilton.
	Frank Conant,	4712	Concord,	Aug. 4, 1853	May 22, 1863		
	Eugene Rockwood,	4713	Acton,	Feb. 2, 1856			
	David Shapley,	4714	Wilmington, Del.,	Nov. 17, 1858			
	Eva Cora,	4715	"	Dec. 15, 1865			
	Eda Flora,	4716	"	Dec. 15, 1865			
	Carrie Luella,	4717	"	Jan. 5, 1868			

CHARLES H. AND LIZZIE M. (TILTON) SHAPLEY. 4711.

	Name	No.	Birthplace	Birth	Death	Marriage	Spouse
	Harrie Tilton,	4718		July 29, 1878			

ELNATHAN AND ELIZABETH (TUTTLE) JONES. 4692.

	Name	No.	Birthplace	Birth	Death	Marriage	Spouse
	Frank Herman,	4719	So. Acton,	Oct. 5, 1853			
	Jennie Sophia,	4720	"	Oct. 15, 1856	May 22, 1857		
	James Elnathan,	4721	"	July 16, 1858	Apr. 28, 1860		
	Carrie Evelyn,	4722	"	Mar. 3, 1863			
	Ann Sophia,	4723	"	May 20, 1865	Jan. 26, 1868		

HON. JOHN AND CLARISSA (JONES) FLETCHER. 4483.

	Name	No.	Birthplace	Birth	Death	Marriage	Spouse
82	James, Rev.,	4724	Acton,	Sept. 5, 1823		Oct. 10, 1849	Lydia Middleton Woodward; 1824–1877; dau. Rev.
	Clarissa Jones,	4725	"	Nov. 1, 1825	Sept. 13, 1826		[Henry and Lydia (Middleton).
82	John, Hon.,	4726	"	Aug. 8, 1827		Apr. 25, 1850	Martha Taylor; '28–'82; d. Silas & Sophia (Hapgood).
82	Edwin, {	4727	"	Oct. 14, 1829		Apr. 29, 1858	1. Mary Jenkins; 1833–1863; d. Thos J. & Mary (McFarlan).
82	{	4728				Jan. 23, 1867	2. Susan Smith; 1838–; d. Chas. & Susan D. (Hodgkins).
	Clarissa Jones,	4729	"	Nov. 24, 1831	Apr. 21, 1845		
82	Abigail Billings,	4730	"	Dec. 25, 1835		May 3, 1857	Henry M. Smith.
85	Quincy Adison,	4731	"	Dec. 23, 1846		Nov. 9, 1881	Lauretta Kelly.

REV. JAMES AND LYDIA M. (WOODWARD) FLETCHER. 4724.

	Name	No.	Birthplace	Birth	Death	Marriage	Spouse
	Mary Wheelock,	4732	Danvers,	Feb. 6, 1851			
	James,	4733	"	Jan. 18, 1853	Dec. 10, 1858		
	Henry Woodward,	4734	"	Sept. 22, 1855	Dec. 31, 1858		

HON. JOHN AND MARTHA (TAYLOR) FLETCHER. 4726.

	Name	No.	Birthplace	Birth	Death	Marriage	Spouse
82	Silas Taylor,	4735	Acton,	Feb. 18, 1854		July 21, 1879	Sarah Frances Robbins; 1854–; dau. Elbridge & Mary
	Clara Sophia,	4735	"	Sept. 28, 1856			[E. (Hapgood).

SILAS TAYLOR AND SARAH FRANCES (ROBBINS) FLETCHER. 4735.

	Name	No.	Birthplace	Birth	Death	Marriage	Spouse
	John Taylor,	4736	Charlestown,	Aug. 3, 1881			

EDWIN AND MARY (JENKINS) FLETCHER. 4727.

	Name	No.	Birthplace	Birth	Death	Marriage	Spouse
	Carrie Evelyn,	4737	Acton,	Jan. 11, 1861	Apr. 27, 1863		

EDWIN AND SUSAN (SMITH) FLETCHER. 4728.

	Name	No.	Birthplace	Birth	Death	Marriage	Spouse
	Evelyn Stanwood,	4738	Acton,	June 5, 1869			

HENRY M. AND ABIGAIL BILLINGS (FLETCHER) SMITH. 4730.

	Name	No.	Birth				
	Hattie Emily,	4739	Jan. 11, 1863				
	Albert Fletcher,	4740	Dec. 24, 1864				
	Martha Fletcher,	4741	Sept. 13, 1867				
	Edwin Fletcher,	4742	Apr. 19, 1872				
	Charles,	4743					

NATHANIEL AND MARY (REDIT) JONES. 484.   (Continued page 83.)

	Name	No.	Birth	Death	Marriage	Spouse
	Elnathan, {	4744	Mch. 29, 1697	July 29, 1772	Sept. 22, 1721	1. Hannah Pierce; 1701–1730.
	(no issue), {	4745			Jan. 13, 1732	2. Rebecca Barrett. No. 13.
	{	4746			Oct. 2, 1740	3. Hannah Brown; –1779.

	Annie,	4747	Aug. 23, 1698		Feb. 15, 1726	Daniel Holden.
	Josiah,	4748	Jan. 19, 1702	June 4, 1741		Elizabeth ——.
	Mary,	4749	Mar. 8, 1700		Oct. 8, 1725	James Houghton.
	Dorcas,	4750	Jan. 17, 1704			
83	Ebenezer,	4751	Feb. 5, 1706			Priscilla ——.
	Elizabeth,	4752	June 25, 1707			
	Susanna,	4753	Mar. 5, 1712			
	Sarah,	4754	Oct. 28, 1715			

EBENEZER AND PRISCILLA ( ) JONES. 4751.

	Hannah,	4755	June 23, 1731			
	Mary,	4756	Feb. 22, 1733	May 31, 1815	Feb. 15, 1759	Jacob Brown; 1736–1816.
	Nathaniel,	4757	Feb. 8, 1737	Died young.		
	Nathaniel,	4758	Oct. 27, 1739			
	Redit,	4759	Mar. 12, 1742	Apr. 10, 1826	Apr. 15, 1768	1. Hannah Wheeler; –1788.
		4760			Jan. 12, 1762	2. Sarah Lee; 1757–1839.
	Priscilla,	4761	May 19, 1744		Jan. 7, 1768	Amos Jewett.
	Dorcas,	4762	Sept. 20, 1746		Mar. 9, 1769	Moses Haines.
	Ebenezer,	4763	Apr. 8, 1749	1792	Oct. 9, 1767	1. Hannah Fay.
83		4764			May 27, 1769	2. Sarah Fay; 1744–1821.

EBENEZER AND SARAH (FAY) JONES. 4764.

	Elnathan,	4765	Wakefield, Sept. 2, 1770			
	Nathaniel,	4766	" Dec. 29, 1772	May 6, 1857		Lois Alley.
	Hannah,	4767	" 1775	Oct. 10, 1829		Abijah Smith; 1765–1825.
83	Simon,	4768	" Jan. 1, 1780	1833		Rebecca Pool; –1865.
	Sarah,	4769	" Aug. 17, 1784	Oct. 12, 1862	Unmarried.	

SIMON AND REBECCA (POOL) JONES. 4768.

99	Simon,	4770	Wakefield, May 3, 1811		July 2, 1832	Betsey Galucia.
83	Sarah Fay,	4771	" Aug. 16, 1813	Feb. 20, 1849	Unmarried.	
83	Thomas,	4772	" Feb. 7, 1817			Elizabeth Ingalls; 1824–1851. [(Dudley).
83	Chas. Augustus,	4773	" Sept. 30, 1820	Apr. 10, 1884	June 12, 1849	Isanna Brigham; 1825–; d. Eliscom and Experience
	Warren,	4774	" Oct. 7, 1822			
	Loring Parker,	4775	" July 22, 1826		Nov. 5, 1852	Caroline E. Johnson.
83	Henry F.,	4776	" Dec. 29, 1830	Nov. 18, 1884	1855	Hannah E. Clark; 1833–1880.

THOMAS AND ELIZABETH (INGALLS) JONES. 4772.

	Charles Lyman,	4777	Wakefield, Mar. 12, 1847	June, 1852		
	Thomas Milton,	4778	" Aug. 19, 1849			

CHARLES AUGUSTUS AND ISANNA (BRIGHAM) JONES. 4773.

	Daisy Rebecca,	4779	Boston, July 7, 1866		Nov. 5, 1885	William Warren Davis; 1862–; son William and
						Adelia M. (Carter).

HENRY F. AND HANNAH E. (CLARK) JONES. 4776.

	S. E.,	4780	July 9, 1855			
	Herman,	4781	July 17, 1860			

EPHRAIM AND HEPZABAH (CHANDLER) JONES. 485.

	Mary,	4782	June 21, 1704			—— Prescott.
83	Ephraim,	4783	Sept. 20, 1706	Nov. 29, 1756	Sept. 12, 1728	Mary Hayward; 1708–1803.
	Joseph,	4784	1708	Mar. 24, 1709		
	Hepzabah,	4785	May 20, 1710			

EPHRAIM AND MARY (HAYWARD) JONES. 4783.

	Ephraim,	4786	May 1, 1730	Sept. 21, 1787	Nov. 7, 1752	Alice Cutler; 1730–1792.
	Mary,	4787	May 17, 1732		Dec. 29, 1757	1. Stephen Willis.
		4788			Mar. 4, 1762	2. Capt. Isaac Jones.
	Hepzabah,	4789	May 6, 1734	Aug. 10, 1790	May 3, 1753	Benjamin Hall; –1817.
	Rebecca,	4790			Mar. 15, 1757	1. David Wheeler, Jr.
		4791			1762	2. John Wolcott.
	Jonas,	4792	July 10, 1736	July 15, 1817	Sept. 6, 1763	Abigail Hartwell; 1744–1809.
83	Peter,	4793	July 26, 1741		May 2, 1765	Anna Tufts; 1744–.
	Lucy,	4794	Oct. 13, 1745	Feb. 10, 1826	Nov. 9, 1762	Richard Hall; –1827.
	Lois,	4795	Dec. 8, 1747	Mar., 25, 1750		
	Martha,	4796	June 19, 1750	Dec. 22, 1835	May 12, 1770	Ebenezer Hall; –1835.

PETER AND ANNA (TUFTS) JONES. 4793.

83	Samuel,	4797	Medford, Apr. 6, 1766	Dec. 24, 1830	Apr. 2, 1793	Lydia Estabrooks; 1770–1826.
83	Lucy,	4798	" Sept. 16, 1768	Jan. 18, 1847	Sept. 12, 1801	Joshua Cushman; –1834.
84	Peter,	4799	" Dec. 20, 1770	Dec. 15, 1816	June 21, 1796	Catharine Hay.

SAMUEL AND LYDIA (ESTABROOKS) JONES. 4797.

	Roxanna,	4800	June 6, 1801		Oct. 6, 1829	Daniel White.
	Peter,	4801	Sept. 22, 1802		May 7, 1829	Ann Eliza Locke; 1805–.

JOSHUA AND LUCY (JONES) CUSHMAN. 4798.

83	Charles,	4802	Dec. 28, 1802			Jane H. ——.

CHARLES AND JANE H. ( ) CUSHMAN. 4802.

83	Joshua,	4803	Aug. 16, 1828			Louise.
84	Charles Edward,	4804	Jan. 6, 1830			Susan L.
	Henry Hayden,	4805	Mar. 8, 1832			
84	George Webster,	4806	Mar. 9, 1838			Lucy J.
	Howard Sidney,	4807	July 6, 1841	May 17, 1863		

JOSHUA AND LOUISE ( ) CUSHMAN. 4803.

	Jennie Louise,	4808	Sept. 1, 1859	Jan. 6, 1875		
	Mary Allerton,	4809	Sept. 3, 1866			

CHARLES EDWARD AND SUSAN L. ( ) CUSHMAN. 4804.

	Fred Howard,	4810	Oct. 20, 1868			

GEORGE WEBSTER AND LUCY J. ( ) CUSHMAN. 4806.

	Alvin Wayland,	4811	June 24, 1872			
	Robert,	4812	Mar. 10, 1881			

PETER AND CATHARINE (HAY) JONES. 4799.

84	Catharine,	4813	Charlestown, Apr. 12, 1797	May 30, 1817		
84	Anna Tufts,	4814	" Feb. 9, 1799	Dec. 23, 1883	Oct. 10, 1821	Samuel Draper; 1787–1863.
	Lucy,	4815	" July 29, 1802	Oct. 16, 1853	Oct. 3, 1822	Wm. Austin; 1778–1841; s. Nath. and Marg't (Rand).
	Mary Hay,	4816	" Mar. 12, 1805	Jan. 8, 1827		[Jane (Mackintosh).
102	Peter Cushman,	4817	" Aug. 10, 1808	May 23, 1885	Oct. 20, 1831	Jane Mackintosh Baldwin; 1811–1876; d. Josiah and
	Elizabeth Mary,	4818	" June 7, 1811	1833	Apr. 10, 1831	Charles Berkeley Johnson; 1805–.

SAMUEL AND ANNA TUFTS (JONES) DRAPER. 4814.

	Catharine Jones,	4819	Charlestown,	Dec. 15, 1874	Unmarried.	
	Edw'd Lafayette,	4820	" Jan. 23, 1826		June 5, 1861	Emma Adeline Hunt; 1840–'75; d. Arad and Adeline.
	Sarah Mercy,	4821	"			
	Lucy Austin,	4822	"			
	Anna Elizabeth,	4823	"			
	Samuel, Jr.,	4824	"	Nov. 22, 1876		
	George Bartlett,	4825	"			
	William Austin,	4826	"			

WILLIAM AND LUCY (JONES) AUSTIN. 4815.

	Edward,	4827	Charlestown, July 29, 1823			
84	Lucy Jones,	4828	" Dec. 27, 1825		June 2, 1847	George A. Whiting.
84	Francis Boylston,	4829	" Sept. 6, 1827		Feb. 17, 1857	Ellen L. Whiting.
84	James Walker,	4830	" Jan. 8, 1829		July 18, 1857	Ariana E. Sleeper; dau. John S.
	Catharine Jones,	4831	"	Died young.		
	Charles,	4832	"	Died young.		

GEORGE A. AND LUCY JONES (AUSTIN) WHITING. 4828.

	Leslie,	4833	Charlestown, Dec. 8, 1848			
	George A.,	4834	" May 23, 1853			
	William Austin,	4835	" Aug. 5, 1855			
	Lucy A.,	4836	" Aug. 15, 1858			
	Ethel,	4837	" May 4, 1869			

FRANCIS B. AND ELLEN L. (WHITING) AUSTIN. 4829.

	William Russell,	4838	Andover, Nov. 3, 1857			
	Charles,	4839	Charlestown, Apr., 1860	Apr., 1860		
	Lucy,	4840	" Aug. 18, 1861		Oct. 13, 1886	Herbert L. Harding.
	Francis Boylston,	4841	" July 24, 1864			
	Jas. Walker, 2d,	4842	" July 16, 1866			
	Ellen Louise,	4843	" July 4, 1869			
	Richard,	4844	" May 6, 1873			

JAMES W. AND ARIANA E. (SLEEPER) AUSTIN. 4830.

	Herbert,	4845	Honolulu, S. I., May 6, 1859			
	Charles,	4846	" Aug. 16, 1862	Nov. 16, 1862		
	Walter,	4847	" Nov. 11, 1864			
	William Francis,	4848	" May 29, 1867	July 12, 1886		
	Edith,	4849	Boston, Dec. 5, 1873			

DEA. GEORGE AND REBECCA (BARRETT) MINOTT. 530–1896.

	Rebecca,	4850	Concord, Feb. 4, 1768	Apr. 13, 1858	Sept. 13, 1792	William Hayward.
37	Dorcas,	4851	" Apr. 19, 1769	Sept. 25, 1798	Dec. 1, 1796	James Barrett. No. 1904.
21	Lucy,	4852	" Apr. 22, 1770			Abel Barrett. No. 857.

JONES AND NANCY MARIA (WRIGHT) TUTTLE. 4386.

	Eugene Francis,	4853	Boston, July 26, 1858			[(Cutler).
	Mary Lizzie,	4854	" Oct. 3, 1863		Oct. 31, 1882	Joseph Parker Snelling; 1851–; son Jos. and Jane F.

BENJAMIN NEWTON AND ANN (HILL) WEBBER. 4055.

	Benj. Pillsbury,	4855	Lowell, July 5, 1838	Sept. 1, 1840		
	Mary Elizabeth,	4856	" Apr. 5, 1840	Jan. 2, 1841		
	Newton,	4857	" Oct. 12, 1846	Nov. 12, 1846		
	Annie Cora,	4858	" Nov. 12, 1856			

CHARLES KINGMAN AND MARY ELIZABETH (BAYLEY) ADAMS. 4018.

	Emma Jane,	4859	Bangor, Me., Nov. 1, 1852			
	Lizzie Hudson,	4860	" Aug. 23, 1855			[L. (Weston).
84	Charles Herbert,	4861	" Feb. 6, 1859		Jan. 10, 1884	Sarah Lois Lord; 1859–; dau. Charles E. and Caroline
	Frank Augustus,	4862	" Dec. 2, 1862			
	George Kingman,	4863	" Mar. 14, 1867			

CHARLES HERBERT AND SARAH LOIS (LORD) ADAMS. 4861.

	Lester Dwight,	4864	Bangor, Me., Nov. 10, 1884			

WILLIAM HENRY AND MARY CATHARINE (ADAMS) KIRKPATRICK. 4023.

	William Adams,	4865	Bangor, Me., Dec. 6, 1860			
	Charles Edward,	4866	" Feb. 14, 1865	May 28, 1867		
	Fred Hudson,	4867	" Aug. 25, 1868			
	Nettie Mabel,	4868	" Dec. 10, 1871			

DAVID AND BETSEY (ADAMS) HEARD. 3989. *(Continued page 85.)*

100	Augustus,	4869	Wayland, Feb. 16, 1819		Feb. 20, 1843	Maria French.

100	David,	4870	Wayland, Aug. 9, 1820	Nov. 4, 1850	Nov. 24, 1842	Nancy K. Hemingway.
100	Eliza Ann,	4871	" Nov. 7, 1823		June 15, 1851	Abraham Andrews Edwards, M. D.; 1796–1867; son
	Adison Adams,	4872	" Nov. 16, 1825	Oct. 20, 1826		[Abraham and Rebecca (Houghton).
	Edwin Hartwell,	4873	" Oct. 3, 1827	Oct. 20, 1857		
	Francis,	4874	" Aug. 29, 1829			H. Elizabeth Hunt.
	Mary Adams,	4875	" Mar. 6, 1832			
	Susan,	4876	" Mar. 29, 1834		Oct. 10, 1867	Robert B. Thomas.
100	Charles Baldwin,	4877	" May 29, 1836		Sept. 4, 1872	Helen M. Cushing.
	Ellen,	4878	" Feb. 16, 1839			
	Edward,	4879	" Nov. 29, 1840	Sept. 29, 1841		

JOB PAGE AND TABITHA ABRAHAM (JONES) WEBBER. 4053.

	Timothy Jones,	4880	Marblehead, Feb. 16, 1824	Jan. 15, 1838		
85	Woodward Ab'h'm,	4881	Lincoln, Dec. 12, 1826		May, 1856	Hannah Lucretia Waters.
	Henry Page,	4882	Lowell, Mar. 7, 1831			
	James Park,	4883	Fitchburg, Mar. 11, 1838	Mar. 29, 1842		
85	Lizzie Jones,	4884	Lowell, Sept. 24, 1840	Mar. 11, 1868	Nov. 20, 1860	Josiah Whitney Brown.

WOODWARD ABRAHAM AND HANNAH LUCRETIA (WATERS) WEBBER. 4881.

	Jos. Woodward,	4885	Weymouth, Oct. 6, 1856			
	Walter Page,	4886	Abington, Jan. 3, 1861			
	Lizzie Jones,	4887	" July 2, 1862			
	Anna Lucretia,	4888	New York, N. Y., Feb. 5, 1866			
	Maria Louisa,	4889	Fitchburg, Feb. 9, 1867			

JOSIAH WHITNEY AND LIZZIE JONES (WEBBER) BROWN. 4884.

	Mary Chase,	4890	Worcester, June, 1862	Apr., 1863		
	Alice,	4891	Balt., Md., Jan. 2, 1864	Oct., 1864		

EPHRAIM AND SARAH (TAYLOR) POTTER. 560.

85	Ephraim,	4892	Concord, Sept. 17, 1755	Jan. 19, 1825	Mar. 12, 1780	Elizabeth Eustis; 1754–1829; d. John & Eliz. (Coffin).
	Sarah,	4893	" Jan. 17, 1757		July 17, 1781	Samuel Lewis.
	Stephen,	4894	" June 18, 1758			
87	Jacob,	4895	" Aug. 12, 1759	Apr. 22, 1842	Nov. 11, 1783	Lucy Brooks; 1760–1844; dau. Luke.
	Mary,	4896	" Dec. 1, 1762	Nov. 10, 1822		

EPHRAIM AND ELIZABETH (EUSTIS) POTTER. 4892.

85	Mary,	4897	Concord, Nov. 28, 1780	Aug. 1, 1833	Jan. 9, 1814	John Dodge; –1840.
85	Wm. Eustis,	4898	" Mar. 15, 1782	Oct. 8, 1843	Dec., 1806	Alice Bass; 1786–1871.
86	Ephraim,	4899	" Oct. 28, 1784	Oct. 5, 1826		Mary Ann Barry; –1864.
	Elizabeth,	4900	" Aug. 28, 1786	Feb. 23, 1861	Unmarried.	
	Isaac,	4901	" Mar. 9, 1788	1825		
	David,	4902	" Apr. 6, 1789	June 4, 1829	Unmarried.	[(Hosmer).
86	Susan Bradshaw,	4903	" May 5, 1791	June 19, 1876	Jan. 9, 1814	Tilly Holden; 1786–1860; son Dan'l and Miliscent
	Daniel,	4904	" Feb. 20, 1793	May 29, 1810		
87	Asa,	4905	" July 11, 1794	June 18, 1876	Dec. 29, 1816	Sarah (Berry) Buswell; –1856.

JOHN AND MARY (POTTER) DODGE. 4897.

85	Charles Henry,	4906	Concord, Nov. 20, 1814		Mar. 13, 1841	Caroline Silsby Rumrill; 1817–.
	Mary Elizabeth,	4907	" Oct. 14, 1815	Mar. 24, 1839		[Bethia (French).
85	Solomon Haskell,	4908	Cambridge, Mar. 1, 1817	May 25, 1886	Apr. 21, 1842	Nancy French Everett; 1819–1859; d. Manning and

CHARLES HENRY AND CAROLINE SILSBY (RUMRILL) DODGE. 4906.

	Caroline Augusta,	4909	Feb. 12, 1843	Oct. 8, 1880	Jan. 19, 1872	W. H. Haley.
	Mary Elizabeth,	4910	Mar. 20, 1845	Oct. 11, 1846		
	Emma Frances,	4911	Jan. 7, 1847			
	Hayw'd Cushing,	4912	Dec. 24, 1848		Oct. 17, 1878	Winifred McIntyre.
85	Solomon Potter,	4913	June 27, 1852			
	Chas. Franklin,	4914	Dec. 16, 1864			

HAYWARD CUSHING AND WINIFRED (McINTIRE) DODGE. 4912.

	Marion Winifred,	4915	Roxbury, Feb. 28, 1885	July 7, 1886		

SOLOMON HASKELL AND NANCY FRENCH (EVERETT) DODGE. 4908.

	Solomon Everett,	4916	Cambridgep't, May 33, 1843	Dec. 21, 1844		[A. (Lambert).
	John Albert,	4917	" Oct. 15, 1844	Apr. 17, 1863		
89	Edward Everett,	4918	" Dec. 21, 1845		June 12, 1872	Mary Elizabeth Hartz; 1847–; dau. John P. and Mary
	Mary Elizabeth,	4919	" Dec. 13, 1847	Nov. 27, 1852		[Martha B. (Smith).
	Ellen Amelia,	4920	" Dec. 19, 1849	Sept. 27, 1850		
85	Alice French,	4921	" Oct. 17, 1854		Dec. 2, 1873	John Kelley Simpson, Jr.; 1847–; son John K. and

QUINCY ADISON AND LAURETTA (KELLY) FLETCHER. 4731.

	Nellie Clarissa,	4922	Apr. 1, 1883			
	Mabel Blanche,	4923	May 23, 1886			

JOHN KELLEY, JR., AND ALICE FRENCH (DODGE) SIMPSON. 4921.

	John Kelley, 3d,	4924	Arlington, May 14, 1876			
	Alice May,	4925	" May 18, 1878			
	Everett Oakes,	4926	" June 16, 1885			

WILLIAM EUSTIS AND ALICE (BASS) POTTER. 4898.

86	William Eustis, {	4927	Quincy, Dec. 31, 1807	Dec. 5, 1868	Feb. 20, 1827	1. Lucy Tilden; 1808–1836. [Eliz. (Foster).
86		4928			Oct. 30, 1833	2. Elizabeth Foster Lewis; 1812–1863; dau. John and
101	Susan Bird,	4929	Boston, Feb. 7, 1810		Apr. 30, 1826	George Stillman Smith; 1804–1870; son Samuel and
						Sally (Kelley).
86	Mary Ann,	4930	" Feb. 12, 1812		Jan. 1, 1837	Thomas Osborne; 1803–1853; son George.
86	Emeline Eliza,	4931	" July 26, 1815		Jan. 10, 1836	Ignatius Sargent; 1810–; s. John and Hannah (Taft).
	Alice,	4932	" 1820	1829		
86	Almira,	4933	" May 27, 1821		Sept. 1, 1840	Ira Perham; 1812–1870; son William and Susan.

WILLIAM EUSTIS AND LUCY (TILDEN) POTTER. 4927.

	Name	No.	Birthplace, Date		Death	Marriage	Spouse
	William Francis,	4934	Canton,	Sept. 9, 1827			
	Lucy Ann,	4935	"	July 31, 1829	Aug. 3, 1829		
	Ann Maria,	4936	"	Oct. 10, 1830	Dec. 28, 1830		
86	George Doane,	4937	Boston,	June 19, 1833		July 17, 1853	Lois Cole; 1827–; d. Willard & Betsey (Pickering).

WILLIAM EUSTIS AND ELIZABETH FOSTER (LEWIS) POTTER. 4928.

	Name	No.	Birthplace, Date		Death	Marriage	Spouse
86	William Eustis,	4938	Quincy,	Oct. 16, 1835		Aug. 31, 1865	Sarah W. Spencer; 1846–; d. John & Mary (Harris).
86	Elizabeth Foster,	4939	Boston,	Apr. 3, 1837		Aug. 2, 1855	Benj. Franklin Rollins; 1827–; son Meshack W. and
	Alonzo Lewis,	4940	"	June, 1839	1854		[Eliz. (Pierce).
99	John Thomas, {	4941	"	Sept. 13, 1847		1866	1. Emma Frances Mayo. [and Sarah E. (Tyler).
99	{	4942				Jan. 9, 1873	2. Lilly Washington Stevens; 1855; d. Seymour W.

GEORGE DOANE AND LOIS (COLE) POTTER. 4937.

	Name	No.	Birthplace, Date		Death	Marriage	Spouse
99	George Henry,	4943	Boston,	June 30, 1855		Feb. 3, 1881	Mary Jane Campbell; 1855–; d. Robt. J. and Sarah
	Edwin Rockwood,	4944	"	Aug. 8, 1857			[(Campbell).
	Benj. Francis,	4945	"	July 8, 1859	Apr. 8, 1862		
	Ida Frances,	4946	"	May 23, 1863		Oct. 7, 1885	John Edw'd Hislop; 1860–; s. Dan'l C. & Hannah E.
	Herb't Raymond,	4947	"	Jan. 6, 1870			

WILLIAM EUSTIS AND SARAH WILLIAMS (SPENCER) POTTER. 4938.

	Name	No.	Birthplace, Date	Death	Marriage	Spouse
	Samuel Eustis,	4948	Scituate, May 3, 1867	Sept. 15, 1869		
	Edward Foster,	4949	Boston, July 15, 1869			
	Willard Thomas,	4950	" Nov. 11, 1873			
	Charles Delmore,	4951	Scituate, Apr. 22, 1875			
	Elizabeth Anna,	4952	Topeka, Kan., Dec. 30, 1882			

BENJAMIN F. AND ELIZABETH FOSTER (POTTER) ROLLINS. 4939.

	Name	No.	Birthplace, Date	Death	Marriage	Spouse
	Annie Elizabeth,	4953	Boston, Apr. 13, 1859	Oct. 23, 1870		
	Bertha Frances,	4954	Chelsea, Sept. 23, 1872			

THOMAS AND MARY ANN (POTTER) OSBORNE. 4930.

	Name	No.	Birthplace, Date	Death	Marriage	Spouse
104	Walter Scott,	4955	Prov., R. I., May 21, 1840	June 5, 1851		
	Henry Faxon (Moore by adoption), {	4956	Nashua, N.H., Mar. 10, 1842		June 1, 1858	Julia A. Moore; dau. Samuel and Julia A.

IGNATIUS AND EMELINE ELIZA (POTTER) SARGENT. 4931.

	Name	No.	Birthplace, Date	Death	Marriage	Spouse
	Daniel Raymond,	4957	Machias, Me., Apr. 13, 1836	June 17, 1837		
	Mary Alice,	4958	" Sept. 6, 1837	Nov. 6, 1839		
86	Daniel Bartlett,	4959	Calais, Me., Aug. 27, 1839		Oct. 17, 1870	Fanny Menow Knowles.
	Mary Alice,	4960	" Feb. 27, 1841	Oct. 18, 1846		[E. (Lees).
86	Henry Clay,	4961	Machias, Me., June 2, 1843		July, 1861	Alice Bruce Heminway; 1843–1875; d. Wm. & Eliz.
	John,	4962	" Apr. 9, 1845	Aug. 17, 1846		[M. (Patton).
86	Ignatius Manlius,	4963	" Aug. 30, 1847		Apr. 29, 1872	Helen Maria Campbell; 1845–; d. Alex. F. and Julia
	John Dudley,	4964	" Sept. 6, 1849	May 19, 1859		[(McPhail).
86	Charles,	4965	" May 21, 1852		Dec. 20, 1880	Ada Maria Leeland; 1857–; d. Enoch S. & Margaret
	Winthrop,	4966	" Aug. 8, 1857	Dec. 14, 1857		

DANIEL BARTLETT AND FANNY MENOW (KNOWLES) SARGENT. 4959.

	Name	No.	Birthplace, Date	Death	Marriage	Spouse
	Winthrop,	4967	Omaha, Neb., Aug. 17, 1872			
	Mary Kennedy,	4968	" Sept. 5, 1874			

HENRY CLAY AND ALICE BRUCE (HEMINWAY) SARGENT. 4961.

	Name	No.	Birthplace, Date	Death	Marriage	Spouse
	John Dudley, 2d,	4969	Machias, Me., Dec. 18, 1861			

IGNATIUS MANLIUS AND HELEN MARIA (CAMPBELL) SARGENT. 4963.

	Name	No.	Birthplace, Date	Death	Marriage	Spouse
	Paul Dudley,	4970	Machias, Me., May 8, 1873			
	Grace Emeline,	4971	" Mar. 25, 1875			

CHARLES AND ADA M. (LEELAND) SARGENT. 4965.

	Name	No.	Birthplace, Date	Death	Marriage	Spouse
	Daniel,	4972	Portland, Me., Aug. 25, 1884			

IRA AND ALMIRA (POTTER) PERHAM. 4933.

	Name	No.	Birthplace, Date	Death	Marriage	Spouse
	Julia Heath,	4973	Boston, Dec. 6, 1841	Aug. 2, 1867		

EPHRAIM AND MARY ANN (BARRY) POTTER. 4899.

	Name	No.	Birthplace, Date	Death	Marriage	Spouse
	Mary Ann,	4974	Concord, Feb. 12, 1817	Died in infancy.		
	Mary Jane,	4975	" Feb. 5, 1819	May 22, 1847	Dec. 22, 1844	James B. Shipley.
86	Ephraim Barry,	4976	" Jan. 27, 1821		Dec. 15, 1842	Rebecca B. Watts; 1822–; 1868.

EPHRAIM B. AND REBECCA B. (WATTS) POTTER. 4976.

	Name	No.	Birthplace, Date	Death	Marriage	Spouse
	Adaline Rebecca,	4977	Concord, Sept. 9, 1844	May 11, 1876	Unmarried.	
	Abby Ann,	4978	" Aug. 8, 1847	July 14, 1875	Unmarried.	[Harriet (Tukey).
86	Charles Atwood,	4979	" Jan. 30, 1850		May 23, 1869	Hattie Eliza Purrington; 1845–; dau. Cornelius and

CHARLES ATWOOD AND HATTIE E. (PURRINGTON) POTTER. 4979.

	Name	No.	Birthplace, Date	Death	Marriage	Spouse
	Mary Addie,	4980	Lynn, July 9, 1870			
	Carrie Brooks,	4981	" Mar. 29, 1872			
	Nellie,	4982	" Feb. 26, 1874			
	William Herbert,	4983	" Nov. 16, 1875			
	Eugene,	4984	" Sept. 26, 1877			
	Georgia,	4985	" June 13, 1880			
	Arthur,	4986	" Mar. 18, 1883			

TILLY AND SUSAN BRADSHAW (POTTER) HOLDEN. 4903.

	Name	No.	Birthplace, Date	Death	Marriage	Spouse
	Susan Eustis,	4987	Concord, Jan. 21, 1825			[(Binney).
	John Albert,	4988	" Jan. 30, 1827			
86	Marshall Henry,	4989	" Mar. 4, 1829		Sept. 5, 1855	Mary Elizabeth Garfield; 1821–; d. Daniel and Polly
	Mary Elizabeth,	4990	" Dec. 29, 1833			

MARSHALL HENRY AND MARY E. (GARFIELD) HOLDEN. 4989.

	Name	No.	Birthplace, Date	Death	Marriage	Spouse
104	Henry Emerson,	4991	Concord, Sept. 11, 1859		Oct. 25, 1883	Annie Hayden Smith; 1859–; dau. Lorenzo G. and
	Clara Brigham,	4992	" June 14, 1864			[Olive (Nye)

ASA AND SARAH (BERRY-BUSWELL) POTTER. 4905.

	Name	No.	Birth	Death	Marriage	Spouse
87	Sarah Ann Robie,	4993	Concord, N. H., Nov. 1, 1817	Feb. 14, 1870	Unmarried.	
	Elizabeth F. A.,	4994	" Feb. 19, 1819	Mar. 18, 1819		
	Isabella Gordon,	4995	" June 5, 1820		July 10, 1850	William Taylor Andrus; 1825–; son Benjamin and
	Harrison Otis,	4996	" July 1, 1821	Jan. 11, 1827		[Clarissa (Taylor).
	Lorenzo,	4997	Chester, N. H., Mar. 20, 1823	Apr. 3, 1823		

WILLIAM T. AND ISABELLA GORDON (POTTER) ANDRUS. 4995.

Name	No.	Birth	Death	Marriage	Spouse
Charles Potter,	4998	New York, N. Y., Sept. 22, 1852	Aug. 2, 1853		

JACOB AND LUCY (BROOKS) POTTER. 4895.

	Name	No.	Birth	Death	Marriage	Spouse
87	Sarah,	4999	Concord, Sept. 19, 1784	Dec. 17, 1880	Apr. 10, 1802	Reuben Gates; 1780–1855; son Reuben and Sally
	Lucy,	5000	" Mar. 28, 1786	Sept. 7, 1815	Unmarried.	[(Fuller).
87	Lydia Brooks,	5001	" Aug. 6, 1789	Apr. 21, 1865	Sept. 2, 1813	Isaac Howe; –1868.
	Sophia (no issue),	5002	" Jan. 15, 1791	Jan. 30, 1879		1. Jacob Manning.
	(no issue),	5003			June 2, 1840	2. William L. Cogswell; 1803–1879.
	Silas,	5004	" Feb. 11, 1793	Apr. 10, 1820	Unmarried.	
	Maria (no issue),	5005	" May 22, 1797		Jan. 15, 1824	Isaac Staples; 1790–1866. [Nancy (Williams).
87	Henry,	5006	" May 12, 1799	Mar. 30, 1876	Aug. 15, 1843	Abigail Livermore Giles; 1811–; d. Capt. Benj. and
87	Dexter, Rev.,	5007	Leominster, Jan. 9, 1803	Apr. 2, 1881		1. Ulyetta Sabine. [and Eliz.
87		5008			May 15, 1845	2. Sarah Louisa Cogswell; 1813–1860; dau. Northend

REUBEN AND SARAH (POTTER) GATES. 4999.

Name	No.	Birth	Death	Marriage	Spouse
William,	5009	Sept. 24, 1808		Sept. 7, 1848	Mary Norton Clay; 1819–; d. John and Sally (Norton).

ISAAC AND LYDIA BROOKS (POTTER) HOWE. 5001.

Name	No.	Birth	Death	Marriage	Spouse
Isaac Gustavus,	5010	1869			

HENRY AND ABIGAIL LIVERMORE (GILES) POTTER. 5006.

	Name	No.	Birth	Death	Marriage	Spouse
87	Henry Staples,	5011	Somerville, May 31, 1845		Sept. 8, 1869	Sophia Grace Robbins; 1847–; d. Charles and Martha
	Wm. L. Cogswell,	5012	Boston, July 23, 1848		Jan. 1, 1873	Nellie Florence Bigelow. [M. (Maxwell).
	Emily Florence,	5013	Cambridge, May 22, 1850		June 23, 1881	Wm. Wilberforce Sias; 1845–, s. Wm. & Chloe B. (Hall).

HENRY STAPLES AND SOPHIA GRACE (ROBBINS) POTTER. 5011.

Name	No.	Birth	Death	Marriage	Spouse
Henry Staples, Jr.,	5014	Boston, Nov. 5, 1870			
Alexander Carleton,	5015	Cambridge, Aug. 27, 1873			
Gracie Florence Cogswell	5016	Boston, Aug. 27, 1878			

REV. DEXTER AND ULYETTA (SABINE) POTTER. 5007.

Name	No.	Birth	Death	Marriage	Spouse
Ulyetta Sabine,	5017	New Haven, Ct., June 9, 1839	Dec. 15, 1859	Unmarried.	

REV. DEXTER AND SARAH L. (COGSWELL) POTTER. 5008.

	Name	No.	Birth	Death	Marriage	Spouse
87	Sophia E. C.,	5018	Hampstead, L. I., Oct. 5, 1848	May 3, 1878	Dec. 21, 1871	E. Morris Stiger; 1839–.
	Maria Louisa C.,	5019	" Apr. 26, 1850	Apr. 28, 1850		
87	Maria Louisa F.,	5020	" Aug. 9, 1851	Apr. 10, 1875	June 25, 1874	Charles S. Moore; 1852–.
	William Henry,	5021	New York, N. Y., Oct. 7, 1854	Nov. 27, 1857		
	Charles N. C.,	5022	" July 16, 1859	Oct. 11, 1859		

E. MORRIS AND SOPHIA ELIZABETH COGSWELL (POTTER) STIGER. 5018.

Name	No.	Birth	Death	Marriage	Spouse
Frances Ann,	5023	Brooklyn, N. Y., Nov. 23, 1872			
William Dexter,	5024	" Dec. 20, 1873			
Grace Cogswell,	5025	" Oct. 22, 1876			

CHARLES S. AND MARIA LOUISA FREDERICA (POTTER) MOORE. 5020.

Name	No.	Birth	Death	Marriage	Spouse
Louisa Maria F.,	5026	Cambridge, Apr. 10, 1875			

JAMES AND LYDIA (POTTER) RUSSELL.. 562.

	Name	No.	Birth	Death	Marriage	Spouse
	Lydia,	5027	Concord, Nov. 2, 1765		Nov. 6, 1788	James Giles; 1767–1839.
	Mary,	5028	" July 10, 1767	Jan. 15, 1799	Unmarried.	
87	Elizabeth,	5029	" Jan. 25, 1769	Nov. 14, 1839	Aug. 12, 1790	Daniel Wheat.
87	Hannah,	5030	" July 20, 1770	Feb. 16, 1868	Aug. 9, 1792	1. Jesse Green.
	(no issue),	5031				2. Stephen Blood; 1770–1836.
87	Susanna,	5032	" Feb. 27, 1773	Nov. 20, 1831	Jan. 6, 1795	Reuben Duren; 1769–1819.
88	James,	5033	" May 9, 1775	June 5, 1858	Aug. 27, 1797	Mary Butler; 1779–1863; d. Jos. and Mary (Kidder).
89	Jacob,	5034	" Dec. 25, 1776	May 5, 1851	Oct. 5, 1800	Susanna Giles; 1778–1856.

DANIEL AND ELIZABETH (RUSSELL) WHEAT. 5029.

Name	No.	Birth	Death	Marriage	Spouse
Susanna,	5035				
Lucinda,	5036	Nov. 9, 1794		Nov. 16, 1820	Thomas Green.
Elizabeth,	5037				

JESSE AND HANNAH (RUSSELL) GREEN. 5030.

	Name	No.	Birth	Death	Marriage	Spouse
	Ephraim,	5038	Carlisle, June 30, 1800	Nov. 10, 1824	Unmarried.	
87	Charles,	5039	" June 30, 1800	Feb. 16, 1843	Sept., 1828	Lydia Hastings; –1885.

CHARLES AND LYDIA (HASTINGS) GREEN. 5039.

	Name	No.	Birth	Death	Marriage	Spouse
	Charles E.,	5040	Lowell, May 2, 1830	Aug., 1830		
	Elizabeth,	5041	" May 5, 1832			
96	Jennie,	5042	" May 17, 1833		June 6, 1855	Adison Churchill.

REUBEN AND SUSANNA (RUSSELL) DUREN. 5032.

	Name	No.	Birth	Death	Marriage	Spouse
87	Isaac,	5043	Carlisle, June 6, 1795	May 27, 1835	July 4, 1816	Mary Blood; 1796–1873.
	George,	5044	" Oct., 1803	May 9, 1804		

ISAAC AND MARY (BLOOD) DUREN. 5043.

	Name	No.	Birth	Death	Marriage	Spouse
88	George Frederick,	5045	Carlisle, Apr. 13, 1817		July 6, 1843	Lucy A. F. Pease; 1822–.
	Mary Elizabeth,	5046	" Dec. 12, 1818	Apr. 24, 1843		
	Susan Maria,	5047	" June 4, 1820	Sept. 20, 1844		
88	Martha Augusta,	5048	" Jan. 14, 1822		Apr. 14, 1844	Nathaniel Hutchinson.
88	Nancy Blood,	5049	" Jan. 3, 1824	Sept. 13, 1853	Apr. 21, 1842	Prescott Nickles; –1884.

GEORGE FREDERICK AND LUCY A. F. (PEASE) DUREN. 5045.

88	Isaac Frederick,	5050	Carlisle,	Oct. 31, 1844		Jan. 22, 1879	Mary Lewis; 1850–.
	Geo. Thompson,	5051	"	May 29, 1850	July 24, 1851		
88	Herman Leslie,	5052	"	Jan. 30, 1852		Apr. 16, 1879	Lottie Lewis; 1850–.
	Chas. Marshman,	5053	"	Apr. 9, 1854	Sept. 28, 1854		
	Geo. Rozalvin,	5054	"	May 18, 1858			
	Mary Francivilla,	5055	"	Mar. 27, 1865			

ISAAC FREDERICK AND MARY (LEWIS) DUREN. 5050.

Arthur Frederick,	5056	Sept. 7, 1885		

HERMAN LESLIE AND LOTTIE (LEWIS) DUREN. 5052.

Roy Leslie,	5057	Oct. 26, 1881		

NATHANIEL AND MARTHA AUGUSTA (DUREN) HUTCHINSON. 5048.

Hiram Nathaniel,	5058	Mar. 29, 1846		Apr. 7, 1870	Elizabeth Brown.

PRESCOTT AND MARY B. (DUREN) NICKELS. 5049.

88	George Prescott,	5059	Apr. 5, 1843	Oct. 19, 1884	Nov. 18, 1869	Sarah Abbie Daniels.
	Camilla Alesta,	5060	June 22, 1853	Aug. 22, 1853		

GEORGE PRESCOTT AND SARAH ABBIE (DANIELS) NICKELS. 5059.

Charles Albert,	5061	July 17, 1875		
Camilla Alesta,	5062	July 2, 1878		
Mary Elizabeth,	5063	July 15, 1881		

JAMES AND MARY (BUTLER) RUSSELL. 5033.

88	Wm. Lamb't, M.D.,	5064	Carlisle,	Oct. 28, 1799		June 2, 1836	Mary Ann Warren; 1816–; dau. Calvin and Caroline
88	Emerson,	5065	"	Sept. 13, 1802	Nov. 13, 1845	Apr. 12, 1830	1. Prudence Chapman; –1838. [(Carter).
		5066				1840	2. Charlotte E. Wyman.
88	Mary Ann,	5067	"	Oct. 3, 1804	Feb. 7, 1854	Apr. 12, 1832	Capt. David Butler; 1809–1885. [tha G. (Chapin).
88	Jas. Sullivan, A.M.,	5068	"	Mar. 23, 1807		Oct. 4, 1842	Eliz. Chapin Bartlett; 1813–1866; d. Waitt and Mar-
88	Geo. Wash'n, Hon.,	5069	"	Aug. 9, 1809		Jan. 1, 1835	1. Susan Faulkner; 1811–1847; dau. Nathaniel.
89		5070				May 16, 1849	2. Catharine Emily Smith; 1828–1861; dau. Solomon
		5071				June 20, 1865	3. Lydia (Baker) Waite; 1819–. [and Catharine.

DR. WILLIAM LAMBERT AND MARY ANN (WARREN) RUSSELL. 5064.

88	Caroline Griswold,	5072	Barre,	Mar. 3, 1838		June 21, 1860	William Howland; 1822–1880. [gail S. (Jenney).
	Mari Anne,	5073	"	Mar. 21, 1850		June 21, 1880	John C. Bartholemew; 1848–; son Gardner and Abi-
	William Calvin,	5074	"	May 10, 1868	May 21, 1876		

WILLIAM AND CAROLINE GRISWOLD (RUSSELL) HOWLAND. 5072.

William Russell,	5075	Lynn,	Feb. 19, 1863	
Bertha Morton,	5076	"	June 10, 1867	

EMERSON AND PRUDENCE (CHAPMAN) RUSSELL. 5065.

88	Mary Ann,	5077	Lowell,	Oct. 19, 1830		Feb. 26, 1849	Edwin Jones; son Edward and Betsey (Hill).
	Lucy Jane Chapman,	5078	"	Jan. 23, 1832			1. Frank Bailey.
		5079					2. Noah Bennett.
	Geo. Emerson,	5080	"	June 14, 1833	Aug. 9, 1833		
	Charles Perley,	5081	"	Oct. 28, 1836		Unmarried.	
88	James Sullivan,	5082	"	Nov. 10, 1837			Sarah Ellen Estes; –1884; d. Wm. and Mary (Bisbee).

EDWIN AND MARY ANN (RUSSELL) JONES. 5077.

	William Edmund,	5083	Chester, N.H.,	June 17, 1850		June 13, 1881	Amanda Bell; dau. James D. and Eliza (Morse).
88	Ellen Elizabeth,	5084	"	Nov. 25, 1856		Feb. 9, 1878	James T. Watts; son Freeman and Eliz (Wheeler).
	Edwin Plummer,	5085	"	July 8, 1860			
	Mary Ida,	5086	"	Aug. 4, 1864			

JAMES T. AND ELLEN E. (JONES) WATTS. 5084.

Alma Jones,	5087	Aug. 19, 1878		
Leroy Plummer,	5088	Jan. 21, 1883		

JAMES SULLIVAN AND SARAH ELLEN (ESTES) RUSSELL. 5082.

Geo. Emerson,	5089	Jan., 1866		
Charles Perley,	5090	May., 1869		
Addie,	5091	Aug. 31, 1877		

CAPT. DAVID AND MARY ANN (RUSSELL) BUTLER. 5067.

	Rockwood David,	5092		Dec. 5, 1834	Sept. 22, 1865	Apr. 16, 1862	Helen Baldwin.
	Orlando,	5093			Died young.		
	Annette Eudora,	5094	Pelham, N.H.,	June 17, 1842		Feb. 24, 1869	Henry W. Burton.
88	Francis Edward,	5095	"	July 30, 1844		Nov. 2, 1874	Elizabeth J. Doak; 1848–.
	Geo. Sullivan,	5096	"	June 26, 1848			

FRANCIS EDWARD AND ELIZABETH J. (DOAK) BUTLER. 5095.

Arthur Frank,	5097	Jan. 13, 1881		

JAMES SULLIVAN AND ELIZABETH CHAPIN (BARTLETT) RUSSELL. 5068.

	Elizabeth Bartlett,	5098	Lowell,	Sept. 11, 1843	Dec. 6, 1869	
	Mary Butler,	5099	"	Apr. 15, 1846		
	James Bartlett,	5100	"	June 5, 1850		
88	Martha Louisa,	5101	"	Nov. 9, 1855	Dec. 22, 1879	Hiram J. Potter; 1852–.

HIRAM J. AND MARTHA L. (RUSSELL) POTTER. 5101.

James Russell,	5102	Lowell,	Nov. 28, 1880	
Helen Leslie,	5103	"	July 22, 1883	

HON. GEORGE WASHINGTON AND SUSAN (FAULKNER) RUSSELL. 5069. (Continued page 89.)

	George Faulkner,	5104		Dec. 25, 1835	Jan. 24, 1837	May 12, 1862	1. Anna Thompson; –1864.
	James William,	5105	Roxbury,	June 10, 1837		Feb., 1869	2. Pluma Fowler.
		5106					
	Frances Jane,	5107		Nov. 29, 1838	Mar. 12, 1840		
	Francis Faulkner,	5108		Feb. 4, 1841			
	Susan Maria,	5109		Sept. 22, 1847	Aug. 26, 1848		

HON. GEORGE WASHINGTON AND CATHARINE E. (SMITH) RUSSELL. 5070.

	George Albert,	5110		Apr. 12, 1851	Dec. 12, 1856		
	Henry Martin,	5111		Aug. 15, 1852	May 29, 1854		
	John Herbert,	5112		Nov. 17, 1855		Mar. 2, 1885	Katharine Field.
	Edward Smith,	5113		Oct. 3, 1861			

JACOB AND SUSANNA (GILES) RUSSELL. 5034.

89	Miranda,	5114	Carlisle,	Jan. 9, 1801	July 2, 1880	Feb. 9, 1830	John Dummer; 1792–1865; s. John & Susanna (Duty).
89	Susan,	5115	"	Dec. 24, 1802	Feb. 14, 1841	1825	Thomas Blake.
89	Milo,	5116	"	Jan. 20, 1805		Nov. 1, 1827	1. Elizabeth P. Rice; –1876.
		5117				Apr. 26, 1878	2. Hannah Russell.
89	Francis,	5118	"	Feb. 1, 1807		Oct. 17, 1833	Mary White; 1805–.
	Samuel Jacob,	5119		1810			1. Lucy Jewell.
		5120					2. Mary Hotchkins.
89	Lydia,	5121	"	Mar. 8, 1812		Oct. 4, 1836	Dexter Mussey.

JOHN AND MIRANDA (RUSSELL) DUMMER. 5114.

	John,	5122	Lowell,	Oct. 30, 1830	June 25, 1848		
	Mary,	5123	"	Mar. 7, 1832	Apr. 28, 1835		
	Mehitable,	5124	"	Oct. 18, 1833	Apr. 24, 1851		[M. (Lee).
89	Edward,	5125	"	Feb. 20, 1841		Mar. 20, 1879	Sarah Maria Barrows; d. Prof. Elijah P. and Sarah

EDWARD AND SARAH M. (BARROWS) DUMMER. 5125.

	William Barrows,	5126	Newbury, June 27, 1880		
	Edward Lee,	5127	Waltham, June 18, 1883		

EDWARD EVERETT AND MARY ELIZABETH (HARTZ) DODGE. 4918.

	Alice Everett,	5128	Madison, Kan., Mar. 7, 1874	
	William Irving,	5129	" Nov. 11, 1875	
	Edward,	5130	" Dec. 28, 1877	
	Annie,	5131	" Dec. 16, 1880	
	Edith,	5132	" Jan. 24, 1883	

THOMAS AND SUSAN (RUSSELL) BLAKE. 5115.

89	Marinda Russell,	5133	Boston,	June 30, 1826	July 5, 1852	June 3, 1847	Michael Homer Mandell.
	Thos. Franklin,	5134	"	Nov. 5, 1828	Apr. 22, 1842		
	Susan Maria,	5135	"	Nov. 5, 1828			1. John Baker.
		5136					2. Smith Chapin.
89	Fred'k William,	5137	"	Oct. 3, 1831		Mar. 19, 1856	Caroline L. Adams.

MICHAEL H. AND MARINDA R. (BLAKE) MANDELL. 5133.

	Mary Dummer,	5138	Lowell, Feb. 17, 1848	Nov. 27, 1873	Handel Stedman Robbins; 1830–.

FREDERICK WILLIAM AND CAROLINE L. (ADAMS) BLAKE. 5137.

89	Mary Anna,	5139	Jan. 6, 1857	Feb. 15, 1879	John M. Jewett.
	Susan Parker,	5140	Dec. 1, 1858	July 2, 1885	Rev. James H. Childs.
	Carrie Louisa,	5141	Mar. 10, 1863		

JOHN M. AND MARY A. (BLAKE) JEWETT. 5139.

	Robert Arthur,	5142	Norway, Me., Aug. 14, 1881
	Harrold Blake,	5143	" Aug. 29, 1885

MILO AND ELIZABETH P. (RICE) RUSSELL. 5116.

	Mary Elizabeth,	5144	Groton,		Oct. 5, 1845		
89	Sarah Rebecca,	5145	"	Apr. 1, 1830		June 29, 1854	William M. Shattuck.
	T. Stillman,	5146	"	Oct. 2, 1831			
	William Melvin,	5147	"	Mar. 12, 1833			
	John Francis,	5148	"	Jan. 12, 1838			
	James Lewis,	5149	"	Dec. 10, 1839			
	Frances L.,	5150	"	July 28, 1843	Oct. '13, 1843		
	Elizabeth Olive,	5151	"	Sept. 7, 1845			—— Irving.
	Charles,	5152	"	Apr. 5, 1847			
	Henry Oliver,	5153	"	Apr. 7, 1848			

WILLIAM M. AND SARAH REBECCA (RUSSELL) SHATTUCK. 5145.

	Ellen L. T.,	5154	Pepperell,	Aug. 22, 1857	
	Mark W.,	5155	"	Feb. 28, 1861	
	Ansel M.,	5156	Groton,	June 7, 1863	

FRANCIS AND MARY (WHITE) RUSSELL. 5118.

	Mary E.,	5157	July 6, 1835	Dec. 6, 1866	Joseph G. Tenney.
89	Francis Calvin,	5158	Apr. 3, 1837	Aug. 29, 1870	Mary E. Smith.
89	Henry H.,	5159	Mar. 5, 1842	1863	Dida Lord.

FRANCIS C. AND MARY E. (SMITH) RUSSELL. 5158.

	Louisa W.,	5160	June 29, 1873
	Francis Smith,	5161	June 8, 1876

HENRY H. AND DIDA (LORD) RUSSELL. 5159.

	Francis Lord,	5162	Apr. 10, 1866

DEXTER AND LYDIA (RUSSELL) MUSSEY. 5121. (Continued page 90.)

	Maryetta D.,	5163	Mar. 25, 1840	Nov. 5, 1862	Almagro Palmerlee.

	Nathan D.,	5164		Mar. 21, 1838		May 15, 1865	1. Mary A. Dewey.
		5164½				Apr. 7, 1871	2. Mary Drake.
	George D.,	5165		Dec. 2, 1841		Dec. 29, 1862	Amelia Chamberlain.
	Martha I.,	5166		Nov. 2, 1845		Nov. 22, 1878	Frank Hotchkiss.
	Josephine P.,	5167		Sept. 30, 1851			
	Harvey E.,	5168		Mar 18, 1849		Nov. 25, 1884	Ella Lyon.

JONAS AND PERSIS (BARRETT) POTTER. 565–1898.

90	Samuel,	5169	Concord,	Oct. 14, 1767	Oct. 29, 1831	Mar. 11, 1788	Lucy Hosmer. No. 5992. [Lydia (Billings).
91	Rebecca,	5170	"	Feb. 24, 1770	Dec. 15, 1826	Feb. 12, 1792	1. Charles Weston; 1769–1811; son Stephen, Jr., and
		5170				Nov. 7, 1815	2. Josiah Merriam; 1755–1832.
	Persis,	5171	"	Jan. 10, 1772	June 3, 1792	Feb. 12, 1792	Levi Parks.
	Elizabeth,	5172	"	July 15, 1775	Oct. 14, 1806	Unmarried.	
	Lucy,	5173	"	Jan. 21, 1779	Mar. 6, 1854	Unmarried.	

JONAS AND SARAH (JONES) POTTER. 566.

93	Jonas,	5174	Concord,	Oct. 16, 1784	July 3, 1868	May 7, 1812	Sarah Melvin; 1790–1851; dau. Jacob and Sarah
65	Sally,	5175	"	Sept. 24, 1788	May 6, 1810	Oct. 11, 1807	Joshua Brown. No. 3648. [(Dexter).
93	John,	5176	"	Nov. 18, 1793	Mar. 15, 1875	Oct. 18, 1818	Sybil Gay Flagg; 1801–1865; dau. Dan. and Phebe
	James,	5177	"	Mar. 14, 1800	Jan. 9, 1802		[(Stevens.)

SAMUEL AND LUCY (HOSMER) POTTER. 5169–5998.

	Nathan,	5178	Concord,	Aug. 31, 1789	May 13, 1813	Unmarried.	
	Dorcas (no issue),	5179	"	Feb. 29, 1791	Aug. 15, 1840	Sept. 21, 1820	Thomas R. Warren; 1798–1861.
	Sewell,	5180	"	May 30, 1794			
	Silas,	5181	"	July 17, 1797	Died at sea.	Unmarried.	
90	Tilly,	5182	"	June 14, 1800	July 7, 1872	1823	1. Ellen Van Sickel; 1806–1833.
90		5183				1835	2. Mrs. Eliza Foulk; 1804–.
	James,	5184	"	Mar. 9, 1803	Apr., 1842		
90	Francis,	5185	"	July 21, 1805	Oct. 27, 1876	Dec. 7, 1828	Mary Hayward. No. 3860. [Lucy (Wesson).
90	Samuel,	5186	"	Sept. 18, 1807	May 24, 1875	Feb. 3, 1828	Jane Smith Baird; Nov. 19, 1806–; dau. Lewis and

TILLY AND ELLEN (VAN SICKEL) POTTER. 5182.

	Tilly Augustus,	5187	Erie, Pa.,	Mar. 3, 1824	1857	Unmarried.	
90	Louisa Jarvis,	5188	"	Feb. 16, 1828		June 19, 1848	T. T. Morris; 1822–.
	Dorcas,	5189	"	May 16, 1830	June 21, 1830		

TILLY AND ELIZA (FOULK) POTTER. 5183

	Mary E. (by adoption),	5190		July 12, 1850			

T. T. AND LOUISA JARVIS (POTTER) MORRIS. 5188.

90	Francis Tilly,	5191	Pittsb'g, Pa., July 21, 1849			Oct. 28, 1875	Jennie Eva Bachtell; 1854–.
90	Rob't Stevenson,	5192	" Nov. 24, 1851			May 1, 1877	Alice Burckholter.
90	Ella Virginia,	5193	" Sept. 9, 1853		Aug. 30, 1880	Oct. 18, 1877	B. O. Hanger.
90	Laura Louisa,	5194	Penora, Ia., Dec. 29, 1855		Aug. 18, 1882	Sept. 17, 1884	E. H. Gottwalt.
90	Harry Monfort,	5195	Carrolton, Ia., Apr. 3, 1858			Aug. 17, 1879	Amy Towne; 1861–.
90	William Thomas,	5196	" Mar. 11, 1860			July 8, 1880	Anna Thuregood; 1861–.
	John Augustus,	5197	" Feb. 2, 1862			May 20, 1884	Estella Kirk; 1864–.
	Carrie,	5198	" Nov. 5, 1863			May 28, 1884	Emilé Tousch; 1861–.
	Mary,	5199	Des Moines, Ia., May 29, 1866		May 8, 1867		
	Freddie Herbert,	5200	" Dec. 13, 1870				

FRANCIS T. AND JENNIE E. (BACHTELL) MORRIS. 5191.

	Roy Bachtell,	5201		June 4, 1879			

ROBERT STEVENSON AND ALICE (BURCKHOLTER) MORRIS. 5192.

	Louisa,	5202		Mar. 1, 1880			
	Laura,	5203		Jan. 2, 1884			

B. O. AND ELLA V. (MORRIS) HANGER. 5193.

	Maud,	5204		Oct., 1879			

E. H. AND LAURA L. (MORRIS) GOTTWALT. 5194.

	George M.,	5205		Feb. 2, 1875			

HARRY M. AND AMY (TOWNE) MORRIS. 5195.

	Maud,	5206		June 12, 1880			
	Gussie,	5207		Oct. 21, 1881			

WILLIAM T. AND ANNA (THUREGOOD) MORRIS. 5196.

	Ella,	5208		Aug. 21, 1881			

FRANCIS AND MARY (HAYWARD) POTTER. 5185–3860.

	William Francis,	5209	Concord,	Feb. 26, 1830			[wood).
	Mary Jane,	5210	"	Dec. 22, 1832		Mar. 21, 1866	Sylvester Lovejoy; 1832–; s. Selah and Miriam (Hey-

SAMUEL AND JANE S. (BAIRD) POTTER. 5186.

90	Charles F., Dea.,	5211	Concord,	Mar. 29, 1829		Mar. 14, 1860	Helen A. Spear; Aug. 23, 1836–; dau. Henry T. and
90	Silas Warren,	5212	"	Feb. 2, 1831	July 28, 1878	Mar. 27, 1853	Celana A. Parker; –1861. [Hepzibeth P. (Fernald).
91	Harriet Jane,	5213	"	June 8, 1833		June 21, 1849	1. Stephen Perkins; 1828–1854. [(Adams).
91		5214				Nov. 8, 1857	2. Amos Part'ge Oliver; 1823; s. Forbes and Nancy
91	Samuel Lewis,	5215	Sudbury,	Sept. 24, 1838		Jan. 1, 1860	Charlotte B. Beakel; 1839–; d. Chester and Martha D. (Ames).
91	James Henry,	5216	"	Aug. 21, 1840		Jan. 18, 1862	Abbie Weltha Walker; 1859–; d. Wm. and Miriam H.
	Lucy Baird,	5217	"	Mar. 25, 1842	Feb. 28, 1846		[(Hawkins).
91	Aline Augusta,	5218	"	Feb. 10, 1846		May 21, 1863	Henry Newcomb; 1841–; s. Jas. and Sarah G. (Rice).

DEA. CHARLES FRANCIS AND HELEN AUGUSTA (SPEAR) POTTER. 5211.

	Mary Goddard,	5219	Somerville, Mar. 10, 1864				
	Henry Austin,	5220	Brighton, July 24, 1869				

SILAS WARREN AND CELANA A. (PARKER) POTTER. 5212.

(Continued page 91.)

91	George Warren,	5221	Stow,	Dec. 13, 1853		Mar. 21, 1877	Lizzie Jane McLaughlin; 1857-; dau. John and Eliza J. (Ackerman).
91	Ida Frances,	5222	Windham, Me., Oct. 10, 1856	July 2, 1883		Mar. 31, 1874	John Bargoon Parsell; 1848-; son Richard H. C. and [Eliza A. (Ely).
	Laura Louise,	5223	Cleveland, O., May 7, 1860	Aug. 31, 1861			

GEORGE WARREN AND LIZZIE JANE (McLAUGHLIN) POTTER. 5221.

	Geo. Warren, Jr.,	5224	Acton,	May 25, 1878			
	John Samuel,	5225	"	May 21, 1880			
	Frank Rich,	5226	"	Aug. 14, 1883			

JOHN BARGOON AND IDA FRANCES (POTTER) PARSELL. 5222.

	Carrie Louisa,	5227	Ohio,	July 20, 1875			
	Alice Emma,	5228	"	Nov. 6, 1876	Jan. 10, 1882		
	Warren Clay,	5229	"	Aug. 3, 1879			

STEPHEN AND HARRIET JANE (POTTER) PERKINS. 5213.

91	James Orrin,	5230	Acton,	June 25, 1850		Oct. 20, 1880	Ida May Moran; 1858-; d. John and Margaret (Lotta).
91	Harriet Jane,	5231	Stow,	July 2, 1852		Oct., 1870	Chas. LeRoy Sawyer; 1850-; s. John B. & Louisa S. (Newton).

AMOS PARTRIDGE AND HARRIET JANE (POTTER-PERKINS) OLIVER. 5214.

91	Lucy Potter,	5232	Barre,	Mar. 14, 1859		Sept. 20, 1876	Norman Richardson; 1852-; s. Jesse C. and Mary F.
	Cora Aline,	5233	Oakham,	Apr. 13, 1861		Aug. 25, 1886	John Bargoon Parsell. No. 5222. [(Pratt).
	Frank Edward,	5234	"	Nov. 4, 1864			

JAMES ORRIN AND IDA MAY (MORAN) PERKINS. 5230.

	Cora Aline,	5235	Eden Prairie, Minn., Oct. 15, 1882				
	Laura Mary,	5236	Devil's Lake, Dak., Apr. 23, 1885				

CHARLES LEROY AND HARRIET JANE (PERKINS) SAWYER. 5231.

	Ralph LeRoy,	5237	Worcester, Oct. 3, 1872	Nov. 7, 1886			
	Barbara Inez,	5238	Dakota, July 1, 1880				
	Blanche Louisa,	5239	" Sept. 18, 1882				

NORMAN AND LUCY POTTER (OLIVER) RICHARDSON. 5232.

	Marion Grace,	5240	Concord,	Jan. 31, 1880			

SAMUEL LEWIS AND CHARLOTTE BUNDY (BEAKEL) POTTER. 5215.

	Helen Frances,	5241	Cleveland, O., Aug. 24, 1861			June 2, 1886	Elmer Huston Libert; '58-; s. Geo. & Phebe A. (Huston).

JAMES HENRY AND ABBY W. (WALKER) POTTER. 5216.

	Jas. Willie (by adoption),	5242	New Braintree, Mar. 22, 1863				

HENRY AND ALINE AUGUSTA (POTTER) NEWCOMB. 5218.

91	Minnie Baird,	5243	Barre,	Mar. 1, 1864		Dec. 24, 1883	Frank Urbanus Rich, M. D.; 1857-; son Raymond S. and Eleanor J. (Grant).

DR. FRANK U. AND MINNIE B. (NEWCOMB) RICH. 5243.

	Ethel Belle,	5244	Maynard,	Apr. 21, 1886			

CHARLES AND REBECCA (POTTER) WESTON. 5170.

91	Charles,	5245	Lincoln,	Apr. 22, 1794	Dec. 31, 1873	Apr. 14, 1819	Lois Coburn; 1795-1871.
	Mary,	5246	"				
91	Persis,	5247	"	Sept. 10, 1792	Apr. 13, 1853		Charles Warren; 1788-1870.
	Sally,	5248	"	Aug. 26, 1801	1829	Unmarried.	
92	Eri,	5249	"	Sept. 24, 1803	Aug. 19, 1875	Apr. 1, 1827	Emily Fiske; 1806-; dau. Jonas and Abigail (Pierce).
92	Rebecca,	5250	Littleton,	Oct. 24, 1796	Dec. 11, 1874	1819	Geo. W. Garfield; 1797-1880.
	Hiram,	5251	"	Apr. 20, 1806	1838	Unmarried.	
93	Jonas,	5252	Lincoln,	Nov. 1, 1808		May, 1839	Adaline A. Verry; 1808-.

CHARLES AND LOIS (COBURN) WESTON. 5245.

	Ann Maria,	5253	Weston,	Apr. 21, 1820	Mar. 6, 1846	Unmarried.	
	Charles Dexter,	5254	"	Sept. 24, 1822		Sept. 9, 1856	Nancy Maria Sanborn; 1827-; d. Ashael and Abigail [(Lovejoy).
	Sarah Jane,	5255	"	Jan. 7, 1825	Oct. 22, 1828		
	Frederick,	5256	"	Jan. 12, 1828	Mar. 9, 1884		

CHARLES AND PERSIS (WESTON) WARREN. 5247.

91	Persis Barrett, {	5257	Brookline, June 19, 1812	May 31, 1878	Sept. 27, 1831	1. William Lane; 1806-1836.	
91		5258	"		Mar. 10, 1839	2. William Clark Pope; 1809-1874.	
92	Charles Wright,	5259	"	Apr. 25, 1814	Jan. 16, 1874	June 14, 1835	Hannah B. Haven; 1817-.
92	Joseph Augustus,	5260	"	Aug. 14, 1816	Mar. 4, 1875	Apr. 16, 1839	Alice Boyce Hanson; 1817-.
92	Caroline Rebekah,	5261	"	Nov. 1, 1817	Oct. 7, 1876	Sept. 6, 1836	Josiah Wetherbee; 1811-1883. [Sally (Wyman).
92	Geo. Washington,	5262	"	Jan. 18, 1820		Aug. 14, 1862	Sarah Boynton Warren; 1835-; dau. Nehemiah and
92	Sarah Elizabeth,	5263	Weston,	Sept. 15, 1822		Nov. 28, 1844	Wm. Livermore; 1819-; son Jonathan and Eunice.
92	Cornelius Weston,	5264	"	Nov. 7, 1825		Jan. 6, 1853	Martha Ann Washburn; 1835-; dau. Charles & Martha
92	John Franklin, {	5265	"	July 13, 1829		July 10, 1859	1. Sarah A. Viles; 1830-1879. [(Murdock).
		5266				June 24, 1885	2. Georgianna Kendall; 1836-.
	William Francis,	5267	"	Mar. 7, 1836		Unmarried.	
	Jonas Potter,	5268	"	July 27, 1839	Jan. 12, 1853		

WILLIAM AND PERSIS BARRETT (WARREN) LANE. 5257.

91	Geo. Henry Willard,	5269	Fitchburg, June 30, 1833	Aug. 7, 1858	April, 1857	Frances M. Viles.	
92	Emory William,	5270	" Oct. 8, 1834		Oct. 2, 1860	Ellen Eliz. Warren; d. Nehemiah & Sally (Wyman).	
91	Franklin Wilder,	5271	" Jan. 25, 1836		July, 1857	Sarah A. Daniels; 1841-; d. Chas & Han'h (Turner).	

WILLIAM CLARK AND PERSIS BARRETT (WARREN-LANE) POPE. 5258.

	Warren Lane,	5272	Roxbury, Dec. 5, 1842			Aug. 25, 1864	Mary Harriet Treat; 1846-; dau. Shubael & Mary H. (Parker).

GEORGE HENRY W. AND FRANCES M. (VILES) LANE. 5269.

	Georgie Frances,	5273	Chelsea, April, 1858				

FRANKLIN WILDER AND SARAH A. (DANIELS) LANE. 5271.

	Frank Elliot,	5274	Charlestown, Dec., 1857	Died at sea.			

EMORY WILLIAM AND ELLEN ELIZABETH (WARREN) LANE. 5270.

	Name	No.	Birth		Marriage	Spouse
	Emory Warren,	5275	Waltham,	Oct. 21, 1861		
	Ida Persis,	5276	"	Mar. 29, 1863		
	Alice Boynton,	5277	"	Sept. 27, 1870		

CHARLES WRIGHT AND HANNAH B. (HAVEN) WARREN. 5259.

	Name	No.	Birth		Marriage	Spouse
92	Hannah Elizabeth,	5278	Boston,	Nov. 12, 1840	Oct. 23, 1858	Jonathan Peirce, Jr.; 1836–; son Jonathan.
	Charles Henry,	5279	"	Mar. 9, 1847		[(Learoyd).
92	Persis Louisa,	5280	"	Mar. 22, 1842	Oct. 26, 1865	Ephraim Stearns, Jr.; 1839–; s. Ephraim & Rachel
92	Frederick W.,	5281	"	Feb. 24, 1849	Dec. 13, 1868	1. Julia Etta Lee; –1879.
92		5282			Dec. 20, 1882	2. Jennie Church Thomas.

JONATHAN, JR., AND HANNAH E. (WARREN) PIERCE. 5278.

	Name	No.	Birth		Marriage	Spouse
92	Lucy Elizabeth,	5283	Boston,	June 15, 1860	Aug., 1880	George A. Haven.

GEORGE A. AND LUCY E. (PIERCE) HAVEN. 5283.

	Name	No.	Birth
	Charles H.,	5284	Apr. 5, 1885

EPHRAIM, JR., AND PERSIS L. (WARREN) STEARNS. 5280.

	Name	No.	Birth	
	Charles Ephraim,	5285	Waltham,	Apr. 27, 1868
	Rachel Learoyd,	5286	"	Jan. 23, 1873

FREDERICK W. AND JULIA ETTA (LEE) WARREN. 5281.

	Name	No.	Birth	
	Hannah Etta,	5287	Elgin, Ill.,	Nov. 20, 1869
	Edward F.,	5288	"	Sept. 3, 1873

FREDERICK W. AND JENNIE C. (THOMAS) WARREN. 5282.

	Name	No.	Birth
	Hattie May,	5289	Elgin, Ill., Feb. 26, 1884

JOSEPH AUGUSTUS AND ALICE BOYCE (HANSON) WARREN. 5260.

	Name	No.	Birth	Marriage	Spouse
	Alice E.,	5290	June 16, 1846		
	Joseph Edward,	5291	Sept. 6, 1848	Sept. 3, 1873	Emma F. Metcalf.

JOSIAH AND CAROLINE R. (WARREN) WETHERBEE. 5261.

	Name	No.	Birth		Marriage	Spouse
	Josiah Warren,	5292	Waltham,	Feb. 2, 1839		
	Charles Henry,	5293	"	Mar. 19, 1842		[(Haynes).
104	Albert,	5294	"	Dec. 28, 1845	Oct. 31, 1867	M. Susan Wetherell; 1844; dau. Benj. C. and Anna
	Eliot Jewett,	5295	"	July 15, 1851		
	John Franklin,	5296	"	Sept. 21, 1853		

GEORGE W. AND SARAH B. (WARREN) WARREN. 5262.

	Name	No.	Birth
	George Frederick,	5297	Waltham, June 27, 1866

WILLIAM AND SARAH ELIZABETH (WARREN) LIVERMORE. 5263.

	Name	No.	Birth		Marriage	Spouse
92	William Warren,	5298	Brighton,	July 6, 1846	Apr. 20, 1870	Nellie May Sawyer; 1853–; dau. William H. and Lydia B. (Skilling).

WILLIAM WARREN AND NELLIE MAY (SAWYER) LIVERMORE. 5298.

	Name	No.	Birth	
	Lizzie Maud,	5299	Brighton,	Feb. 15, 1871
	Bertrand Warren,	5300	"	May 14, 1873
	Henry Claflin,	5301	"	June 12, 1877
	Florence May,	5302	"	Aug. 12, 1879

CORNELIUS WESTON AND MARTHA ANN (WASHBURN) WARREN. 5264.

	Name	No.	Birth		Death
	Cornelius Weston,	5303	Boston,	Dec. 15, 1854	Jan. 4, 1858
	Martha Nellie,	5304	"	Jan. 26, 1858	
	Persis Maria,	5305	"	Sept. 20, 1859	
	Chas. Washburn,	5306	"	Oct. 29, 1862	

JOHN FRANKLIN AND SARAH A. (VILES) WARREN. 5265.

	Name	No.	Birth		Death	Marriage	Spouse
	John F.,	5307	Weston,	Aug. 24, 1860	Sept. 7, 1860		
	Florence A.,	5308	"	Aug. 12, 1862		Jan. 1, 1884	Franklin Holbrook; 1858–.
	George P.,	5309	"	Sept. 20, 1864	Dec. 9, 1868		
	Edward L.,	5310	"	Dec. 29, 1865	Dec. 10, 1868		
	Ida F.,	5311	"	Oct. 3, 1869			

ERI AND EMILY (FISKE) WESTON. 5249.

	Name	No.	Birth	Death	Marriage	Spouse
	Emily Augusta,	5312	July 8, 1828	Oct. 30, 1866		
	Addie L.,	5313	July 18, 1834	May 25, 1863		James E. Keyes.

JAMES E. AND ADDIE L. (WESTON) KEYES. 5313.

	Name	No.	Birth
	Elliot Weston,	5314	May 18, 1863

GEORGE W. AND REBECCA (WESTON) GARFIELD. 5250.

	Name	No.	Birth		Marriage	Spouse
92	George Chesley,	5315	Weston,	Jan. 12, 1820		
	Cynthia G.,	5316	"	Feb. 27, 1822		Daniel Davis; 1816–1882.
	Caroline R.,	5317	"	Dec. 26, 1824		
	Emily,	5318	"	Dec. 12, 1827	June 3, 1877	Hartwell H. Hale.
92	Hiram,	5319	"	May 8, 1829	Oct. 21, 1856	Lydia Ann Underwood.
	Abbie C.,	5320	"	Aug. 1, 1831	Sept. 24, 1868	Chesley Jenness.
	Daniel,	5321	"	Nov. 27, 1833		
93	Martha Maria,	5322	"	June 30, 1836	Sept. 12, 1861	Asa Norman Wheeler; 1836–.
	Sarah Persis,	5323	"	Aug. 25, 1838	Dec. 24, 1867	Jerome T. Beal; 1831–.

DANIEL AND CYNTHIA G. (GARFIELD) DAVIS. 5316.

	Name	No.	Birth	Death	Marriage	Spouse
	Herbert Whitney,	5324	Mar. 2, 1848		Apr. 26, 1877	Viola Estelle Erskine; 1857–.
	Waldo Emerson,	5325	Dec. 20, 1849			
	Frank Orrin,	5326	June 22, 1852	Oct. 22, 1852		

HIRAM AND LYDIA ANN (UNDERWOOD) GARFIELD. 5319.

(Continued page 93.)

	Alfred Hiram,	5327	Weston,	June 12, 1858			
	Alice Maria,	5328	"	Jan. 28, 1860			
	Walter,	5329	"	July 19, 1863			

ASA NORMAN AND MARTHA MARIA (GARFIELD) WHEELER. 5322.

	Ida Josephine,	5330		July 2, 1864			
	Eugene Clifton,	5331		May 26, 1866			
	Ernest Newman,	5332		Oct. 25, 1867	Sept. 1, 1868		
	Eva Louisa,	5333		Aug. 9, 1869			

JONAS AND ADALINE A. (VERRY) WESTON. 5252.

	Charles J.,	5334		July 25, 1842	Sept., 1842		
93	Alice P.,	5335		Jan. 22, 1844		Dec. 5, 1865	Micajah Scarborough; 1843–; son Wm. and May J.
	Persis A.,	5336		Feb. 3, 1846			
	Hannah A.,	5337		Oct. 16, 1850		Sept., 1872	Walter S. Sawyer.

MICAJAH AND ALICE P. (WESTON) SCARBOROUGH. 5335.

	Albert G.,	5338	Lynn,	May 11, 1867			

JONAS AND SARAH (MELVIN) POTTER. 5174.

93	Mary Batchelder Davis (by adoption),	5339	Lowell,	Oct. 23, 1826		Sept. 9, 1849	{ Willard Thomas Farrar; 1828–; son Sumner and So-[phia (Bruce).

WILLARD T. AND MARY B. (POTTER) FARRAR. 5339.

93	Willard Sumner,	5340	Concord,	Aug. 5, 1850		Sept. 25, 1873	Addie Sophia Hopkins; d. Geo. & Lucy (Kempton).
	Sarah Sophia,	5341	"	May 11, 1853		May 11, 1871	George Harvey Hopkins; 1846–; son Geo. and Lucy [(Kempton).
	Charles Stuart,	5342	"	Oct. 20, 1861	Sept. 20, 1862		

GEORGE H. AND SARAH S. (FARRAR) HOPKINS. 5341.

	George Willard,	5343	Concord,	Feb. 4, 1872			
	Isabel Gertrude,	5344	"	Dec. 29, 1874			

JOHN AND SYBIL GAY (FLAGG) POTTER. 5176.

93	Sarah,	5345	Concord,	Jan. 27, 1820	Dec. 28, 1878	Apr. 15, 1838	Frederick Roullard; 1812–.
	Sophia Morse (no iss.),	5346	"	Mar. 9, 1821	Jan. 21, 1875	Apr. 9, 1840	Louis Roullard; 1815–.
	Phebe Stevens,	5347	"	May 22, 1823	Mar. 6, 1841		
93	Rebecca Brown,	5348	"	Mar. 12, 1825		Jan., 1845	Hugh Cash; 1809–; son John and Nancy (Accles).
94	Charles Hubbard,	5349	"	July 29, 1827	June 21, 1860	July 1, 1851	Luella Page; 1824–. [rich).
94	Daniel Flagg,	5350	"	May 7, 1830		Mar. 16, 1853	Louisa E. Gray; 1830–; dau. Oliver and Mary (Good-
	John Henry (no issue),	5351	"	Aug. 23, 1836	Feb. 14, 1874	Apr. 28, 1859	Sarah (Follett) Vialle; 1826–; d. John and Deborah.
	Lucy,	5352	"	Dec. 12, 1840		Mar. 25, 1862	George Dudley Tufts; 1835–; son Dudley H. and
	Eliza Pierce, {	5353	"	Apr. 28, 1844		Apr. 29, 1869	1. Melville LeForest Jones. [Mary E. (George).
		5354				Apr. 28, 1881	2. Alfred Hammersly; 1840–; s. John & Eliza (Gill).

FREDERICK AND SARAH (POTTER) ROULLARD. 5345.

93	Sarah Ann,	5355	Acton,	Feb. 16, 1839		May 6, 1863	John White.
93	George, {	5356	"	Jan. 29, 1842		Jan. 29, 1867	1. Clara M. Dunnells; 1847–1874.
		5357				Nov. 26, 1874	2. Emma R. Dunnells; 1856–.
93	Mary Etta,	5358	"	Jan. 15, 1844		Apr. 12, 1874	John Byam.
	Albert,	5359	"	Dec. 21, 1845		Dec. 1, 1871	Georgia Farmer.
93	Lyman,	5360	"	Oct. 11, 1848		May 9, 1872	Lucy Emma Hanson.
	Waldo,	5361	"	Apr. 26, 1851		Apr. 23, 1873	Susie E. Godfrey; 1852–1885.
	Granville,	5362	"	June 6, 1854			
	Frederick,	5363	"	Feb. 1, 1857			
	Elmer,	5364	"	Jan. 27, 1865			
	Cora,	5365	"	Jan. 31, 1867			

JOHN AND SARAH ANN (ROULLARD) WHITE. 5355.

	Carrie E.,	5366	No. Acton,	Jan. 11, 1864			
	J. Sidney,	5367	"	July 31, 1866			

GEORGE AND CLARA M. (DUNNELLS) ROULLARD. 5356.

	George Frederick,	5368		Oct. 29, 1867			
	Charles,	5369		Sept. 7, 1869			
	Gertrude,	5370		Oct. 18, 1871			
	Clarence,	5371		Apr. 1, 1874	Feb. 20, 1875		

JOHN AND MARY ETTA (ROULLARD) BYAM. 5358.

	Estella M.,	5372		Sept. 20, 1875			

LYMAN AND LUCY E. (HANSON) ROULLARD. 5360.

	Dana Hanson,	5373		Feb. 25, 1873	Sept. 28, 1877		
	Eva Sargent,	5374		Aug. 22, 1874			
	James Lyman,	5375		June 30, 1876			
	Ernest Boardman,	5376		July 1, 1877	Jan. 2, 1882		
	Sarah Emma,	5377		Aug. 16, 1879	Apr. 8, 1882		
	Ethel Lavina,	5378		Feb. 5, 1882			
	Herman Granville,	5379		Nov. 27, 1883			

HUGH AND REBECCA B. (POTTER) CASH. 5348.

	Charles Henry, {	5380	Concord,	June 4, 1847		1868	1. Charlotte E. Davis; –1870.
		5381	"			1884	2. Angie B. Phillips.
	Albert,	5382	"	Apr. 10, 1850			
93	Nellie Frances,	5383	"	Apr. 21, 1852		June 5, 1879	M. B. C. Cummings.
	Annie Phebe,	5384	"	Nov. 16, 1857			
	George Herbert,	5385	"	Oct. 25, 1859			
	Mary Elizabeth,	5386	Acton,	July 20, 1863			

M. B. C. AND NELLIE F. (CASH) CUMMINGS. 5383. (Continued page 94.)

	Lucy May,	5387	Acton,	June 20, 1880			
	Charles M.,	5387	"	July 6, 1881			

	Estella A.,	5388	Acton,	Sept. 10, 1882		
	Herbert S.,	5389	"	Sept. 11, 1883		

CHARLES HUBBARD AND LUELLA (PAGE) POTTER. 5349.

94	John Sargent, {	5390	Acton,	July 23, 1852	Sept. 21, 1873	1. Susie R. Harris; 1848–1876.
94		5391				2. Mrs. Adelaide A. Moody; 1856–.
	Horace Page,	5392	"	Nov. 8, 1855	Apr. 1, 1876	Charlotte M. Thayer; 1856–.
	Chas. Hubbard,	5393	"	Nov. 29, 1857		

JOHN SARGENT AND ADELAIDE A. (MOODY) POTTER. 5391.

	Philip,	5394	Acton,	June 21, 1884		

HORACE PAGE AND CHARLOTTE M (THAYER) POTTER. 5392.

	Lottie Luella,	5395	Acton,	Mar. 29, 1879		
	Charles Horace,	5396	"	Mar. 23, 1881		

DANIEL FLAGG AND LAURA E. (GRAY) POTTER. 5350.

94	John Henry,	5397	Littleton,	Aug. 19, 1854	Dec. 13, 1879	Edith May Tuttle; 1859–; dau. Chas. F. and Adelia
	Clara Augusta,	5398	"	July 1, 1857		[(Pike).

JOHN HENRY AND EDITH MAY (TUTTLE) POTTER. 5398.

	Edith Addie,	5399		Dec. 14, 1880	Dec. 20, 1880	
	Elsie May,	5400		Aug. 9, 1882	Feb. 7, 1883	
	Eunice May,	5401	Concord,	Aug. 26, 1884	Sept. 13, 1884	

JOHN AND GRACE (POTTER) PRESCOTT. 613–568.

	Jonathan,	5402	Concord,	Apr. 4, 1767	Apr. 13, 1800	Aug. 13, ——	Rebecca Meriam.
94	Samuel Potter,	5403	"	Mar. 19, 1769	Sept. 2, 1820	June 7, 1798	Elizabeth Brown. No. 3645.
	John,	5404	"	Sept. 27, 1770	Oct., 1792	
	Abigail,	5405	"	Sept. 30, 1771		
	Abel,	5406	"	Feb. 23, 1773	Dec. 19, 1821	1795	Mary Perry.
	Grace,	5407	"	July 25, 1774		

SAMUEL POTTER AND ELIZABETH (BROWN) PRESCOTT. 5403.

94	Nathan,	5408	Concord,	Nov. 29, 1798		Feb. 15, 1825	Catharine Kendall; 1801–; dau. Asa.
94	Lucy Brown,	5409	"	Mar. 31, 1801	Sept. 29, 1877	Mar. 14, 1820	Joseph Chandler Green; 1799–1844; son Isaiah and
61	Sophronia,	5410	"	Dec. 11, 1802		Apr. 13, 1826	Herman Brown. No. 3403. [Hannah (Chandler).
95	Almira,	5411	"	Sept. 26, 1805		June 3, 1830	Stephen Farrar; 1802–.
60	Elizabeth,	5412	"	Jan. 15, 1808	Oct. 11, 1866	May 5, 1831	Edmund Brown. No. 3346.
95	Sarah,	5413	"	Feb. 25, 1810	July 18, 1863	Mar. 13, 1834	Abner Marion; 1809–1858; son John C. & Martha (Carter).
95	Humphrey, {	5414	"	Feb. 26, 1814		Nov. 29, 1838	1. Martha Marion; 1820–1849; d. John C. & Martha (Carter).
96		5415				Aug. 22, 1850	2. Mary Taylor; 1817–; d. Abel & Sarah (Hodgman).

NATHAN AND CATHARINE (KENDALL) PRESCOTT. 5408.

	Almira,	5416	Concord,	Dec. 15, 1825		Nov., 1854	John Milton Merriam.
94	Nathan Otis,	5417	"	Oct. 18, 1827		Jan. 17, 1850	Lucy Ann Richardson; 1825–; dau. Abraham.
94	Mary Elizabeth,	5418	"	June 25, 1830		1851	Wilder Reed.
94	Geo. Henry, {	5419	"	June 25, 1830		Mar. 1, 1853	1. Emily Taylor; –1864.
		5420				1865	2. Fanny McClunge.
	Martha H.,	5421	"	June 25, 1833		Nov., 1854	S. H. Hill.
94	Ann Maria,	5422	"	June 25, 1833	Feb. 27, 1866	Sept., 1854	James Wilson.

NATHAN OTIS AND LUCY ANN (RICHARDSON) PRESCOTT. 5417.

	Clarence Marcellus,	5423	Fitchburg,	Mar. 20, 1851		
	Flora Marcella,	5424	"	Oct. 1, 1853		
	Linnæus Clayton,	5425	"	Aug. 24, 1855		
	Idella Etola,	5426	"	July 14, 1857		
	Estella Viola,	5427	"	July 14, 1857		
	Etta Eudora,	5428	"	May 27, 1861	Jan. 20, 1865	
	Corra Orilla,	5429	Nashua, N. H., Apr. 20, 1863		

WILDER AND MARY ELIZABETH (PRESCOTT) REED. 5418.

	Lizzie Maria,	5430	Mason, N. H., Nov. 27, 1852	Aug. 13, 1854		
	Emily C.,	5431	" June 27, 1854		Feb. 2, 1875	Fred A. Drake.
	Abbie J.,	5432	" Aug. 21, 1857		Nov. 25, 1876	George Edwards.
	Ida Bell,	5433	Sharon, N. H., Apr. 6, 1861		Mar. 23, 1883	Clarence W. Osborn.
	George Prescott,	5434	" Oct. 28, 1864		Nov. 7, 1884	Mattie Maria Hill.
	Willie E.,	5434½	East Jaffrey, N. H., July 18, 1868		

GEORGE HENRY AND EMILY (TAYLOR) PRESCOTT. 5419.

	Linnæus,	5435				
	Charles Henry,	5436		Jan. 19, 1855		
	Nella Olivia,	5437		Feb. 27, 1857		
	Georgian'a Estelle,	5438		June 20, 1859		
	Edith,	5439		Aug. 4, 1861		

JAMES AND ANN MARIA (PRESCOTT) WILSON. 5422.

	Mary Lizzie,	5440				
	Robert Edgar,	5441				
	Mary Josephine,	5442				
	George Eddy,	5443				
	Martha Maria,	5444				

JOSEPH CHANDLER AND LUCY BROWN (PRESCOTT) GREEN. 5409. (Continued page 95.)

95	Charles,	5445	Carlisle,	Oct. 19, 1820		Oct. 19, 1848	Emma Heller Jasper.
	Josiah Chandler,	5446	Dudley,	June 18, 1822	Feb. 21, 1845	
	Joseph Adams, {	5447	Concord,	Dec. 15, 1824			1. Harriet Ricker Mason; –1850.
		5448					2. Anna Whiting Mason; –1862.
	George,	5449	"	Feb. 4, 1827	Mar. 2, 1827	
95	George Prescott,	5450	"	July 20, 1828		July 5, 1853	Lucy Ellen Mason.
95	Alden,	5451	Berwick, Me., Mar. 12, 1831		Mar. 26, 1856	Eliza Victoria Metzgar.

95	Lucy Hannah,	5452	Fayette, Me., Aug. 8, 1836		May 11, 1856	Ira Lewis Mason.
	Albert,	5453	"	May 24, 1862		

CHARLES AND EMMA HELLER (JASPER) GREEN. 5455.

Mary Emma,	5454	No. Turner, Me., Aug. 2, 1849		Dec. 23, 1866	Stephen Henry Rose.
Charles Edwin,	5455	" Mar. 5, 1851	Apr. 14, 1851		
Ida Ella,	5456	" Apr. 25, 1852		June 22, 1878	John Alcock Tustin.
Charles Edwin,	5457	Bethel, O., Feb. 21, 1854	July 14, 1873		
Myrtie Elma,	5458	" Mar. 19, 1859			
Ira Eugene,	5459	" Nov. 24, 1861			
Albert Ethelbert,	5460	" Mar. 27, 1866			

GEORGE PRESCOTT AND LUCY ELLEN (MASON) GREEN. 5450.

Effie M.,	5461	No. Turner, Me., July 29, 1854
Cora M.,	5462	Bethel, O., Feb. 27, 1861
Bennie B.,	5463	Williamsburg, O., Oct. 3, 1866
Eddie M.,	5464	Bethel, O., Mar. 7, 1868
Fernando S.,	5465	" Apr. 7, 1871
Isaiah F.,	5466	Clarksville, O., Mar. 3, 1875

ALDEN AND LUCY ELLEN (MASON) GREEN. 5451.

Callie Dimmit,	5467	Bethel, O., Apr. 5, 1858
William Albert,	5468	Felicity, O., Mar. 30, 1862
Arthur Sherman,	5469	Turner, Me., July 25, 1868

IRA LEWIS AND LUCY HANNAH (GREEN) MASON. 5452.

Albert Leslie,	5470	Bethel, O., Oct. 29, 1857	Feb. 23, 1859		
Flora Ethel,	5471	" Jan. 16, 1860		Jan. 1, 1884	Walter B. Jones.
Carrie Alberta,	5472	" July 23, 1862		Feb. 13, 1881	James M. Dillingham.
Henry Irving,	5473	Turner, Me., Dec. 16, 1865			
Ira Luther,	5474	" Aug. 18, 1870			
Walter Evans,	5475	" Apr. 28, 1881			
William Evarts,	5476	" Apr. 28, 1881			

STEPHEN AND ALMIRA (PRESCOTT) FARRAR. 5411.

Geo. Humphrey,	5477	Aug. 25, 1831	Nov. 3, 1861	Carrie M. Colby.
Erwin Otis,	5478	Aug. 30, 1833	Dec. 4, 1860	Mary Ann Colby; 1844-.
Lizzie,	5479	Sept. 17, 1835		
Alden Prescott,	5480	Jan. 26, 1838	Apr. 10, 1866	Mrs. Mary Ann Bachelder.
Sarah Boardman,	5481	Apr. 23, 1840		
Walter Judson,	5482	Aug. 11, 1845		
Nathan Edson,	5483	Aug. 30, 1849		

ABNER AND SARAH (PRESCOTT) MARION. 5413.

95	Ann Melina,	5484	Burlington, Jan. 26, 1835	Jan. 13, 1862	Lever't Milton Chase; 1832-; s. Sam'l & Sally (Gilley).
95	Abner Prescott,	5485	" Aug. 12, 1836	Dec. 24, 1863	Eliza S. Covell; 1840-1867. [J. (Fay).
95	Nathan Henry,	5486	" Sept. 25, 1838	June 19, 1876	Sarah Augusta Tidd; 1838-; dau. Jonathan and Sarah
95	Edwin Theodore,	5487	" May 14, 1841	Mar. 29, 1864	Affa Bond; 1848-; dau. Chas. and Lydia W. (Tidd).
95	Horace Eugene, M.D.	5488	" Aug. 3, 1843	Jan. 14, 1880	Cath'ne Louise Sparhawk; 1848-; d. Geo. & Sus'n'a (Jacks'n).
95	Otis Humphrey, M.D.	5489	" Jan. 12, 1847	Dec. 27, 1879	Car'line Eud'ra Jo'ns'n; 1855-; d. Jas.W.& Sus'n A, (Smith).
95	Sarah Elizabeth,	5490	" May 10, 1851	Jan. 21, 1874	Edwin Sewall Davis, 1848-; s. Amos B. & Eleanor P. (Tyler).

LEVERETT MILTON AND ANNA M. (MARION) CHASE. 5484.

Sarah Marion,	5491	Burlington, June 30, 1863	
Harry Waldemar,	5492	W. Newton, Jan. 23, 1866	
Mary Evalina,	5493	Roxbury, Feb. 9, 1868	Sept. 22, 1868
Charles Samuel,	5494	" Oct. 16, 1869	
Georgianna Melina	5495	" Jan. 15, 1875	

ABNER PRESCOTT AND ELIZA S. (COVELL) MARION. 5485.

Eliza Maria,	5496	Burlington, Feb. 16, 1866

NATHAN HENRY AND SARAH AUGUSTA (TIDD) MARION. 5486.

Henry Seward,	5497	Burlington, Dec. 22, 1877	Mar. 9, 1880
Horace Humphrey,	5498	N. Woburn, July 22, 1879	June 15, 1880
Jonathan Tidd,	5499	" Apr. 27, 1881	Aug. 10, 1881
Marshall Prescott,	5500	" Apr. 27, 1881	Aug. 10, 1881

EDWIN THEODORE AND AFFA (BOND) MARION. 5487.

Alonzo Bond,	5501	Burlington, Dec. 20, 1864	Apr. 28, 1876
Charles Quincy,	5502	Ayer, Sept. 29, 1866	
Otis Daniel,	5503	N. Woburn, Feb. 17, 1877	
Nelson Bond,	5504	" Aug. 28, 1879	

DR. HORACE EUGENE AND CATHARINE LOUISE (SPARHAWK) MARION. 5488.

Eva Prescott,	5505	Brighton, Oct. 17, 1880
Gardner Sparhawk	5506	" Dec. 14, 1884

DR. OTIS HUMPHREY AND CAROLINE EUDORA (JOHNSON) MARION. 5489.

Jas. Willis Johnson	5507	Brighton, Dec. 5, 1880

EDWIN SEWALL AND SARAH ELIZABETH (MARION) DAVIS. 5490.

Horace Amos,	5508	Brighton, Nov. 14, 1874	
Edna Prescott,	5509	" Nov. 11, 1875	July 21, 1885
Carrie Louise,	5510	" June 9, 1885	

HUMPHREY AND MARTHA (MARION) PRESCOTT. 5414.

	Martha Elizabeth,	5511	Burlington, Mar. 16, 1840	July 13, 1864	Henry C. Robbins, M. D.
96	John Humphrey,	5512	" Oct. 16, 1841	May 3, 1866	Lydia Jane Osgood; 1846-.
	Lucy Brown,	5513	" July 2, 1849		—— Todd.

HUMPHREY AND MARY (TAYLOR) PRESCOTT. 5415.

	Name	No.	Birth	Death	Marriage	Spouse
	Josiah Bartlett,	5514	Burlington, Sept. 16, 1851			
	William Arthur,	5515	" Aug. 11, 1857			

JOHN HUMPHREY AND LYDIA JANE (OSGOOD) PRESCOTT. 5512.

	Name	No.	Birth	Death	Marriage	Spouse
	Fred'k Marion,	5516	Boston, Jan. 19, 1869			
	John Osgood,	5517	Lowell, July 2, 1871			
	Annie Farnam,	5518	" June 26, 1873			
	Samuel Osgood,	5519	" Dec. 5, 1875			
	Norah Louisa Araline,	5520	" Aug. 21, 1877			
	Nathaniel Parker,	5521	" Mar. 16, 1880			
	Robert Dearborn,	5522	Somerville, Oct. 27, 1881			

ADISON AND JENNIE (GREEN) CHURCHILL. 5042.

	Name	No.	Birth	Death	Marriage	Spouse
	Minnie C.,	5523	Exeter, N.H., May 28, 1856	May 31, 1856		
	Charles Sidney,	5524	Lowell, July 4, 1857	June 8, 1866		
	Adison, Jr.,	5524	" Oct. 4, 1860			
	LaForeste Edgar,	5525	" Nov. 9, 1862			

CAPT. JOHN AND PHEBE (BREWER) JONES. 4284.

	Name	No.	Birth	Death	Marriage	Spouse
	Betty,	5526	Ashby, Feb. 8, 1755	Mar. 10, 1759	Oct., 1770	Huldah Hancock.
	James, Col.,	5527	" May 15, 1756	Jan., 1828	Apr. 15, 1777	Ralph Hill.
	Mary,	5528	" June 16, 1758			
	Samuel,	5529	" June 27, 1761	Dec. 18, 1762		
	Samuel,	5530		1811		
	John, {	5531	" Mar. 12, 1768	July 11, 1826	July 19, 1791	1. Lydia Turner; –1810.
		5532			1811	2. Martha Bates; –1827.
	Elisha,	5533	" Apr. 15, 1770	Nov. 21, 1809	Mar. 27, 1793	Persis Taylor; 1768–; dau. Abraham.
96	Amos, {	5534	" Oct. 7, 1772		1800	1. Rachel Young.
96		5535			Aug. 4, 1808	2. Sarah Getchell.
	Daniel,	5536	" Apr. 4, 1775	Oct. 31, 1808	1800	Lucy Shepley.
	Phebe,	5537	" Mar. 20, 1777		Feb. 23, 1797	Lemuel Shepley.

AMOS AND RACHEL (YOUNG) JONES. 5534.

	Name	No.	Birth	Death	Marriage	Spouse
	Jonas,	5538	Madison, Me., June 13, 1801			
96	Huldah,	5539	" June 13, 1803		June 24, 1821	Capt. Herbert Savage.
96	Rachel Young,	5540	" Feb. 26, 1805	Apr. 20, 1846	1830	John Blackden; 1880–; d. Wm. and Mary (Oakes).
97	Amos Young,	5541	" Feb. 27, 1807	1840		Sybil W. Stevens.

AMOS AND SARAH (GRETCHELL) JONES. 5535.

	Name	No.	Birth	Death	Marriage	Spouse
97	Timothy B.,	5542	Madison, Me., June 8, 1809		Feb. 17, 1841	Sarah P. Messer.
	Phebe P.,	5542	" Sept. 23, 1811	Oct. 23, 1833		
97	John D.,	5543	" May 3, 1814		Aug. 7, 1853	Mary S. Rand.
	Adaline B.,	5544	" Oct. 9, 1816			Enoch Messer.

CAPT. HERBERT AND HULDAH (JONES) SAVAGE. 5539.

	Name	No.	Birth	Death	Marriage	Spouse
	Mandana Dusen,	5545	Anson, Me., Apr. 28, 1822			Christopher Holmes.
	Louisa Bradford,	5546	" July 2, 1823			
	Salome H.,	5547	Kingfield, Me., May 9, 1824		Oct. 19, 1843	Charles C. Hapgood.
	Albin K. P.,	5548	Anson, Me., July 26, 1826	Mar. 26, 1847		
	Cyrus,	5549	" Mar. 22, 1828	Nov. 22, 1837		
	Mark C.,	5550	" Jan. 15, 1830			
	Amos J.,	5551	Emden, Me., Sept. 3, 1832			
	Stephen Decatur,	5552	Anson, Me., Mar. 16, 1835			
	Betsey,	5553	" Nov. 17, 1837	Aug. 17, 1841		

JOHN AND RACHEL Y. (JONES) BLACKDEN. 5540.

	Name	No.	Birth	Death	Marriage	Spouse
96	John, Jr.,	5554	Anson, Me., Sept. 8, 1830		Jan. 1, 1852	Mitty Weston Cookson; 1833–.
96	Corydon Campbell Young	5555	" May 23, 1832		Sept. 10, 1853	Charlotte Kendall.
	Ethan Allen, {	5556	" Mar. 20, 1834		Jan. 15, 1861	1. Ella L. Getchell; d. Jonah & Sarah O. (Getchell).
		5557			Dec. 18, 1878	2. Maria Josephine Richmond; 1838–1885; d. Gideon
96	Amelia Theodora,	5558	Madison, Me., Apr. 10, 1836	Apr. 8, 1869	1854	Austin Mills. [B. and Hannah W. (Pendleton).
	Owen Oakes,	5559	" June 16, 1838			
96	Goff Manter, {	5560	" Oct. 7, 1840			1. Annie Electa McCoslin; 1852–.
		5561				2. Ella W. Morrison; 1852–.
	Allison,	5562	" June 14, 1844			Olive Tibbets.

JOHN, JR., AND MITTY WESTON (COOKSON) BLACKDEN. 5554.

	Name	No.	Birth	Death	Marriage	Spouse
	Dora Sibyl,	5563	Hamden, Me., Nov. 2, 1854	Sept. 25, 1874	Oct. 11, 1872	Daniel Blaisdell Small.
	Perry Decatur,	5564	Carmel, Me., Dec. 26, 1859			
	Lillian May,	5565	" May 8, 1867			
	Amy Florence,	5566	" Oct. 28, 1877	Feb. 18, 1878		

CORYDON C. Y. AND CHARLOTTE (KENDALL) BLACKDEN. 5555.

	Name	No.	Birth	Death	Marriage	Spouse
	Clara Maria,	5567	Norridgewock, Me., July 1, 1856			William H. Snead.
	Annie Bell,	5568	Skowhegan, Me., July 8, 1859			Levi B. Boynton.
	Fred Fenno,	5569	" Feb. 8, 1865	Dec. 31, 1884		

AUSTIN AND AMELIA T. (BLACKDEN) MILLS. 5558.

	Name	No.	Birth	Death	Marriage	Spouse
	Charles Edward,	5570	Apr. 10, 1856		Dec. 31, 1877	Delia Sutton; 1856–.

CHARLES EDWARD AND DELIA (SUTTON) MILLS. 5570.

	Name	No.	Birth	Death	Marriage	Spouse
	Gracie,	5571	Aug. 14, 1878			
	Frank Charles,	5572	Nov. 6, 1879			
	Clarence Edward,	5573	Nov. 20, 1882			

GOFF MANTER AND ANNIE E. (McCOSLIN) BLACKDEN. 5560.

	Name	No.	Birth	Death	Marriage	Spouse
	Jennie Florence,	5574	Etna, Me., May 31, 1872			
	Lydia Ann,	5575	" Oct. 3, 1874			

AMOS YOUNG AND SYBIL W. (STEVENS) JONES. 5541.

David Young,	5576	Madison, Me.				
Almira Celestia,	5577	" Feb. 14, 1834				
Prentis Mellin,	5578	" Aug. 6, 1838				
Amos,	5579	" 1839				

TIMOTHY B. AND SARAH P. (MESSER) JONES. 5542.

Adelaide L.,	5580	Madison, Me., Feb. 6, 1843		Sept. 18, 1869	Mark Getchell.
Amos R.,	5581	" Dec. 30, 1845			
Sarah C.,	5582	" Apr. 20, 1847	Oct. 21, 1848		
Jared Williams,	5583	" Sept. 11, 1849			
Samuel M.,	5584	" May 31, 1854		Nov. 3, 1880	Lillie V. Cummings.

JOHN D. AND MARY S. (RAND) JONES. 5543.

97	Sarah Rand,	5585	July 15, 1854		Jan. 14, 1871	Edmond Farbush
97	Augusta L.,	5586	Sept. 5, 1855		Oct. 19, 1876	Samuel S. Day.
	Thomas M.,	5587	July 7, 1857	Sept. 14, 1858		
	Sewall K.,	5588	Nov. 1, 1859			
	John A.,	5589	Aug. 23, 1861			
	Ulysses G.,	5590	Sept. 22, 1865			
	Mary E.,	5591	Mar. 13, 1867		Feb. 5, 1885	Manning E. Titcom.
	Charles D.,	5592	Jan. 27, 1870			
	Carrie M.,	5593	May 2, 1872			
	Franklin C.,	5594	Apr. 27, 1874			
	Albert H.,	5595	Nov. 16, 1876			
	Ernest J.,	5596	Dec. 15, 1879			

EDMOND AND SARAH R. (JONES) FARBUSH. 5585.

Artemus W.,	5597	Aug. 4, 1873	
Bertha M.,	5598	Aug. 2, 1875	
Angelia L.,	5599	Aug. 21, 1880	
Nellie M.,	5600	Mar. 13, 1883	

SAMUEL S. AND AUGUSTA L. (JONES) DAY. 5586.

Mabel M.,	5601	June 16, 1878	
Eugene G.,	5602	Dec. 22, 1881	

BENJAMIN AND CYNTHIA (LEWIS) CONANT. 4087.

97	Abbie Davis,	5603	Boston, Sept. 26, 1830	May 25, 1864	Wm. Allen Norris; 1828–; s. Rob't & Love (Hallett).

GEORGE W. AND ANNA (STEVENS) CONANT. 4093.

Abigail Ann,	5604	Boxboro, May 3, 1830	Apr. 5, 1886	May 25, 1871	George G. Winch; son Daniel.
George,	5605	" July 30, 1831	Jan. 31, 1834		
Sarah Sophia,	5606	" Dec. 2, 1833			
Mary Isabella,	5607	Bolton, Dec. 6, 1835			
Francis Stevens,	5608	Lunenburg, July 6, 1838	Sept. 19, 1844		
Susan Elizabeth,	5609	" Feb. 15, 1841	Oct. 29, 1865		
Harriet Maria,	5610	" July 2, 1848			

LEVI, JR., AND ANNA WHITNEY (MEAD) CONANT. 4094.

97	Benjamin,	5611	Dublin, N. H., July 28, 1837		Jan. 7, 1861	Clara Maria Newhall; 1833–; dau. Reuben and Emily (Rugg).
97	Sherman,	5612	" Dec. 21, 1839		Jan. 12, 1866	Frances H. Dewey; d. Frederick F. & Hannah (Pratt).
	Henry,	5613	" Dec. 18, 1843	May 17, 1848		[G. (Gibbs).
97	Ellen Sherwin,	5614	Littleton, July 19, 1846		Aug. 3, 1870	Francis Edward Ballard; son Francis G. and Abby
97	Anna Jane,	5615	" Nov. 16, 1848		Aug. 30, 1871	Judge John Henry Hardy; 1847–; son John and Hannah (Farley).
97	Amelia Brick,	5616	" July 11, 1851		Sept. 16, 1875	Thomas Heber Wakefield; 1850–; son Thos. L. and [Jane (Perry).
	George Arthur,	5617	" Mar. 31, 1854	Oct. 26, 1883	Unmarried.	
	Levi Leonard,	5618	" Mar. 3, 1857		July 24, 1884	Laura Mehitable Chamberlain; 1853–; dau. John [and Mehitable B. (Morse).
	Elmer Kimball,	5619	" June 30, 1862			

BENJAMIN AND CLARA MARIA (NEWHALL) CONANT. 5611.

Flora Carrie,	5620	Cambridge, Nov. 10, 1863	Apr. 29, 1871	
Daisy Adelle,	5621	" May 31, 1872		
Emily Kimball,	5622	" Oct. 6, 1874	Dec. 4, 1874	

SHERMAN AND FRANCES H. (DEWEY) CONANT. 5612.

Anna Whitney,	5623	Jacksonville, Fla., Oct. 15, 1867	Jan. 13, 1880	
John Sherman,	5624	Tallahassee, Fla., June 10, 1876		

FRANCIS EDWARD AND ELLEN SHERWIN (CONANT) BALLARD. 5614.

Alice Gibbs,	5625	Lexington, June 2, 1872	
John Francis,	5626	" July 26, 1873	
Edith,	5627	" Aug. 16, 1875	
William Henry,	5628	" Jan. 31, 1879	
Walter Clark,	5629	" Mar. 18, 1881	

JUDGE JOHN HENRY AND ANNA JANE (CONANT) HARDY. 5615.

Henry Ballard,	5630	Arlington, Dec. 11, 1872	Aug. 9, 1873	
John Henry, Jr.,	5631	" June 10, 1874		
Horace Dexter,	5632	" Feb. 28, 1877		

THOMAS HEBER AND AMELIA BRICK (CONANT) WAKEFIELD. 5616.

Harrold Hardy,	5633	Dedham, Feb. 20, 1881	

HENRY AND HARRIET A. (BLOOD) CONANT. 4095.

Susie J.,	5634 / 5635	Apr. 11, 1840	Oct. 23, 1867 / Apr. 11, 1882	1. Alfred Dana Wright; 1835–1876; s. Milo & Betsey (Ames). / 2. Caleb Richardson; '24–; s. Henry & Charlotte (Batchelder).

WILLIAM AND JOANNA (DAVIS) HARTWELL. 3982.

99	William, Jr.,	5636	Bedford, Jan. 12, 1797		Nov. 30, 1826	Ruhamah Webber; 1802–1879; dau. Asa & Eliot R. (Lane). [(Greer).
99	Amos, Dea.,	5637	" Aug. 3, 1798	July 25, 1870	June 20, 1822	Louisa Hodgman; 1802–1878; dau. Thomas & Sarah
104	Benjamin Farley,	5638	" June 8, 1800	Dec. 14, 1884	Nov. 13, 1828	1. Lucy Webber; 2. Mary F. Fitch, Jan. 20, 1835;
	Joseph,	5639	" Apr. 7, 1802	Aug. 16, 1868		[3. Mrs. Nancy Brooks, Nov. 17, 1875.
	Isaac (no issue),	5640	" Mar. 1, 1804	Dec. 6, 1884		
	Mary Joa'na (no issue),	5641	" May 17, 1806		June 19, 1862	Lucy Frost; 1819–; dau. Benj. & Bulah (Hodgman).
98	John Batchelder,	5642	" June 27, 1808		Nov. 3, 1863	Rob't Bartley; 1797–1867; s. Rob't. [(Simpson).
					July 14, 1832	Julia Ann Harrington; 1810–; d. Samuel and Mary

JOHN BATCHELDER AND JULIA ANN (HARRINGTON) HARTWELL. 5642.

98	John Henry,	5643	Boston, Jan. 16, 1835		Nov. 21, 1861	Emeline Augusta Stearns; 1839–1883; dau. Leonard and Hannah (Wilson).
98	Chas. Frederick, {	5644 5645	Arlington, Mar. 29, 1844		Mar. 29, 1866 Mar. 29, 1884	1. Mary Jane Boothby; d. Eli & Mary Jane (Pierce). 2. Annie Augusta (Jordan) Webster; d. George W. and Emeline (Noyes).

JOHN HENRY AND EMELINE AUGUSTA (STEARNS) HARTWELL. 5643.

	George Henry,	5646	Arlington, Aug. 22, 1864		.	
	Addie Augusta,	5647	" Oct. 29, 1866			
	Charles Tilden,	5648	" Dec. 18, 1868			
	Julia Almira,	5649	" Jan. 14, 1871			

CHARLES FREDERICK AND MARY JANE (BOOTHBY) HARTWELL. 5644.

	Fred'k William,	5650	Arlington, Mar. 20, 1868			
	Walter Chandler,	5651	" May 2, 1870			
	Herbert Eugene,	5652	" Mar. 12, 1872			
	Gertrude Eugene,	5653	Somerville, Nov. 14, 1874			

ANTHONY AND BETSEY (HUBBARD) VAN DORN. 1868.

	Elizabeth,	5654	Brattleboro, Vt., June, 1817			
	Charles Barrett,	5655	" 1819	1821		
	Moses T.,	5656	" Jan. 12, 1821	1885		
	Harriet,	5657	" Jan. 8, 1823			—— Brown.
	Charles Anthony,	5658	" Jan. 3, 1825			

WILLIAM AND BETSEY (SWAIN) LYMAN. 1914.

	Electa G.,	5659				H. Lindsley.
	Meliscent.	5660				J. Gillette.
	Lucy H.,	5661		1874		I. Potter.
	Betsey C.,	5662				D. Stanley.
	William H.,	5663		1849		
	Olive W.,	5664	Oct. 28, 1823		Mar. 26, 1874	Allen Bacon.
	Martha P.,	5665				

GEORGE WALLACE AND CHARLOTTE E. (BEDLOW) ADAMS. 2438.

	Mary Coleman,	5666	Brooklyn, N.Y., Nov. 28, 1873			

REV. JOHN COLEMAN AND MIRIAM PRIEST (HOVEY) ADAMS. 2440.

	Katharine,	5667	Chicago, Ill., Apr. 3, 1866			

SAMUEL AND LUCINDA (CONANT) MEAD. 4092.

	Lucinda,	5668	Boxboro', July 22, 1828			Dana C. Howe.
	Albert,	5669	" Apr. 23, 1830			
	Alfred,	5670	" Feb. 10, 1832			
	Abbie Conant,	5671	" Apr. 2, 1834			
	Anna Rebecca (no issue),	5672	" Jan. 2, 1836	Apr. 26, 1860		—— Harding.
	Mary Stevens,	5673	" June 20, 1840	Dec. 22, 1846		

ROBERT GARDNER AND REBECCA (CONANT) WILSON. 4088.

98	John Overing,	5674	Hopkinton, May 30, 1821		Nov. 23, 1843	Mary Morse; 1820–; dau. Jesse & Betsey (Coolidge).
98	Mary Ann Bigelow,	5675	" Aug. 10, 1822		Oct. 24, 1849	Edwin Coolidge Morse; 1819–1886; son Jesse and
	Robert Gardner,	5676	" Mar. 4, 1824			[Betsey (Coolidge).
98	Joseph Warren,	5677	" Jan., 1826		Feb. 9, 1859	Julia V. Phelps; 1837–; d. Erastus R. & Nancy M. (Wilmot).
98	Rebecca Frances,	5678	Bedford, N.H., Nov. 11, 1834	Mar. 25, 1866	1855	Theodore Hill Mansfield. [liam Cobb.
98	Charles Oscar,	5679	Harvard, Mar. 20, 1838	Jan. 24, 1822	Dec. 25, 1861	Susan M. Reid Cobb; 1840–1885; adopted dau. Wil-

JOHN OVERING AND MARY (MORSE) WILSON. 5674.

104	Edward Horatio,	5680	Natick, Oct. 10, 1845	Apr. 17, 1882	Oct. 10, 1871	Ella Myra Coolidge.
	John Howard,	5681	" Mar. 9, 1847		May, 1877	Carrie Ives Dawson.
104	Mary Lizzie,	5682	" May 12, 1851		Dec. 26, 1877	Frederick Herbert Ripley.
	Nellie Frances,	5683	" Apr. 24, 1857			

EDWIN C. AND MARY A. B. (WILSON) MORSE. 5675.

	Eugene Edwin,	5684	Natick, Aug. 4, 1850	Feb. 11, 1851		
	Edwin Wilson,	5685	" Mar. 29, 1855		Sept. 14, 1881	Florence LaBelle Stone.
	Charles Wilson,	5686	" Aug. 14, 1860	July 23, 1861		

JOSEPH W. AND JULIA V. (PHELPS) WILSON. 5677.

	Eugene Phelps,	5687	New Haven, Ct., Nov. 12, '59	June 29, 1867		
	Joseph Warren.	5688	Norwalk, Ct., June 26, '61	June 29, 1867		
	Robert Gardner,	5689	" Mar. 18, 1886			
	Henry Hamilton,	5690	" Feb. 26, 1868			

THEODORE H. AND REBECCA F. (WILSON) MANSFIELD. 5678.

	Walter Gardner,	5691	Natick, June 24, 1857	March, 1864		
	Warren Wilson,	5692	" July, 1858			
	Mary Frances,	5693	" Oct. 24, 1861			

CHARLES OSCAR AND SUSAN M. (COBB) WILSON. 5679.

(Continued page 99.)

	Harry Maxwell,	5694	Apr. 26, 1863			
	Charles Edwin,	5695	July 14, 1866			

	Name	No.	Birth			Spouse
	John Overing, 2d,	5696		July 12, 1872		
	Maria Louise,	5697		Sept., 1880	Sept., 1880	.

NATHAN AND SUKEY (DAVIS) CONANT. 3832.

	Name	No.	Birth			Spouse
	Lucius,	5698	Guilford, Vt., Aug. 19,'18	Sept. 24, 1850	Nov. 7, 1843	Mary M. Hutchins.
	Susan,	5699	" Mar. 31, 1821	Mar. 8, 1848	Unmarried.	
	Caroline C.,	5700	" Aug. 7, 1823		Dec. 25, 1845	George W. Penniman; 1821-1874.
	Maria B.,	5701	" Aug. 22, 1831	July 11, 1848		

NAHUM AND ELIZA A. (GIBSON) CONANT. 3839.

	Name	No.	Birth			Spouse
102	Nahum,	5702	Cambridge, Aug. 23, 1833	June 26, 1867	Aug. 23, 1857	Elmira W. Dougherty; -1862.
102	Eliza A.,	5703	Dec. 28, 1835	May 28, 1860	Nov. 24, 1853	Edmund Sherman Tuttle; -1860.
	Amelia C.,	5704	Sept. 20, 1838		Oct. 29, 1858	Baron S. Hager.
102	Marcus,	5705	Oct. 24, 1842		June 20, 1867	Ellen J. Leavenworth.
	William,	5706	Oct. 24, 1842	Oct. 24, 1842		
102	Susanna C.,	5707	June 26, 1845		Oct. 30, 1864	George F. Proctor.
102	Robert C.,	5708	June 26, 1845			Sarah M. Burbank.

SIMON AND BETSEY (GALUCIA) JONES. 4770.

	Name	No.				Spouse
	George W.,	5709				
	Sarah E.,	5710				Abel L. Goodwin.
	Charles W.,	5711				
	Mary A.,	5712				
	Sarah E.,	5713				
	Willie F.,	5714				
	Simon W.,	5715				

ANTHONY M. AND SARAH MARIA (WAIT) STRONG. 4432.

	Name	No.	Birth			Spouse
	Charles Henry,	5716	May 27, 1833		Jan. 15, 1857	Margaret Matilda Teller.
	Richard M.,	5717	1835	1863		
	Robert, Rev.,	5718	Nov. 20, 1836		Jan. 6, 1875	Villa Marquis.
	Elizabeth,	5719	1840		1862	Archibald McClure.
	James Clarke,	5720		Died infancy.		
	John Schoolcraft,	5721		"		

CHARLES AND ANNA (WAIT) SCOVEL. 4434.

	Name	No.	Birth			Spouse
	Minerva Wait,	5722	July 16, 1836		Oct. 4, 1860	William Lyon.
	William Nelson,	5723	Oct. 31, 1842	Feb. 27, 1844		
	Anna,	5724	Feb. 15, 1847	Mar. 5, 1848		

ANDREW JACKSON AND MARTHA (HOSMER) HARLOW. 4212.

	Name	No.	Birth			
	Fred Hurd,	5725	Rochester, N. Y., Feb. 18,1851	June 24, 1870		.

HENRY JOSEPH AND LAURA A. (BALLOU-WHITING) HOSMER. 4213.

	Name	No.	Birth			
	Henry Joseph, Jr.,	5726	Concord, June 8, 1876			

CYRUS AND ANNA E. (PRESCOTT) HOSMER. 4214.

	Name	No.	Birth			
	Cyrus, 4th,	5727	Concord, Oct. 13, 1874			
	Ralph Prescott,	5728	" May 25, 1877			
	George Salisbury,	5729	" Oct. 25, 1879			

JOHN THOMAS AND EMMA F. (MAYO) POTTER. 4941.

	Name	No.	Birth			
	Abbie,	5730	1869	1874		

JOHN THOMAS AND LILLY W. (STEVENS) POTTER. 4942.

	Name	No.	Birth			
	Arthur Seymour	5731	Lynn, Jan. 11, 1874			

GEORGE H. AND MARY J. (CAMPBELL) POTTER. 4943.

	Name	No.	Birth			
	George Edwin,	5732	Boston, Oct. 18, 1882			

WILLIAM, JR., AND RUHAMAH (WEBBER) HARTWELL. 5636.

	Name	No.	Birth			
	William Webber,	5733	Concord, Oct. 2, 1827			
	Joanna Elvina,	5734	" Nov. 1, 1829			
	Lydia Elizabeth,	5735	" Mar. 15, 1835			

DEA. AMOS AND LOUISA (HODGMAN) HARTWELL. 5637.

	Name	No.	Birth			Spouse
	Sarah Joanna,	5736	Bedford, Aug. 31, 1823	Nov. 19, 1823		
99	Mary,	5737	" Mar. 19, 1825		Nov. 27, 1845	Josiah Bacon Gleason. [(Gardner).
99	Sarah,	5738	" Feb. 24, 1829		Jan. 1, 1851	Royal Turner Bryant; 1825-; son Nathan and Mary.
100	Edward Amos,	5739	" Sept. 23, 1828		Oct. 13, 1860	Almira Chamberlain; 1834-; d. Phineas W. & Almira (Hatch).
99	William Green,	5740	" Dec. 1, 1834		June 11, 1868	Clara Augusta Smith; 1842-1885; d. Sam'l and Eliz. (Locke).
	Abbie Louise,	5741	" June 15, 1839			[vinia (Munroe).
100	Frederick Alonzo,	5742	" June 13, 1841		Nov. 23, 1865	Lavinia Augusta Nichols; 1843-; d. Sylvester and La-

JOSIAH B. AND MARY (HARTWELL) GLEASON. 5737.

	Name	No.	Birth			Spouse
	Henry Josiah,	5743	Billerica, Mar. 17, 1847			
	Freder'k Eugene,	5744	" Apr. 13, 1848		Nov. 26, 1885	Louise Upton.

ROYAL T. AND SARAH (HARTWELL) BRYANT. 5738.

	Name	No.	Birth			Spouse
	Edward Turner,	5745	Bedford, Oct. 21, 1851			
102	Sarah Louise,	5746	Billerica, June 20, 1853		Nov. 20, 1879	Whitney Foster; 1852-; s. Jos. and Lydia A. (Dutton)
	Mary Emma,	5747	" July 31, 1855		June 20, 1880	John A. Wight; 1849-; son Eleazar G. & Phebe W.
	Ida Flora,	5748	" Mar. 17, 1857			[(Carter).
	Arthur Walter,	5749	" Mar. 14, 1859			
	Hartwell Irving,	5750	" Oct. 24, 1862		May 4, 1886	Margarite Annie Hilton.

WILLIAM G. AND CLARA A. (SMITH) HARTWELL. 5740.

	Name	No.	Birth			
	Edith Smith,	5751	Bedford, Oct. 5, 1872			
	Clara Howard,	5752	" Nov. 25, 1877			
	Lillie,	5753	" Mar. 7, 1880			

EDWARD A. AND ALMIRA (CHAMBERLAIN) HARTWELL. 5739.

Walter Chamberl'n	5754	Quincy, Ill., Dec. 8, 1861	Aug. 13, 1862		
Carrie Louise,	5755	Chicago, Ill., Aug. 4, 1864			
Lydia Cornelia,	5756	" Nov. 29, 1867			
Almira Florence,	5757	" July 23, 1869			
Abbie Gertrude,	5758	" Oct. 6, 1871			
Mary Belle,	5759	" May 23, 1875			
Edw. Chamberl'n	5760	" Nov. 12, 1876	July 12, 1877		

FREDERICK A. AND LAVINIA A. (NICHOLS) HARTWELL. 5742.

Fannie Taylor,	5761	Woburn, Aug. 13, 1868			
Henry Gardner,	5762	" Aug. 24, 1871			
Herbert Cabot,	5763	" Mar. 18, 1873			
William Winn,	5764	" Sept. 1, 1874			
Florence May,	5765	" May 21, 1876			
Ernest Nichols,	5766	" Feb. 25, 1878			
Edward Amos,	5767	" Sept. 17, 1879			

AUGUSTUS AND MARIA (FRENCH) HEARD. 4869.

Martha Ellen,	5768	Sudbury, Apr. 26, 1846	Feb. 19, 1845		
Maria Josephine,	5769	" Oct. 8, 1851	Sept. 15, 1880	Unmarried.	
Mary Elizabeth,	5770	" June 21, 1852		June 3, 1874	James Fred Dean.
Emma Estelle,	5771	" Mar. 5, 1853		Mar. 1, 1877	Lyman Belcher.
Nellie,	5772	" Jan. 23, 1856		Nov. 28, 1875	Charles E. Nutting.
Eva May,	5773	Wayland, Mar. 5, 1858	Apr. 22, 1859		
Frank Cushing,	5774	" May 14, 1862			
Eva,	5775	Francest'wn, N.H., May 11, 1867			

DAVID AND NANCY K. (HEMINWAY) HEARD. 4870.

100	David Herbert,	5776	Holliston, Jan. 23, 1847	Mar. 13, 1847		
	Edward Burnap,	5777	" Mar. 21, 1848	Aug. 7, 1851		
	David Herbert,	5778	" Mar. 21, 1848		June 15, 1870	Emma C. Brooks.
	Alberti Harrison,	5779	" June 4, 1850	June 6, 1854		

DAVID H. AND EMMA C. (BROOKS) HEARD. 5776.

David,	5780	W. Medway, Sept. 5, 1871	Nov. 18, 1876		
Joel Bertie,	5781	" July 5, 1874			
Alvin David,	5782	" Jan. 30, 1877	Sept. 2, 1877		
Jennie Ethel,	5783	" Apr. 13, 1879			

DR. ABRAHAM A. AND ELIZA A. (HEARD) EDWARDS. 4871.

Clarence,	5784	Concord, Feb. 6, 1852			[Eliz. S. (Mulford).
John Houghton,	5785	" Jan. 26, 1858		Apr. 8, 1886	Anselia Arelina Robie; 1859–; dau. John W. and

CHARLES B. AND HELEN M. (CUSHING) HEARD. 4877.

Wayland Cushing,	5786	Florida, Jan. 31, 1874	Feb. 3, 1874		
Betsey,	5787	" Jan. 30, 1875			

HENRY AND ELIZA (ABRAMS) JORDAN. 980.

100	Caleb Davis,	5788	Mar. 29, 1831		June 20, 1854	Jane Elizabeth Price.
100	William Abrams,	5789	May 12, 1834		Mar., 1854	Anna Mary King.

CLIFTON ASHTON AND ELIZA (ABRAMS–JORDAN) GARRETT. 981.

100	Annie Abrams.	5790	Nov. 10, 1847		Dec. 15, 1868	Joseph Lynn Elgin.

CALEB DAVIS AND JANE ELIZABETH (PRICE) JORDAN. 5788.

100	Charles Henry,	5791	May 2, 1855		Sept. 12, 1882	Ida Belle Madison.
	Martha Abrams,	5792	Oct. 1, 1857			
100	Capitola Black,	5793	Nov. 27, 1859		Apr. 5, 1882	George Foster Wells.
100	Elizabeth Wooley,	5794	Sept. 24, 1861		Oct. 10, 1883	Robert Irwin Paine.
	Caleb Davis, Jr.,	5795	July 5, 1865			
	Annie Elgin,	5796	Aug. 31, 1868			
	Lillian May,	5797	Oct. 2, 1873			
	Edith Maria,	5798	Apr. 10, 1878	May 21, 1880		

CHARLES HENRY AND IDA BELLE (MADISON) JORDAN. 5791.

Clifford Robert,	5799	Sept. 5, 1883			
Florence Brent,	5800	July 15, 1885			

GEORGE FOSTER AND CAPITOLA BLACK (JORDAN) WELLS. 5793.

Effie May,	5801	Feb. 22, 1883			
Jennie Elizabeth,	5802	Oct. 2, 1884			

ROBERT IRWIN AND ELIZABETH (JORDAN) PAINE. 5794.

Robert Irwin, Jr.,	5803	Mar. 17, 1885			

WILLIAM ABRAMS AND ANNA MARY (KING) JORDAN. 5789.

James Crehove,	5804	Jan. 5, 1855	1860		
Anna Eliza,	5805	1858	1860		
Wm. Abrams, Jr.,	5806	1859	1885		
Mary Crehove,	5807	Mar. 31, 1867			

JOSEPH LYNN AND ANNIE ABRAMS (GARRETT) ELGIN. 5790.

John Garrett,	5808	Nov. 12, 1869			
William Clifton,	5809	Feb. 14, 1872			

CALVIN B. AND HARRIET M. (WILLETT) ORCUTT. 3282.

Mary Willett,	5810	June 20, 1875			
Russell Barber,	5811	Oct. 12, 1883			

SAMUEL AND MEHITABLE (PIPER) CONANT. 3831.

	Name	No.					Notes
	Nancy,	5812					—— Wetherbee.
	Rebeccah,	5813					—— Newton.

NATHAN AND REBECCA (CONANT) BROOKS. 3834.

		No.	Place	Born	Died	Married	Spouse
	Nathan,	5814	Acton,	Mar. 27, 1822	May 19, 1822		
	Rebecca,	5814	"	May 1, 1823		Mar. 15, 1849	Joseph A. Smith.
102	George, {	5815	"			Jan. 3, 1877	1. Catharine Comstock; –1874.
		5815					2. Mrs. Isabel M. Jacobs.
	Henry,	5816	"	Dec. 30, 1829			Hannah Homer.

JOHN HINCKLEY AND NANCY ROBBINS (JONES) SANDERS. 4490.

		No.	Place	Born	Died	Married	Spouse
101	Chas. Barton, M D.,	5817	Lowell,	Feb. 19, 1844		June 4, 1871	1. Clara Augusta Butterfield; –1877.
101		5818					2. Lizzie Sophia Taylor; 1853–; dau. Moses and Mary
101	Nancy Emma,	5819	Berwick, Me., June 11, '50				John Prushia. [E. (Stearns).
	Edgar Rand,	5820	"	Dec. 9, 1865			

DR. CHARLES BARTON AND CLARA AUGUSTA (BUTTERFIELD) SANDERS. 5817.

		No.	Place	Born	Died	Married	Spouse
	Walter Barton,	5821	Acton,	Oct. 16, 1875	Aug. 18, 1877		
	Clara Butterfield,	5822	"	Aug. 11, 1877	Sept., 1877		

DR. CHARLES BARTON AND LIZZIE SOPHIA (TAYLOR) SANDERS. 5818.

		No.	Place	Born	Died
	Ralph Barton,	5823	Acton,	Dec. 4, 1883	
	Richard Stearns,	5824	"	June 26, 1886	

JOHN AND NANCY EMMA (SANDERS) PRUSHIA 5819

		No.
	Florence Emma,	5825
		5826

GEORGE STILLMAN AND SUSAN BIRD (POTTER) SMITH. 4929.

		No.	Place	Born	Died	Married	Spouse
	Francis Wayland,	5827	Machias, Me., May 8, 1828	July 5, 1829			
	Francis Wayland,	5828	"	July 10, 1831			Abby (Goodwin) Bradbury; dau. Geo. N.
	Georgianna,	5829	"	Nov. 15, 1833	Apr., 1834		
	Harriet Emeline,	5830	"	June 5, 1835	May 28, 1842		
	Horace Potter,	5831	"	July 27, 1837	Sept., 1838		
	Horace Potter,	5832	"	Apr. 14, 1839			Lydia Murray.
	Almira,	5833	"	Mar. 16, 1840	June 2, 1842		[Olive (Pike).
	Eliza'th McAlister,	5834	"	Dec. 14, 1841		Nov. 13, 1865	Abraham Leonard Clark; 1837–; s. Capt. Tristram and
101	Alice Maria,	5835	"	June 9, 1844		Jan. 18, 1866	Charles Freeman Smith; 1841–; s. James and Dorothy
	Winfield Scott,	5836	"	Oct. 9, 1845	Jan. 21, 1847		[(Elliott).
	George Stillman,	5837	Boston,	July 7, 1847	Dec. 25, 1849		
	Daniel Webster,	5838	Chelsea,	May 27, 1849	Jan. 27, 1850		
	Susan Bird,	5839	Biddeford, Me., Dec. 10, '50	Jan. 5, 1851			
	Emeline Sargent,	5840	"	Apr. 27, 1852			William H. Johnson; son Samuel H.
	Eunice Frances,	5841	"	Sept. 29, 1853	Aug., 1854		

CHARLES F. AND ALICE M. (SMITH) SMITH. 5835.

		No.	Place	Born	Died
	Howard Freeman,	5842	Biddeford, Me., June 16, '71	July 3, 1873	
	Howard Freeman,	5843	"	July 20, 1873		

CHARLES HENRY AND NELLIE LOUISE (TUTTLE) FAIRBANKS. 4703.

		No.	Place	Born
	Alice Tuttle,	5844	Acton,	July 5, 1886

EDWIN A. AND MIRANDA (BUTLER) JONES. 4496.

		No.	Place	Born	Died
	Frederick,	5845	Hudson,	Mar. 29, 1864	Mar. 30, 1864
	Walter Augustine,	5846	"	May 9, 1865	
	Alice Emma,	5847	"	June 28, 1869	

FRANCIS AND ANN ELIZABETH (ROBBINS) JONES. 4493.

		No.	Place	Born	Married	Spouse
101	Wilbur Francis,	5848	Acton,	Nov. 12, 1854	Sept. 12, 1876	Ellen Merrill; 1856–; d. Seth W. & Hulda A. (Cutler).

WILBUR F. AND ELLA (MERRILL) JONES. 5848.

		No.	Place	Born
	Vernal Merrill,	5849	Hudson,	July 11, 1878
	Vertram Francis,	5850	"	Dec. 5, 1883

LUTHER AND SUSANNA (KELLY) JONES. 4638.

		No.	Place	Born	Died
	Florence Kelley,	5851	So. Yarmouth, Sept. 27, 1848	Nov. 27, 1850	
	Loretta,	5852	"	Jan. 6, 1850	Dec. 17, 1878
	Millard Fillmore,	5853	"	Feb. 20, 1851	
	Elizabeth Kelley,	5854	"	July 19, 1852	
	Robena,	5855	"	Sept. 6, 1855	

TIMOTHY AND LUCY (DAVIS) HARTWELL. 3980.

		No.	Place	Born	Died	Married	Spouse
104	George, {	5856	Littleton,	Mar. 17, 1791	June 6, 1853	Oct. 14, 1830	1. Sally Whitney; –1829.
		5856				1816	2. Deborah Young; –1853.
101	Joseph,	5857	"	Oct. 5, 1792	July 19, 1852		Nancy Watts; 1793–1853.
102	Charles, {	5858	"	Jan. 16, 1796	Feb. 19, 1882	Dec. 18, 1821	1. Lucy Lawrence; 1798–1846.
102		5859				Oct. 11, 1848	2. Louisa A. Marble; 1817–.
81	Timothy, Jr.,	5860	Ashby,	Jan. 2, 1798	Sept. 16, 1854	June 19, 1828	Lucinda Eleanor Jones. No. 4634.
	Lucy,	5861	"	Jan. 26, 1800	Mar. 3, 1815		
103	Mary Ann,	5862	"	Apr. 2, 1802	Mar. 15, 1825	May 25, 1821	Obed Symonds; 1796–1833.
	Eleaz'r Davis (no iss.),	5863	"	Nov. 2, 1804			Eunice Woods.
	John,	5864	"	Nov. 6, 1807			
103	Lydia Ruth Porter	5865	"	Dec. 1, 1810		Jan. 29, 1827	Obed Symonds; 1796–1833.

JOSEPH AND NANCY (WATTS) HARTWELL. 5857.

		No.	Place	Born	Died	Married	Spouse
	Lucy,	5866	Groton,	Jan. 5, 1817	Oct. 27, 1836	Jan. 5, 1848	Hannah Page; –1867.
	George,	5867	Littleton,	Apr. 10, 1822	Jan. 3, 1868		
	Nancy Watts,	5868	"	Apr. 30, 1826	Nov. 4, 1833		
	Mary Jane,	5869	"	Oct. 9, 1828		Feb. 24, 1844	Byron E. Bartlett.
	Lydia Ann,	5870	"	Feb. 5, 1831		Oct. 17, 1850	Nahum W. Mower.
	John Henry,	5871	"	Nov. 18, 1834		July 4, 1856	Sarah F. George.

CHARLES AND LUCY (LAWRENCE) HARTWELL. 5858.

	Name	No.	Birth	Death	Marriage	Spouse
102	Mariah L.,	5872	Sept. 29, 1822	Mar. 22, 1883	May 4, 1839	Timothy Hinds.
102	Lucy Ann,	5873	July 2, 1824	Mar. 16, 1879	Jan., 1849	Moses Wheeler.
102	Charles Newton,	5874	Nov. 3, 1825		Sept. 18, 1860	Lucy R. Woods.
	Clara,	5875	Dec. 16, 1827	Feb., 1854	Aug. 12, 1851	Clark James Lewis.
103	Huldah,	5876	Feb. 20, 1831	June 23, 1874	May 5, 1848	David Kendall Wallace; 1826-.
102	Sarah,	5877	June 16, 1835		Nov. 8, 1855	Joseph W. Stone.

CHARLES AND LOUISA A. (MARBLE) HARTWELL. 5859.

	Name	No.		Birth	Death	Marriage	Spouse
	Albert Newell,	5878	Ashby,	Feb. 28, 1850		June 14, 1874	Loma Susan Des Rochers.
102	Hosea Adams,	5879	"	Mar. 25, 1852		Sept. 19, 1875	Alice Streater Wilker.
	Frank Waldo,	5880	"	Dec. 27, 1853			[(Ralfe).
102	Clara Louisa,	5881	"	Sept. 6, 1856		Nov. 25, 1875	Elwood Edson Adams; 1851-; son Daniel and Lucy
	Fred Augustus,	5882	"	Mar. 15, 1863	Aug. 23, 1865		

TIMOTHY AND MARIA L. (HARTWELL) HINDS. 5872.

Name	No.				Spouse
Sophrona,	5883				Charles H. Wise.
Dora,	5884				Alonzo Hoyt.
Emma,	5885				Julius Wheeler.

MOSES AND LUCY ANN (HARTWELL) WHEELER. 5873.

Name	No.				Spouse
	5886				George L. Marble.

CHARLES N. AND LUCY R. (WOODS) HARTWELL. 5874.

Name	No.
Clara,	5887
Emma,	5888
Minnie,	5889
Flora,	5890
Fannie,	5891

JOSEPH W. AND SARAH (HARTWELL) STONE. 5877.

Name	No.				Spouse
Charles O.,	5892				
Lucie E.,	5892½				Charles Marden.

GEORGE AND CATHARINE (COMSTOCK) BROOKS. 5815.

Name	No.		Birth	Death
Stephen George,	5893	Concord,	Nov. 14, 1850	
Nathan H.,	5894	"	Dec. 17, 1853	Dec. 2, 1873
Francis A.,	5895	"	Sept. 1, 1855	
Mary A.,	5896	"	Nov. 21, 1857	Dec. 9, 1863
Fredson Perley,	5897	"	Apr. 10, 1860	
Herman Elbert,	5898	"	Nov. 29, 1865	
Cora A.,	5898½	"	June 12, 1869	Sept. 22, 1869

HOSEA A. AND ALICE S. (WILKER) HARTWELL. 5879

Name	No.		Birth
Abbie Mabel,	5899	Ashburnham,	Feb. 3, 1878
Arthur Lewis,	5900	"	May 13, 1882
Clarence Wilker,	5901	Gardner,	Oct. 1, 1885

ELWOOD E. AND CLARA L. (HARTWELL) ADAMS. 5881.

Name	No.		Birth	Death
Ethel Emma,	5902	Gardner,	Mar. 15, 1879	May 24, 1880

EDMUND S. AND ELIZA A. (CONANT) TUTTLE. 5703.

Name	No.	Birth	Death	Marriage	Spouse
Julien Sherman,	5903	Nov. 20, 1854	1856		
Julius Herbert,	5904	Mar. 7, 1857		Nov. 17, 1881	Jennie C. Carroll.
Fred'k Adalbert,	5905	Jan. 14, 1859			

MARCUS AND ELLEN J. (LEAVENWORTH) CONANT. 5705.

Name	No.	Birth
Ida May,	5906	May 25, 1869
Lulu Belle,	5907	Dec. 3, 1874
Marcus,	5908	Nov. 26, 1881

NAHUM AND ELMIRA W. (DOUGHERTY) CONANT. 5702.

Name	No.	Birth
Laura Louisa,	5909	June 5, 1858

ROBERT C. AND SARAH M. (BURBANK) CONANT. 5708.

Name	No.	Birth
J. Edwin,	5910	June 10, 1870
Eva L.,	5911	Mar. 2, 1874

GEORGE F. AND SUSANNA C. (CONANT) PROCTOR. 5707.

Name	No.	Birth
Lizzie A.,	5912	Nov. 22, 1865
Herbert F.,	5913	June 29, 1871

WHITNEY AND SARAH L. (BRYANT) FOSTER. 5746.

Name	No.		Birth	Death
Joseph Herbert,	5914	Lexington,	Sept. 18, 1880	Dec. 20, 1884

JOHN AND MARY STRATTON (JONES) MEAD. 4488.

Name	No.	Birth	Death
John Baldwin Thayer,	5915	1861	
Stephen Origin,	5916	1868	
Mary Abigail Read,	5917		May 14, 1886
James Murray,	5918		June, 1872

CHARLES AND JULIA MARIA (BARRETT) MARSH. 1735.

	Name	No.		Birth	Marriage	Spouse
102	Edith Barrett,	5919	Boston,	Mar. 24, 1863	Oct. 21, 1884	George Hayward Binney; 1861-; s. Henry P. and
	Mabel Minott,	5920	"	Mar. 4, 1867		[Josephine (Hayward).
	Charles Reuben,	5921	"	Mar. 2, 1872		

GEORGE HAYWARD AND EDITH BARRETT (MARSH) BINNEY. 5919.

Name	No.		Birth
Geo. Hayward, Jr.,	5922	Boston,	Jan. 20, 1886

LORENZO AND MARY (STOW) EATON. 1086.

	Name	No.	Birthplace, Date	Death	Marriage	Spouse
	Harriet Louisa,	5923	Concord, Dec. 30, 1845			
	Mary Stone,	5924	" Nov. 18, 1849			

DANIEL HEALD AND LYDIA (HOSMER) WOOD. 2054-4215.

	Name	No.	Birthplace, Date	Death	Marriage	Spouse
	Cyrus Hosmer,	5925	Concord, Apr. 23, 1862	Apr. 27, 1862		
	Fannie,	5926	Poughkenamon, Pa., Sept. 23, 1863			
	Fred Harlow,	5927	Concord, Oct. 2, 1871			
	Bessie Hosmer,	5928	Montclair, N.J., Aug. 27, 1874	Feb. 23, 1875		

FRANCIS AND CHARLOTTE LOUISA (JONES) BROWN. 4492.

	Name	No.	Birthplace, Date	Death	Marriage	Spouse
	Charlotte Frances,	5929	Stow, Aug. 23, 1844			Lucius C. Tolman; –1885.
	Betsey Eliza,	5930	" Oct. 8, 1846			
	John Henry,	5931	" July 8, 1849			
103	James Perry,	5932	" Apr. 16, 1851		Dec. 25, 1882	Laura Ann Jones. No. 4420.
	Frank Pierce,	5933	" Aug. 11, 1853	Feb. 24, 1884		
	Usher Jones,	5934	Acton, Apr. 12, 1861	July 27, 1886		
	Fred Aaron,	5935	Stow, Aug. 13, 1863			
	Nettie Elmira,	5936	" June 24, 1867			

JAMES PERRY AND LAURA ANN (JONES) BROWN. 5932-4420.

	Name	No.	Birthplace, Date	Death	Marriage	Spouse
	Lizzie Jones,	5937	Acton, Mar. 12, 1885			

PETER CUSHMAN AND JANE MACKINTOSH (BALDWIN) JONES. 4817.

	Name	No.	Birthplace, Date	Death	Marriage	Spouse
103	William Parker,	5938	Boston, Aug. 28, 1832	Nov. 21, 1835	Jan. 1, 1856	Lucy Anna Mudge; 1832–; dau. Alfred and Lucy A. [(Kinsman).
	Mary Elizabeth,	5939	" Feb. 5, 1834			
	Jane Elizabeth,	5940	" Nov. 21, 1836			
103	Peter Cushman, Jr.,	5941	" Dec. 10, 1837		May 12, 1862	Cornelia Hall; 1842–; dau. Edwin O. and Sarah.
	Catharine (no issue),	5942	" Nov. 11, 1839		June 27, 1872	Henry Kirk Hobart; 1836–; s. Benj. W. and Eliz. A. [(Wood).
	Lucy Ann,	5943	" Feb. 22, 1842			
103	Sarah Frances,	5944	" Aug. 10, 1844		Jan. 10, 1866	John Adams Kenrick; 1839–; s. John A. & Mary S. (Stedman).
103	George Bartlett,	5945	Newton, Aug. 12, 1848		July 26, 1881	Susan Elizabeth Johnson; 1857–; dau. Erasmus and
	Edward Draper,	5946	Boston, Oct. 25, 1850			[Sarah C. (Murdough).

WILLIAM PARKER AND LUCY ANNA (MUDGE) JONES. 5938.

	Name	No.	Birthplace, Date	Death	Marriage	Spouse
103	Fred'k Kinsman Mudge,	5947	Boston, Nov. 11, 1856		Jan. 1, 1883	Helen May Wilde; 1863–; dau. Jos. D. and Helen M. (Litch).

FREDERICK K. M. AND HELEN M. (WILDE) JONES. 5947.

	Name	No.	Birthplace, Date	Death	Marriage	Spouse
	Alfred Wilde,	5948	Melrose, Nov. 3, 1883			

PETER CUSHMAN, JR., AND CORNELIA (HALL) JONES. 5941.

	Name	No.	Birthplace, Date	Death	Marriage	Spouse
	Edwin Austin,	5949	Honolulu, S. I., May 16, '63			
	Ada,	5950	" Oct. 26, 1869			
	Alice,	5951	" Jan. 15, 1881			

JOHN ADAMS AND SARAH FRANCES (JONES) KENRICK. 5944.

	Name	No.	Birthplace, Date	Death	Marriage	Spouse
	Mabel Frances,	5952	Newton, Oct. 24, 1866			
	John Adams, Jr.,	5953	" Feb. 11, 1871	Oct. 4, 1872		
	John Adams, Jr.,	5954	" Apr. 24, 1874	Sept. 28, 1876		
	Jennie,	5955	" Jan. 18, 1877			

GEORGE BARTLETT AND SUSAN ELIZABETH (JOHNSON) JONES. 5945.

	Name	No.	Birthplace, Date	Death	Marriage	Spouse
	Henry Seaver,	5956	Newton, July 2, 1882			
	Gertrude Bartlett,	5957	" Nov. 23, 1883			

CHARLES HENRY AND LIZZIE EDNA (JONES) MARTIN. 4668.

	Name	No.	Birthplace, Date	Death	Marriage	Spouse
	Hattie Mabel,	5958	Cambridge, Feb. 3, 1877			

DAVID KENDALL AND HULDAH (HARTWELL) WALLACE. 5876.

	Name	No.	Birthplace, Date	Death	Marriage	Spouse
103	Huldah Elvina,	5959	Rindge, N.H., Aug. 6, 1848	Dec. 4, 1858		
	Clara Ella,	5960	" July 12, 1852		July 3, 1871	Clement Philemon Flint; 1849–; son David and Pru
	Sarah Anna,	5961	" July 15, 1854	Jan. 17, 1858		[dence (Whitcomb).
	Emma Maria,	5962	Winchendon, Aug. 4, 1856	Jan. 14, 1859		

CLEMENT PHILEMON AND CLARA ELLA (WALLACE) FLINT. 5960.

	Name	No.	Birthplace, Date	Death	Marriage	Spouse
	Charles Monroe,	5963	Winchendon, Dec. 12, 1873			
	Theron Clement,	5964	" Apr. 7, 1876			
	Leon David,	5965	" May 10, 1880			
	Emma Hulda,	5966	" Oct. 6, 1884			

OSCAR A. AND ELIZABETH F. (BROWN) JONES. 4621.

	Name	No.	Birthplace, Date	Death	Marriage	Spouse
	Arthur Drew,	5967	Boston, Aug. 13, 1877			

LOWELL A. AND SARAH A. (PARMENTER) JONES. 4622.

	Name	No.	Birthplace, Date	Death	Marriage	Spouse
	Ada Maria,	5968	Acton, Sept. 17, 1872			

FRANK AND ADA I. (JONES) MARSHALL. 4626.

	Name	No.	Birthplace, Date	Death	Marriage	Spouse
	Irving Franklin,	5969	May 28, 1879			
	Carl Bertrand,	5970	Aug. 11, 1882			

OBED AND MARY ANN (HARTWELL) SYMONDS. 5862.

	Name	No.	Birthplace, Date	Death	Marriage	Spouse
104	Obed Augustus,	5971	Ashby, June 8, 1822	Dec. 31, 1875	June 15, 1843	Mary Wright; 1822–1875.

OBED AND LYDIA RUTH PORTER (HARTWELL) SYMONDS. 5865.

	Name	No.	Birthplace, Date	Death	Marriage	Spouse
101	Mary Ann,	5972	Ashby, Aug. 19, 1829		July 18, 1849	Charles W. Whitcomb; 1830–1882.
	Lydia Jane,	5973	" Sept. 28, 1831	Feb. 14, 1853		
	Sarah Maria,	5974	" Feb. 12, 1834	Mar. 15, 1838		

CHARLES W. AND MARY ANN (SYMONDS) WHITCOMB. 5972.

Mary Ann,	5975	Ashby,	Mar. 19, 1850	Jan. 12, 1871	June 1, 1869	Elbridge Gipson; 1849–.
Perry C.,	5976	"	Jan. 19, 1852			
Hattie R.,	5977		Nov. 28, 1854		Nov. 6, 1879	Edward H. Fletcher; 1853–.

NATHAN BROOKS AND ELIZABETH (BROWN) STOW. 1089.

Mary Caroline,	5978	Concord,	Oct. 2, 1857	June 5, 1858		

OBED AUGUSTUS AND MARY (WRIGHT) SYMONDS. 5971.

Mary Angeline,	5979	Acton,	Sept. 29, 1844			
Emory Augustus,	5980	"	June 1, 1846	July 17, 1868		
James Adison,	5981	"	Mar. 17, 1848		Dec. 20, 1874	Flora C. Harlow; 1855–.
Sophia Emma,	5982	"	Nov. 25, 1853			

(104)

JAMES ADISON AND FLORA C. (HARLOW) SYMONDS. 5981.

Elaine C.,	5983	Acton,	Oct. 1, 1881			
Esteane D.,	5984	"	Aug. 29, 1884			

CHARLES L. AND ESTELLE MAY (PHILLIPS) JONES. 4623.

Chester Elwyn,	5985	Arlington,	May 4, 1881			
Leon Roscoe,	5986	"	Mar. 16, 1886	Mar. 19, 1886		

JOHN H. AND LUCY F. (BARRETT) CHAPMAN. 2129.

Grace Chetwoode,	5987	Concord,	July 10, 1880			

HENRY LIVINGSTON AND MARY H. (BARRETT) SHATTUCK. 2619.

Kate Elizabeth,	5988	Concord,	June 6, 1852	Aug. 6, 1861		

ALBERT AND M. SUSAN (WETHERELL) WETHERBEE. 5294.

Harry Josiah,	5989	Waltham,	May 11, 1869			
Fred Benjamin,	5990	"	June 28, 1871			

NATHAN AND BEULAH (HOSMER) HOSMER. 3790.

Beulah,	5991	Concord,	Feb. 2, 1764	May 10, 1785		
Lucy,	5992	"	Jan. 3, 1766	Dec. 1, 1857	Mar. 11, 1788	Samuel Potter. No. 5169.
Meliscent,	5993	"	July 25, 1768			Dea. Francis Jarvis.
Silas,	5994	"	Sept. 30, 1770			Polly Puffer.
Nathan,	5995	"	Apr. 20, 1773			Patty Brown.
Elizabeth,	5996	"	Sept. 10, 1775	Aug. 8, 1822		
Stephen,	5997	"	May, 1778	July 17, 1778		

(90)

HENRY A. AND ELIZA (LEIGHTON) BARRETT. 2616.

Mary Leighton,	5998	Concord,	Jan. 3, 1867	Mar. 23, 1868		

HENRY EMERSON AND ANNIE HAYDEN (SMITH) HOLDEN. 4991.

Edna Gray,	5999	Concord,	May 31, 1885	June 4, 1885		
Bertha H.,	6000	"	Apr. 10, 1886	Apr. 12, 1886		

BENJAMIN AND MARY FOWLE (FITCH) HARTWELL. 5638.

Lucy Webber,	6001	Bedford,	Jan. 16, 1837	Oct. 2, 1860	Nov. 25, 1858	Hanibal S. Pond.
Mary Elzina,	6002	"	Feb. 21, 1829		Jan. 1, 1861	Matthew R. Fletcher.

GEORGE AND SALLY (WHITNEY) HARTWELL. 5856.

Sarah Ann,	6003	Mason, N. H.,	Aug. 28, '22	Oct., 1857		Samuel Warner Shattuck.
George Whitney,	6004	"	Apr. 4, 1824	Sept. 6, 1857	Unmarried.	
Emily Augusta,	6005	Townsend,	Oct. 9, 1827		Mar. 2, 1847	Silas Wetherbee; –1885.

(104)

SILAS AND EMILY AUGUSTA (HARTWELL) WETHERBEE. 6005.

George,	6006 / 6007	Townsend,	Dec. 12, 1847		Apr. 16, 1872 / May 18, 1875	1. Roselthe Melissa Rowley; –1873. / 2. Margaret Grace Hannah Hayter; 1853–.
Frank,	6008	Ashby,	June 4, 1850		May 5, 1875	Ellen Rosella Wright; 1855–.
Kate,	6009	"	Sept. 15, 1852			
Charles,	6010	"	May 30, 1855		June 15, 1881	Hattie Augusta Whitney.
Emma,	6011	"	Oct. 2, 1857		Aug. 15, 1880	Harrold E. Spaulding.
Jennie,	6012	"	July 13, 1860			
Abbie,	6013	"	July 30, 1863	Jan. 8, 1882		
Fred,	6014	"	Nov. 3, 1865			
Mary,	6015	"	Jan. 2, 1868			
Annie,	6016	"	Apr. 8, 1870	Feb. 22, 1873		
John,	6017	"	Jan. 18, 1873			
Florence,	6018	"	Dec. 21, 1875	Oct. 14, 1876		

(104)

GEORGE AND MARGARET G. H. (HAYTER) WETHERBEE. 6007.

Mabel Gertrude,	6019	Fitchburg,	May 5, 1876			

HENRY FAXON AND JULIA A. (MOORE) MOORE. 4956.

Fred Albert,	6020	Framingham,	Aug. 14, '59	Dec. 9, 1861		
Walter Henry,	6021	"	June 8, 1861	Dec. 13, 1861		
Frank,	6022	Berlin,	July 10, 1862	June 20, 1865		
Morris,	6023	Hudson,	Feb. 9, 1866	Aug. 12, 1867		
Robert Henry,	6024	Framingham,	May 2, 1875			
Beula,	6025	New York, N. Y.,	Oct. 28, 1885			

EDWARD H. AND ELLA M. (COOLIDGE) WILSON. 5680.

Helen Howard,	6026		Jan. 4, 1876			
John Edward,	6027		July 20, 1879			

FREDERICK H. AND MARY M. (WILSON) RIPLEY. 5682.

Helen Louise,	6028		Oct. 22, 1878	Mar. 15, 1879		
Grace Wilson,	6029		June 24, 1880			
Freder'k Edward,	6030		Dec. 25, 1882	Jan. 29, 1884		

OLD FAMILIES, CONCORD, MASSACHUSETTS.

BARRETT.

HUMPHREY BARRETT[1] settled in Concord in 1639; admitted a freeman, May 6, 1657. It is supposed that he came from the county of Kent, England. There came with him a wife and three sons, John, Thomas, and Humphrey, Jr. Respecting the son John, it is not definitely known where he settled. Shattuck supposes him to have been of Marlboro. The records of probate, however, show that John Barrett of Marlboro had a brother William Barrett of Cambridge, and Thomas Barrett of Marlboro, formerly of Cambridge.

Thomas Barrett, here mentioned, in his will, Jan. 16, 1672, made a little before his death, names brothers John and William, and a sister Lydia Cheever. As Humphrey, Sr., had a son Thomas, who was drowned in the North River at Concord, in 1652, leaving a son Oliver, who died in 1671, and a daughter Mary, who married James Smedley, both of these children being mentioned in the wills of Humphrey Barrett and his wife Mary Barrett as their grandchildren, it therefore follows that John Barrett of Marlboro was not a son of Humphrey Barrett of Concord.

Humphrey Barrett's farm was some three hundred acres or more; his house-lot of twelve acres was near the centre of the town. The old house was on what is now known as Monument Street.

HUMPHREY BARRETT, Jr.[4], born in England, 1630, and came to Concord with his parents. He married Elizabeth Paine in 1661; issue by this marriage, a daughter Mary, who married Josiah Blood[51]. His wife, Elizabeth Paine, died in 1674, and in 1675 he married Mary Potter[545], a daughter of Luke Potter, one of the first settlers in Concord. Thus Humphrey Barrett, Jr., and Mary Potter, his wife, became the common ancestors of the Concord branch of the Barrett family of New England. Their sons, Joseph and Benjamin Barrett, married the sisters Rebecca and Lydia Minott, respectively, daughters of James and Rebecca (Wheeler) Minott[501] of Concord.

Humphrey Barrett, Jr., was a deacon of the church in Concord; admitted a freeman, May 24, 1662; was deputy and representative to the General Court, 1691, and ensign of the foot company. Major Gen. Gookin, in 1685, reported to the General Court that the Concord train band "had but one commissioned officer that officiates in that company, viz., Left. Buss, who is very aged, and not well able to conduct the affairs of ye great company, therefore, having informed himself as the fittest man to supply the place of ensign for that company, did propose to the court, Humphrey Barrett, who was a freeman, and of ye church at Concord, a sergeant of that company, that the court would make him ensigne of Concord foot company." He was appointed and approved of Oct. 14, 1685.— *Walcott's Colonial Period.*

CAPT. JOSEPH BARRETT[9], the eldest son of Humphrey Barrett, Jr., was one of the original grantees of Grafton, Mass., having granted to him May 7, 1728, 121 1-2 acres of land. He was a farmer, as well as largely engaged in the business enterprises of the day. He was town treasurer, 1634 to 1739, commissioned captain of foot company, May 7, 1732. He married Rebecca Minott[506].

BENJAMIN BARRETT[10] was also one of the original grantees of Grafton, receiving 131 1-2 acres of land, April 25, 1728. He was a farmer, and engaged in business enterprises with his brother, Capt. Joseph Barrett. His wife was Lydia Minott[507].

LIEUT. OLIVER BARRETT[14] was born in Concord; moved to Bolton, Mass., and settled where the place is now known as the Barrett Homestead. He was a farmer, and served as a lieutenant in the Revolution. He married Hannah, daughter of John and Mary (Brown) Hunt.

JOHN BARRETT[17] was in the fight at North Bridge, Concord, April 19, 1775. He married Lois, daughter of Joshua and Lydia (Wheeler) Brooks, and lived in Concord.

DEA. THOMAS BARRETT[20] was engaged with his brother, Col. James Barrett, largely in business affairs, accumulating thereby a considerable property. He was a man noted for his piety and mildness of manners. "On the morning of the 'Concord fight,' the British seized and abused several aged and unarmed men; among these was Dea. Thomas Barrett. Not daunted by the scenes of that morning, he spoke of the mother country's unkind treatment of the Colonies, and protested against the violence of the soldiers, who threatened to kill him as a rebel; he calmly replied, 'You need not take that trouble, for I am old and will soon die of myself.' Touched by this reply, they said, 'Well, old daddy, you may go in peace.'"— *Harper's Magazine*, 1875.

The epitaph on his tombstone thus records his virtues: "In him the Christian graces shone uncommonly bright. Unfeigned love and distributive charity ran through his sentiments and actions. The blessing of the widow, the fatherless, the poor, and those ready to perish, came upon him. His talents as a deacon and private Christian were superior, and so exercised as to leave behind him a sweet remembrance f his name; so nearly did he imitate his Saviour, that it may be said with truth he had the spirit of Christ, which the judgment-day, we trust, will better show than any human testimony."

His wife was Mary Jones[428.1]. He was born in Concord in 707, and died in 1779.

Col. James Barrett[21], of Concord, Mass., "the distinguished commander of the Provincial troops in the 'Concord fight,' April 19, 1775, where the first forcible resistance was made to British aggression." Col. Barrett occupies a very interesting and prominent place in the Revolutionary history. From his lips proceeded the first orders to an American force to march against and engage the soldiers of the king. He was in command at the North Bridge on the 19th of April, 1775, by virtue of his commission, and where was presented every characteristic necessary to constitute a battle. The historic record says that after the council of officers and citizens on the hill had "resolved to march into the centre of the town to defend their homes, or die in the attempt," "Col. Barrett immediately gave orders to march by wheeling from the right." That he comprehended the magnificent results that were to follow from those brief authoritative words, that he saw in those few hundreds of militia and minute-men the aroused and advancing ranks of freedom, and in that threatened bridge their narrow and inevitable way, would, perhaps, be too much to claim; but we may presume that he who so immediately proceeded to carry into effect the resolution of his fellow-citizens, his imagination kindling with gleams of those visions that drew from Adams, as he heard the guns at Lexington, the exclamation, 'Oh, what a glorious morning is this!" felt that the order involved far more than its immediate and obvious consequences. His affidavit, four days after, on the 23d of April, made when it was still doubtful in what light the transaction would be received by the government, is simple and bold, reading like a military despatch: "I, James Barrett, of Concord, colonel of a regiment of militia, in the county of Middlesex, do testify and say, that on Wednesday morning last, about daybreak, I was informed of the approach of a number of the regular troops to the town of Concord, where were some magazines belonging to the Province, where there was assembled some of the militia of this and the neighboring towns. I ordered them to march to the North Bridge, so called, which the regulars had passed and were taking up; I ordered said militia to march to said bridge and pass the same, but not to fire on the king's troops, unless they were first fired upon. We advanced near said bridge, when the said troops fired upon our militia, and killed two men dead on the spot, and wounded several others, which was the first firing of guns in the town of Concord. My detachment then returned the fire, which killed and wounded several of the king's troops."

Col. Barrett was a son of Benjamin and Lydia (Minott) Barrett, and his wife was Rebecca Hubbard[462]. The following in reference to Col. James Barrett is from Shattuck's "History of Concord": "Having early in life embraced those principles of religion which are calculated to make men respected, useful, and happy, and having arrived to mature age in an important period of our history, he received from his townsmen frequent marks of their confidence in civil and military life. In 1768, he was chosen representative to the General Court, and was re-elected each year until 1777. He was also a member of many of the county and State conventions held during that important period, and a member of each of the Provincial Congresses. When it was decided to collect and deposit military stores at Concord, Col. Barrett was appointed to superintend them, and aid in their collection and manufacture. He accepted the office of colonel of the regiment of militia organized in March, 1775, and was in command on the 19th of April, though then sixty-four years of age.

"Of the various committees chosen by the State, county, or town, for raising men, procuring provisions, etc., he was usually a member." He died April 11, 1779.

Rebecca Hubbard (Barrett)[462.21], the wife of Col. James Barrett, was a woman of great energy, moral and intellectual worth. The following is from "Harper's Magazine," 1875: "Capt. Parsons, with the other three companies, proceeded to Col. Barrett's, one mile and a half to the northwest, to destroy the stores there; they reached his home about eight o'clock, and just after Col. Barrett had left on his return to the rendezvous. Capt. Parsons said to Mrs. Barrett, 'Our orders are to search your house and your brother's from top to bottom.' She was requested to provide refreshments for the soldiers. . . . Mrs. Barrett was offered compensation for the refreshments, but she refused to take any, remarking, 'We are commanded to feed our enemies.' They threw some money into her lap, which she finally retained, saying, 'This is the price of blood.' . . . She had concealed some musket balls, cartridges, and flints in casks in the attic, and covered them with feathers; they were not discovered. Mrs. Barrett was a great-granddaughter of Rev. Peter Bulkeley, the first minister of Concord."

BROOKS.

Thomas Brooks[91] was a freeman, 1636, and came to Concord about that time, having, as it is believed, come from London, England. He was representative in Concord seven years. His daughter Mary married Capt. Timothy Wheeler[629] of Concord.

Joshua Brooks[93], of Concord, married Hannah, daughter of Capt. Hugh Mason of Watertown. "He was a tanner in Lincoln. He is the ancestor of nearly all of the name in Concord and Lincoln." His son, Noah Brooks, married Dorothy Potter[543]. His daughter, Grace Brooks, married Judah Potter[546].

BROWN.

THOMAS BROWN[125] was in Concord about 1640, but from what part of England he came is not definitely known. His son Thomas[131] was town clerk of Concord.

BULKELEY.

REV. PETER BULKELEY[167] came from Bedfordshire, England, 1635. He was associated with Major Simon Willard in the settlement of Concord. They brought with them from England twelve other families.

BUTTRICK.

WILLIAM BUTTRICK[193] came to Concord in 1635. "He served the town for many years honorably as a sergeant, a post then of distinction." His son Samuel married Elizabeth Blood[47], and they were the grandparents of Major John Buttrick[217].

MAJOR JOHN BUTTRICK[217] "was one of the officers in command on the 19th of April, 1775, and his name will be handed down to posterity with distinguished honor for the noble stand he took, and the bravery he manifested in leading a gallant band of militia-men on to meet the invading enemy at the North Bridge, and for beginning the first forcible resistance to British arms. He then returned the fire by commanding his own company to fire, saying, 'Fire! fellow-soldiers; for God's sake, fire!' and discharged his own gun the same instant. He was buried in 1791, with military honors."

CONANT.

LOT CONANT[227], a great-grandson of the celebrated Roger Conant of Salem, Mass. He came to Concord soon after 1700. His son, Silas Conant, married Lois Potter[567].

DAVIS.

DOLOR DAVIS[253] came, it is probable, from Kent, England. He was in Cambridge, 1634; removed to Concord from Barnstable in 1655. His wife was Margery Willard[697], a sister of Lieut. Simon Willard[698].

SAMUEL DAVIS[259] settled in the part of Concord which was afterward set off as Bedford. He was a freeman, March 21, 1689-90. His son, Eleazer Davis[248], married Eunice Potter[549].

SIMON DAVIS[272] married Hannah (Potter) Brown[552]. He was a grandson of Lieut. Simon and Mary (Blood) Davis[265 36].

FARRAR.

JOHN FARRAR[287] and JACOB FARRAR[288] were proprietors in Lancaster, 1653.

GEORGE FARRAR[295], son of Jacob Farrar of Lancaster, settled in Concord in 1692. He lived upon land then owned by his father, which land is still owned by his descendants, being now in the town of Lincoln. He married Mary How. Of their sons, George married Mary Barrett[11], and Samuel married Lydia Barrett[22].

DEA. SAMUEL FARRAR[303] lived and died upon the home place in Lincoln. Was a selectman of Concord in 1754, and after the town of Lincoln was set off from Concord, he was town clerk and representative for many years of the new town. He was chairman of the first committee of correspondence, and of the Middlesex Convention of Aug. 30, 1774; also a member of the first Provincial Congress, which met Oct. 11, 1774. He took part in the "Concord fight," April 19, 1775, although being then sixty-six years of age. He was the youngest son of George Farrar, who settled in Concord, 1692, and succeeded him as deacon of the church. His wife was Lydia Barrett[22].

JUDGE TIMOTHY FARRAR[319] of New Ipswich, N. H., graduate of Harvard College, 1767. "He taught school in Concord, Lincoln, and Framingham, then settling as a teacher in New Ipswich in 1770, also becoming a freeholder there in 1771. His farm and the school divided his attention till the War of the Revolution brought to him public trusts, 1774 to 1775. He was first selectman, and town clerk, Jan. 24, 1776. He was commissioned Justice to the Court of Common Pleas; the youngest of the twenty-nine appointed at that time. From April, 1778, to May 20, 1782, he was a member of the convention for framing a new constitution; from 1779 he was one of the thirty-two councillors till the new constitution went into operation in June, 1784. Appointed March, 1791, to the bench of the Supreme Court. Appointed Chief Justice of that court, 1802, resigning in April, 1803, and accepting a reappointment to Court of Common Pleas, continued until 1813. In 1816 he retired from the judiciary, after a continuous service of over forty years. During this time he had been Presidential elector four times, and in 1804 was appointed a trustee of Dartmouth College, holding this office for more than twenty years. He was repeatedly nominated and urged to become a candidate for Congress, and for governor of New Hampshire. He lived to be one hundred and one years seven months and twelve days of age, outliving all his collegiate contemporaries, and all the ante-Revolutionary graduates of Harvard College, the one hundred and fifty-three officers of the civil list in 1776, and the thirty-two councillors of the Revolution."

JONES.

JOHN JONES[473] came from Cambridge to Concord about 1650. His eldest son, Samuel Jones, married Elizabeth Potter[544].

MINOTT.

JAMES MINOTT[501], a grandson of George Minott[404], married Rebecca, daughter of Captain Timothy Wheeler[628]. He lived in Concord, practised medicine, was a captain, justice of peace, representative, and eminently a useful citizen. He had a family of ten children, some of whom by marriage became connected with the Adams, Barrett, Brooks, Brown, Prescott, Wheeler, and others of the old families in Concord.

DEA. GEORGE MINOTT[530] of Concord. He married, successively, Rebecca Barrett[1896], Elizabeth Barrett[849], and Mrs. Lydia (Barrett) Mann[1559]. He commanded a company in the Revolution at the taking of Burgoyne, and at several other engagements. He was made a deacon of the church in 1779, and served in that office until his death.

POTTER.

LUKE POTTER[536], born in England about 1608, was among the original settlers of Concord, taking up land in the south quarter. His house-lot consisted of six and one half acres on both sides of Heywood Street (then known as "Potter's Lane"). His wife Mary died in 1644; he married a second time the same year, Mary, daughter of Walter Edmunds. He was one of the first deacons of the church, and took an active part in the affairs of the town, during the fifty years succeeding its settlement. It is only by his son Judah, who married Grace Brooks[103], that the name Potter is perpetuated in the records of Concord. Of his other children, Mary married Humphrey Barrett, Jr.[4], Dorothy married Noah Brooks[102], Elizabeth married Samuel Jones[474], and son Samuel married Mary Wright, and was killed by the Indians in the "Sudbury fight"; he died without issue. Luke Potter died in 1697.

PRESCOTT.

JONATHAN PRESCOTT[1578] was the ancestor of the Concord branch of this distinguished family.

COL. CHARLES PRESCOTT[596], who married Elizabeth Barrett[16], was born in 1711, and died in 1779. He was a selectman in Concord six years, and represented the town nine years in the General Court. Also a colonel of militia, serving three years in the War of the Revolution. He was at times a justice of the peace, and always an influential and highly honored citizen, holding many important trusts.

RUSSELL.

JAMES RUSSELL[562], a son of James and Susanna (Farrar) Russell of Concord, and great-grandson of Benjamin Russell, who came to Concord in 1860 (he being a son of William Russell, who settled in Cambridge in 1640), built a house in the south part of the town. which is still standing; that location is now in the town of Carlisle. James Russell married Lydia Potter[562].

WILLARD.

MAJOR SIMON WILLARD[698] was one of the distinguished leaders in the first settlement of the town of Concord. He came from Kent, England, and was associated with the Rev. Peter Bulkeley in the first purchase of the land from the natives.

BALL.

REV. GEORGE S. BALL[760] of Upton, Mass., a Unitarian minister, born in Leominster, Mass., graduated at Meadville Theological School in 1847. He was ordained over the society at Ware, remaining until 1849; in 1850, at Upton, Mass.; and next as associate pastor with Dr. Kendall at Plymouth, Mass.. returning in 1856 to Upton. Chosen representative from Upton and Northbridge in 1861, he resigned from this office to serve as chaplain in the 21st Regiment. After the war he was again a representative, also a State senator. He was a member of the commission to revise the Constitution in 1852.

BARRETT.

PROF. ALBERT TENNISON BARRETT[2959] of Winchester, Tenn., a graduate of University of Rochester, 1869, receiving the highest award then given at the University, viz., the first prize, "Davis Gold Medal." Since 1871, he has been Professor of Mathematics in Mary Sharp College at Winchester, the eldest college for women in America, requiring a long course of Latin, Greek, and higher mathematics to obtain a diploma. He received the degree of LL.D. from the Southwestern Baptist University at Jackson, Tenn.

AMOS BARRETT[2812], of Kingsville, Ohio, was born in Paris, Oneida Co., N. Y. His parents removed the winter after his birth to Pomfret, N. Y., near his paternal grandparents' residence. At the age of fourteen he was removed with his parents to Kingsville, Ohio, and lived in that place until his death. In 1827 he married Annis M. Brown, of Fredonia, N. Y. They raised a family of six sons and four daugh-

Amos Barrett.

ters, all of whom are now living, excepting two daughters who died in childhood. His early life was devoted principally to farming; later in life he engaged in manufacturing, trading, and fire insurance. He never lost sight of the fact that a thorough education was the greatest boon that he could bestow upon his children, and to this end he worked with all his ability, with the prayerful and devoted co-operation of his wife. He joined the Baptist Church while young, and always remained a devoted and consistent member, holding the office of deacon for many years. He was strictly a temperate man, never using liquor or tobacco in any form, an honest and an upright citizen, beloved and respected by all his acquaintance. In 1877 he celebrated his golden wedding, at the residence of his son, Rev. A. J. Barrett, D. D., of Rochester, N. Y., at which time he sang in a clear voice to his faithful wife a song composed for the occasion by C. W. Haywood, of Cleveland, Ohio, the music written by his son, Clinton S. Barrett; a part of this song is appended to this sketch. Amos Barrett died at his residence in Kingsville in 1886.

I.

Just fifty years ago, wife,
  You were my blooming bride;
I led you to the altar, wife,
  My heart aglow with pride;
I thought you fairer than the dawn,
  And purer than the snow;
But you, somehow, are dearer now
  Than fifty years ago.

II.

Since fifty years ago, wife,
  Within our humble home
What changes have we seen, wife!
  What sunshine and what gloom!
But still, through all the varying scenes
  Of gladness and of woe,
Your love shone bright, with calmer light
  Than fifty years ago.

V.

Just fifty years ago, wife,
  With faith in God's good-will,
We took each other's hand, wife,
  To climb life's rugged hill;
Now we'll go down the other side,
  With feeble steps and slow,
While faith's bright star beams brighter far
  Than fifty years ago.

AMOS BARRETT,[1563] of Concord, Mass., was at the "Concord fight," in the ranks; he was afterwards a captain of militia in Concord. He moved after his marriage to Union, Maine, becoming one of the first settlers of that town.

REV. AMOS JUDSON BARRETT[2952], a graduate of the University of Rochester, N. Y., and has received the degrees of A. B., A. M., and D. D. He taught school in Nunda and Little Falls, N. Y., Kingsville, Ohio, and then in Roch-

ester, N. Y. He is now the pastor of the Lake Avenue Baptist Church, Rochester, N. Y.

ASA BARRETT[747] was born in Bolton, Mass.; removed to Lancaster, and for many years was associated with Ephraim Fuller in the manufacture of wire. He afterward moved to Baltimore, Md. He held a captain's commission in the militia of Massachusetts, and was drafted in the War of 1812. An active and useful citizen, who lived to the age of ninety-one.

DR. BENJAMIN BARRETT[2594], of Northampton, Mass., a graduate of Harvard College, 1819, of Medical School, 1822. Afterwards he studied medicine with Drs. Warren and Jackson, beginning the practice at Northampton in 1823, and continuing until 1846. He was a member of the State Legislature, 1842 to 1844, and after this elected to the State Senate.

BENJAMIN BARRETT[2646] served in the Revolutionary War, fought in the battles of Bennington and Cross Plains.

HON. CHARLES BARRETT[1048], of Grafton, Vt., is a graduate of Dartmouth, class 1852. He has represented his town in the General Assembly, 1861–62 and 1876–79; senator from Windham County, 1864 to 1869, and again, 1877 to 1882.

COL. CHARLES BARRETT[1174], of Ashburnham, Mass. At the age of twenty-one he settled in Ashburnham, after completing his apprenticeship at the blacksmith trade in 1809, when there were but eleven dwelling houses in the village. He built a shop, and a dwelling in which he resided for twenty-nine years. In 1835, he built the house where his son, Col. George Barrett, now resides. He early in life identified himself with all the societies and organizations for the material and moral interests of the town. In 1824 he was elected colonel of the Ninth Regiment of Massachusetts Volunteer Militia. He was for many years a selectman and assessor, and in 1827 and 1834 was representative to the General Court. He was one of the principal promoters in building the Congregational church in Ashburnham, and was often chosen to fill various parish offices. After he was seventy years old he canvassed the town on foot to obtain subscriptions to defray parish expenses. He placed himself on the side of total abstinence as early as 1827 or 1828, and proved by his example that a man could perform a hard day's labor without alcoholic stimulants. He was a man of good morals and strict honesty, and set an example by his pure life worthy of imitation. About 1835 he gave up his business of blacksmithing, and was engaged as a contractor and builder, acquiring interests in many of the enterprises of the place, and for many years was proprietor of a grain mill. Col. Charles Barrett during his long life was always pleasant, courteous, and gentlemanly in his intercourse with his neighbors, possessed of an unselfish nature, a warm heart, and kindly feeling toward his fellow-men. Col. Barrett was a member of the Masonic order for some seventy years. When a young man he had his life insured for $1000, and when ninety-six years old, having outlived the limit of his policy, the company paid him the amount of his insurance.

CHARLES BARRETT[1559], of New Ipswich, N. H., "from his youth possessed an enterprising spirit, and while a young man, in connection with his brother, built the grist and saw mills in what is now Mason Village, N. H. In 1764 he came to New Ipswich, N. H. At the commencement of the Revolution, Mr. Barrett, by energy and industry, had made himself one of the most prominent men of the town; but, like several of our leading men, he had strong doubts of the measures then adopted by the ardent Whigs. Having always been accustomed to state his opinion boldly and fearlessly, he often became involved in controversies with many of the patriot party, and a large part of the people branded him as an enemy of his country; and at one time party feeling ran so high that his principles were discussed in town meeting. The people soon found that honest opinions, however strongly expressed, should not be punished; and as the honesty of Mr. Barrett's principles had never been questioned, he soon acquiesced in the measures of the new government, and paid his full share towards carrying on the war; he regained his popularity and the confidence of his townsmen. He was elected a delegate to the convention to ratify the Constitution of the United States, and was afterwards a member of the Senate; he served as councillor for one or more terms; was chosen representative, annually, for fourteen years, which, more than anything else, shows the confidence of his townsmen. Soon after the Revolution he obtained the grant of a township of land in Lincoln County, Maine, which was for a long time called Barrett's town; afterwards incorporated, and named Hope. Here he spent much of his time, and was the means of inducing many persons to emigrate there from this and the neighboring towns, to whom he freely distributed lands. In 1790 he was engaged with J. Jameson in erecting extensive mills on the falls of Georgis River. He also projected an extensive course of improvements of this river, so as to enable loaded boats to reach this township from ti le water. He built upon the river the first series of locks constructed in New England, and probably in this country. . . . He had an interest in the glass-house on the Mountain, and was one of the subscribers to the Academy, and made to it a donation of a tract of wild land in Camden, Maine, which was afterwards sold by him as agent of the institution. He may be said to be the father of the cotton manufacture in the place, as Mr. Robbins, a practical machinist, came here at his suggestion, and they, in connection with Benjamin Champney, erected the first cotton mill in the State. Though Mr. Barrett had received but a very ordinary education, he possessed a very strong mind, and had

informed himself so as to converse well on almost any subject."—*From Kidder's History of New Ipswich, N. H.*

CHARLES BARRETT[1714], of New Ipswich, N. H., graduated at Dartmouth College, 1794; "began a business life as a co-partner with Samuel Appleton. Mr. Appleton left the business for a wider field in Boston. In a few years after, he was followed by Mr. Barrett, whose ample means and business habits brought him an esteemed circle of acquaintance and friends. Here he pursued an extensive commercial trade through the trying times which our commerce passed, in that era of non-intercourse, embargo, and war, with varied success, till 1814, when he returned, with his family, to his native town, to enjoy once more the retirement of his beautiful mansion, which he had erected during the time of his former residence. In 1819, Mr. Barrett was induced to purchase an interest in the old cotton factory. Being associated with several gentlemen, he procured an act of incorporation, under the title of the "Water Loom Factory Company." Here they erected a large building. This promising to be a good investment, two other companies were formed, of which Mr. Barrett was the head and principal manager. These establishments were built near the High Bridge and at Mason Village, with which he was connected during his life. Mr. Barrett's life was an active one; like his father, he disliked to see an idle man. He was the principal in establishing the bank, and it was mainly from his exertions that the Unitarian church was erected, as also many other public improvements. He was elected to fill various town offices, and for many years was the town's representative in the General Court."— *From Kidder's History New Ipswich, N. H.*

CHARLES BARRETT[1722] was born in Boston, Mass. At the age of five he had a severe illness; the medicine given to him destroyed his hearing. He was educated at the asylum for deaf-mutes at Hartford, Conn. In 1852, when the "New England Gallaudet Association of Deaf-Mutes" was formed, Mr. Barrett was chosen its treasurer; which office he continued to hold, by repeated election, until his death. He was of a particularly sunny and genial temperament, uniformly lively and happy; honest and upright in his dealings, he won the confidence and esteem of all. He was married to Abby Beals Harrt of Boston. She was remarkable for her great fidelity and charming manner of interpreting the conversation of those about them to her husband. Her father, Edmund Hartt, was the builder of the frigate "Constitution"; he also designed and superintended the building of the "Boston" frigate, 1799. Mr. Barrett was for a short time engaged in business in New Ipswich, N. H., whither his parents had removed, occupying a brick house in Bank Village, erected for him by his father at the time of his marriage. At the death of his mother, he came into possession of the Barrett homestead at New Ipswich, and occupied that until 1848, when he sold it to his brother George, and

Charles Barrett

removed to Boston. The following beautiful tribute was paid to his memory, at the time of his death, 1862: "To all who were permitted to know him, his short and comparatively uneventful life suggests many sweet and beautiful memories, — memories of gracious, kindly intercourse, of serene cheerfulness, of Christian content. Kind and courteous to all, conscientious in the discharge of his duties, it was in the sacred circle of home that the purity and beauty of his character shone with the brightest and clearest light. He was indeed the sunshine of that home, gladdening all who entered it, lavishing warmth and light with an unconscious bounty that was its chiefest charm. Nature had been so bountiful to him in the rich gifts of the heart and soul, that one scarcely remembered his privations. The closed avenues shut out much that might have pained his childlike gentleness of heart and tarnished his rare purity of soul; while in the sweet and sacred silence his spirit grew like a white flower in the deep, quiet woods, reaching towards the great source of light and life. The flower has withered and fallen to the earth, but the mortal germ within still lives to bloom and flourish in the new world and the new life."

CAPT. CHARLES BARRETT[2352], of New York, engaged at the age of fourteen as a sailor, continuing upon the sea for nine years until 1844. He graduated at Yale College, 1852; after this taking a three years' course at Union Theological Seminary. From 1855 to 1876 he was a ship-master in the India, China, and Pacific trades. He was in the fleet at the taking of Fort Fisher, as a delegate of the Christian Commission, the only man serving therein without pay. He is now conducting a Christian mission in the city of New York.

CLARENCE TYNAN BARRETT[2323] entered the service of the United States on the 2d of August, 1862, as second lieutenant of the One Hundred and Fifty-sixth New York Volunteers; promoted to adjutant, rank of first lieutenant, Jan. 31, 1863, and to aide-de-camp, rank of captain, May 27, 1864, for gallant and meritorious service during the campaign against the city of Mobile and its defence; promoted Nov. 26, 1865, to brevet major. He resigned from the service, and now resides at West New Brighton, N. Y.

CAPT. CLINTON SAMUEL BARRETT[2955], of Chattanooga, Tenn., was educated principally at the Academy, Kingsville, Ohio; subsequently a student in Nunda, N. Y., Literary Institution, in which institution he was promoted to the faculty. Capt. Barrett served in the army, Company H, Fifteenth Missouri Volunteers, then joining the United States Military Telegraph Corps, remaining until the close of the war. Is now travelling passenger agent for the St. Louis, Missouri and Southern Railroad, and also general land agent for the Fort Smith and Little Rock Railroad.

DANIEL BARRETT[1568] settled in Camden, Me., about 1792, where he purchased of Wm. Molineaux on Beauchamp Neck,

built a house, and afterwards married. He was of a retiring disposition, and seldom allowed himself to be put forward for any public place. He was noted for his upright character, sound judgment, exactness, energy, and industry. He was a class leader in the Methodist Episcopal church for many years, or until his death. He was largely interested in farming, stock raising, and the manufacture of lime, owning several lime-kilns and wharves, and also in ship-building, building and owning several vessels, among which was the brig "Eagle." His greatest undertaking was the building of a turnpike around Mount Beatter, one that will remain a monument to his industry and perseverance, as he has expressed it in one of his deeds, "as long as oaks grow and water runs." He obtained a charter, June 23, 1802, of the General Court of Massachusetts, which was entitled "An Act authorizing Daniel Barrett to make a Turnpike Road over Megantehook Mountain, in the town of Camden, in the county of Lincoln." This roadway he kept in repair and collected the tolls until 1834, when he sold it to the towns of Camden and Lincolnville.

EZRA BARRETT[1179], born in Ashby, Mass., settled after his marriage in Warren, N. H. He was for many years a deacon in the Congregational church. He was greatly esteemed for his thorough Christian and business integrity, dignified and gentlemanly deportment. He was extensively engaged in the manufacture of various farming implements for the New England market, in use at the time, he having invented the Concord scythe snaith, and also a lathe for turning wood by a pattern. He was much interested in common schools, and in improving the construction of their houses. He published a singing book for Sunday-school use. His wife was Rhoda Johnson, a daughter of Col. Reuben and Rhoda Johnson. He died in 1843.

EDWARD HARRIS BARRETT[1289], of Minneapolis, Minn., settled in Springfield, Ill., and lived there until 1854, when he removed with his wife and three sons to Minnesota Territory. He built the first log-cabin on the prairie west from Winona, then a town of three buildings, — a frame hotel, a log-cabin serving as a dwelling, a store and post-office (the mail being often carried in the postmaster's hat), and an unenclosed warehouse. The Indians had been taken from that part of the prairie the previous year. Mr. Barrett's cabin was, like all others in the new country, nightly filled with Eastern travellers, curious to see the wonders of the far-famed Territory. During the prevalence of cholera in the spring of 1855, a large colony of Dunkards emigrated from Indiana, and many died on the way and after reaching Minnesota, before they could provide comfortable shelter. Four of a family, with six children, died at Mr. Barrett's in four days. The funeral, the first public religious service held in town, was at the cabin, and was succeeded by a weekly Sunday school, organized and conducted by Mr. Barrett, and Sunday services by the pastor of the colony and various preachers of any denomination who came around. The first day school met there, also the earliest town meetings, courts, and elections, Mr. Barrett holding several town, county, State, and United States offices. He left his farm to obtain better school and religious privileges, and moved farther west, to Wasioja, in 1866, thence to Minneapolis, where he and his son Frank had previously established the Asbestine Stone Company, for manufacturing artificial stone.

GEORGE MINOTT BARRETT[1963], of Grafton, Vt., was clerk for many years in Grafton for his uncle, Capt. John Barrett, and succeeded to the business, which he conducted for nearly fifty years successfully, and gained the esteem of all that had relations with him. He died in 1883.

GEORGE BARRETT[1718], born in New Ipswich, N. H., was for a time clerk for his cousin, Henry Melville, in Nelson, N. H., where he lived for several years, then returning to New Ipswich, where he for a time kept a store. He afterwards removed to Boston, entering into a copartnership with Silas Bullard (they were agents for the sale of cotton goods which were made at the factories in New Ipswich, Mr. Barrett's father being a large owner in these factories), continuing until the death of Mr. Bullard, in 1835. He resided in Boston seven years after his marriage, then returning to New Ipswich, living at the family mansion until the death of his mother. He succeeded Mr. Ainsworth as cashier of the bank at New Ipswich, and retained that position until illness obliged him to resign. After his election, he removed to the Bank Village, where the bank was then located; it was removed to its present location about the year 1845. Soon after this his brother Charles removed to Boston, and as it was George Barrett's great wish to own Forest Hall, the family homestead in New Ipswich, he purchased it, and lived there the remainder of his life. Although devoted to his business, he found great pleasure in beautifying his fine country home. All kinds of country pursuits gave him keen enjoyment. His business qualifications were very fine, and his honesty and uprightness were such that persons often said of him, " His word is as good as his bond." A man of kindest heart and most generous impulses, and all of the many whom he numbered among his friends entertained for him the highest esteem and regard. One of his marked tastes was his great love of Shakespeare. He read and reread Shakespeare's plays, and could recite whole pages from his works. He died in 1862, after a painful illness of two years, which he bore with great fortitude. His wife still survives him, and lives in the old homestead, Forest Hall. A very pleasing incident in Mr. Barrett's life was his interview with Samuel Appleton, Esq., of Boston. Mr. Appleton's letter, and Mr. Barrett's account of the interview, are as follows : —

BOSTON, May 27, 1850.

GEORGE BARRETT, Esq.

Dear Sir, — I will thank you to call on me, at my house in Boston, as it is convenient for you so to do (it may be, perhaps, for their inter-est), respecting the descendants of my early friend, your grandfather, the late Hon. Charles Barrett. Please write me and say when probably you will call on me. Very respectfully,

Your friend and humble servant,

SAMUEL APPLETON.

" On receipt of the above, I made arrangements and started for Boston. I called on Mr. Appleton, and he said : ' Your grandfather met me in the street, when I was young and very poor, and took a fancy to me (for what reason I do not know, nor can I conceive to this day). He had large quantities of land in Maine, and sent me, with others, to settle the town of Hope. The others were to pay one hundred dollars each, for their farms; mine he gave me, but I did not like it, and returned. He still fancied me, and told me he would put me into trade. He did. He built a store for me, lent me sufficient money, gave me an unlimited letter of credit on Samuel Parkman of Boston, took me with his own family to board, and told me that if I lost the money he was satisfied; if I never paid him for board he was satisfied; that I might pay him part of profits, if I pleased, or not. In fact, left it all to me to do as I pleased. Mr. Barrett was the origin of the wealth of our family, for if it had not been for him, I probably should never have gone to Boston.' He then inquired how many heirs my father's sister, Mrs. Dana, had. I told him five. He knew we had but three. He then said : ' I want to make some small presents on account of my early friend, your grandfather, the Hon. Charles Barrett, and I propose five thousand dollars for yourself, your brother Charles, and Mrs. Hersey.' He handed me a check for that amount on the Columbian Bank, and the following receipt, in his own handwriting, to sign : —

Received of Samuel Appleton, Five Thousand Dollars, which sum is given, as he says, for the kindness and patronage he received from my grandfather, the Hon. Charles Barrett, in early life, when he was young and poor. I promise to pay over to my sister, Mrs. Hersey, one third of it, and to my brother, Charles Barrett, one third. It will stand thus: —

For Mrs. Hersey	$1,666.67
For Charles Barrett	1,666.67
For myself, George Barrett	1,666.66
	$5,000.00

BOSTON, May 29, 1850.

" He also requested me to see Gen. James Dana, my cousin, and tell him to call, and he would receive a check for five thousand dollars."

The following notice appeared in the Boston *Daily Advertiser:* "Samuel Appleton, Esq., has recently bestowed ten thousand dollars upon the descendants of an early friend. It is pleasing to record this act of private munificence, which reflects so much honor upon the heart of the generous donor."

GEORGE MINOTT BARRETT[2152], of Staten Island, N. Y., settled at first in Malden, Mass. He was connected with his brother William's dye-house, and about 1818 visited Staten

Geo. Barrett

George H. Barrett

Island, N. Y., in company with his brother William, Wm. Tileston, and Farnham Hall, for the purpose of selecting a suitable location for erecting a dye-house. They purchased about sixteen acres of land on the north shore of the island, and immediately commenced to erect suitable buildings, organized and commenced work 1819. In 1824, the business having proved successful, was organized into a stock company, under the name of the "New York Dyeing and Printing Establishment," under which name the business is still continued. Mr. Barrett was appointed chief superintendent, and held the position for many years, being a director until his death.

GEORGE HUBBELL BARRETT[2937] of Oakland, Cal. He left his home at the age of fifteen; attended school at Kingsville Academy one year; he taught school during two winters, and was a part of the time a clerk in a store in Springfield, Pa., until he was eighteen years of age; he then moved to Wisconsin, from thence to California, and there engaged in farming. In the time of the War of the Rebellion he was orderly sergeant of cavalry in the Home Guards, the State having armed ten thousand men for home safety, in the absence of the regulars. He moved, in 1875, from San Pueblo to Oakland.

HUMPHREY BARRETT[788] was born at the Barrett homestead in Bolton. He was for many years successful at the watch-making trade. He moved to Lancaster, where he was the postmaster for more than thirty years, and at the same time continuing in the watch-making trade. In 1884 he went to Eustis, Fla., and died there the following year.

HUMPHREY BARRETT[553] owned and lived upon the farm where his ancestor, Humphrey Barrett, settled in 1640. A farmer, managing his farm with prudence and economy, making the returns profitable. He was assessor of taxes 1783, town treasurer 1792–93. He died in 1827, without issue, willing nearly all of his property to his nephew, Albert B. Heywood.

HENRY BARRETT[2382] of Malden, Mass., after the death of his father in 1834, formed a company with his brothers William and Simon H., and Henry Jaques, to continue the dyeing business at Malden. Upon the death of William, about four years later, the company was reorganized, with Mr. Barrett and his brothers Simon H., Augustus, and Aaron as members. About 1844, Simon H. and Augustus relinquished their interests, after which time Mr. Barrett and his brother Aaron carried on the business until the death of Aaron, 1878; Mr. Barrett continuing it alone till the present time, his son, Richard S., now having the principal management of the business. The works were removed in 1882 to Somerville, Mass. Mr. Barrett was for several years president of the Middlesex Savings Bank, and has been personally interested in the welfare of his native town.

HON. JOSEPH BARRETT[1911] of Concord, Mass., a grandson of Col. James Barrett, of Revolutionary fame; his mother was Miliscent Estabrook, granddaughter of Rev. Joseph Estabrook, who was for years a minister of the town, and whose ancestry traces back to the Rev. Peter Bulkeley, the first minister in Concord. He received such educational advantages only as were afforded by the common schools, with the addition of a few months spent at the Westford Academy. While yet a boy he gave promising indications of the physical powers that he was to be so noted for in after years. When about fifteen years of age, with his father upon his back, a man who weighed two hundred and sixty pounds, he forded the Assabet River. He learned the trade of leather dresser in New Haven, Conn., of his brother-in-law, and carried on that kind of business in Concord before his majority. Appointed deputy sheriff of the county and keeper of the jail at the age of twenty-five. In this capacity he became familiarly known, it falling generally to his lot to arrest the desperate characters. Many stories are told of his fearless courage and feats of strength required in executing the duties of this office. He was also, about this time, elected captain of the military company known vulgarly as the "Old Shad," then in a state bordering on insubordination, and under his discipline reduced to perfect subjection. In 1822 he became the owner of the famous "Lee Farm," of four hundred acres; added to this was one hundred acres of outlying land; this, with his large sheep farm in New Hampshire, made him one of the most extensive farmers of the State, keeping hundreds of sheep and cattle; scores of horses and oxen grazed upon his hills or labored in tilling his lands. He excelled in his various undertakings; his product of wool was of the finest, winning the first prizes at the fairs; and in the great ploughing matches with the farmers, "Squire Joe," as he was familiarly called, was sure to come out ahead. He made large quantities of cider each season, often five hundred barrels or more. As instances of his strength, it is told that he could lift, unaided, a barrel of cider over the wheels and into his wagon. He one time shouldered and carried up two flights of stairs a bag containing over eight bushels of shelled corn. Though upwards of six feet in height and weighing about two hundred and fifty pounds, he handled pitchforks, hoes, and other small tools about his farm with great strength, but with ease and natural facility; could dance as lightly upon the floor as those of slighter build; and it was his wont to enter church during prayer-time without disturbing the worship. He was always very active in the town offices; was chairman of the board of assessors, chairman of the board of selectmen, president of the fire association, and fire-warden, president of the Middlesex Agricultural Society, and held other minor offices. In 1831 he was elected to the State Legislature, and again, frequently, in subsequent years. In 1845 elected Treasurer and Receiver-General of the State, and was re-elected four times, being in the office at the time of his death. Joseph Barrett was a Concord product, purely; all his ancestry in this country were of Concord origin, or settlers of the town.

A man of temperate habits, warm-hearted, generous, and possessing those traits of character which endeared him alike to both family and friends. He died suddenly, of heart disease, in his seventy-first year, in 1849.

HON. JONATHAN FAY BARRETT[2124], of Concord, in his youth attended Mrs. Bliss' private school in Concord. While in attendance there he was the playmate and class-mate of Judge Hoar; the friendship then formed was firmly cemented in the intercourse of riper years. At a public meeting, held in the Concord Town Hall during the congressional contest between Judge Hoar and Gen. Butler, Mr. Barrett's love and esteem for his old schoolmate manifested itself in an eloquent and fiery attack upon the Judge's maligners, which few who heard will ever forget. He was one of the famous class of Harvard College, 1837. In 1855, Mr. Barrett, with Thomas W. Pierce, and other Boston capitalists, became interested in railroad enterprises, and went to Galveston, Texas, where he originated and afterwards became the president of the Buffalo Bayou, Brazos and Colorado Railroad, running between Galveston and Harrisburgh, and now a part of the great Texas Central Railway system. In religious matters he was somewhat of a free-thinker, but friendly to the church and its people, and an attendant at the Unitarian church in his native town for several years.

ISRAEL BARRETT[2645], of Oneida County, N. Y., served in the operations against Nova Scotia in Capt. Ward's company, and was taken prisoner September, 1775; he also served in the War of the Revolution.

JAMES BARRETT[1839], the eldest son of Col. James Barrett, was born in Concord, in the old block-house now known as the Prescott Barrett Homestead, and made famous as the hiding-place for military stores on the 19th of April, 1775. He certainly began life in an exceedingly small way, for it is related that at the time of his birth he was placed, without squeezing, into a quart tankard; but, like the oak, he was not daunted by so small a beginning, for on arriving at manhood he measured fully six feet, being broad-shouldered and strong. While a young man he worked on his father's farm, getting his education from the schools of the town. July 4, 1758, being then twenty-five years of age, he married Miliscent Estabrook, granddaughter of the Rev. Joseph Estabrook. He settled on the farm now known as the Geo. M. Barrett Homestead, the house he built, where he ever afterward lived. He assisted his father in the preparations to resist the British in 1775, and was a participant in the "Concord fight." Hearing that a company of the invaders were on their way to search his house and that of his father, and realizing that his wife and seven little children were left unprotected, he mounted his horse and rode with all speed to their assistance. On reaching home, he found his house locked and its occupants gone. It seems his wife, hearing that the enemy were coming, had gathered her husband's papers,

and their little stock of silver, placing them in a bushel basket, then depositing the baby on top she started with her burden for the woods, followed by the rest of the children, where her husband found her. A kind and indulgent father, his children were brought up in the strictest manner. A religious man, he believed and insisted that no work should be done, other than was necessary, after sundown on a Saturday, but that the evening before the Sabbath should be spent in prayer and meditation. He required all his household to attend church, and his daughters were never allowed to receive callers on Sunday. He was an extensive farmer, and one of the leading men of the town; he transacted a good deal of legal business for his neighbors, as lawyers were then a rarity; he was noted for his business ability and strict integrity. He was a justice of the peace, and a member of the first, last, and most of the intermediate Revolutionary committees of correspondence. He represented his town several times in the General Court. He died in his sixty-fourth year, and was buried in the Hill burying-ground.

MAJOR JAMES ATWATER BARRETT[2118] served throughout the Rebellion, having enlisted in July, 1861, as first sergeant in Company H, Forty-eighth Regiment, New York Volunteer Infantry, and was mustered out Sept. 1, 1865. Sergeant Barrett was promoted to second lieutenant Dec. 29, 1862, and to first lieutenant July 23, 1863; receiving then a furlough of two months, he visited his home in Concord, Mass., returning to his regiment in September. He was wounded in battle June 2, 1864, at Cold Harbor; then, after a furlough of three months spent at the North, he rejoined his regiment at Petersburg, Va. Captain Barrett married Jane Farmer[4262]. He died at his home in Brooklyn, N. Y., Dec. 14, 1885.

CAPT. JOHN BARRETT[1025]. Born in Mason, N. H., he lived during his minority upon his father's farm, removing to Grafton, Vt., about 1805, then engaging in mercantile business with Nathan Wheeler. He at once took an active part in the affairs of the town; he was chosen a selectman in 1807, and for several years succeeding; chosen a representative to the General Assembly in 1811, and re-elected five terms. The business copartnership of Wheeler & Barrett continued about ten years, after which Mr. Wheeler remained at the old stand, and Mr. Barrett built the brick building (now the town house), which he occupied as a store until 1828, when he retired from business, having accumulated a handsome property, and gained a thorough and honest business reputation. Always an active member of the Congregational society, he became a member of the church in 1833. When that society was divided, he was prominent as a member of the South Congregational Society, contributing a large share of the funds required in building the church. He was State senator, 1841 and 1842. He died in 1856.

Jos. Barrett
Concord

Rev. John Barrett[1116], familiarly known in life as Father Barrett, a faithful minister of the Gospel, graduated at Williams College, 1810. He was employed for a time by the Evangelical Society, and was ordained at Mesopotamia, Ohio, 1827. He died without issue, in 1849.

John Lyman Barrett[1134] of Greeley, Col., a graduate of Burr Seminary, Manchester, Vt., 1847. He taught school several years in Georgia and Louisiana; was admitted to the bar, 1855, beginning law practice at Farmersville Union Parish, La. He was a member of the Constitutional Convention of Louisiana, 1868, and removed to Greeley, 1874.

Rev. John P. Barrett[2520], of Farmington, Ill., fitted for college at Watertown High School, graduating from Havard College, 1864; spent one year at Andover Theological Seminary, when ill health compelled him to abandon study. From 1865 to 1876 he entered into business connections at Boston, St. Louis, and Chicago. In 1877 he graduated from the Chicago Theological Seminary, and was ordained and settled as pastor of the Congregational church at Manchester, Iowa, 1877; at Hennepin, Ill., 1881; thence to Farmington, Ill., where he is now preaching. He also served for a short time with the Christian Commission.

Capt. John Miller Barrett[1575] of Baltimore, Md., a captain of militia, and took a prominent part in the defence of Baltimore in the War of 1812, raising a company of his own, which did valuable service, in recognition of which Congress gave him a commission in the Regular Army as lieutenant, Fourth Regiment. He was stricken with yellow fever, and died, leaving an enviable reputation as a soldier. His monument at Baltimore bears the following inscription: "John M. Barrett, Lieut. 5th Reg. U. S. Infantry and Commissary U. S. A., died in passage from New Orleans to Mobile, Oct. 16, 1819. A defender of Fort McHenry and Lieut. of the 38th U. S. Infantry of the line during the War of 1812."

John Leahy Barrett[1578], of Baltimore, Md., resided in New York City from 1844 to 1869, when he returned to Baltimore and engaged with his brother Minott in the gilding trade. He is now retired from business.

Lieut. Jonas Barrett[1162], born in Concord, settled in Ashby (then Townsend) in 1760, when the town was a wilderness; built a log-hut and began clearing his farm; in 1764–5 he built his dwelling-house, which is still standing. Lieut. Barrett was one of the leading men of the town; he was a selectman of Townsend, 1767, and in May, 1768, was elected selectman of the new town, Ashby, and re-elected 1773 and 1774; assessor, 1769; treasurer, 1771 to 1774; town clerk, 1772–74; constable, 1775. He died in Ashby, 1803.

Jonas Stone Barrett[1621] is mentioned in the "History of Belfast, Me.," as having a peculiar religious belief, which he set forth in a pamphlet entitled "New Views of the Bible, and its Abuses by the Priests," which was published in 1842. He removed to California, and died there in 1864.

Capt. Joseph Barrett[1012] removed from Concord to Mason, N. H., before that town was incorporated, and settled upon the farm which is still owned by his descendants. He was an industrious farmer, and had the esteem of his fellow-citizens. He was town clerk fourteen years, first selectman fourteen years, town treasurer twelve years, and representative four years. He died in 1831.

Rev. Joshua Barrett[1117], a graduate from Dartmouth College, 1810. He studied theology and engaged in preaching and as a missionary, and was ordained over the Second Church at Plymouth, Mass., Jan. 11, 1826. He died 1868.

Rev. Luther G. Barrett[2518] at the age of ten went to reside with a relative in Sturbridge, Mass. Here, at the age of twelve, he was converted and baptized into fellowship with the Baptist Church. At sixteen he entered the High School in Watertown, his native place, thence to Harvard College, graduating in 1862; also graduated from the Newton Theological Seminary, class of 1865. While a student at the seminary, he spent most of the winters 1864 and 1865 in the service of the Christian Commission, in the army before Richmond; was ordained to the ministry at Watertown, Sept. 7, 1865. Ill health now compelled a rest, during which he made the tour of Europe. In September, 1867, he accepted the pastorate of the Baptist church in Weston, Mass.; called to Winchester, Mass., 1870; in 1875 to a Baptist church in New York City; in July, 1878, to the church in South Abington, Mass; in July, 1880, of the Pleasant Street Baptist Church, Concord, Mass.

Myron Erastus Barrett[2950] of Niles, Mich. He was a teacher of writing in Cochrane Commercial College, in Detroit, Mich., in 1856, and afterwards established a college at Kingsville, Ohio, conducting it successfully until it was destroyed by fire. He then moved to Niles, Mich., and is principal and proprietor of Barrett's Commercial College, St. Joseph's, Mich.

Col. Nathan Barrett[1894] was the second son of Col. James Barrett, born in Concord, and was the first of the name on Ponkatasset Hill, or Barrett's Hill, as sometimes called, he having come into possession of this estate in 1761. He married Meriam, a daughter of Dr. Simon Hunt, and raised a family of fifteen children, all of whom grew to manhood and womanhood. He was a man of high character, prominent in public affairs, public-spirited, energetic, and charitable. At "Concord fight" he was captain of the third militia company, and while in pursuit of the Britsh was wounded in the arm. His great-grandson, Edwin S. Barrett, of Battle Lawn, Concord, has in his possession five commissions given to this ancestor, viz.: ensign's commission, dated March 26, 1776, from George III., by Gov. Francis Bernard; captain's commission, July 10, 1773, also from George III., by Gov. Thomas Hutchinson; major's commission, Feb. 14, 1776, signed by the Council of Massachusetts Bay; lieutenant-colonel's commission, May 3, 1779, also signed by the Council; and a further lieutenant-colonel's commission, July 1, 1781, given by John Hancock, the first governor. "On the retreat from Concord of the British, April 19, 1775, Major Pitcairn was wounded, and fell from his horse. The animal was captured by the Americans, and subsequently sold at Concord. On the back of his horse was Major Pitcairn's holster, containing his pistols. Capt. Barrett bought them, and offered them to Gen. Washington, then in command of the Provincial army around Boston. Gen. Washington declining to accept them, Capt. Barrett then presented them to Gen. Israel Putnam, who used them until the close of the war, when they came into the possession of the general's son, and were by him willed to a grandson of the general, John P. Putnam. These were exhibited at the Centennial. They are about one foot in length, made of steel, with flint-lock attachments of the Revolutionary period."

NATHAN BARRETT[2140], known as the second Nathan Barrett, was born on Ponkatasset Hill, in Concord. He was not, like his immediate ancestors, active in the military calling, being affected with a slight lameness. As an energetic business man he had few superiors; with a strong mental grasp, he was equal to all emergencies of life; his counsel and advice were always in demand. Benevolent in disposition, ever ready to aid the needy, he died greatly lamented. His wife was Mary Jones[4291].

CAPT. NATHAN BARRETT[2155], the third Nathan, and the last of his race on Ponkatasset Hill. Capt. Barrett carried on during his life the large farm left to him from his ancestors, and the title of "Honest Nathan" was given to him by his neighbors and friends. Being kind-hearted, charitable, and a thorough Christian gentleman, he earned the high esteem of his townsmen. He was twice married; first to Mary S. Fuller, and a second time to his cousin, Lucy A. Barrett[2514].

COL. NATHAN BARRETT[2215], of Staten Island, N. Y., was colonel of New York militia about 1830. He was a Christian and a philanthropist, highly esteemed and beloved. It was due to his exertions that the county house of his county was greatly improved.

NATHAN M. BARRETT[2283] was a soldier in the War of the Rebellion; enlisted in Company I, One Hundred Fifty-sixth Regiment New York Volunteers, serving three years and four months. He was at the battles of Winchester, Fisher

Hill, and Cedar Creek. At Augusta, Ga., he received, with several others, a commission as first lieutenant from Gov. Seymour of New York, as a complimentary testimonial. He was discharged Nov. 15, 1865. In 1866 he crossed the plains, and for two years thereafter was engaged in gold mining.

NATHAN F. BARRETT[2326], of New York, enlisted in the One Hundred and Fifty-sixth Regiment, Company I, New York State Volunteers, Sept. 19, 1862; served in the Nineteenth Army Corps in Louisiana under Banks through the Port Hudson and Red River campaigns. He joined Sheridan's army at Washington, about August, 1864, and was in the Shenandoah campaign throughout. He was wounded at Cedar Creek in the left arm; joined Sherman's army at Savannah, and was in a division of Nineteenth Army Corps which relieved Gen. Geary at Savannah; was again in Sherman's army at Goldsboro, N. C., and was there at Johnston's surrender. Mustered out of service at Hart's Island, New York, Nov. 9, 1865, holding commissions of second and first lieutenants and sergeant-major. He is now a professor of landscape engineering. He designed the well-known town of Pullman, Ill.

MAJOR OLIVER BARRETT[744], of Bolton, lived in the old Barrett homestead; held a major's commission in the militia of Massachusetts, and filled various offices of trust in the town and parish.

DR. PERRY GORDON BARRETT[2951] graduated an M. D. at the Buffalo, N. Y., Medical College, then settled at Walnut Creek, Kan., remaining there until after the death of his first wife. He entered the United States Army in 1862, at Corinth, Miss., under contract until a vacancy for surgeon should occur. His first commission was assistant surgeon of the Seventh Ohio Volunteer Corps. He was taken a prisoner at Rogersville, Tenn., and incarcerated in Libby Prison, at Richmond, Nov. 10, 1863. His treatment while a prisoner was such as characterized that infamous prison. Gen. Neal Dow and Col. Streight were prisoners on the same floor at the time, in other departments. He remained for three weeks in Libby Prison, until his exchange. After a furlough of two weeks, he was ordered to join the command, near Knoxville, Tenn. He attempted to do so; the deprivations and cruelties of his prison life had so affected his health that he was obliged to go into the hospital at Camp Nelson, near Lexington, Ky., and did not recover till the following spring, joining the command at the time of the exciting chase after Morgan and his command, June 13, 1864. At the time of his promotion to the position of surgeon of the Thirty-first United States Colored Troops he was ordered to join the forces then commanded by Gen. Grant, before Richmond and Petersburg, Va., where he remained in service until after the surrender of Lee. After this, his regiment was ordered to Texas, remaining during

Richd Bauitt

Sam.ˡ Barrett

the summer on the east bank of the Rio Grande, at various points for a distance of two hundred miles; returning with his regiment to Hartford, Conn., Dec. 1, 1865, where he was mustered out of service. He resumed the practice of medicine at Erie, Pa., 1867, thence removed to Hood River, Oregon, in 1871.

CAPT. RICHARD BARRETT[2125], of Concord, Mass., derived his education from the public schools of the town, spending his spare time upon his father's large farm, taking a great interest in its affairs. He joined the Concord Artillery in 1837, thus following in the footsteps of his forefathers; elected captain at the age of twenty-two, and holding that position nearly all the time until 1871. At the time of election to the captaincy of the Artillery, there was great rivalry existing between it and the Infantry, both famous organizations, thus necessitating incessant labor and energy in each of the captains of these organizations to endeavor to bring his company to the head. At the time of his father's death, in 1849, he became the owner of the "Lee Farm," which he sold some years later. He was in the grain business in Boston, and subsequently in the lumber business at Manchester, Vt., returning to Concord in 1855. In the War of the Rebellion he was captain of the Concord Artillery, Company G, Forty-seventh Regiment Massachusetts Volunteers, in the Department of the Gulf, under Gen. Banks. Returning in 1863, he occupied a position in the United States marshal's office in Boston. In 1864 he became secretary and treasurer of the Middlesex Mutual Fire Insurance Company, still occupying the position; twice elected to the Legislature, in 1859 and 1879; always a Republican, and a loyal supporter of his party. In early life, he was one of the selectmen, and for many years chairman of the board of assessors. He was greatly interested in the Middlesex Agricultural Society, and for some years its treasurer. Capt. Barrett resides on a fine farm, situated at the foot of Ponkatasset Hill, about one mile from the centre of the town.

CAPT. RICHARD FAY BARRETT[2130], of Concord, Mass., spent a few of his early years with his uncle in Providence, going from thence to New York City, where he remained several years, then returning to Concord to take a position in the Middlesex Mutual Fire Insurance Company's office, and is now the assistant secretary of that company. Capt. Barrett was for several years captain of the Concord Artillery and Infantry Company attached to the Fifth Regiment Massachusetts Volunteer Militia. He has held the office of selectman and other town offices.

ROSWELL BARRETT[793] of Bolton, Mass., a farmer, land surveyor, and justice of the peace, residing upon the Barrett homestead in Bolton. Mr. Barrett taught school for twenty-five years, and for more than forty years has been a member of the school committee, and has also held nearly every office

within the gift of the town and parish. He married his cousin, Sarah Josephine Barrett[841].

DEA. SAMUEL BARRETT[1562] of Concord, Mass. The following is from the *New England Chronicle*, Dec. 14, 1775: "We hear from Concord, that a fine laboratory for gun making is set up there, by Dea. Barrett, where every branch of that business is carried on; as the laboratory has the advantage of a water power, the boring, grinding, and polishing are done by that means."

MAJOR SAMUEL BARRETT[2717] of Jamestown, N. Y. During his minority he resided with his sister in Newfane, Vt., who had married Eli Crosby, Esq. He settled in Jamestown in 1816; after his marriage he was for a time landlord of the Cass House, a hotel then standing where now is the Jamestown House. Major Barrett soon became a leading citizen, and was a prominent man in all business matters pertaining to the town during his long life. When a young man he was a candidate, in opposition to the late Gen. Risley, for the office of sheriff, on the Clintonian ticket. He was at times member of various mercantile copartnerships, one of the directors of the Chautauqua County Bank at the time of its organization. In 1835 he was elected president of the bank, to succeed Hon. E. T. Foot, its first president, who then resigned; this position he retained to the time of his death. For several years supervisor of Jamestown, and one year member of the State Assembly; filling all of these various positions creditably. A man of useful common-sense and sound judgment, of unquestioned integrity in public life, commanding also the confidence and respect of his associates in all the relations of life. He celebrated his golden wedding in 1868.

STEPHEN BARRETT[1899], of Concord, Mass., was a farmer and kept a tannery. He was a selectman, 1802 to 1807, and deputy representative, 1811.

STEPHEN BARRETT[2535], of Shirley, Mass., learned the trade of tanning with his father. He bought a tannery in Shirley in 1801, removed there and continued in the business until his death.

STEPHEN BARRETT[2643] of Sangersfield, N. Y. He was one of the original settlers in Paris, N. Y., being the third person to locate there in 1789. He remained in Paris six years, and then moved to Sangersfield, N. Y. He was a selectman in Paris, also justice in the town of Mohawk. He was a soldier in the War of the Revolution for three years.

STEPHEN BARRETT[2803] moved with his parents in 1804 to Chautauqua County, N. Y. He was a soldier in the War of 1812, in Capt. Martin B. Tuft's company, of New York State Militia. He moved with his family to Kingsville, Ohio, in 1821. In 1838 he moved, with a wife and nine daughters, to Beloit, Wis., near which place he had taken up a claim of land the previous year. One of his first efforts, after settling in his new home, was to aid in the organization of a Baptist church, his family making more than one half of the original membership. He and his wife continued to be members of this church until their death. In 1861, having been prosperous in their undertakings, they gave up housekeeping and lived until their deaths with their children. They were buried in Silver Lake Cemetery, Portage, Wis. Mr. Barrett was familiarly known as Dea. Barrett. Having a very large number of friends and acquaintance, his aid and counsel were sought by those in need, and none ever left him, on such occasions, regretfully. He lived a truly religious life.

PROF. STEPHEN P. BARRETT[2953], of Lincoln, Neb., received his early education at the Kingsville Academy, beginning teaching in 1851, and taught in their order at the following places : Plymouth, Ohio, Raysville and Waterbury, Pa., Geneva and Harpersfield, Ohio, and in 1855 in Nunda, N. Y., Literary Institution ; following this he entered the University of Rochester, graduating in the classical course July, 1859, degree of A. B., subsequently, in 1864, the degree of A. M. He was principal of boys' school, Chattanooga, Tenn., two years ; public schools, Buchanan, Mich., seven years ; schools of the "Dalles," Oregon, four years ; Baker City Academy, Oregon, three years ; and now principal of High School, Lincoln, Neb.

CAPT. THEODORE A. BARRETT[2452] of Brooklyn, N. Y. Mr. Barrett, when a boy, worked upon his step-father's farm and in the office of the *Yeoman Gazette* until about 1834 (his father was at one time editor of the *Yeoman Gazette* and Concord *Freeman*, published at Concord, Mass.), when he ran away from home and shipped in the United States Navy at Charlestown, and was drafted to the frigate "Potomac," for the Mediterranean station ; arriving at that station, he was promoted to ship-yeoman. He followed the sea, being promoted in the various grades and given the command of a ship in 1844. In 1861 he took the command of a steamer to be fitted out to capture blockade runners. Before the day he was to report for duty, he was attacked by inflammatory rheumatism, and compelled to resign the command.

WILLIAM BARRETT[2148], of Malden, Mass., served an apprenticeship at the clothing trade with a Mr. Minott of Billerica, where he learned something of the trade of dyeing. After finishing his trade he went to Charlestown, Mass. ; here he made the acquaintance of a Mr. Thompson, an Englishman, who was in the dyeing business in a small way. Mr. Barrett engaged with him and gained a thorough knowledge of the business, and afterwards came to have an interest in the business. Mr. Thompson neglected the work, being a man of unsteady habits. Mr. Barrett then determined to start for himself alone, and looking for a suitable location for

the growing business, he removed to Malden in 1804, and established his dye-works in that place. About 1808 he engaged in copartnership with Meshack Shattuck, as Barrett & Shattuck. This firm was dissolved at the death of Mr. Shattuck (by suicide), Dec. 11, 1811, Mr. Barrett continuing alone until his death. In 1816 all of his buildings were burned, they being of wood ; he immediately rebuilt of brick, and of considerably enlarged capacity. His profitable business he left to his sons. Mr. Barrett was a public-spirited man, and took a forward part in any enterprise for the benefit of his town.

BROWN.

REV. ADISON BROWN[3402] graduated at Cambridge, 1826. He studied for the ministry at the Cambridge Theological School, and was settled over the Unitarian church and society of Brattleboro, Vt., 1832. He was a faithful pastor and well-beloved minister of the church for many years ; his health failing, he was obliged to relinquish preaching for a while. Recovering his health partially, he established a school in Brattleboro, which he carried on for some years. He then became editor of the *Vermont Phœnix*, and was connected with that paper till nearly the close of his life. He never relinquished the ministry ; he loved his profession and continued to preach, as opportunity offered and health permitted, up to within a year or two of his death, which occurred in 1872. He was an upright man, respected and loved by all who knew him.

AMOS BROWN[3327], of New Ipswich, N. H., was a farmer, and for a few years after his marriage he kept a store on the turnpike near his residence. In religious belief he was a Baptist, and for many years was a deacon of the Baptist church, thus following in the footsteps of his father. He was always particular to have daily family worship. He married his cousin, Hannah Brown[3032], who was always a faithful sympathizer with her husband in his religious opinions. Both were constant in attending church. Amos Brown did much toward the support of the church. He built a Baptist church mostly at his own expense, and paid largely toward the support of the minister. He was for some time a selectman of his town.

LIEUT. CYRUS BROWN[3123] was a civil engineer. He entered the Union Army soon after the breaking out of the Rebellion, and was promoted to the office of lieutenant in the One Hundredth New York Volunteers. He was wounded at the storming of Fort Wagner, near Charleston, S. C., July 18, 1863 ; he remained on the battle-field all night, protecting himself by burrowing in the sand ; was captured by the Confederates in the morning and taken five miles to Charleston, where his shattered leg was amputated. In five days he was exchanged and taken to a hospital near New York, where he died Aug. 13, 1863.

LIEUT. CYRUS W. BROWN[3094], of Joliet, Ill., entered the Union Army in 1862. In 1863 he received his lieutenant's commission in the Third Pennsylvania Colored Regiment. He served in the approaches that compelled the evacuation of Fort Wayne, Morris Island, in 1864 ; also was with Gen. Seymour's expedition into Florida ; he served as an adjutant in the regiment. He has been four years State's attorney for Mill County, Ill.

CAPT. GUY A. BROWN[3081], of Lincoln, Neb., is reporter for the Superior Court of Nebraska and State librarian. He enlisted in the Union Army, 1862, and served therein till the close of the war. He was a captain in the Ninth New York Artillery.

HERMAN BROWN[3403] was for many years deacon in the Baptist church, following thus in the footsteps of his father and grandfather. His high religious and moral character was made known by his life and works.

REV. JOHN BROWN[3025] received a good education in the grammar schools of Concord. He was a Baptist, and frequently in his early life preached in various places, whenever he received a call to do so. He removed, in 1817, from his farm in Sharon, N. H., with his family to Alexander, N. Y.

JOHN W. BROWN[3070], of Batavia, N. Y., is a farmer. Has been elected several times to minor offices in his town, and five times to the office of supervisor ; and has for two terms represented the county in the State Legislature.

JOHN J. BROWN, M. D.[3116], of Sheboygan, Wis. Educated himself for a physician, and practised medicine for several years. He has made several trips to tropical climes to gather specimens of conchology and botany ; has devoted part of his time to teaching ; has taken an active part in public questions and occupied places of public trust.

REV. JOHN S. BROWN[3405] of Lawrence, Kan. A graduate of Phillips Academy, Exeter, N. H., and Union College, 1834. He taught school until he was settled as minister over the First Congregational Society and Church at Fitzwilliam, N. H., in 1844 ; removing from thence to Ashby, Mass., and with his family, to Lawrence, Kan., in 1857.

REV. JOSEPH BROWN[3030] was educated for the ministry, and settled first in 1795 in Shapleigh, Me., over the Congregational church. He removed to Alfred, Me., in 1805 ; to Cavendish, Vt., about 1812, continuing in the ministry until his death.

JOSHUA L. BROWN[3067] was at first a farmer, afterwards studied law, and held successively the office of deputy county clerk, county treasurer, county judge and surrogate.

CAPT. JOSIAH BROWN[3023] was a man of marked ability and influence, a true patriot and devoted Christian. He was at the battle of Bunker Hill, and his company was the last to retreat before the British regulars. He often related the following incident. He said : "After we had orders to retreat, a brave youth of seventeen, who had fought by my side all day, had just loaded his gun and returned the ramrod to its place, when a British officer rode up flourishing his sword, and exclaimed, ' My boy, lay down your arms ; we 've won the day !' The young brave, nothing terrified, drew up his gun and shot the officer down, and retorted, 'Then G—— d—— you, you 've lost it!' and fled amidst a storm of bullets fired at him, escaping without harm." Five of his children settled in Whitingham, Vt., viz., Josiah, Joseph, Jonas, Amos, Nathan, and Sarah, who had married her cousin, Reuben Brown. These families were all farmers, men of note and influence at that age, taking an active interest in the current events of the time, and did much towards supporting institutions the best calculated to promote permanent good to the people.

REUBEN BROWN[3033] moved with his family from New Ipswich, N. H., to Whitingham, Vt., about the year 1800. He lived in Whitingham till somewhere near 1811, then removed to Canada, and lived in Brownsville, a town named after Reuben Brown, that part of the country being newly settled ; he bought four hundred acres of good land, became prosperous and raised a large family. He married his cousin, Sarah Brown[3326].

REV. NATHAN BROWN, D D.[3514], was born at New Ipswich, N. H., June 22, 1807, and died in Yokohama, Japan, Jan. 1, 1886. His boyhood was passed in Whitingham, Vt., whither his parents removed the year after his birth. Here his scholarly instincts began to develop in childhood, accompanied by an unusual concentration of character. A strict conscientiousness showed itself as a marked trait almost from infancy. His relations to the unseen Father and the realities of the spiritual life were early revealed to him, and at the age of nine he was baptized on profession of his faith by Rev. Jonathan Wilson. To these gifts were added a powerful physical constitution, strengthened by the out-door labors of a farmer's son. When sixteen years of age he entered Williams College, and graduated at twenty, in September, 1827, the valedictorian of a class of thirty members. The three following years were mainly occupied in teaching. From 1829 to 1831 he was associated in the Bennington Seminary with his college friend and classmate, Rev. James Ballard, whose sister Eliza, daughter of Capt. William Ballard of East Claremont, Mass., he married May 6, 1830.

During the year 1831, Mr. Brown was editor of the *Vermont Telegraph*, a religious journal published at Brandon. While there the way was opened for his entrance upon the foreign-missionary work, and the following winter was spent in preparatory study at Newton, Mass. He was ordained at Rutland, Vt., Aug. 15, 1832, and sailed for Burmah on Dec. 22 of that year, reaching Calcutta in May, and Maulmain in June, 1833. The next year he made a missionary tour up the Irrawaddy as far as Ava, distributing Christian books and tracts, and found the people generally ready to receive them, though in some cases the heathen rulers manifested hostility. Being appointed to establish a new mission in Assam, Mr. Brown left Burmah in August, 1835, and travelled inland up the Brahmaputra River seven hundred miles from Calcutta to Sudiya, a post near the northeastern frontier of the province, which it was hoped would prove a stepping-stone to China, whose seaports were then closed against foreigners. He labored in Assam for twenty years, mastering the language without dictionary or grammar, and enduring, with his heroic wife, the perils and hardships of pioneer missionary life, in a region then beyond the safeguards of civilization. Among their experiences in India were a night attack and massacre at Sudiya, by the Khamtis, in January, 1839; the sickness and death of their three eldest children (one of whom they buried at Maulmain on the day of their departure); the desecrated grave of their first-born thrice opened by robbers for treasure, and left to wild beasts; repeated personal illness from fevers of the country and cholera; until at last, with health broken down, Dr. and Mrs. Brown returned to America in 1855, leaving behind them many weeping converts as the fruit of their sufferings and labors, and those of their associates. In addition to his other manifold missionary labors, Dr. Brown had translated the New Testament into Assamese. As a translator, he worked from the originals, with conscientious fidelity as to both text and translation, and his versions of the New Testament, both in Assamese and Japanese, while based on the requirements of the best modern scholarship, have already passed the tests of time and service. As an Oriental linguist, his characteristic was a comprehensive grasp of varied languages in their relationships to each other, resulting from patient research and an intuitive apprehension of lingual affinities. Among the languages to which he had given special study during this period of his life were the Burmese, the Shan and its cognates, and the Sanscrit, with several of its living dialects, including, of course, the Assamese. As a missionary, his scheme of work was thorough and far-reaching, taking into account the intellectual, social, industrial, and moral elevation of the races for whom he labored. Discovering the foundations of the heathen religions to be based on a corrupted fabulous literature, he early apprehended the importance of undermining those foundations by planting the seeds of scientific, historic, and religious truth; and relied on the press and schools as next in importance to the living preacher. With this view, he established *The Orunodoi* (Dawn of Day), an attractive monthly illustrated magazine, in the Assamese language. While broad in aim, he was remarkably practical and thorough in details. In Burmah and Assam he travelled from village to village, distributing tracts, becoming acquainted with the natives, and preaching;

winning the affection even of fierce savages of the hills by his gentle, unostentatious friendliness. His return to America, which seemed the overthrow of the hopes of a lifetime, proved ultimately to be the introduction to a second and not less important mission, in behalf of the enslaved blacks of his own land. In 1856, Dr. Brown was called to the editorship of *The American Baptist*, an anti-slavery journal in New York City; which post he held for fifteen years, during the stormiest period of the nation's history. His instincts and convictions had always been on the side of freedom; from early manhood he was an abolitionist; and he took up this new duty with all the zeal and religious enthusiasm which characterized his missionary work in foreign lands. His editorials, before and during the war, attracted attention by their vigor and clearness. Recognized as one of the leading spirits in the anti-slavery movement, he was appointed in 1862, with Cheever and Goodell, to wait upon President Lincoln and urge upon him the emancipation of the slaves. During this period of his life, after the assassination of President Lincoln, he wrote an allegorical history of the Civil War, entitled "Magnus Maharba." Meanwhile his interest in philological studies continued unabated, and he organized an association called "The American Philological Society," one object of which was to promote a system of scientific phonetics adapted to all languages. In this phonetic form, as well as in the ordinary spelling, "Magnus Maharba" was published.

In May, 1871, Dr. Brown lost the devoted companion of his toils, whose health had not, like his, recovered from the effect of the sufferings she had undergone. The awakening of Japan and calls for missionaries to that country soon led the veteran to resume his life-work as a foreign missionary; and in 1872 he was designated by the Baptist Missionary Union to Japan, for which field he set sail from San Francisco, in January, 1873. He had married, in July, 1873, Charlotte Amelia Worth, widow of William Marlitt, Esq. She, with her two little daughters, accompanied him to Japan. Although now sixty-five years of age, he entered upon and completed this third great work of his life with unabated energy; and in August, 1879, his translation of the New Testament, from Greek into vernacular Japanese, was in print. This he afterwards revised and published, both in the vernacular and scholars' editions, and issued other Scriptures and tracts, being assisted for a time in the work of publication and distribution by his son, William Pearce Brown. He believed the Kana, or vernacular, to be the chief reliance of the missionary press, in reaching the great mass of the people; and his publications, in this character, as well as in Romanized Japanese, have had a large circulation.

At the close of the year 1885, his Japanese Hymn Book was completed, forming an appropriate period at once to his missionary, linguistic, and literary labors. The poetic "gift and faculty divine" was his, and in the intervals of his multiplied duties, bursts of sacred song welled up from his lov-

Nathan Brown

ing and enthusiastic spirit in the Eastern tongues, which had become to him like his own; and they are sung, to-day, by converts from heathenism, in Assam, Burmah, and Japan. At the age of nineteen, while still an undergraduate at Williams College, he had written that heart-stirring reveille, "The Missionary Call," which strikes the key-note of a life of remarkable unity and completeness, inspired throughout, from youth to age, by a single controlling principle, "the love of man, founded on the love of God." The following is the correct text of the poem as originally published: —

My soul is not at rest. There comes a strange
And secret whisper to my spirit, like
A dream of night, that tells me I am on
Enchanted ground. Why live I here? The vows
Of God are on me, and I may not stop
To play with shadows, or pluck earthly flowers,
Till I my work have done, and rendered up
Account. The voice of my departed Lord,
Go TEACH ALL NATIONS, from the eastern world
Comes on the night air, and awakes my ear.

And I will go. I may not longer doubt
To give up friends and home and idol hopes,
And every tender tie that binds my heart
To thee, my country! Why should I regard
Earth's little store of borrowed sweets? I sure
Have had enough of sorrow in my cup
To show that never was it His design,
Who placed me here, that I should live in ease,
Or drink at pleasure's fountain.

          Henceforth, then,
It matters not, if storm or sunshine be
My earthly lot, bitter or sweet my cup;
I only pray, God fit me for the work;
God make me holy, and my spirit nerve
For the stern hour of strife. Let me but know
There is an Arm unseen that holds me up,
An Eye that kindly watches all my path,
Till I my weary pilgrimage have done;
Let me but know I have a Friend that waits
To welcome me to glory, and I joy
To tread the dark and death-fraught wilderness.

And when I come to stretch me for the last,
In unattended agony, beneath
The cocoa's shade, or lift my dying eyes
From Afric's burning sands, it will be sweet
That I have toiled for other worlds than this;
I know I shall feel happier than to die
On softer bed.

          And if I should reach heaven;
If one that hath so deeply, darkly sinned;
If one whom ruin and revolt have held
With such a fearful grasp; if one for whom
Satan has struggled as he hath for me,
Should ever reach that blessed shore, oh, how
This heart will flame with gratitude and love!
And through the ages of eternal years,
Thus saved, my spirit never shall repent
That toil and suffering once were mine below.

WILLIAM R. BROWN[3456], of Larned, Kansas, has held the positions of district judge, member of the House of Representatives at Washington, and register at United States Land Office at Lawrence, Kan.; a graduate of Union College, 1862.

WM. G. BROWN[3517] of Stevens Point, Wis. He was fitted for college at New Hampton, N. H., and at Bennington Seminary, of which latter institution his brother, Rev. Dr. Nathan Brown, was then an associate principal. He entered Williams College in 1833; poor health prevented his finishing the course. He taught school at Bennington, Vt., Shelburne Falls and Holyoke, Mass., and in 1840 became editor of the *Vermont Telegraph*, afterwards of the *Voice of Freedom*, both anti-slavery papers, published at Brandon, Vt. 1856 to 1858 was editor of Chicopee *Journal*, published at Chicopee, Mass. He is the author of several poems that have attained a wide circulation. The best known of these poems are "A Hundred Years to Come" and "Mother, Home, and Heaven."

CHURCHILL.

GARDNER A. CHURCHILL[1513], of Boston, Mass., was appointed an acting ensign, United States Navy, 1862, and served in the navy for three years. He formed, in 1866, with Mr. H. T. Rockwell, the firm of Rockwell & Churchill, printers, of Boston. He moved to Dorchester, 1868; has represented that town two terms in the Legislature, and was one year trustee of Danvers Hospital.

CROSBY.

SAMUEL COBB CROSBY[2721], of Jamestown, N. Y., came to Jamestown in 1832, and for a year thereafter was employed as a clerk in the post-office, E. T. Foote being the postmaster. Subsequently he was in business with Mr. N. Lowry; afterwards kept a general store, firm name S. C. Crosby & Co.; also for a time engaged in business with his brother-in-law, Zalmon Keeler. In 1855 he went out of the mercantile trade; subsequently, however, in 1863, he, with the late Bradford Burlin, established the first coal-yard in Jamestown. This was an experiment. Previous to this, wood had been the only fuel used in this section. Mr. Crosby has held offices of public trust during the years of his active business life, all of which were faithfully administered.

DANIELS.

FRANCIS DANIELS[1045]. In his early days he was a merchant near Plainfield, Vt. For nearly twenty years he was engaged in the cotton trade in Mobile and New Orleans, returning to reside in Grafton, Vt., about 1850. He took an active interest in local affairs, and was a generous supporter of all public enterprise which seemed worthy in his judgment. His private benefactions to the poor were liberal and frequent. He contributed largely to the support of the Congregational church. He was an ardent Republican of the original abolition type. He represented his town in the State Legislature, 1858–59, and again in 1863–64, serving a part of the time on the Committee on Banking. At the beginning of the war he advocated strongly the policy of arming the blacks, and in the latter part of the summer of 1861, at a public meeting in Grafton, Vt., he introduced a series of resolutions, requesting President Lincoln to arm the blacks, and advocated the measure in a spirited speech. He died in Grafton, 1877. His wife was Lucy Barrett[1045].

FRANCIS BARRETT DANIELS[1040] of Dubuque, Iowa, graduate at Phillipsburg Academy, Andover, Mass., class 1867, Harvard College, class 1871, and Columbia College Law School, class 1874. Is practising law at Dubuque, Iowa, where he was a Presidential elector in 1880.

DAY.

LIEUT. MURRAY SIMPSON DAY[1771], of the United States Navy, was a son of Hannibal Day, and son-in-law of Gen. George S. Greene. From 1873 to 1876, Lieut. Day, by consent of the United States government, served the Japanese government in organizing and starting a government Coast Survey similar to the United States Coast Survey. Lieut. Day died Dec. 27, 1878, on board the United States ship "Vandalia," on the voyage from Gibraltar to New York.

DANA.

HON. SAMUEL DANA[1715], of Groton, Mass., was identified with the history of his native town for nearly fifty years. He studied law at the office of his father and Judge John Lowell in Boston; was admitted to the bar in 1789, and opened an office in Groton, where he gained an extensive practice, becoming a leader of the Middlesex bar. Butler's "History of Groton" says of him: "He was a popular speaker, able advocate, and successful practitioner. Mr. Dana was the first postmaster of Groton. There was a mail once in each week; the quarterly receipts for the first year (1800) amounted to three dollars. He was also captain of the North Company in Groton, composed of Democrats, the South Company being Federalists, commanded by Hon. Timothy Bigelow, who was the lawyer usually pitted against Mr. Dana in the more important suits of the day. He was appointed county attorney for the county of Middlesex in 1807, holding the office for four years, when he received the appointment of chief justice of the Court of Common Pleas, holding the position for ten years. He was representative to the General Court for two years, 1802–3, and was elected to the Senate for nine successive years, during eight of which he was president of that body. In the fall of 1814 he was elected a representative to fill the vacancy in Congress, and was a delegate to the convention for altering and amending the State Constitution in 1820–21. In 1825–26 he again represented the town in the Legislature. He removed to Charlestown in 1808, where he, with his family, resided for

five years. Mrs. Dana's health being delicate, and she being unable to bear the east winds, he returned to his native town, purchasing a farm of some three hundred acres, upon which he introduced the most approved agricultural implements. He was one of the first members of the Middlesex Agricultural Society at Concord, Mass. He was also much interested in the growth of wool, and in company with others imported the first merino sheep into this country. He spent the winter of 1824–5 in Washington, and there organized the New England Society for the Improvement of Wool. Mrs. Dana is remembered as being tall and singularly graceful in her movements, and noted for her beauty of form and feature, her culture and refinement, lovely disposition, and powers of conversation." He died in Charlestown, Mass.

HON. JAMES DANA[1544] of Boston, Mass. Mr. Dana graduated at Harvard College, 1830, and is a counsellor at law in Boston. He was mayor of the city of Charlestown for three years, beginning in 1858. During his term of office the Mystic Water Works, for the supply of Charlestown and contiguous municipalities, was established, also the Charlestown Public Library. He was appointed clerk of the courts in Middlesex County, to fill a vacancy, and served until his successor was elected and qualified. He held a commission as an officer in the Massachusetts State Volunteer Militia for twelve years, viz., commander of the Charlestown Light Infantry, brigade-major on the staff of Gen. Joshual Butterick of Concord, colonel of Fourth Regiment of Infantry, and general in Third Brigade, Second Division.

GEN. JAMES JACKSON DANA[1747], of Washington, D. C., received from President Franklin Pierce a commission as lieutenant in the United States Fourth Regiment of Artillery, and was engaged in operations against the Seminole Indians in Florida, and in the disturbances in Kansas, and subsequently served at various points with his regiment in Nebraska, Minnesota, and Utah. At the outbreak of the Southern Rebellion he was appointed regimental quartermaster, and ordered from Camp Floyd, Utah, where he was serving with the light battery of his regiment, to headquarters at Fort McHenry, Baltimore. He was soon after appointed assistant quartermaster, with rank of captain United States Army, and placed in charge of the transportation branch of the Washington quartermaster's depot, covering an area of more than one hundred acres, on which were the extensive stables for thousands of horses and mules, hospitals for the treatment of the wounded animals, shops and storehouses where army wagons, ambulances, harness, and articles pertaining to land transportation were received, stored, repaired, and manufactured, and issued to the Army of the Potomac and the troops around Washington. His official expenditures were by the millions, and his employees numbered upwards of five thousand. The lamented Gen. Reynolds, commanding the First Army Corps, having applied for him as chief quartermaster, with rank of

colonel, on his staff, he was so appointed, and was engaged in the campaign of Chancellorsville, and at Gettysburg, where Gen. Reynolds received the untimely fatal shot. Capt. Dana was brevetted major, lieutenant-colonel, colonel, and brigadier-general for faithful and meritorious services in the quartermaster's department during the war, and was promoted major and quartermaster, Jan. 18, 1867, and lieutenant-colonel and deputy quartermaster, Feb. 13, 1882. Gen. Dana served after the war in charge of a division in the office of the quartermaster-general; subsequently as chief quartermaster Department of the Lakes, of the Department of Arizona and New Mexico, in charge of the clothing depot at Schuylkill Arsenal, Philadelphia, and as depot quartermaster at sundry places. He was also in charge, at Nashville, Tenn., of the investigation of claims of loyal citizens for property taken by and used for the armies of the United States in Tennessee during the Rebellion; afterwards he served as chief quartermaster, Department of the South, whence he was ordered to duty in the general office at Washington. On the 9th of April, 1885, having reached the age of sixty-four years, by operation of act June 30, 1882, he was retired from active service, holding at the time the rank of lieutenant-colonel and deputy quartermaster-general, United States Army.

EVERETT.

Col. John M. Everett[1409], of Foxboro, Mass., was a farmer; he also held a number of public offices: colonel of the State militia, justice of the peace, trial justice, and a member of the board of selectmen and school committee; in 1846 was representative to the Legislature. In 1850 he made a survey of Foxboro (his native town), and from it drew a map of the town. In 1871, feeling the effect of age upon him, he sold his farm and removed to Wrentham, and soon after became blind. After submitting to several painful operations, three of which were unsuccessful in bringing sight, discouraged by his friends and knowing that his chances were small, he again sought Dr. Sprague of Boston, for the fourth time, and returned to his home rejoicing with sight restored.

FOSTER.

Isaac Foster[1184] after his marriage moved to New York State in 1817 to the town of Aurelius, where afterward Fosterville, a village of the town, was named for him and his brother. Mr. Foster opened the first store in Fosterville in 1819. He was a justice of the peace for eleven years, and was the first postmaster of Fosterville.

FLETCHER.

Hon. John Fletcher[4726], of Acton, Mass., was a member of the State Legislature, 1862, State Senate, 1870 and 1871.

Rev. James Fletcher[4724], of Acton, Mass., a graduate of Academy at New Ipswich, N. H., Dartmouth College, 1843, Andover Seminary, 1856. Mr. Fletcher has been engaged as a minister in the Congregational society, and also a teacher in academies and seminaries in the State. He married Lydia Middleton Woodward, daughter of Rev. Henry Woodward, one of the first missionaries to Ceylon, and a granddaughter of Prof. Bessaleel Woodward of Dartmouth College.

FROTHINGHAM.

Rev. William Frothingham[1119], a graduate at Harvard College, 1799, in the class with Channing, Tuckerman, and other distinguished Unitarians. He kept a school at Lexington for a time, was licensed to preach June 9, 1801, and ordained pastor of the church at Saugus, Mass., Sept. 26, 1804, remaining there twelve years, and in July, 1819, he was installed over the Congregational church at Belfast, Maine, where his ministry continued twenty-seven years. His wife was Lois Barrett[1119].

GREENE.

Charles Thruston Greene[1769] was a member of the Twenty-second Regiment New York State Militia in service of the United States, also second lieutenant Sixtieth Regiment New York Volunteers, aide-de-camp to his father, Gen. Geo. S. Greene; assistant adjutant-general, 1863. He was in many of the important battles, and lost a leg at the battle of Chattanooga, Tenn., while leading the Third Brigade, Second Division, Second Army Corps, past the batteries at Ringold. He was appointed captain and brevet major in the Regiment of Veteran Reserves for gallant service, and when the regiment was disbanded, he was placed upon the retired list of the army, with the rank of captain mounted.

Capt. Francis Vinton Greene[1773] was a cadet at United States Military Academy, West Point, 1866 to 1870, at the head of his class each year; lieutenant of engineers, captain engineers, United States Army; assistant astronomer and surveyor on the location of the northern boundary line between the United States and Great Britain; military attaché to the United States Legation at St. Petersburg. He has been assistant engineer for the city of Washington since 1879. In addition to his official reports on the movements, organization, etc., of the Russian army in the campaign of 1877–78, he has published "Army Life in Russia," "The Mississippi Campaign of the Civil War."

Gen. George Sears Greene[1743] was born at Apponaug, Warwick, R. I., May 6, 1801. He is a descendant in the sixth generation from Major John Greene, deputy governor of Rhode Island, whose father, John Green, Sr., came from Salisbury, in England, in 1635, settling in Warwick, R. I., 1643.

Gen. Greene graduated at the Military Academy, West

Point, 1823, second in his class, with rank of second lieutenant. Lieut. Greene left the army in 1836 and became a civil engineer, building many railroads in the States of Maine, Massachusetts, Rhode Island, New York, Maryland, and Virginia. In 1856 he served in the Croton Aqueduct Department in the city of New York, building the reservoir in Central Park, raising the High Bridge, and increasing its capacity for bringing water into the city.

Gen. Greene was appointed brigadier-general of volunteers, United States Army, April 28, 1862. He commanded his brigade at Cedar Mountain, Aug. 9, 1862, and was in command of the Second Division of the Twelfth Army Corps in the battle of Antietam, Sept. 17, 1862. Also commanded his brigade at the battle of Chancellorsville, May 1 and 2, 1863; and at Gettysburg, July 2, 1863, with a portion of his brigade he held the right wing of the Army of the Potomac, at Culp's Hill, against a fierce onslaught of more than a division of Confederate troops, thereby averting a terrible disaster which would have resulted from turning the right wing of the army. He was transferred to the Western armies in September, 1863, and in a night engagement at Wauhatchie, near Chattanooga, on Oct. 28, 1863, he was dangerously wounded by a rifle bullet passing through his face and breaking the bones of the jaw. This wound disabled him from active service until January, 1865, when he rejoined Sherman's army in North Carolina, and participated in the engagements preceding Johnson's surrender. He was appointed brevet major-general for his distinguished services, March 13, 1865, and retired from the army in 1866. In 1867 he became chief engineer and commissioner of the Croton Aqueduct Department, and remained such until 1871, when he became chief engineer of public works in Washington, resigning from that position in 1872. He was president of the American Society of Civil Engineers from 1875 to 1877, and since that date has been engaged as consulting engineer on various engineering works.

GEORGE SEARS GREENE, Jr.[1766], of New York, is a civil engineer, and has been engineer in chief, Department of Docks, New York City, from 1875 to the present time.

SAMUEL DANA GREENE[1767], midshipman U. S. Naval Academy, Annapolis, Md., 1855 to 1859; passed midshipman, 1859, to August 31, 1861, when he was promoted lieutenant U. S. Navy; second in command of the iron-clad "Monitor" under Lieut. Worden, and in command when Lieut. Worden was wounded in the fight with the rebel ironclad "Merrimac." He was attached to the "Monitor" till she sank off Cape Hatteras. He was lieutenant-commander and commander, and constantly on duty until his death.

GOWING.

JOHN KENDALL GOWING[2549], of Shirley, Mass., was a prominent resident of Shirley during his life. He was a selectman four years, was county commissioner, and represented his town in the Legislature one year.

HALL.

EVELYN MAY BARRETT HALL[2752], wife of Elial F. Hall, was of unusual mental endowments; she was thorough in her knowledge, unostentatious in her bearing, and possessed great character as well as the gentlest of spirits. She was a dependence wherever she was placed. Having no children of her own, her sympathy and help went out in a large measure to the families of her brothers and sisters, and entered into the charitable work with which she was connected in New York City. Her aid here was invaluable. The influence of her character among working women, whom she met with from week to week, was said to have been wonderful for good. She had many devoted friends among these women, who loved her and gained great strength and practical knowledge from her for their common needs. She said to her sister shortly before her death, "This work of mine is not finished; I shall take it with me into the other world." She had a rare gift for literary work, and wrote many valuable articles, notably the description of the first company that navigated Chautauqua Lake. It will find an honored place in the archives of the country. Dr. Taylor, her pastor, closed in the brief funeral service with the following words: "She so gentle, so even-tempered, and so cultured, tried to walk with God."

HOSMER.

REV. GEORGE WASHINGTON HOSMER[4207] was born in Concord in 1803. He studied first at the school in Concord, then taught by the Rev. Samuel Barrett (afterwards minister of the Chardon Street Church in Boston); here he prepared for college, and was admitted to the Freshman class in Harvard College, 1822. He taught a school during his college term in Wayland, Lincoln, and Bolton to help pay his expenses. After graduating he taught school successfully at Plymouth, for about one year, then entering the Divinity School at Cambridge; after this he preached for seven years at Northfield, Mass. He succeeded the Rev. James Freeman Clarke at Louisville, Ky., in 1835. He removed to Buffalo in 1836, and there continued a successful pastorate for thirty years. He became the president of Antioch College, Yellow Springs, Ohio, in 1866, occupying the chair for seven years, when he removed to Newton, Mass., becoming pastor of the Channing Church.

MAJOR JOSEPH HOSMER[4193] of Concord. "In the great events of the Revolution he acted a conspicuous part, always in favor of liberty. Whilst the preliminary measures were under discussion, one of the townsmen made a powerful speech, in which he attempted to ridicule the doings of the 'Sons of Liberty.' Mr. Hosmer immediately replied in a

Charles Augustus Jones

strain of natural, unaffected, but energetic eloquence (for which he was afterwards distinguished), which particularly attracted public attention, and introduced him to public favor. He was a militia officer on April 19, 1775, and the first captain of the Concord Light Infantry Company, and was afterwards promoted to major. He was a representative five years, a senator twelve, being always an active and influential member. He was appointed sheriff of the county in 1792, and sustained the office fifteen years. Major Hosmer was endowed by nature with strong, active powers of mind; and the character he formed enabled him to meet all events with that fortitude which is an earnest of success. Ardent without rashness, bold without presumption, and religious without fanaticism, he was eminently a useful man."

PROF. JAMES KENDALL HOSMER[4217], a minister at Deerfield, Mass., 1860 to 1866 corporal Fifty-second Regiment Massachusetts Volunteers, 1862–63; professor Antioch College, Ohio, 1866 to 1872; State University, Mo., 1872 to 1874; at Washington University, St. Louis, 1874.

HUBBARD.

EBENEZER HUBBARD[1864], of Concord, Mass., lived where he boasted that his grandfather had entertained Washington. 'He was always greatly disturbed in mind because the monument to commemorate the fight at North Bridge was not placed on the opposite side of the river, where the Americans stood that April morning. In his will he left one thousand dollars toward the cost of another monument on that side (which has resulted in the present statue of the minute-man). He also placed six hundred dollars in the hands of the town clerk to build a bridge on the site of the old one." He died unmarried.

HUMPHREY.

JOHN HUMPHREY[1398], a graduate of Bridgewater Normal School, 1855, enlisted in United States Navy, at Charlestown, Mass., June, 1861; subsequently detailed to United States steamship "Cumberland," which started for the scene of action, stopping to bombard Forts Henry and Hatteras, and then proceeded to their station off Newport News at the mouth of the James River, where they were placed with the United States steamship "Congress," to guard the river, and where the historic action took place between them and the rebel iron-clad "Merrimac," and where he fell, one of the first victims; his remains were not recovered.

WILLIAM S. HUMPHREY[1478], of Bridgeport, Conn., engaged in 1835 in the india-rubber trade, then in its infancy. In 1849 he visited California Returning in 1852, he became superintendent of a rubber packing and belting factory in Newtown, where he remained several years. In 1865 he established a business of making steam boilers in Bridgeport,

Conn., a successful business, in which he continued until his death, which resulted accidentally from the falling of a tree.

HUNT.

REUBEN HUNT[850], a son of Simon and Mary (Raymond) Hunt. He was one of the founders of the Congregational Unitarian church in Charlestown; he died in 1816. During his life he had accumulated a large property. His wife was Rebecca Barrett[1850].

SIMON HUNT[868], born in Concord, Mass., 1784, and removed to Camden, Maine, in 1806, where he resided until his death in 1865, a period of nearly sixty years. During the War of 1812, while a British squadron was riding at anchor in the bay, he ventured out in a small boat to reconnoitre the English men-of-war. He was captured, and imprisoned for one week. His wife, Hannah B. (Rogers) Hunt, died in Camden in 1882.

SIMON HUNT[997], of Hudson, Wis. He was born in Camden, Maine, in 1826, received an academic education at home, learned the trade of shoe-making in Georgetown, Mass., removed to Missouri, 1851, and is now engaged in business at Hudson, Wis. His wife, Jane C. (Arey) Hunt, a very estimable lady, died in 1883.

JONES.

CHARLES AUGUSTUS JONES[4773] was born in Wakefield, Mass. He was engaged in the hotel business all his life, having been some years steward of the old Winthrop House in Boston, before it was burned. He was proprietor of the Norfolk House for twenty-five years. It was his pride during many years to say that he was the second oldest hotel-keeper in Boston, Harvey D. Parker being the oldest. He was connected with the Masonic order, and a member of the Joseph Warren Commandery of Knights Templars. Mr. Jones lived in Boston from 1836 to the time of his death, excepting about two years spent in New York. He came to the Norfolk House in 1859. He married Isanna Brigham, and their only daughter married William Warren Davis of Boston.

ELNATHAN JONES[4692] of South Acton, Mass., of the house of Tuttle, Jones & Wetherbee, which was established nearly fifty years ago, and now so well known in South Acton and its vicinity. Mr. Jones was several years in the employment of this house before being admitted to the partnership. He is a man of very successful business abilities, and of the highest integrity; has held some of the minor offices in his town, and has been always deeply interested in the welfare of the Universalist society. His fellow-citizens would have often been glad to elect him to office. He has, however, discouraged all such prominence.

LEWIS.

BETSEY L. (BARRETT) LEWIS[2817] of Lewiston, Wis. She married Edward F. Lewis, and in 1849 they moved to what is now Lewiston, her present home (the town taking its name from that of her husband). At that time the country was in the possession of the Indians, and was before the government had made its survey of the lands. She shared with her husband a conscientious and an active life, both in public and private stations. Mr. Lewis was elected sheriff of the county in 1857, and soon after the breaking out of the war was appointed provost-marshal of the congressional district, and held the office until the close of the war. He died in 1885.

FRANKLIN FILLMORE LEWIS[2831], of Portage, Wis., finished his education in the State Normal School of Wisconsin. He taught school for a time, and was principal of the public schools of Whitewater, Wis., and is now engaged in the manufactory with his brother at Portage, Wis.

JUDSON ADONIRAM LEWIS[2828] enlisted in Company G, Second Regiment Wisconsin Volunteers, at the beginning of the Rebellion; being then under age, his name was taken from the enlistment. The year following, having gained his parents' consent, he again enlisted, and in Company C, Twenty-third Regiment Wisconsin Volunteers. He was with the regiment during its marches and engagements in Kentucky, Tennessee, Missouri, and Mississippi. He was at the siege of Vicksburg, in 1863, and on May 22, at the time of a charge upon the enemies' works, he was shot in the head and killed. He was color-bearer of his regiment at the time. He was buried with others of the killed by the enemy.

STEPHEN BARRETT LEWIS[2830], of Portage, Wis., graduated from the State Normal School of Wisconsin, 1874. He was elected principal of the schools of Clinton, Wis., the same year, and continued in this position for nine years. After this he engaged in the woollen manufacture at Portage, Wis.

MILES.

CAPT. CHARLES MILES[1558] of Concord, Mass., the husband of Ruth Barrett[1558], was in a company of ninety-four minute-men in the Revolution. He commanded his company in the "Concord fight," into which he said he "went with the same seriousness as if he were going to the house of God." He was also in command at Ticonderoga.

MARTIN.

MRS. LIZZIE EDNA (JONES) MARTIN[1668], of Boston, Mass., is an artist and teacher, well known to art lovers of Boston and New York, having been engaged in the work for more than ten years. She has instructed pupils from all parts of the Union in oil, water-color, and china painting. Some of Mrs. Martin's productions have become celebrated, not alone in her own country, a few of her exquisite flower pictures having been collected by London houses to be lithographed for art studies.

MATSELL.

GEORGE WASHINGTON MATSELL[2501], born in New York City, Oct. 25, 1811, and was a pupil of Coates Academy, in that city. At an early age, as a sailor boy, he made several voyages to the West Indies and China. In 1826, he was apprenticed, as designer of patterns, to Messrs. Barrett, Tileston & Co., of the New York dyeing and printing establishment of Staten Island. From 1837 to 1843 was major of the Sixth Infantry of the State of New York; in 1840 appointed police magistrate at the Tombs, New York; after holding that position for five years, was appointed, in 1845, chief of police by Mayor Havemeyer, and under whose able administration he originated the first police system in the United States, bringing together all the information on the subject, from whatever quarters it could be found. From these sources, and from his own practical experiences and observations, was drawn up, in 1845, the first manual of rules and regulations of the police department in the United States. He held the office of chief of police, continuously, under the mayoralties of Havemeyer, Meckle, Brady, Havemeyer (second term), Woodhull, Kingsland, Westervelt, and Wood. He was admitted as a counsellor of the Supreme Court of the State of New York. In 1857 he retired to his farm in Iowa. In 1873 he was appointed superintendent of police, when the Hon. Wm. F. Havemeyer was re-elected for the third term; and in the same year was appointed by him police commissioner, and elected president of the board of police. He died at his residence in Fifty-eighth Street, New York City, and was buried in Trinity cemetery on the bank of the Hudson River. His wife was Ellen M. Barrett[2501], daughter of George M. Barrett[2152].

NOURSE.

MAJOR BARNARD NOURSE[743] was born in Bolton, where he afterwards lived during his life. He was a farmer, and served for several years as a representative in the State Legislature, and held a major's commission in the militia of Massachusetts. He married Hannah Barrett[742].

CALEB NOURSE[750] of Bolton. He was a school teacher for many years, in the latter part of his life engaging in farming. He held nearly every office in his town, — an honored citizen. He died in 1884.

Charles F. Potter

Henry Potts

PIERCE.

REV. JOHN DAVIS PIERCE[2690] of Ypsilanti, Mich. From the age of two years until twenty, he lived with a paternal uncle in Worcester, Mass. After this, obtaining employment as a farm laborer, he saved one hundred dollars; with a like sum, given to him by his grandfather, he started out to acquire an education. The 14th of December, 1817, he walked fourteen miles, buying a Latin grammar on the way, and taking his first lesson in Latin that evening, under Rev. Enoch Pond. He entered Brown University the following September, and by close application, graduated in 1823, in the first eight of his class of thirty-six. He was settled as a pastor in Oneida County, N. Y., in 1823, remaining until 1829, when the Masonic and anti-Masonic contest rendered it necessary for him to close his pastorate. He received a commission from the Home Missionary Society in 1831; in July, of the same year, removed to Marshall, Mich., laboring there as a missionary until July 26, 1836, in which year he was appointed superintendent of public instruction. His first work in this office was to draw up a plan for the organization of the primary schools and of the State University, and the disposal of the primary school and university lands. He presented this plan to the Legislature in January, 1837, when it was adopted with very few amendments. He held this office for five years. In 1842, he returned to the Christian ministry, and continued therein until 1847, when he was elected to the State Legislature; was chairman of the Committee on Federal Relations in the House. He introduced and succeeded in carrying a resolution instructing the Michigan delegation in the national Congress to oppose the introduction of slavery into the Territories. He also prepared and carried the homestead exemption law, the first law of this kind enacted in the United States. In 1850 was a member of the convention for framing a new constitution for the State.

POTTER.

DEA. CHARLES FRANCIS POTTER[5211] of Boston, Mass., born at Concord, and is a descendant from several of the earliest families that settled there; of these, his grandmother was Lucy Hosmer. She was a daughter of Nathan Hosmer, whose wife was Bulah Hosmer, both descendants of James Hosmer, who first settled in Concord. His great-grandfather, Jonas Potter, married Persis Barrett, daughter of Col. James Barrett. Judah Potter, the son of Luke Potter and grandfather of Jonas, married Grace Brooks, daughter of Joshua and Hannah (Mason) Brooks. Mr. Potter is a man of high business integrity and perfect uprightness. Entirely free from all questionable indulgences, his moral and Christian character are without a stain. A Universalist in faith, he honors his profession, and devotes himself assiduously to the promotion of church interests. As an indication of the esteem in which he is held by his Christian acquaintance, it may be noticed that he has been an officer in the Universalist Sunday-School Union, embracing nearly twenty different schools, for twenty-seven years, including the secretaryship for ten years, and all the subordinate offices at different times. He is now president of the Union, and has been often called to preside over other bodies, in which duties he displays rare abilities. Mr. Potter was a deacon in the Universalist church at Brighton.

HENRY POTTER[5006], of Cambridge, Mass., was born in Concord, and was a resident of Cambridge for nearly half a century, and was always an active promoter of any enterprise calculated to benefit his city. One of the original charter members of the Cambridge Horse Railroad Company, and some time its president, it was mainly through his influence and subscriptions that the North Avenue and Arlington branch of that road was built. He was also associated with the birth and growth of the Cambridge Gas Light Company and Water Works, and to the stock of both companies subscribed largely. Mr. Potter was likewise one of the organizers of the Cambridge Market Bank, of which he was president for many years. He was also president of the Harvard Manufacturing Company, and had held the offices of president and director in many institutions, but at the time of his death had relinquished all of these positions excepting the chairmanship of the trustees of the Cambridge Horse Railroad bonds and director in the Gas Light Company, the latter company stoutly declining to accept his resignation, but relieved him from all labor connected with the position. Mr. Potter is remembered as a very benevolent man, always ready to give from his means to the deserving poor, and bestowing his bounty liberally. He was also well known as a merchant of Boston, of the house of Potter & Demmon. He retired from active business in 1865. Mr. Potter married, in 1843, Abigail Livermore Giles, daughter of Capt. Benjamin and Nancy (Williams) Giles, born in Beverly, Mass., Feb. 10, 1811 (see "Giles Memorial," p. 69). Nancy Williams was a daughter of Elisha Williams, who was born 1757, "graduated at Yale College, 1775, received the degree A. M. from Harvard and Yale, and who served on Gen. Washington's staff for a time, and later in life became pastor of the Baptist church in Beverly and died there, 1845" ("History of Williams Family," pp. 165–168, and Bond's "Watertown Genealogies," p. 349). Abigail Livermore, wife of Elisha Williams, born 1758, died 1817. She was eldest daughter of Dea. Elijah Livermore, 1730–1808, a native of Waltham, deacon, chairman, and selectman for a long period. He removed to Livermore, Me., in 1779, of which township he was chief proprietor and first settler. He was emphatically the father of that town, and a man of great worth. — *Bond's Watertown*, p. 346.

HENRY STAPLES POTTER[5011] of Boston, son of Henry and Abigail Livermore (Giles) Potter of Cambridge, is one of the leading merchants of Boston, his house standing at the head of the canning business in New England.

SAMUEL POTTER[5169]. At the time of the "Concord fight," April 19, 1775, he was a lad about seven and a half years of age. His father lived about one mile from the centre of the town, and one and one half miles from the battle-ground. When the British soldiers were scattered over the town on their errands of destruction, as some of them approached the house where he lived, his mother took him and the other two children (both girls) back of the house and hid them in the bushes. Small boy though he was, he took his father's gun, and when the soldiers passed through the house and out at the back door, he raised the gun to fire at them. His mother was quick enough to put her hand under the hammer to prevent the gun from discharging, thus, probably, saving their own lives.

SAMUEL POTTER[5186] was early in life engaged in the manufacture of powder, in which business his rare ability and skill have gained for him the reputation of being the most skilful manufacturer of gunpowder in the country. For nearly forty years he was superintendent of the American Powder Company's Works at Acton, Mass., and for many years was one of its directors. His hair-breadth escapes from death by the explosions at the works were many. Scores of instances could be recounted when he had just left or was about to enter a mill before an explosion took place, which would have blown him to atoms. He passed through all of these dangers, and lived to a good age. All honor to his name and race.

SILAS WARREN POTTER[5212] was all through the War of the Rebellion; he was left for dead on the battle-field of Shiloh, but discovered to be alive the next day by a passing straggler, a Massachusetts man, who had known him at home. He was a prisoner at Libby Prison, and in company with two other prisoners dug a subterranean passage and escaped. Afterwards a captain in the Fifty-ninth Veteran Regiment of Massachusetts; was severely wounded in the head at the battle of the Wilderness. His wounds and shattered constitution were afterwards the cause of his death.

RUSSELL.

JAMES SULLIVAN RUSSELL, A. M.[5068], of Lowell, Mass., now nearly eighty years of age. He studied at Brown University; from this institution he received the honorary degree of A. M. He taught school in the various towns in the State, finally becoming teacher of mathematics in the Lowell, Mass., High School; continued forty-three years, retiring in 1881.

WILLIAM LAMBERT RUSSELL, M. D.[5064], of Barre, Mass., a graduate of Harvard College, is an educated physician; his wife, Mary Ann Warren, is a descendant of Gen. Warren.

SAWYER.

JOEL SAWYER[786] of Bolton, Mass., a watch-maker, which trade he has followed for many years; later in life he has given his attention to that of millwright, having achieved considerable reputation by the thoroughness of his work. He married Sarah Barrett[786].

DR. LEVI SAWYER[749] was a native of Bolton, Mass.; he studied medicine, and practised in South Carolina and Georgia; afterward returning to Bolton, he continued his practice until his death in 1841. His wife was Hannah Norse[749].

SEVER.

COL. JOHN SEVER[1739] of Kingston, Mass. Col. Sever was a leading merchant, ship builder and owner. He was one of the originators and the first president of the Old Colony Railroad. He was very actively engaged in the construction of this road, his services in amicably settling land damages, and in other departments of the road, were valuable and duly appreciated. He was a successful business man, and had few superiors in Plymouth County. He was colonel of a regiment of Massachusetts militia.

MARTHA SEVER[1754], with her sister, Ann D. Sever[1749], volunteered as hospital nurses in 1864. Martha died at the Military Hospital, Beverly, N. J., in 1864. The Grand Army Post of Kingston, Mass., is named in honor of her memory, — "The Martha Sever Post." Her name is also inscribed on the soldiers' monument erected at that place. Her sister continued in the service at the hospital until it was abandoned.

SPALDING.

DR. EDWARD SPALDING[1039] of Nashua, N. H. A graduate from Dartmouth College, 1833. Studied medicine with his father and at the Harvard Medical School. Graduated an M. D., 1837. He has practised in his profession from that date to the present time in Nashua, N. H. Has several times been a member of the city government. Elected mayor in 1864; also elected a trustee of Dartmouth College in 1866. He assumed nearly the entire expense of publishing a history of his native town, Amherst, N. H. He married Dora Everett Barrett[1039].

SWAIN.

CHIPMAN SWAIN[1918]. Until forty years of age lived in the house in which he was born, and for fourteen years was sheriff of Windham, his native county, in Vermont. 1842 to 1845 he was superintendent of the State Prison in Windsor, Vt.

In 1855, at the age of sixty, he removed to Delton, Wis., and entered with much ardor in the work of making him a new home; and thus his life was one of constant enterprise and faithful activity until his death.

JOSEPH SWAIN[1903] was son of Rev. John Swain, who was a noted divine of his day, and for the most part of his life was settled in Wenham, Mass. The great-grandfather of Rev. John Swain was Jeremiah Swain, Jr., who, with his father, came to this country and settled in Reading, Mass., about 1640. He was a major and a noted Indian warrior.

Elizabeth Chipman, the mother of Joseph Swain, was the daughter of John and Rebecca (Neale) Chipman. John Chipman was son of John Chipman, who came from Dorchester, England, 1631.

Hope Howland, the wife of John Chipman, Sr., was the daughter of John and Elizabeth (Tilley) Howland.

John Tilley and wife and their daughter Elizabeth and John Howland came to this country in the "Mayflower."

PRESCOTT SWAIN[1921] of Bronxville, N. Y. Mr. Swain, after the death of his brother James, assumed the name of James, and was known the greater part of his life as James Prescott Swain. He presented to the town of Concord, Mass., some relics of the Revolutionary War, at the centennial anniversary of the "Concord fight," April 19, 1875; he was present on that day, when he contracted a severe cold, from which he died, April 27, 1875.

COPY OF A LETTER FROM JAMES P. SWAIN TO CHARLES THOMPSON, ESQ.

BRONXVILLE, N. Y., March 24, 1875.

CHARLES THOMPSON, Esq.

Dear Sir, — About one hundred and one years ago, Dr. Warren sent a young man, his nephew by marriage, Joseph Swain, son of Rev. Joseph Swain, of Wenham, to Concord, to take charge of the rebel armory. After repairing the guns generally in use, he attempted to make some new ones. For this purpose he returned to Salem to the edge-tool factory of Mrs. Proctor, where he had previously had charge, and secured such tools as were to be had; and among them this anvil, which I now, through you, present to the town of Concord. On this anvil the first gun-barrel was welded in Concord.

Col. James Barrett and his son James had, during the French war, furnished, through the commissary department in Boston, oat meal and some other provisions. This continued on until near 1774. It was a common occurrence for a young staff officer to come to Concord on this business, and while waiting a reply would amuse himself by talking loyalty with James Barrett's oldest daughter, Meliscent, to hear her rebel replies. He asked her what they would do if it should become necessary for the Colonies to resist, as there was not a person who even knew how to make cartridges. She replied that they would use their powder-horns and bullets, just as they shot bears. "That," says the young man, "would be too barbarous; give me a piece of pine, and I will show you how." After whittling the stick to the proper form, he took these scissors, which I now present to the town of Concord, and cut the paper for the pattern cartridge.

The sequel shows how apt a scholar she was, for all the cartridges were made under her superintendence by the young ladies of Concord; her only male assistant was her younger brother, the late Major James Barrett, who drove the last load of cartridges from the house after the British came in sight on the 19th of April, 1775. After the war, Joseph Swain returned to Concord and married Meliscent Barrett, and took these relics to Halifax, Vt., where I came in possession of them.

Yours,

JAMES P. SWAIN.

This letter is copied in manuscript, and in a frame with the scissors mentioned fastened thereon, is now hanging in the Public Library at Concord.

TRUE.

DR. HENRY AYER TRUE[1835]. A graduate of Bowdoin College, 1832. Studied medicine with Drs. Esterbrook of Camden and McLean of Topsham, Me. Attended lectures at Boston and Brunswick, at which latter place he received a medical degree. He was appointed assistant superintending physician of the McLean Asylum at Somerville, Mass., and afterwards was a druggist at New York City. He removed to Marion, Ohio, where ill health obliged him to abandon an extensive medical practice.

TAYLOR.

J. S. D. TAYLOR[1047]. A graduate of the University of Vermont; studied law, and admitted to the bar; principal of an academy at Plattsburg, N. Y., and for some years before his death was associate editor and proprietor of the St. Albans *Message.* He died in 1873. His wife was Susan Hall Barrett[1047].

WHITE.

JOHN H. WHITE[2751] of New York City, "who married Lucy E. Barrett[2751], was a native of New Hampshire, but in his early boyhood his parents settled in Hoosic Falls, Rensselaer County, N. Y., where he was brought up, and which he always regarded as his country home. He was a graduate of the Rensselaer Polytechnic Institute, at Troy, N. Y. He was admitted to the bar in this city in the winter of 1848. In the fall of 1849 he was elected to the Assembly from the First Assembly District of this city, his first vote having been cast for Henry Clay. In 1850, Mr. White was elected school commissioner for the first ward. In 1852 he was the Whig candidate for the office of judge of the Marine Court, in 1854 for the office of recorder, and in 1856 for the office of city judge. People addressed him as Judge White, and he was very generally known by that appellation. He was the only Republican member of the Assembly from this city in the Legislature of 1870. He became a candidate only five days before the election, and it was universally conceded that he was the only Republican who could carry the Eleventh District, which he represented. Mr. White was an active and zealous member of the Republican party during the Rebellion and since that time. For ten years successively he was a member of the Republican general committee of this city. He was a member of the Union League Club, and was one of the founders of the Masonic Lodge known as Kane Lodge. Mr. White was frank, impulsive, sympathetic, generous, and magnanimous even to a fault. In his political, professional, and social relations he was always ready to take the side of the weaker, and to strike rapid and vigorous blows on that side, without pausing to calculate the chances. In his conflicts at the bar he often broke through technicalities and achieved victory, where others, of more erudition but less courage, would have failed. It was this trait of his character which attracted to his side such a host of warm friends and admirers from all classes of people, as was amply attested by the large attendance at his funeral. By his integrity and industry he built up a flourishing business, and left a competency to his family. He will long be remembered in the metropolis as an able lawyer, a loyal and upright citizen, a fearless enemy of injustice and oppression of every kind, a prompt and energetic man of business, a sincere and faithful friend, and a cultivated and conscientious Christian gentleman." — *New York Daily Register.*

WHITNEY.

Lucius Whitney[1359] served during the War of the Rebellion, enlisting as a private in the Seventh Kansas Cavalry Volunteers, and rising through the several grades to first lieutenant and R. C. S. of the regiment. He was upon detached service as staff officer for Col. Hatch, now of the Regular Army, also for Gen. John McNeil. He was also placed in command of the Gratiot Street Military Prison at St. Louis, Mo., and was for some time provost-marshal of the western district of Missouri. After the war he was postmaster nine years at Morris, Ill., and is at present postmaster at Billings, Montana.

WYMAN.

Samuel Wyman[3036], who married Polly Brown, was a farmer and lived in Cavendish, Vt., and later in life moved to Granville, N. Y., and died there in 1855.

WOOD.

Earl S. Wood[1507] of Bridgeport, Conn. Mr. Wood enlisted for three years in the War of the Rebellion, in Company A, Twentieth Regiment Connecticut Volunteers, Col. Ross commanding. In April, 1864, his regiment was assigned to the Third Division, Twentieth Army Corps, under Gen. Hooker. For two weeks his company lay in the front line of intrenchments before Atlanta, within range of the rebel rifles. On the night of Sept. 1, 1864, the rebels evacuated Atlanta. Mr. Wood was one of the detachment sent into the city, to whom the mayor of Atlanta surrendered the city.

INDEX OF NAMES IN GENEALOGICAL TABLES.

A

ABBEY, Alice L., 60.

ABBOTT, Carrie M., 22.

ABRAMS, Eliza, 20; J. S., 20; Louisa D., 20; Martha, 20; Mary E., 20; Wm., 20.

ACKERMAN, Henry, 43.

ALDRICH, Emeline, 60; Howard W., 57; Marianne, 57; Windsor F., 57; William H., 57.

ADAMS, Amos, 78; Betsey, 56, 70; Betsey M., 57; Benjamin, 41, 70; Caroline, 70, 89; Charlotte C., 71; Charles E., 36; Charles H., 84; Charles K., 36, 65, 71; Charles P., 57; Daniel, 13, 70; Elizabeth, 5; Ellen, 36, 57, 71; Elwood E., 402; Emma, 57, 84; Ethel E., 102; Flora F., 70; Forest N., 70; George, 54; George H., 70; George I., 36; George K., 84; George W., 44; Georgianna, 70; Gertie M., 36; Helen, 62; Henry, 70, 71; Howard B., 36; Ira H., 57; Jerusha, 57; Jennie M., 70; John, 12, 13; John C., 44; John G., 43; Josiah Q., 57; Joseph, 12, 70; Katharine, 98; Lester D., 84; Lizzie H., 84; Love, 10; Lovey, 70; Lucy A., 70; Marcella, 57; Margaret, 57; Mary, 12, 70; Mary A., 44; Mary C., 71, 98; Mary J., 70; Myra G., 44; Nellie R., 70; Olive J., 36; Roxalana, 70; Winslow C., 71; Wm. H., 70; Samuel, 56; Samuel L., 56; Sarah, 73; Simon R., 70.

AGNEW, Mary G., 42.

AIKEN, Charles A., 25; Elizabeth, 22; Mary A., 25; Samuel, 25.

ALLEN, David H., 49; Elizabeth, 6; Herman, 49; Jane, 8; Sarah, 60.

ALLEY, Lois, 83.

AMES, Algernon L., 80; Carrie S., 55; Frances H., 31; Frank E., 80; Frank W. F., 80; Frankie, 31; George T., 80; Georgia E., 80; Stella M., 80; Theodore, 79; Winslow, 21.

ANDREWS, Ada, 32; Nellie, 32.

ANDRUS, William T., 87; Charles P., 87.

ANGUS, John S., 72; Marshall P., 73.

APPLETON, Mary, 21.

AREY, Jane C., 20.

ARMSTRONG, Malvina, 53.

ATKINSON, Susanna, 6; Hannah, 6.

ATKINS, Amos, 50; Alice R., 52; Dudley H., 52; Horatio B., 52; Myron B., 52.

ATWELL, George F., 45; Herman, 44, 55; Paul R. G., 45.

ATWOOD, Leroy H., 28; Louisa K., 51.

AUSTIN, Charles, 84; Catharine J., 84; Edith, 84; Edward, 84; Francis B., 84; Herbert, 84; James W., 84; Louisa, 84; Lucy, 84; Richard, 84; Walter, 84; William, 84; William F., 84; William R., 84.

AYER, Polly, 59.

B

BABBETT, Mary A., 33.

BABCOCK, Margaret M., 30.

BACHELDER, Mary A., 95.

BACHTEL, Jennie E., 90.

BACON, Allen, 98; Amanda C., 76; Helen F., 39.

BAILEY, Frank, 88.

BAIRD, Jane S., 90.

BAKER, Abigail, 7; Amos, 14; John, 89; Lydia, 88; Susanna, 65; Tirzah, 39.

BALCOM, Lizzie E, 61.

BALDWIN, Helen C., 88.

BALL, Charles K., 59; Charles T., 69; Clinton D., 16; Experience, 21; George, 59; George E., 69; George S., 16; George W., 16; Lizzie II., 16; Lydia W., 16; Mabel M, 59; Rena E., 69; Ralph, 72; Susan A., 16; Walter S., 16; W. T., 59.

BALLANCE. Charlotte E., 22.

BALLARD, Abigail, 7; Adelia E., 63; Allen G., 97; Dorothy S., 63; Edith, 97; Eliza B., 63; Ellen G., 63; Eliza W., 62; Frances E., 97; Frances W., 63; John F., 97; Jonathan, 62; Julia R., 63; Maria I., 63; Mary A., 63; Nathan B., 63; Susan M., 63; Walter C., 97; William H., 97.

BALLOU, Laura A., 74.

BANCROFT, Anna, 10; E. Dana, 46; Elvira, 21.

BANNISTER, Mary M., 53.

BARDOLPH, Henry C., 55; Lewis, 55.

BARBER, Elizabeth G., 43.

BARNES, A. K., 52; Clarinda, 48; Effie S., 31; Lucy, 73; Susan B., 69; William E., 31; Vira T., 31.

BARRETT, Aaron, 43; Abel, 18, 21, 84; Abel J., 47; Abigail, 16, 21, 34; Abram M., 40; Achsah, 17; Ada L., 46; Adaline, 45; Adaline M., 51; Addie, 32; Adelaide, 53; Adelia, 24; Albert A., 23, 45; Albert P., 24; Albert T., 53; Alberta L., 18; Albion R., 28; Allen A., 32; Alice, 41, 43; Alice H., 30; Alice I., 43; Alice M., 46; Alice S., 54; Alfred W., 34; Almira C., 24; Alonzo, 51; Amanda E., 51; Amanda M., 42, Amelia H., 41; Amos, 26, 30, 31, 34, 40, 51; Amos A., 27; Amos J., 53; Amos W., 40; Angeline L., 27; Ann A., 24; Ann E., 22, 23, 31; Ann W., 44; Anna, 21, 23; Anna E., 50; Anna M., 39, 44, 54; Annie L., 17, 42, 53; Annie M., 42; Annie W. 40; Arabella, 43; Arabella C., 42; Arethusia T., 31; Arthur L., 28; Arvilla L., 22; Asa, 16, 17; Asa S., 21; Augusta, 45; Augusta A., 28; Augusta H., 47; Augusta M., 42; Bathsheba, 16; Becke, 16; Benjamin, 5, 13, 23, 24, 47, 48, 50, 75; Benjamin F., 44, 47; Bertha M., 17; Bethia, 31, 53; Beth Louise, 40; Bessie C., 49; Betsey, 18, 26, 34, 36, 47, 48; Betsey L., 51; Blanch, 33; Benson S., 52; Caleb, 26; Carlos, 22; Caroline, 24, 43; Caroline A., 23, 46; Caroline H., 31; Caroline J., 25; Caroline M., 41, 43; Caroline S., 44; Carrie A. 32; Carrie C., 38; Carrie L., 44; Carrie M., 25, 42; Catharine P., 44; Charles, 13, 18, 21, 23, 30, 31, 32, 33, 34, 37, 40, 43, 46, 50; Charles A., 32, 44, 46; Charles B., 24; Charles C., 30; Charles E., 33, 45; Charles F., 17, 34, 25; Charles G., 25, 38; Charles H., 22, 24, 26, 37, 43, 45; Charles M., 42, 44, 47, 69; Charles N., 42, Charles O., 47; Charles R., 24; Charles S., 21, 40, 46, 52; Charles T., 32; Charles W., 43, Charlie, 40; Clara A., 25; Clara H., 38; Clara F., 39; Clarence T., 42; Clarinda, 50, 53; Clarinda M., 54; Clarissa D., 25; Clifford M., 28; Clinton, 52; Clinton S., 53; Clinton W., 53; Constance M., 50; Cora S., 24; Cordelia M., 42; Cornelia C., 51; Corinne, 50; Cynthia, 23; Cynthia E., 24, 25; Cyrus, 46; Daisey V., 43; Daniel, 22, 30, 31; Daniel N., 23; Daniel T., 31; David, 40, 41; David P., 47; Diantha J., 27; Dora E., 21; Dorcas, 30, 31, 33, 37; Dorcas A., 32; Dorliska, 52; Dorothy, 30; Dudley, 53; Ebenezer H., 34; Edgar C., 25; Edith A., 53; Edith M., 17, 30, 50; Edith O., 52; Edward, 30, 33; Edward B., 44; Edward E., 31; Edward G., 17; Edward H., 31; Edward K., 41; Edward L, 28; Edward S., 24, 42, 47; Edwin, 23; Edwin A., 33; Edwin C., 47; Edwin G., 40; Edwin H., 25; Edwin N., 32; Edwin S., 44; Eleanor D., 30; Electa, 50; Elisha, 21, 48; Elisha B., 21; Eliza, 34, 41; Eliza E., 28; Eliza W., 39; Elizabeth, 5, 13, 14, 18, 26, 34, 43, 46; Elizabeth A, 22; Elizabeth B., 23, 44; Elizabeth E., 44; Elizabeth F., 24; Elizabeth G., 23; Elizabeth J., 25, 47; Elizabeth M., 27; Elizabeth T., 25; Ella S., 25; Ella V., 17; Ellen A, 44; Ellen B., 29; Ellen C., 37; Ellen M., 45; Elmer C., 25; Elsie, 52; Elsie P., 24; Emeline A., 44; Emeline E, 40; Emeline M., 51; Emeline T., 45; Emily A., 25, 37, 45; Emily M., 21, 27, 44; Emily S., 49; Emily R., 28; Emma A., 25, 42; Emma C., 53; Emma J., 38; Emma R., 25; Emerson, 46, 75; E. Pauline, 50; Ephraim, 24, 36, 40, 45; Ephraim A., 43; Ephraim C., 25; Ethel, 44; Ethel C., 42; Eugene, 40; Eunice, 30; Eva E., 50; Eva M., 25; Evelyn M., 50; Everett E., 22; Ezra, 23; Fanney A., 53; Fernand H., 22; Fidelia, 40; Fidelia F., 40; Florence H., 46; Florence H., 46; Florence M., 53; Florinda M., 50; Floy M., 25; Fortuna, 32; Foster H., 45; Frances A., 45; Frances M., 28, 30; Francis, 40, 44; Francis A., 33, 43; Francis H., 45; Francis J., 24; Francis O., 18; Francis R., 18; Frank, 17, 47; Frank H., 17, 22, 25; Frank E., 24, 25; Frank J., 42; Frank M., 22, 40; Frank P., 46; Frank W., 39; Franklin, 41; Franklin H., 44; Franklin N., 40; Franklin W., 22; Fred O., 17; Frederick, 47; Frederick C., 50; Frederick F., 39; Frederick L., 28, 50; Frederick M., 43; George, 32, 45, 46, 51, 37; George A., 24, 25; George B., 23, 25, 31; George E., 46, 47; George F., 38; George H., 24, 25, 37, 44, 53; George H. M., 32; George M., 21, 37, 40; George P., 47; George R., 34, 46; George W., 33, 44, 45; George V., 24, 46; Georgiana, 44; Grace F., 17; Grace C., 25; Grace M., 53; Hannah, 16, 21, 30, 36; Hannah J., 31; Harriet, 23, 34, 42, 46; Harriet B., 43; Harriet E., 23; Harriet P., 51; Harrold F., 34; Harry D., 31; Harry H., 30, 40, 43; Harry E., 40; Hattie, 31; Hattie F., 32; Harvey P., 53; Hayward, 47; Helen, 17; Helen A., 44; Helen J., 40, 46; Helen L., 24, 43; Helen M., 53; Henry, 34, 43, 45, 47, 49, 50, 67; Henry A., 25, 47; Henry C., 30; Henry H., 24, 43, 47; Henry L., 50; Henry M., 23; Henry Q., 25; Henry P., 47; Henry R., 40; Harry W., 18, 25, 49; Hepzabah, 21; Herbert E., 25; Herbert F., 28; Herbert L., 40; Herbert M., 38, 47; Herbert S., 17; Hiram W., 31; Horace F., 40; Horace W., 44; Hulburt, 53; Humphrey, 5, 13, 17, 18, 21, 47; Ida C., 25; Ida M., 28; Inez D., 53; Irene F., 41; Isabella, 45; Isabella T., 28; Israel, 48, 49; Jabez, 17; James, 5, 12, 35, 36, 37, 40; James A., 37, 75; James F., 23, 24, 49; James H., 37, 44; James M., 41, 49; James P., 18; James W., 47; Janet D., 30; Jay A., 53; J. Arthur, 22; Jay C., 53; J. Lewis, 24; Jeanie S., 39; Jennie A., 32; Jennie E., 24; Jennie L., 44; Jennie M., 47; Jessie G., 44; Jessie M., 50; Joel, 22; John, 5, 16, 17, 21, 22, 23, 26, 45, 46; John B., 23, 42; John C., 31; John D., 22; John F., 21, 24, 32; John H., 21; John K., 50; John L., 23, 30, 31; John M., 30; John O., 25; John P., 47; John T., 41, 42, 43; John W., 25; Jonas, 21, 23, 26; Jonas A., 27; Jonas F., 24; Jonas H., 26; Jonas M., 41; Jonas P., 23, 24; Jonas S., 31, 32; Jonathan F., 39; Jonathan H., 47; Joseph, 5, 13, 21, 24, 36, 39; Joseph A., 21; Joseph M., 23; Josephine, 24, 46; Josephine M., 32; Joshua, 22; Joshua P., 23; Jotham, 51; Judson, 53; Julia, 53; Julia A., 45; Julia E., 32; Julia M., 24, 33; Juliet, 25; Juliet M., 33; Lama E., 49; Laura, 37; Laura A., 42; Laura E., 50; Laura K., 31; Laura T., 43; Laura W., 44; Lelia, 53; Leola, 53; Lizzie M., 25; Lois, 21, 22; Louisa, 21, 41, 45; Louisa, A., 42, 43, 45; Louisa B., 43; Louisa C., 17; Louisa G., 17, 44; Louisa R., 42; Lucinda H., 44;

HARMON, Clarissa, 65.
HARRIGAN, Priscilla, 51.
HARRINGTON, Carrie E., 79; Clarence N., 60; Frank N., 79; Freddie B., 60; Jennie E., 60; Julia A., 98; Nellie, 60; Numan, 60; Phineas, 68; William E., 79.
HARRIS, George H., 78; Ida S., 28; Jonathan, 7; Ruth A., 36; S. Sophia, 79; Susie R., 94; Willard L., 28.
HARRT, Abby B., 33.
HART, Gilbert, 57; William, 23.
HARTWELL, Abbie G., 100; Abbie L., 99; Abbie M., 102; Abigail, 11, 83; Addie A., 98; Albert N., 102; Almira F., 100; Amos, 98; Arthur L., 102; Arthur S., 81; Bethia M., 81; Benjamin F., 98; Carrie L., 100; Charles, 101; Charles F., 98; Charles N., 102; Charles T., 98; Chauncey, 81; Clarence W., 102; Clara, 102; Clara L., 102; Clara H., 99; Ebenezer, 10; Edith S., 99; Edward, 10; Edward A., 99, 100; Edward C., 100; Eleazer D., 101; Ellen, 81; Elizabeth, 10, 11; Emily A., 104; Emma, 102; Emma A., 81; Ernest N., 100; Fannie, 102; Fannie T., 100; Flora, 102; Florence M., 100; Frank W., 102; Fred A., 102; Frederick A., 99; Frederick W., 98; George, 101; George H., 98; George W., 104; Gertrude E., 98; Hannah, 11; Henry, 81; Henry G., 100; Herbert C., 100; Herbert E., 98; Herbert H., 81; Herman O., 81; Hosea A., 102; Huldah, 102; Isaac, 98; Joanna E., 99; Jane, 11; John, 10, 11, 101; John B., 98; John H., 98, 101; Jonathan, 7, 10, 11; Joseph, 10, 11, 98, 101; Julia A., 98; Lillie, 99; Lucinda, 81; Lucy, 101; Lucy A., 102; Lucy W., 105; Lydia A., 101; Lydia C., 100; Lydia E., 99 Lydia R., 101; Mabel E., 81; Minnie, 102; Martha, 10; Mariah L., 102; Mary, 10, 11, 99; Mary A., 101; Mary B., 100; Mary E., 104; Mary J., 98, 101; Nancy W., 101; Nathaniel, 10; Nettie E., 81; Rebecca, 11; Ruth, 11; Sarah, 10, 11, 99, 102; Sarah A., 104; Sarah J., 99; Solomon, 70; Timothy, 70; Walter C., 98, 100; William, 10, 11, 70, 98; William G., 99; William W., 99, 100.
HARTZ, Mary E., 85.
HARVEY, Elizabeth, 50; Evelyn, 50; Mary A., 50; Samuel B., 50; Willard, 50; Willard B., 50.
HARWOOD, Hannah, 14.
HASTINGS, Charles, 72; Charles A., 73; Emily P., 73; E. G., 65; Julia A., 65; Minnie A., 65; Nellie E., 73; Percy W., 73; Lydia, 87; Sarah, 87.
HATCH, Cora A., 28; George A., 70; Harry O., 70; Jennie L., 22; Leslie A., 70; Margaret E., 70; Oscar, 70.
HAVEN, Charles H., 92; George A., 92; Hannah B., 91.
HAWES, Mary, 40.
HAWKS, Mary A., 46; Elizabeth S., 48.
HAY, Catharine, 83.
HAYDEN, E. H., 64.
HAYNES, Caleb S., 65; Clifford C., 65; Cyrus H., 65; James, 68; Nathaniel L., 65; Otis B., 65; Philip L., 65.
HAYTER, Margaret G., 104.
HAYWARD, Abial, 11; Ada J., 69; Charles H., 26, 27; Cordelia, 28; Cornelia, 28; Daniel, 68; Dorothy, 11; Ebenezer, 11; Eliza A., 68; Elizabeth C., 69; Elizabeth G., 26, 27; Elizabeth M., 68; Emma E., 77; Ephraim, 26; George, 11; Grace A., 77; Hannah, 9, 11; Harriet R., 68; Helen A., 26; Henry W., 69; James, 11, 68; James E., 68; James A., 26; Jennie E., 26; Joel F., 27; Foster J., 28; John, 11; Joseph, 11, 14; Judith, 11; Laura, 68; Lillian L., 69; Lois C., 68; Lucy A., 26; Lucy W., 68; Martha J., 28; Mary, 7, 9, 11, 15, 34, 68, 83, 90; Mary J., 68; Minnie H., 28; Nancy, 68; Olive, 47; Paul, 23; Poland E., 28; Ralph W., 69; Reuben, 9, 68, 78; Russell S., 68; Samuel, 68; Sarah, 11; Sarah P., 68; Simeon, 11; Stevens, 26, 28; Sylvester, 69; Walter, E., 77; William, 84; William A., 68; William B., 69; William C., 68.
HAZLETINE, Benjamin, 67; Charles B., 67;

Frances, 67; Grace, 67; Louisa, 67; Mary, 67.
HAZLETON, Amelia P., 40; Grace, 32.
HEAL, Albert F., 41; Amos B., 41; Annie E., 41; Augusta H., 41; Caroline H., 41; Caroline L., 41; Caroline M., 31, 41; Charles E., 41; Clara M., 41; Edwin B., 41; Edgar K., 41; Eliza B., 41; Ella B., 41; Ella L., 41; Frank J., 41; Frederick S., 41; George F., 41; George H., 41; Hattie M., 42; Harry E., 41; James, 41; James A., 41; James L., 41; Joseph H., 41; Lizzie E., 41; Lillie S., 41; Louisa, 41; Lydia N., 41; Mary A., 41; Nathan M., 41; Peter P., 41.
HEALD, Mary J., 78.
HEARD, Adison A., 85; Alberta H., 100; Alvin D., 100; Augusta, 84; Betsey, 100; Charles B., 85; David, 70, 85, 100; David H., 100; Edward, 85; Edwin H., 85; Eliza A., 85; Ellen, 85; Emma E., 100; Eva, 100; Eva M., 85; Francis, 85; Frank C., 100; Jennie E., 100; Joel B, 100; Maria J., 100; Martha E., 100; Mary E., 100; Nellie, 100; Susan, 85; Wayland C., 100.
HEMMINWAY, Alice B., 86; Charles A., 70; Charles B., 70; Charles F., 70; E. E., 57; Jennie A., 70; Nancy K., 85.
HERRICK, Benjamin M., 78; George L., 65; Lucy, 58; Mary B., 32; Mary E., 44.
HERSEY, Alfred C., 33; Alfred H., 33; Asa J., 66.
HETT, Mercy, 8.
HEWETT, George M., 44; Horatio N., 44; James D., 44; James P., 44; Maria A., 44; Sophia E., 44.
HEYWOOD, Betsey, 18, 20; Hannah L., 28; Jonas, 18; Jonathan, 47; Rebecca, 18, 20; Samuel, 12.
HICKOK, Clinton W., 52; Myron W., 52.
HIGGINS, Amelia L., 42; Patience, 41.
HIGGINSON, Elizabeth, 14.
HILDRETH, Ella M., 81; James B., 81; Julia V., 81; Maria T., 81; Mary E., 81.
HILL, Ann, 71; Jonathan, 10; Mattie M., 94; Ralph, 94; S. H., 94.
HILLMAN, Francis, 63; Mabel A., 63.
HILTON, Margaret A., 99.
HINCKLEY, Benjamin B., 48; Donald R., 48; Edward B., 48; George B., 48; Henry B., 48; Henry R., 47; Minerva, 77; Rose, 48.
HINDS, Dora, 102; Emma, 102; Sophrona, 102; Timothy, 102.
HISLOP, John E., 86.
HOAR, Daniel, 12; Elizabeth, 14; Mary F., 73; Mercy, 10; Roxalana, 70; Sherman, 38.
HOBART, Henry K., 103.
HOBBS, Alice, 32; George J., 67.
HODGE, Almeda, 53.
HODGES, Susan A., 35.
HODGIN, Catharine, 46.
HODGMAN, Louise, 98.
HOLBROOK, Franklin, 92.
HOLDEN, Bertha H., 104; Clara B., 86; Daniel, 67, 83; David B., 19; Edna G., 104; Eliza J., 22; George W., 19; Henry E., 86; John A., 86; Marshall H., 86; Mary E., 86; Sarah F., 19; Susan E., 86; Tilly, 85; William H., 18; William M., 19.
HOLLENBUCK, Nancy E., 75.
HOLMAN, Nelson, 68; Orissa, 16.
HOLMES, Christopher, 96; Mary E., 55; Julia R., 74.
HOLT, Charlotte A., 45.
HOLYOKE, Mary, 7.
HOOKER, Phebe, 73.
HOMAN, Annie E., 64.
HOMER, Hannah, 101.
HOPKINS, Addie S., 93; George H., 93.
HORTON, Electa M., 49; Nancy, 58.
HORSLEY, Lucy, 60.
HOSMER, Abigail, 11, 14; Amos H., 21; Ann, 11; Anna H., 74; Benjamin, 73; Beulah, 64, 67, 104; Caroline A., 41; Cyrus, 36, 73, 74, 99; Dinah, 73; Dorothy, 11; Edward J., 74; Edward S., 74; Eliot N., 74; Elizabeth, 74, 104; Ella, 74; Ephraim, 12; Ernest C., 74; George J., 74; George S., 18, 99; George W., 74; Hannah, 11, 15; Harriet S., 79; Herbert B., 19; Herbert G., 74; Herbert W., 19; Henry J., 74, 99; Horace R., 68;

James, 11; James K., 74; Jane, 12; Jesse, 14; John, 11, 18; John F., 18; Jonathan, 12; Joseph, 73; Joseph H., 74; Josephine, 74; Josiah, 12; Lavinia, 73; Lucinda, 73; Lucy, 73, 90, 104; Lucius, 82; Lucius E., 82; Lydia, 38, 73, 74; Meliscent, 67, 74, 104; Martha, 74; Mary, 11, 15, 67; Mary L., 74; Nathan, 67, 104; Oliver, 67; Patty, 73; Persis, 73; Prudence, 11, 12; Ralph, 99; Ralph S., 74; Rebecca P., 74; Rufus, 73; Ruth, 11, 74; Sarah, 11; Silas, 67; Stephen, 10, 11, 12, 16, 67, 104; Thomas, 11, 12; Thomas N., 43; Washington, 74; William R., 74.
HOTCHKINS, Frank, 90; Mary, 89.
HOUGHRANT, Fannie, 42.
HOUGHTON, Cyrene, 17; Eleazer, 16; Henry P., 17; James, 83; John, 9; Lucy W., 68; Sarah P., 17.
HOUSEMAN, Susie M., 41.
HOVEY, Mary J., 53; Miriam P., 44.
HOW, Elizabeth, 5; Israel, 12; Mary, 10; Thomas, 11.
HOWARD, Cecil J., 64; Ethan H., 74; Hannah, 12; Henry C., 74; Nathaniel, 15.
HOWE, David, 12; David C., 98; Isaac, 87; John, 20; Mary, 9.
HOWLAND, Bertha M., 88; William, 88; William R., 88.
HUBBARD, Abigail, 12; Betsey, 35; Charles, 35; Daniel, 12; David, 30, 35; Ebenezer, 12, 35; George, 12; Hannah, 12; John, 12; Jonathan, 7, 12; Joseph, 12; Lucy, 12; Mary, 9, 12, 30; Mary B., 35; Nathan, 12; Peter, 12; Rebecca, 5, 12; Samuel, 12; Sarah, 75; Sarah B., 35; Sarah E., 32; Silas, 35; Thomas, 12, 64.
HUBBELL, Phebe, 51; Susan, 50.
HUDSON, Barzilla N., 18; Charlotte, 70; Hannah A., 43; Susan, 34.
HUEY, Arthur B., 20; Emma H., 20; Malcom S., 20; Samuel B., 20; Samuel C., 20; William A., 20.
HULL, Abby A., 33; Joanna, 9.
HUMPHREY, Crawford N., 27; Ella U., 28; Flora U., 27; George A., 28; Hannah H., 27; John, 27; John H., 27; M. E., 28; William S., 28.
HUNSTABLE, Lydia H., 75.
HUNSTON, Frederick L., 30; Joel, 29; Londean, 30.
HUNT, Abel, 27; Ada I., 20; Almira C., 18; Ann M., 18; Betsey, 49; Charles H., 18; Edward J., 20; Elizabeth T., 18; Eliza A., 20; Emeline P., 18; Eva S., 20; Hannah, 5; Hannah R., 20; Harriet P., 18; Humphrey, 20; John, 7; Leonard B., 20; Louisa J., 18; Maranda, 18; Martha A., 18; Mary H., 18; Mary P., 20; Miriam, 35; Ralph H., 20; Reuben, 18, 20; Samuel, 9; Sarah A., 18; Simon, 20; Submit, 10; Thomas H., 20; Walter R., 20.
HUNTINGTON, Constant D., 44; George P., 43; Henry B., 44; James L., 44; Paul S., 44.
HURD, Charles H., 18; Julia, 33.
HUSTON, Abraham G., 52; Raymond B., 52; Nellie A., 52.
HUTCHINS, Anna E., 42; David E., 60; Mary M., 99; Wallace J., 28.
HUTCHINSON, Hiram, 65; Hiram N., 88; Nathaniel, 87; Sabina, 56.
HYDE, Adeline, 73.

I

INGALLS, Elizabeth, 83; Henry, 31; Mary J., 31.
IRWIN, Lottie E., 53.
IVES, Mary W., 54.

J

JACKSON, Albion, 35; D. F., 44; Thomas E., 64.
JACOB, Martha, 15; Isabel M., 101.
JAMES, Amos V., 67.
JAQUITH, Polly, 59.
JARVIS, Eddie B., 45; Francis, 104; Horace B., 45; Isaac F., 45; James E., 45; James H., 45; James O., 45; John H., 45; Lizzie M., 45; Susan M., 45.

142

INDEX OF BIOGRAPHIES.

Made in the USA